Hey! You're Reading in the Wrong Direction!

This is the ***end*** of this graphic novel!

To properly enjoy this VIZ graphic novel, please turn it around and begin reading from ***right to left.*** Unlike English, Japanese is read right to left, so Japanese comics are read in reverse order from the way English comics are typically read.

1
2
3
4
1
2
5
6
7
8
3
4
9
5
142

Follow the action this way

This book has been printed in the original Japanese format in order to preserve the orientation of the original artwork. Have fun with it!

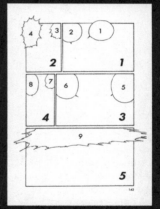

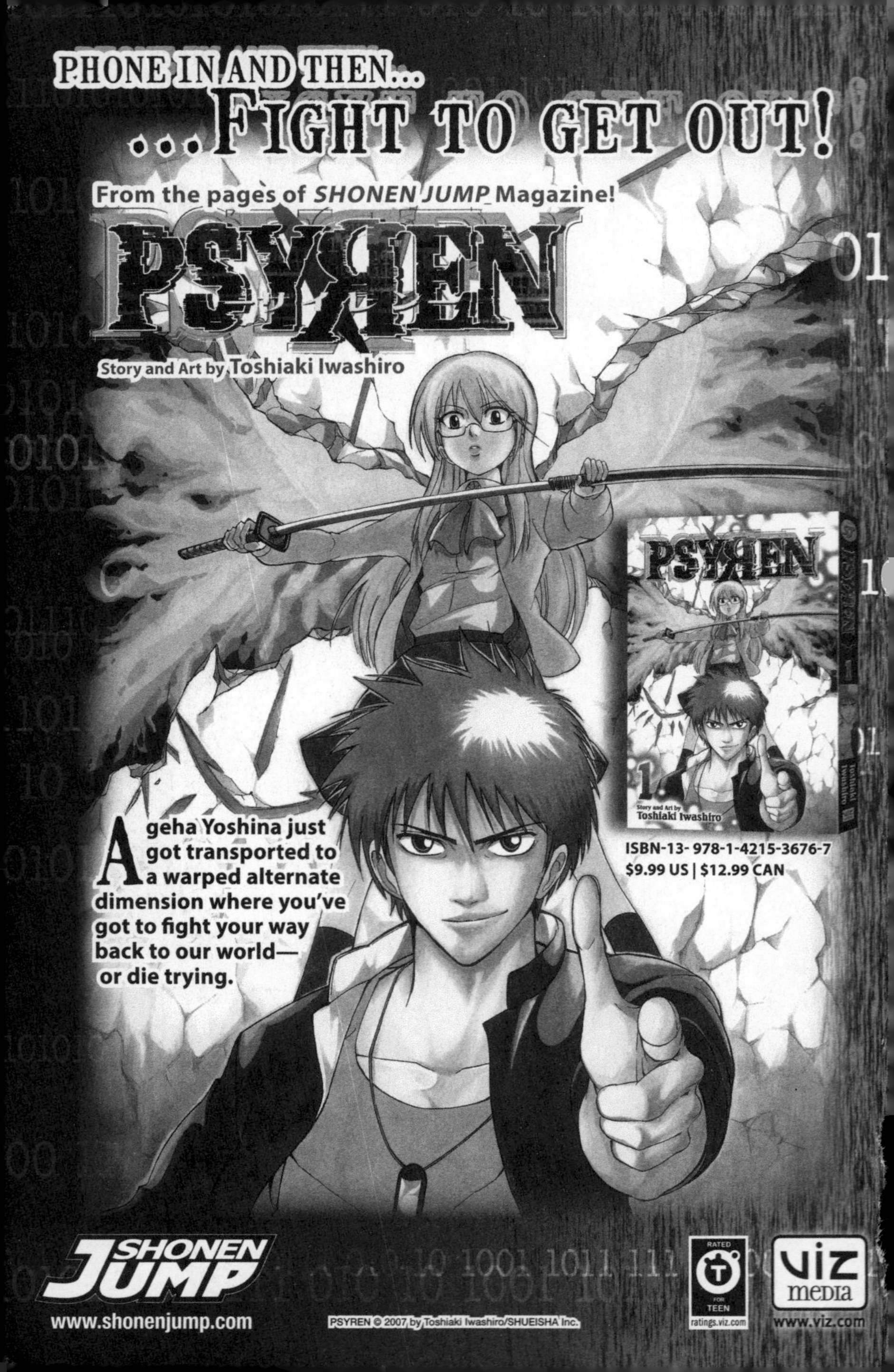

PHONE IN AND THEN...
...FIGHT TO GET OUT!
From the pages of SHONEN JUMP Magazine!
PSYREN
Story and Art by Toshiaki Iwashiro
Ageha Yoshina just got transported to a warped alternate dimension where you've got to fight your way back to our world—or die trying.
PSYREN
1
Story and Art by Toshiaki Iwashiro
ISBN-13- 978-1-4215-3676-7
$9.99 US | $12.99 CAN
SHONEN JUMP
www.shonenjump.com
PSYREN © 2007 by Toshiaki Iwashiro/SHUEISHA Inc.
RATED T FOR TEEN
ratings.viz.com
VIZ media
www.viz.com

MONSTER HUNTER: Flash Hunter
VOL. 1
VIZ MEDIA Edition

Story by Keiichi Hikami
Art by Shin Yamamoto

Translation/John Werry
English Adaptation/Stan!
Touch-up Art & Lettering/John Hunt, Primary Graphix
Cover & Interior Design/Izumi Evers
Editor/Mike Montesa

First published in Japan in 2011 by KADOKAWA CORPORATION ENTERBRAIN
English translation rights arranged with KADOKAWA CORPORATION ENTERBRAIN

Printed in the U.S.A.

Published by VIZ Media, LLC
P.O. Box 77010
San Francisco, CA 94107

10 9 8 7 6 5 4 3 2 1
First printing, April 2016

www.viz.com

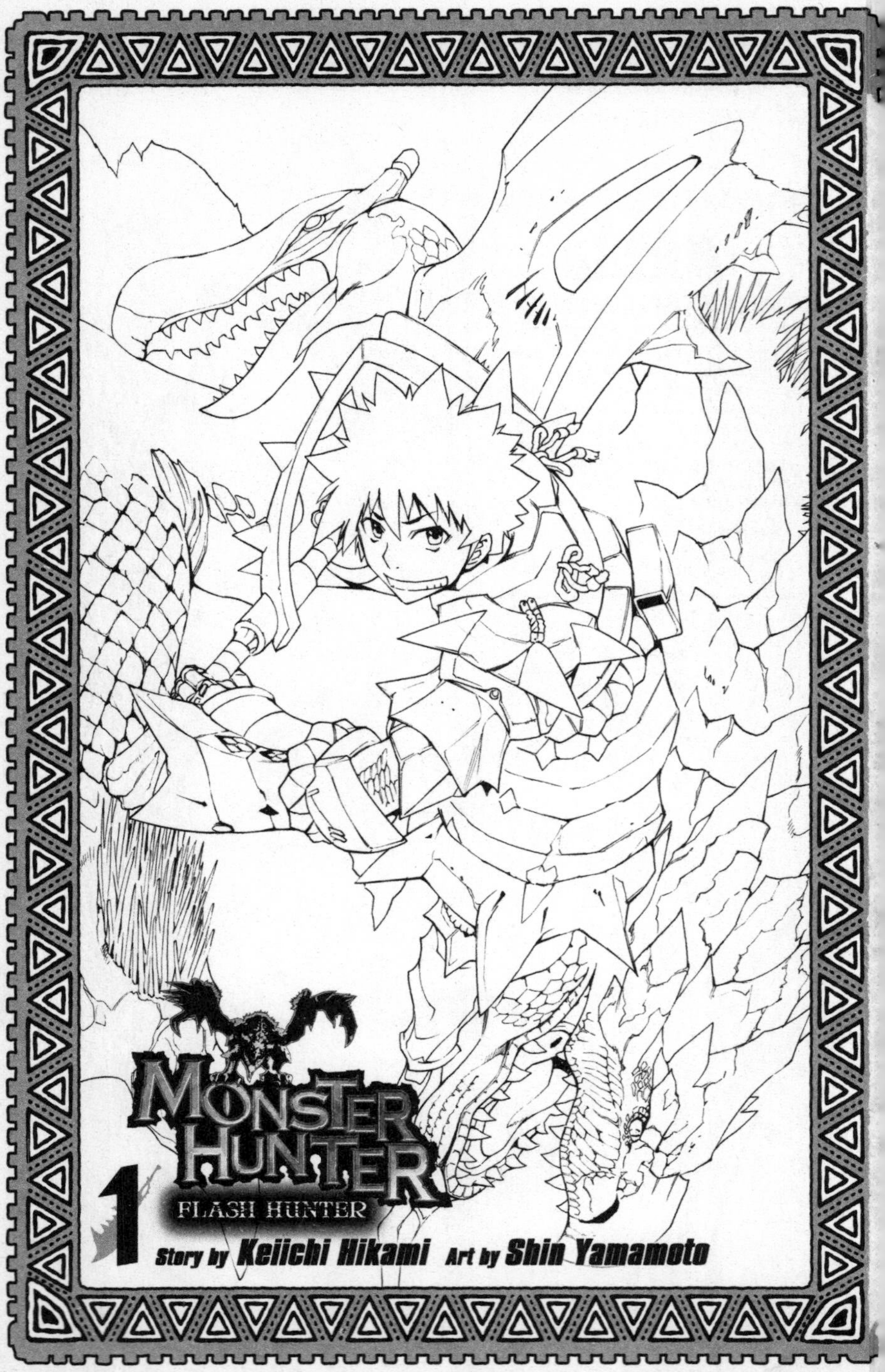
MONSTER HUNTER
FLASH HUNTER
1
Story by Keiichi Hikami Art by Shin Yamamoto

CHARACTERS

RAIGA

Due to his careless personality and reckless behavior, Keres calls him a bullfango (a particularly annoying beast). He's a fledgling hunter who uses a great sword. In order to become the resident hunter who protects the village where he was born and raised, he devotes himself to training in Loc Lac, a frontier land where many hunters gather.

Weapon: Golem Blade +

Armor: Kut-Ku Series (Swordsman)

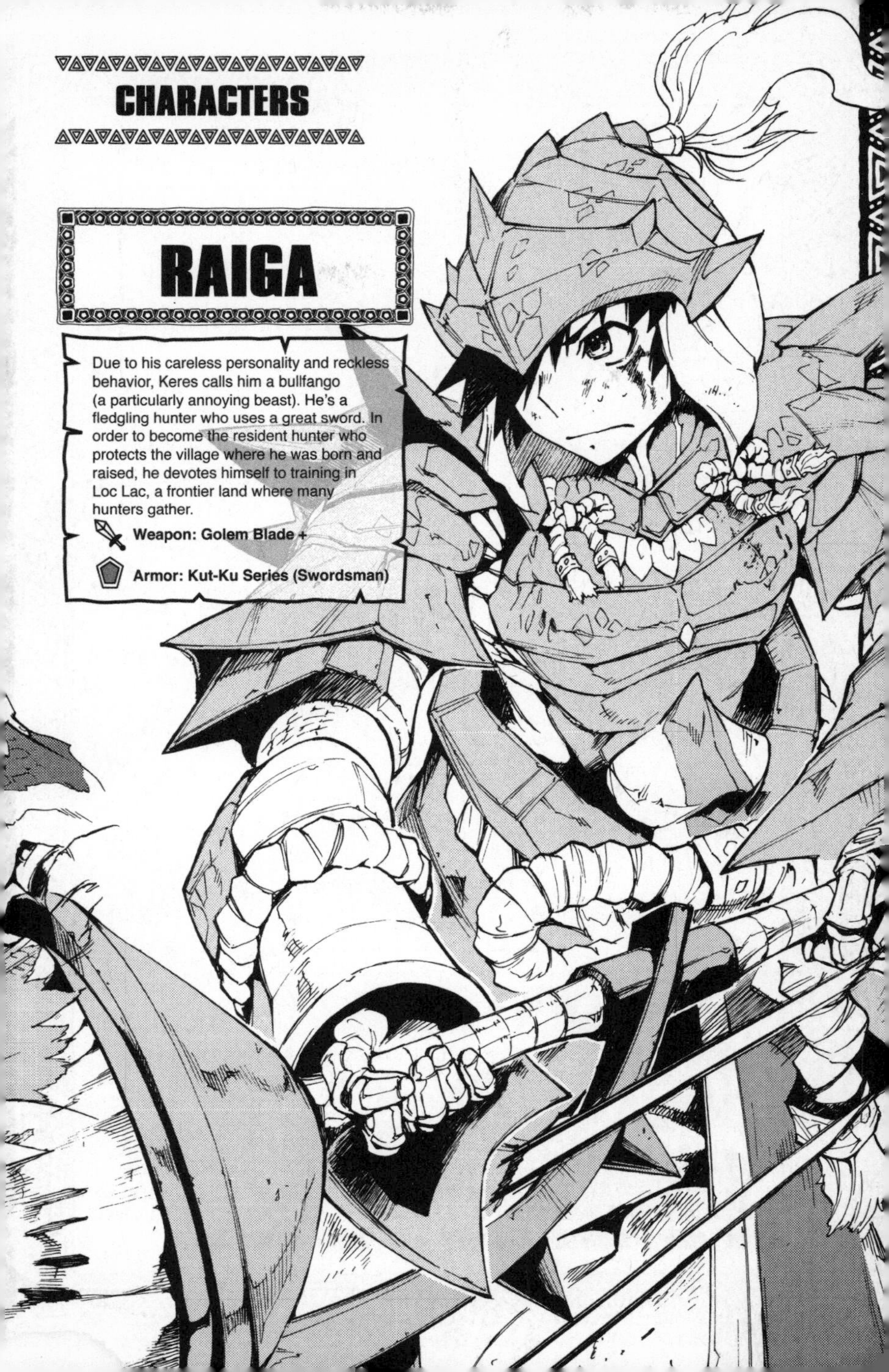

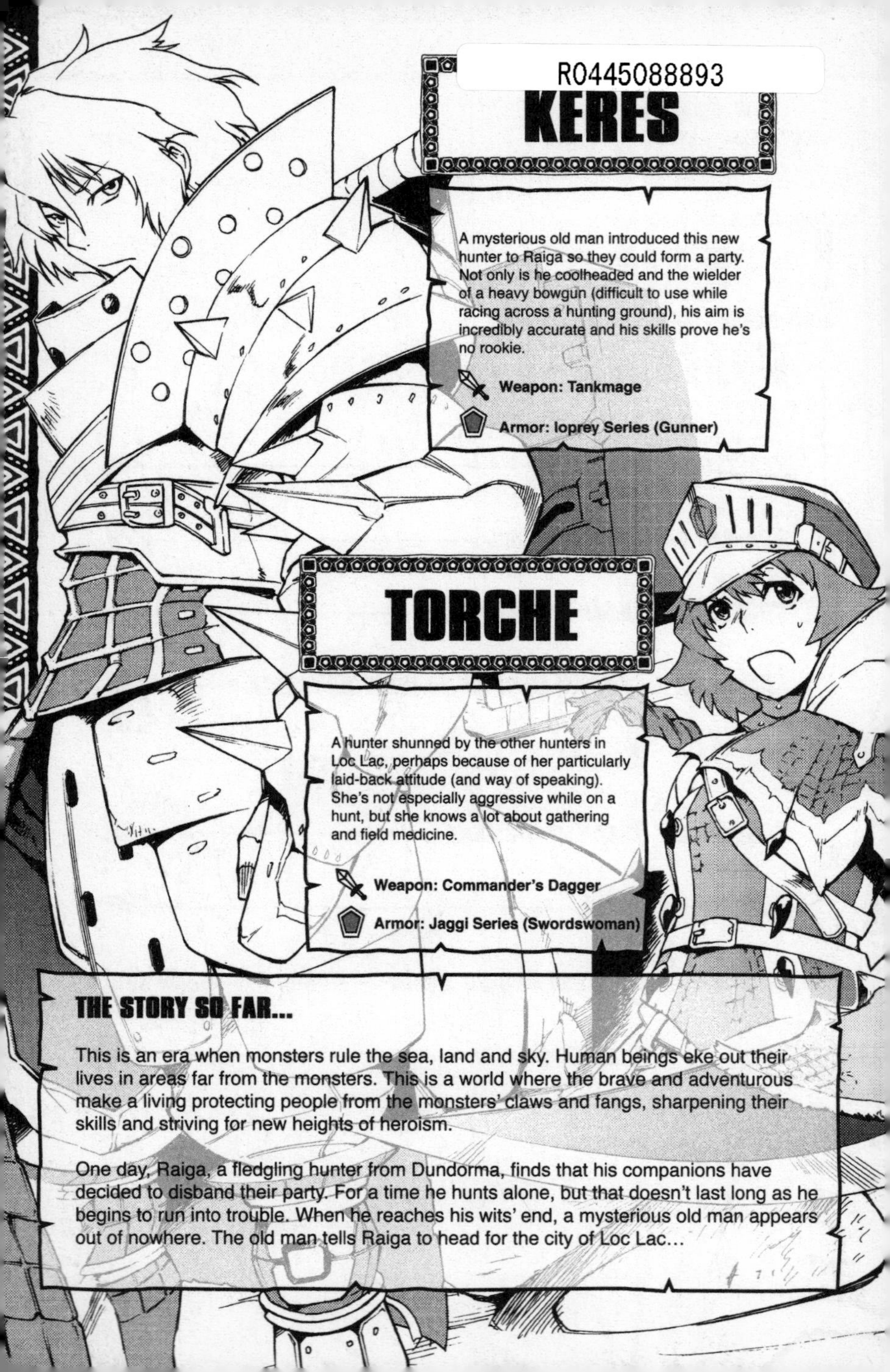

KERES

A mysterious old man introduced this new hunter to Raiga so they could form a party. Not only is he coolheaded and the wielder of a heavy bowgun (difficult to use while racing across a hunting ground), his aim is incredibly accurate and his skills prove he's no rookie.

Weapon: Tankmage

Armor: Ioprey Series (Gunner)

TORCHE

A hunter shunned by the other hunters in Loc Lac, perhaps because of her particularly laid-back attitude (and way of speaking). She's not especially aggressive while on a hunt, but she knows a lot about gathering and field medicine.

Weapon: Commander's Dagger

Armor: Jaggi Series (Swordswoman)

THE STORY SO FAR...

This is an era when monsters rule the sea, land and sky. Human beings eke out their lives in areas far from the monsters. This is a world where the brave and adventurous make a living protecting people from the monsters' claws and fangs, sharpening their skills and striving for new heights of heroism.

One day, Raiga, a fledgling hunter from Dundorma, finds that his companions have decided to disband their party. For a time he hunts alone, but that doesn't last long as he begins to run into trouble. When he reaches his wits' end, a mysterious old man appears out of nowhere. The old man tells Raiga to head for the city of Loc Lac...

Contents

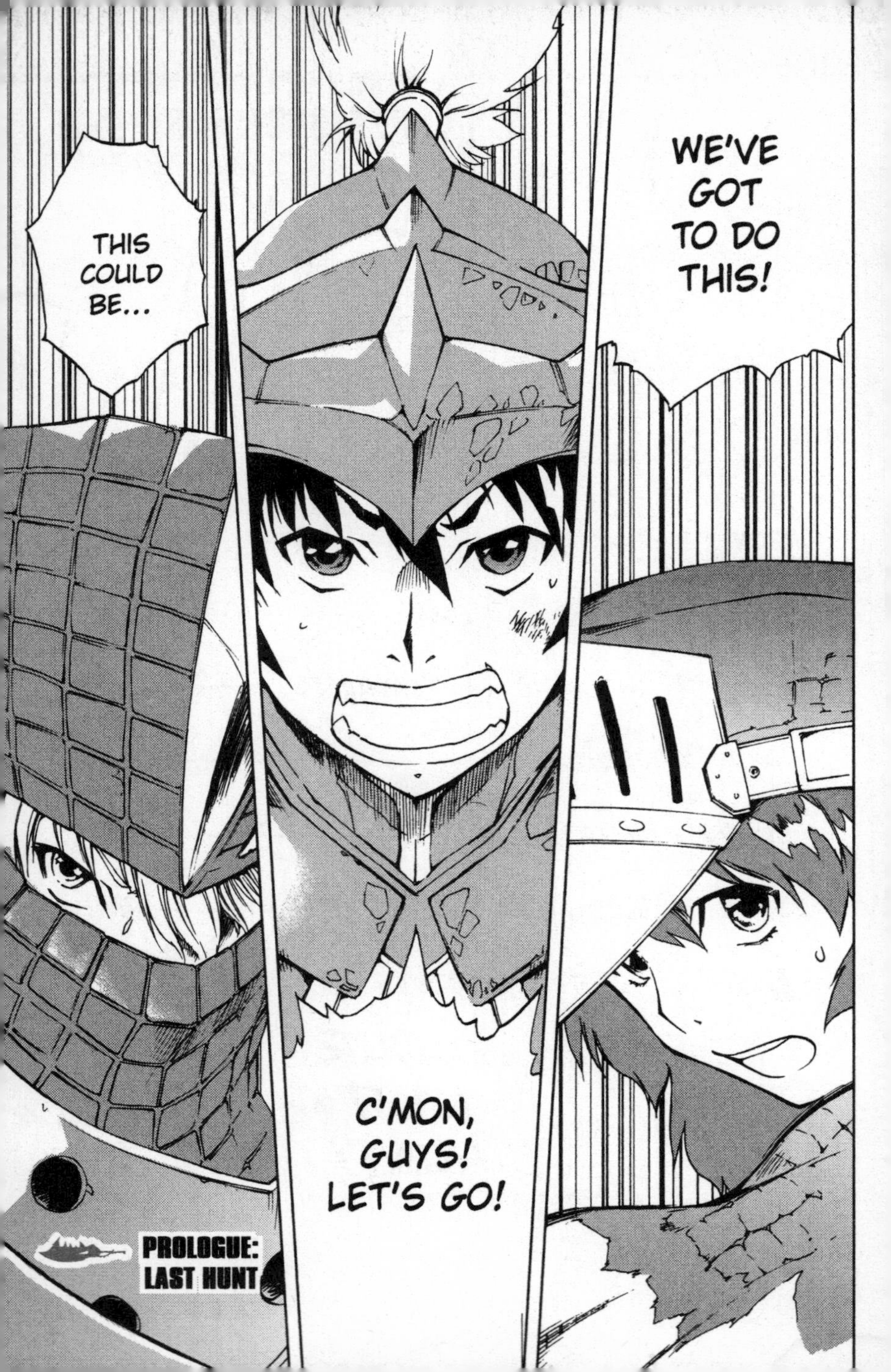
WE'VE GOT TO DO THIS!
THIS COULD BE...
C'MON, GUYS! LET'S GO!
PROLOGUE: LAST HUNT

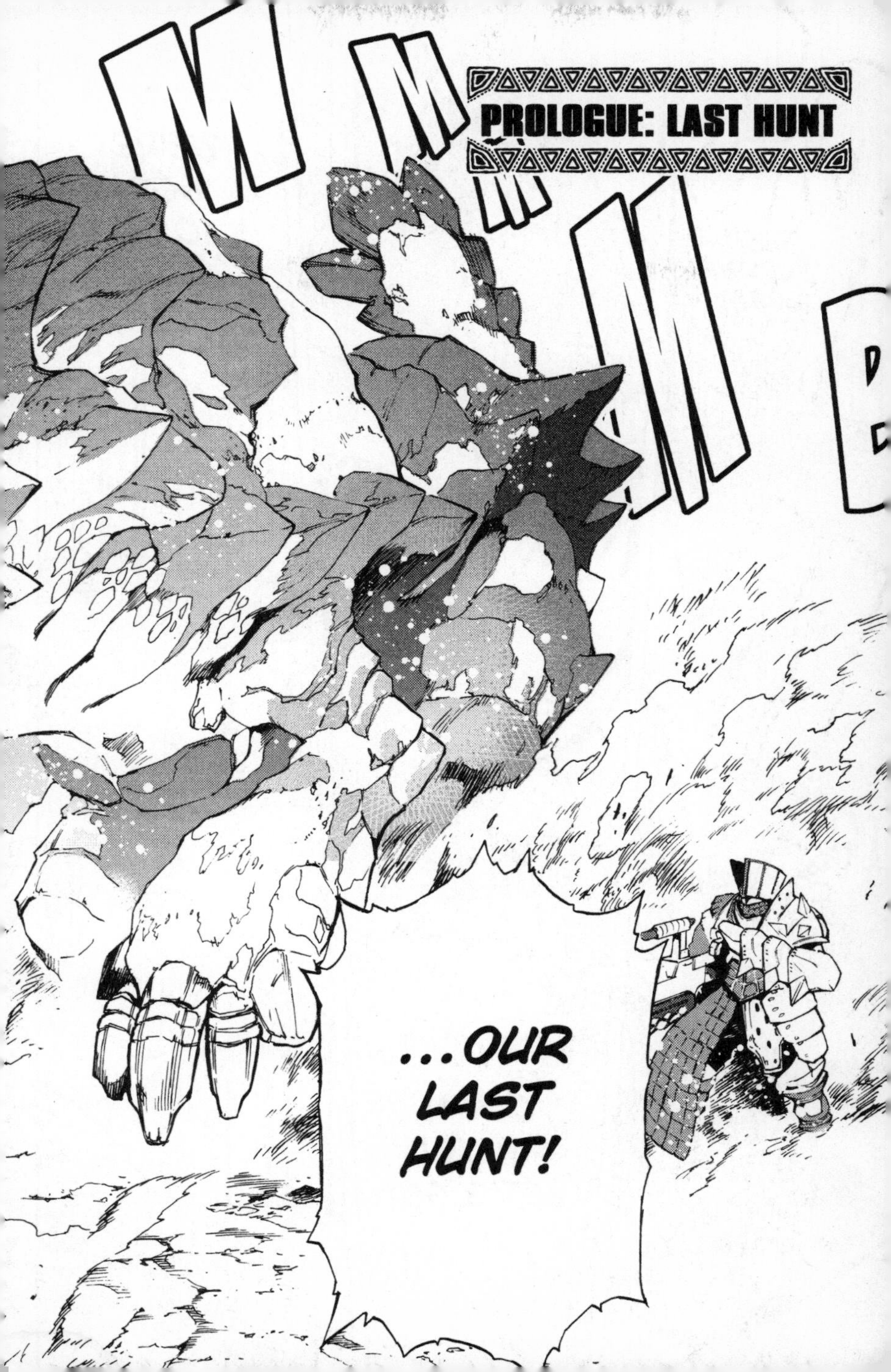

MMMMB
PROLOGUE: LAST HUNT
...OUR LAST HUNT!

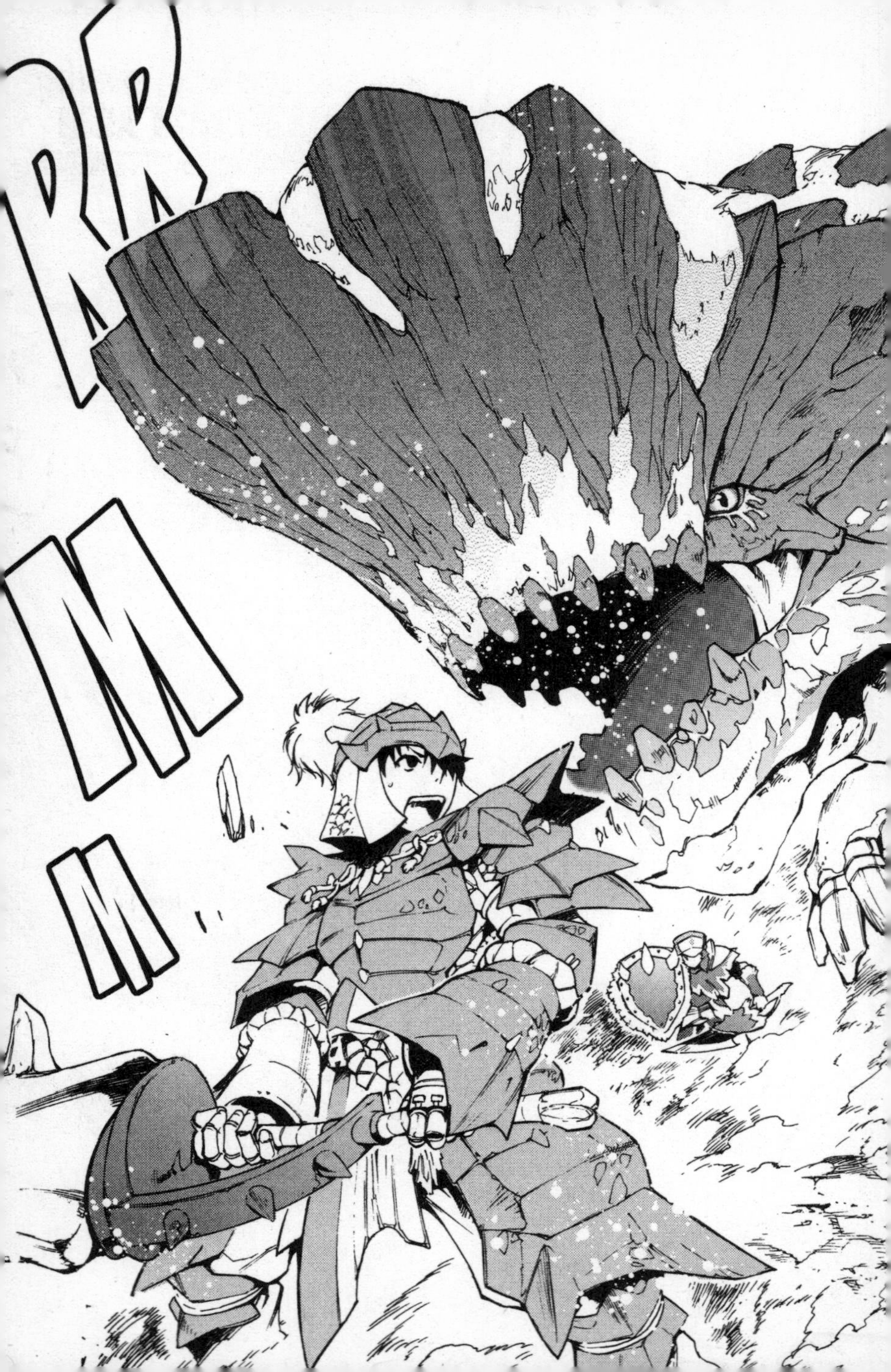
RRMM

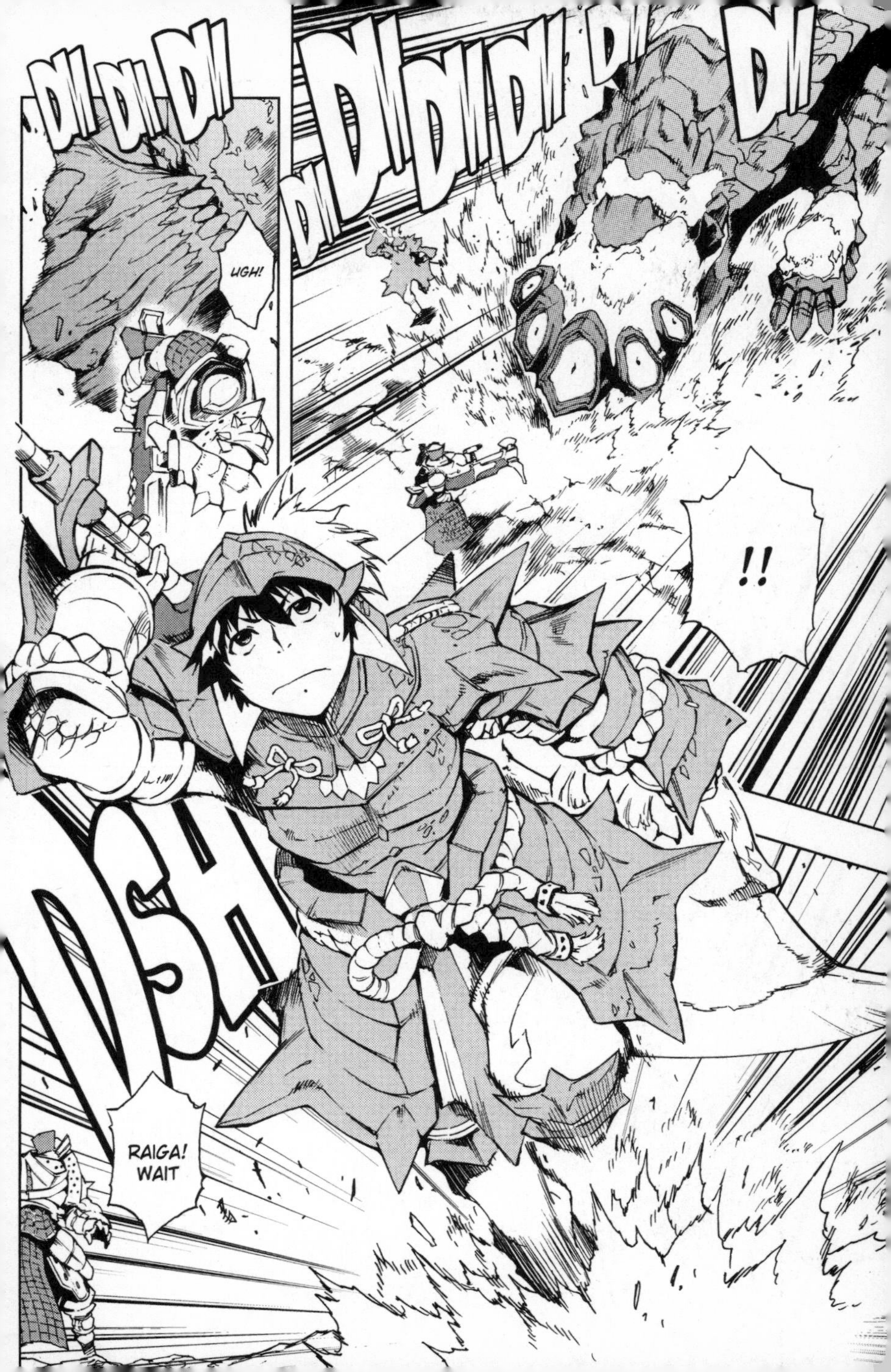
UGH!
!!
RAIGA! WAIT

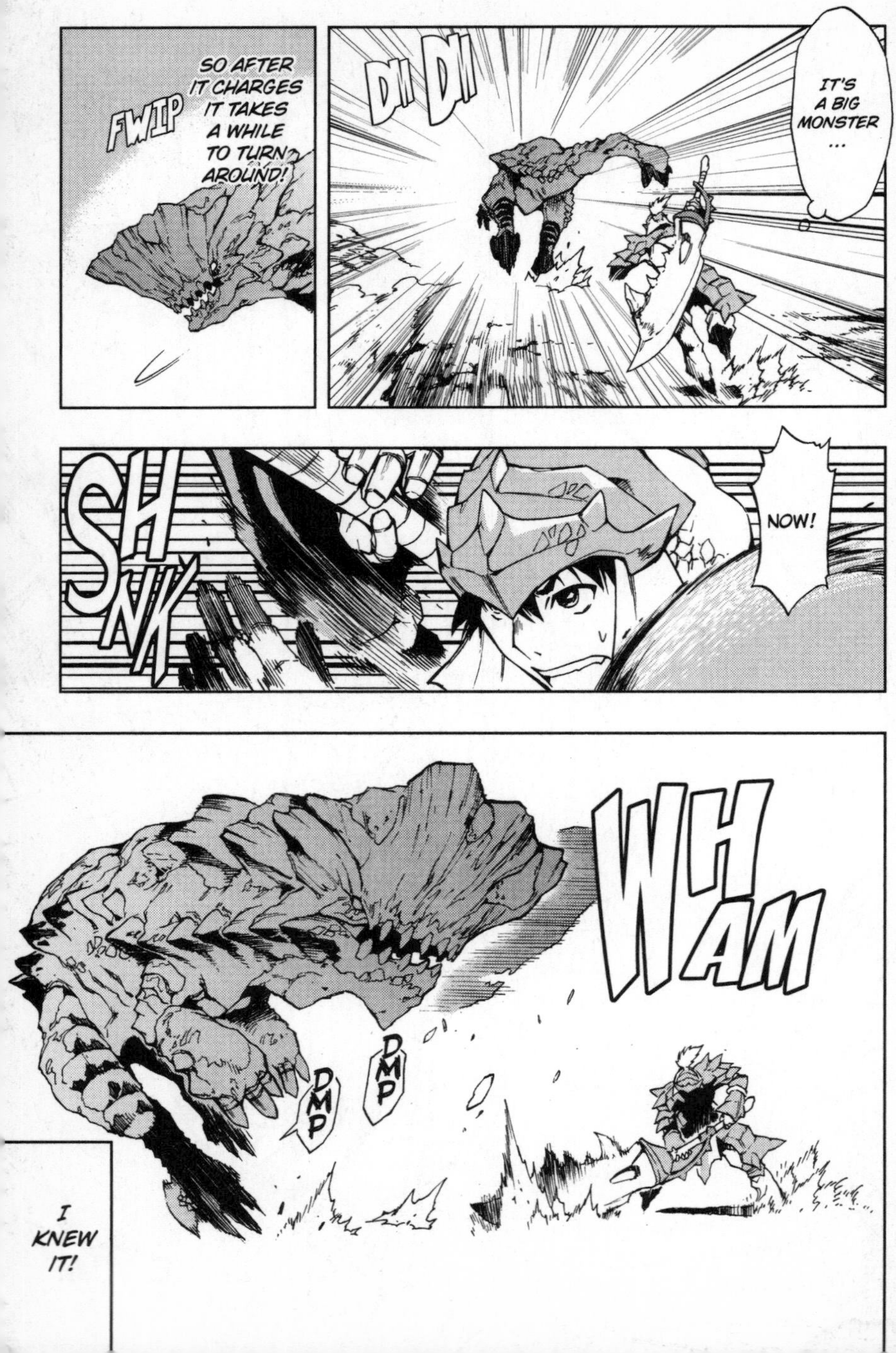
IT'S A BIG MONSTER ...
DM DM
SO AFTER IT CHARGES IT TAKES A WHILE TO TURN AROUND!
FWIP
NOW!
SHNK
WHAM
DMP
DMP
I KNEW IT!

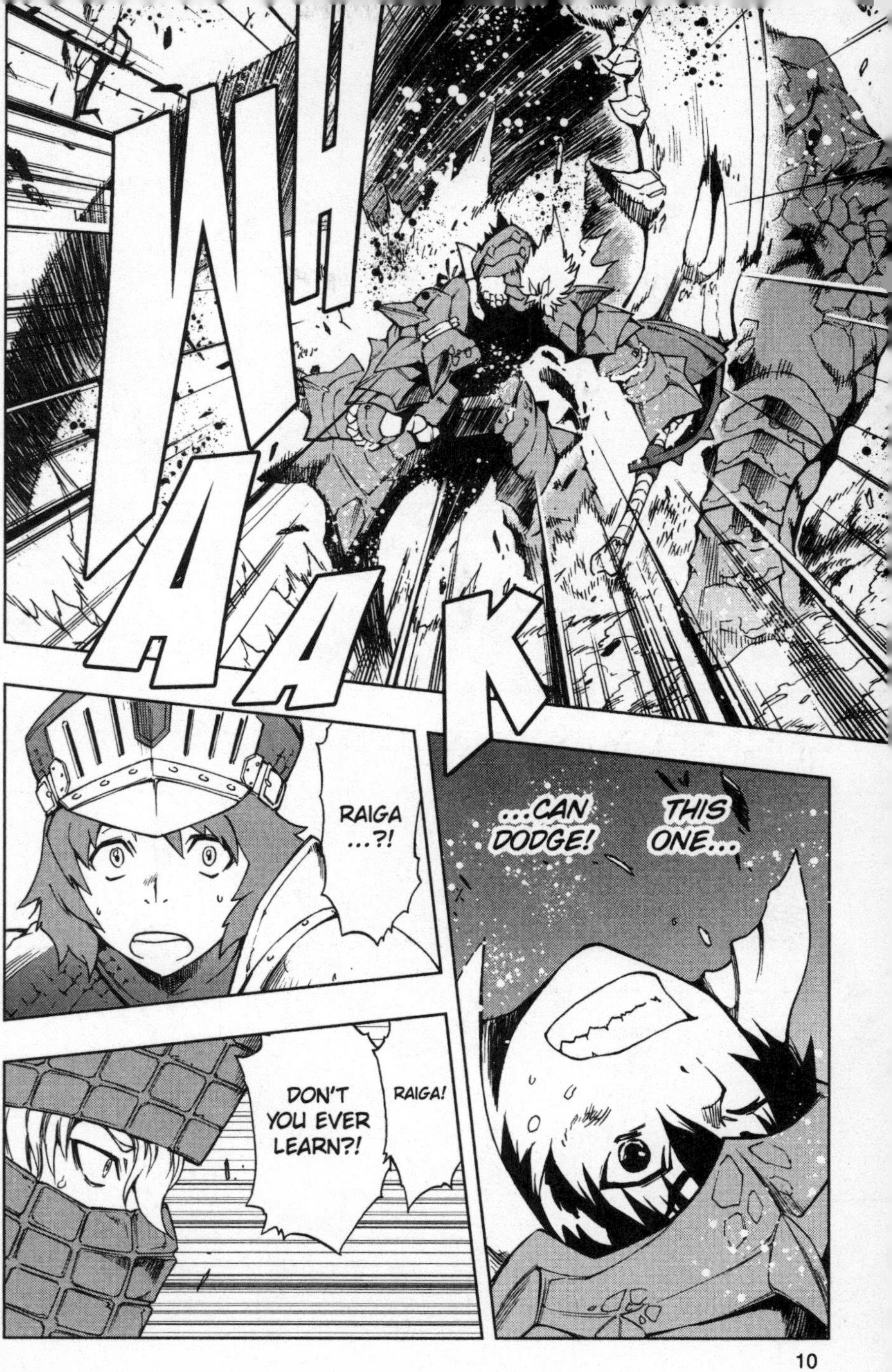
WHAAK
THIS ONE...
...CAN DODGE!
RAIGA ...?!
RAIGA!
DON'T YOU EVER LEARN?!

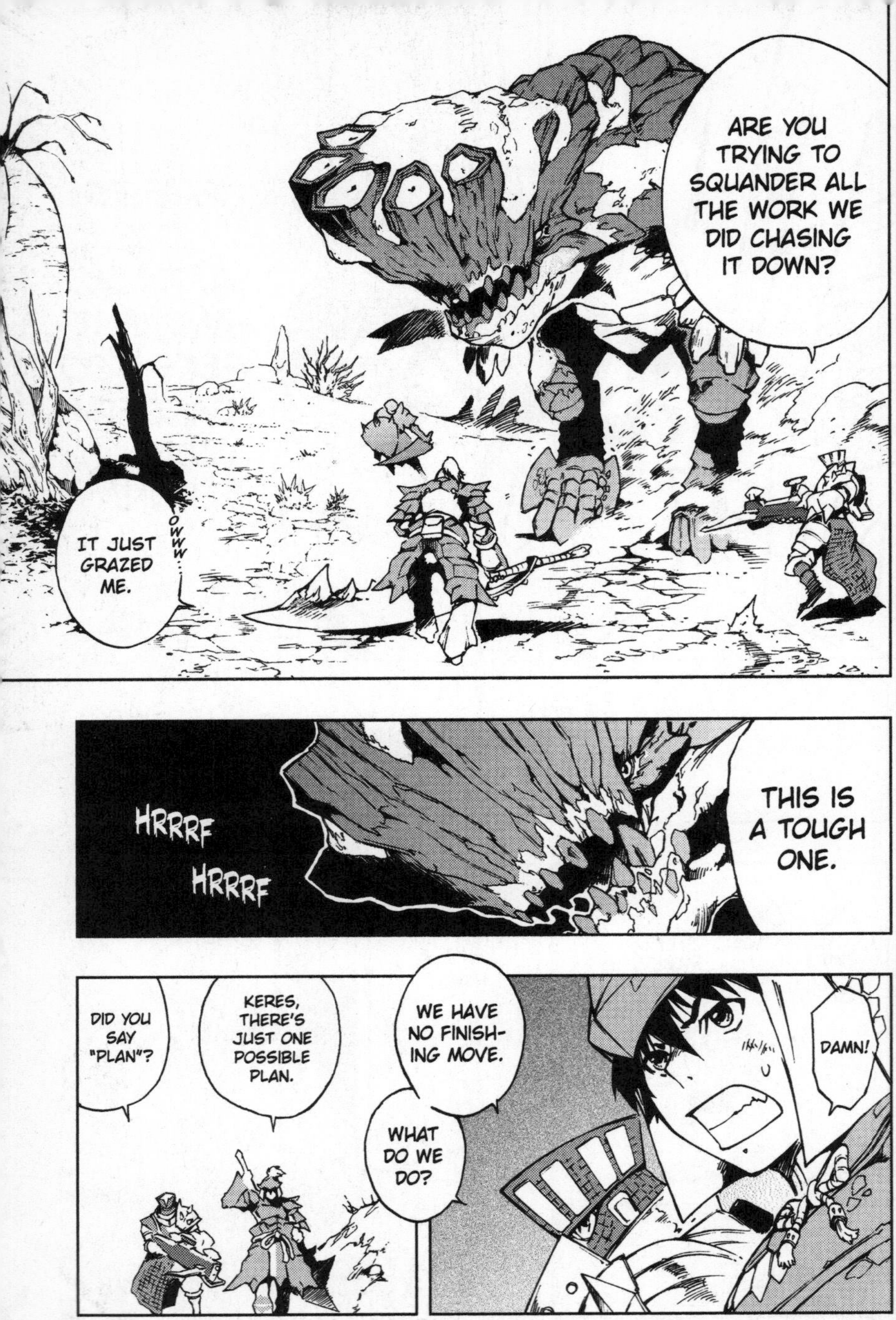
ARE YOU TRYING TO SQUANDER ALL THE WORK WE DID CHASING IT DOWN?
OWWW...
IT JUST GRAZED ME.
THIS IS A TOUGH ONE.
HRRRF
HRRRF
DAMN!
WE HAVE NO FINISH-ING MOVE.
WHAT DO WE DO?
KERES, THERE'S JUST ONE POSSIBLE PLAN.
DID YOU SAY "PLAN"?

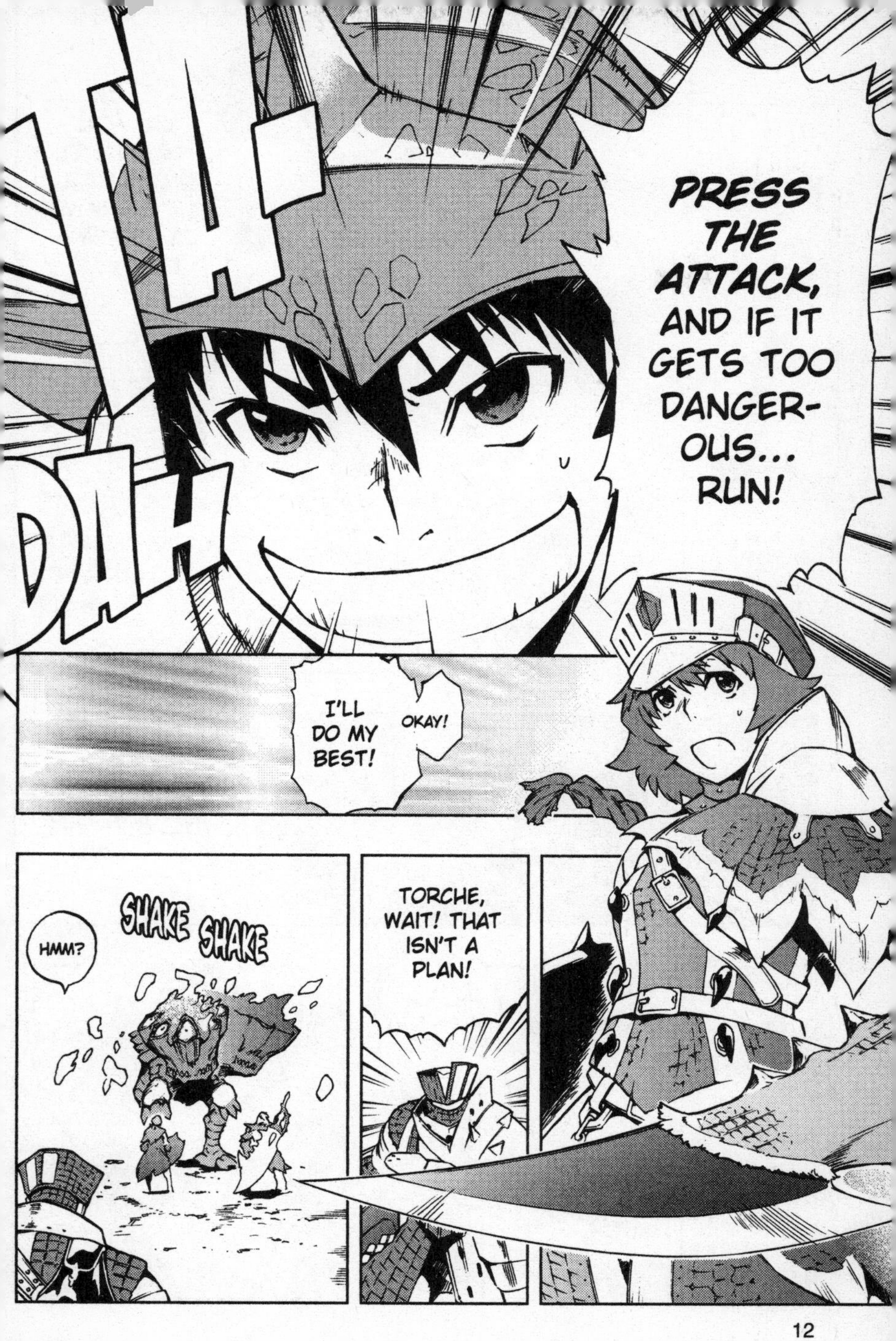
PRESS THE ATTACK, AND IF IT GETS TOO DANGEROUS... RUN!
DAH
OKAY!
I'LL DO MY BEST!
TORCHE, WAIT! THAT ISN'T A PLAN!
SHAKE SHAKE
HMM?

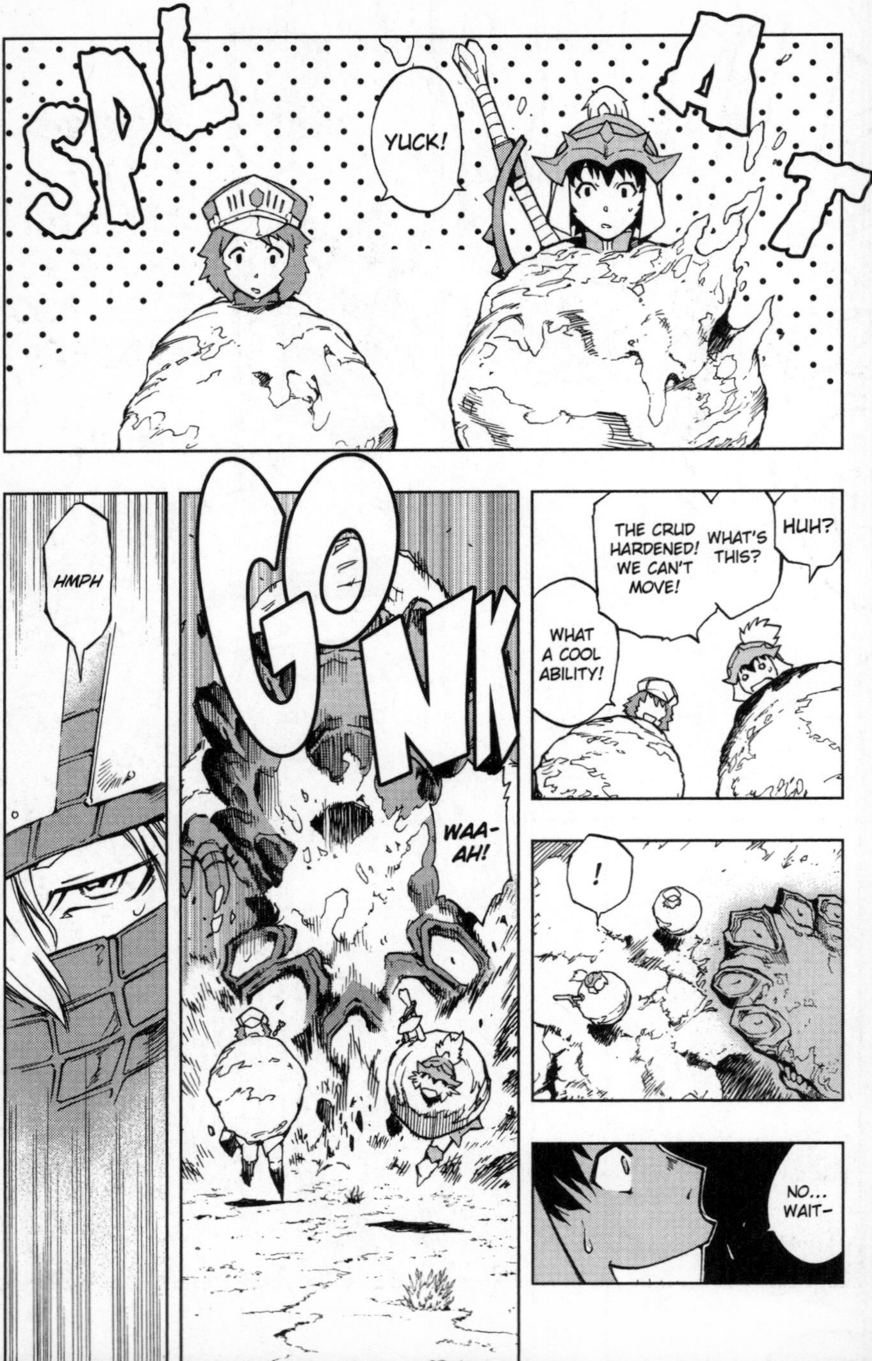
SPLAT
YUCK!
HUH?
WHAT'S THIS?
THE CRUD HARDENED! WE CAN'T MOVE!
WHAT A COOL ABILITY!
!
NO... WAIT-
GONK
WAA-AH!
HMPH

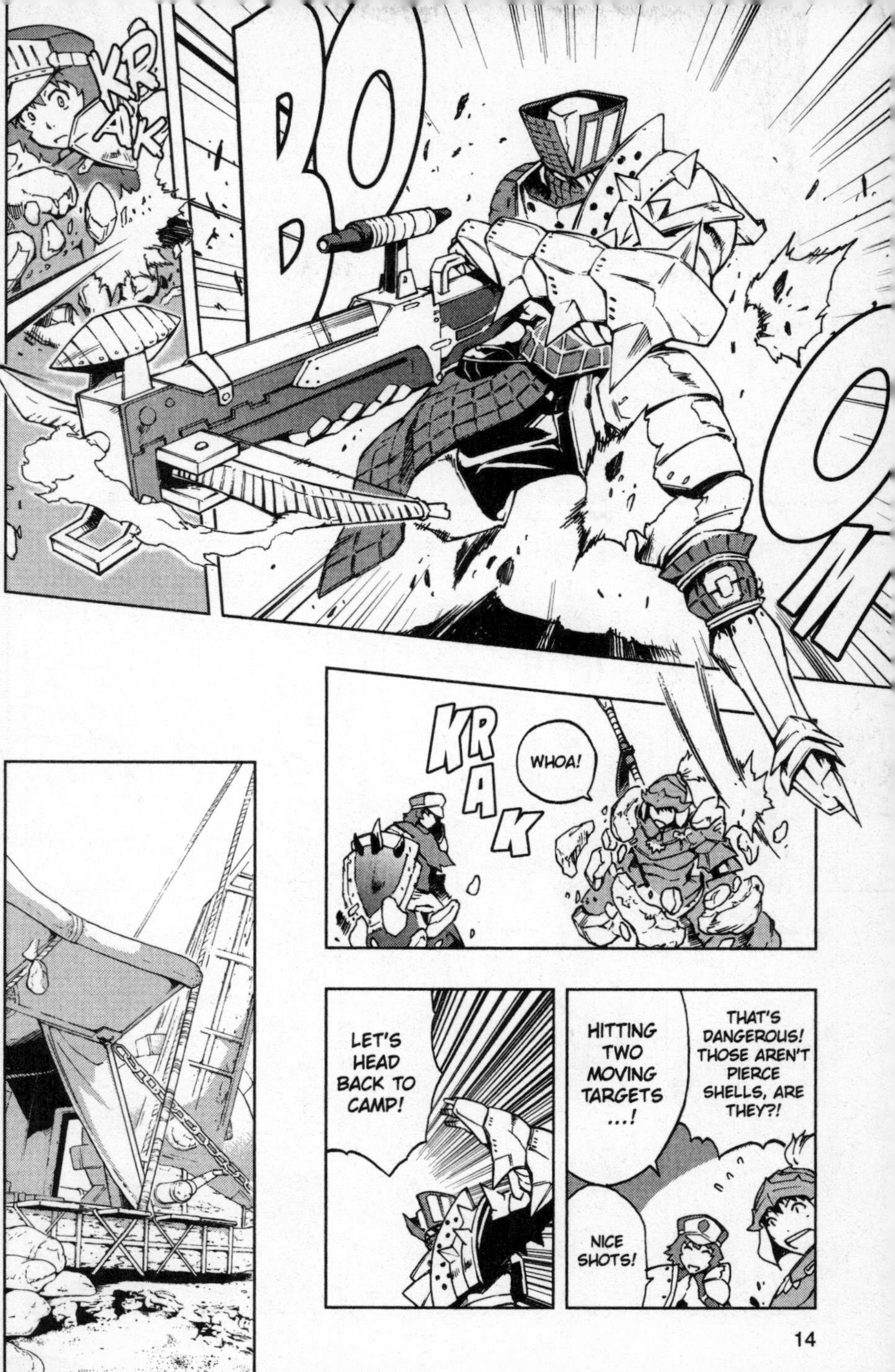
KRAK
BOOM
KRAK
WHOA!
THAT'S DANGEROUS! THOSE AREN'T PIERCE SHELLS, ARE THEY?!
HITTING TWO MOVING TARGETS ...!
NICE SHOTS!
LET'S HEAD BACK TO CAMP!

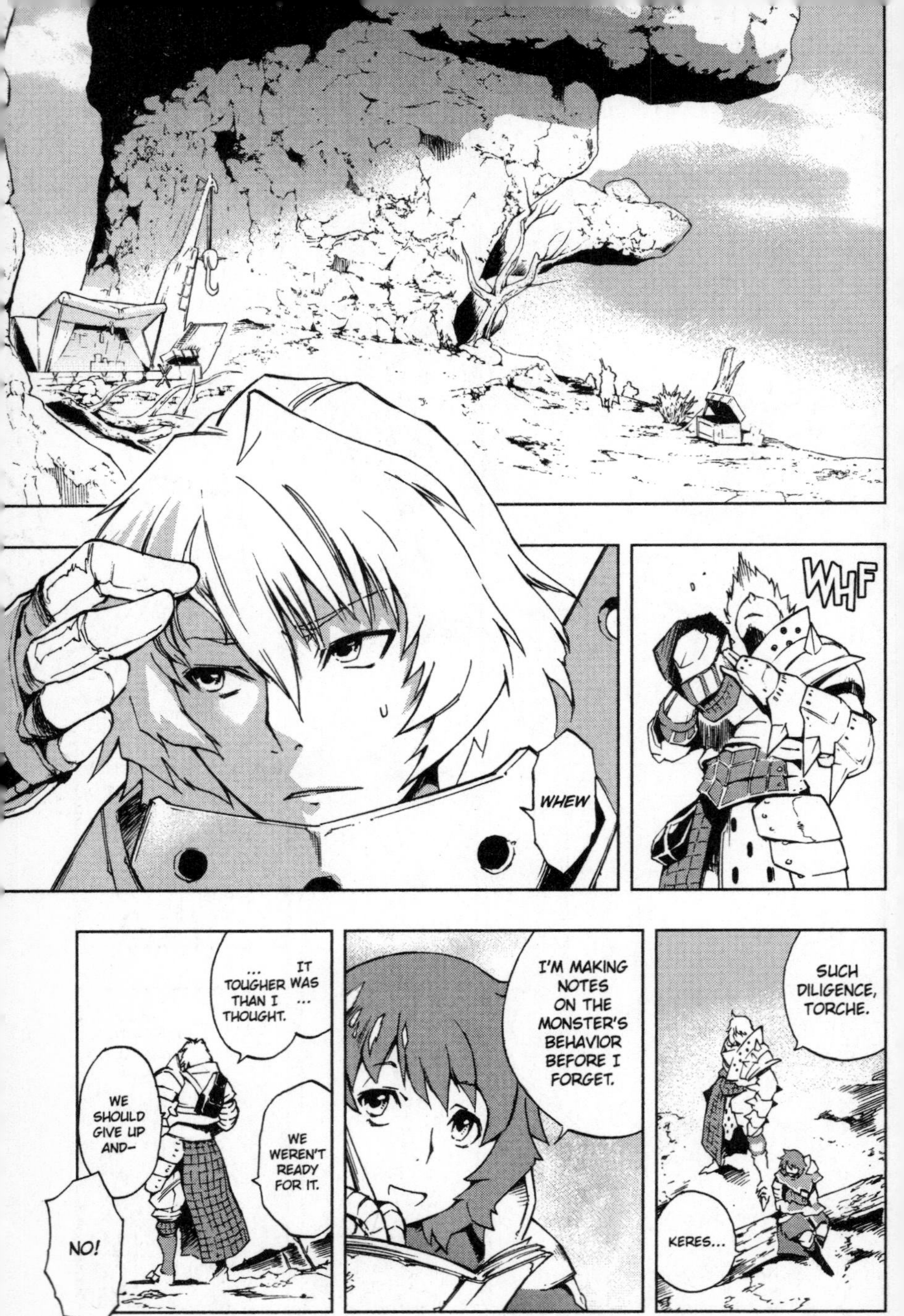
WHF
WHEW
SUCH DILIGENCE, TORCHE.
KERES...
I'M MAKING NOTES ON THE MONSTER'S BEHAVIOR BEFORE I FORGET.
IT WAS ...
... TOUGHER THAN I THOUGHT.
WE WEREN'T READY FOR IT.
WE SHOULD GIVE UP AND–
NO!

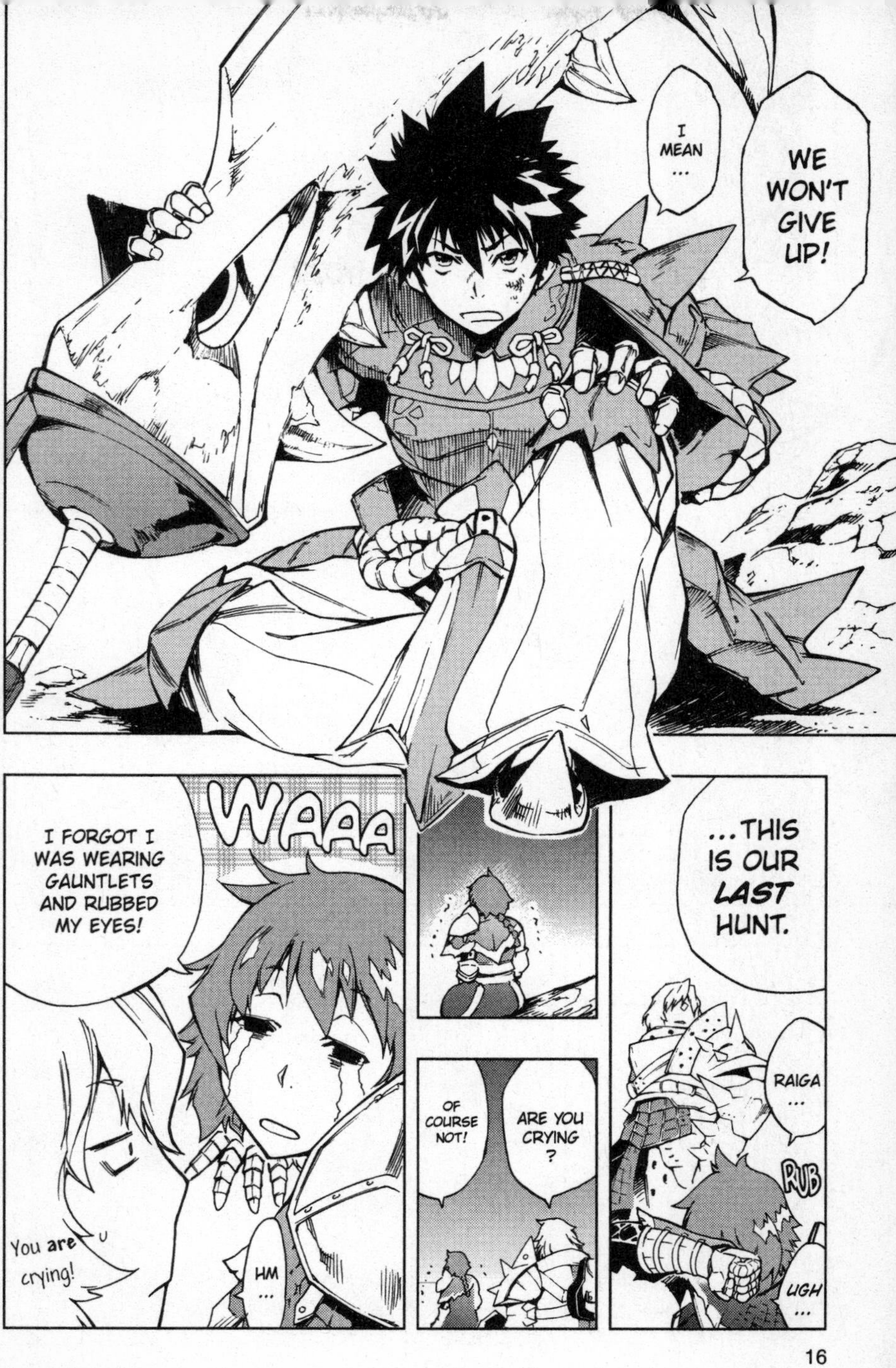
WE WON'T GIVE UP!
I MEAN ...
...THIS IS OUR **LAST** HUNT.
RAIGA ...
RUB
UGH ...
ARE YOU CRYING ?
OF COURSE NOT!
WAAA
I FORGOT I WAS WEARING GAUNTLETS AND RUBBED MY EYES!
HM ...
You **are** crying!

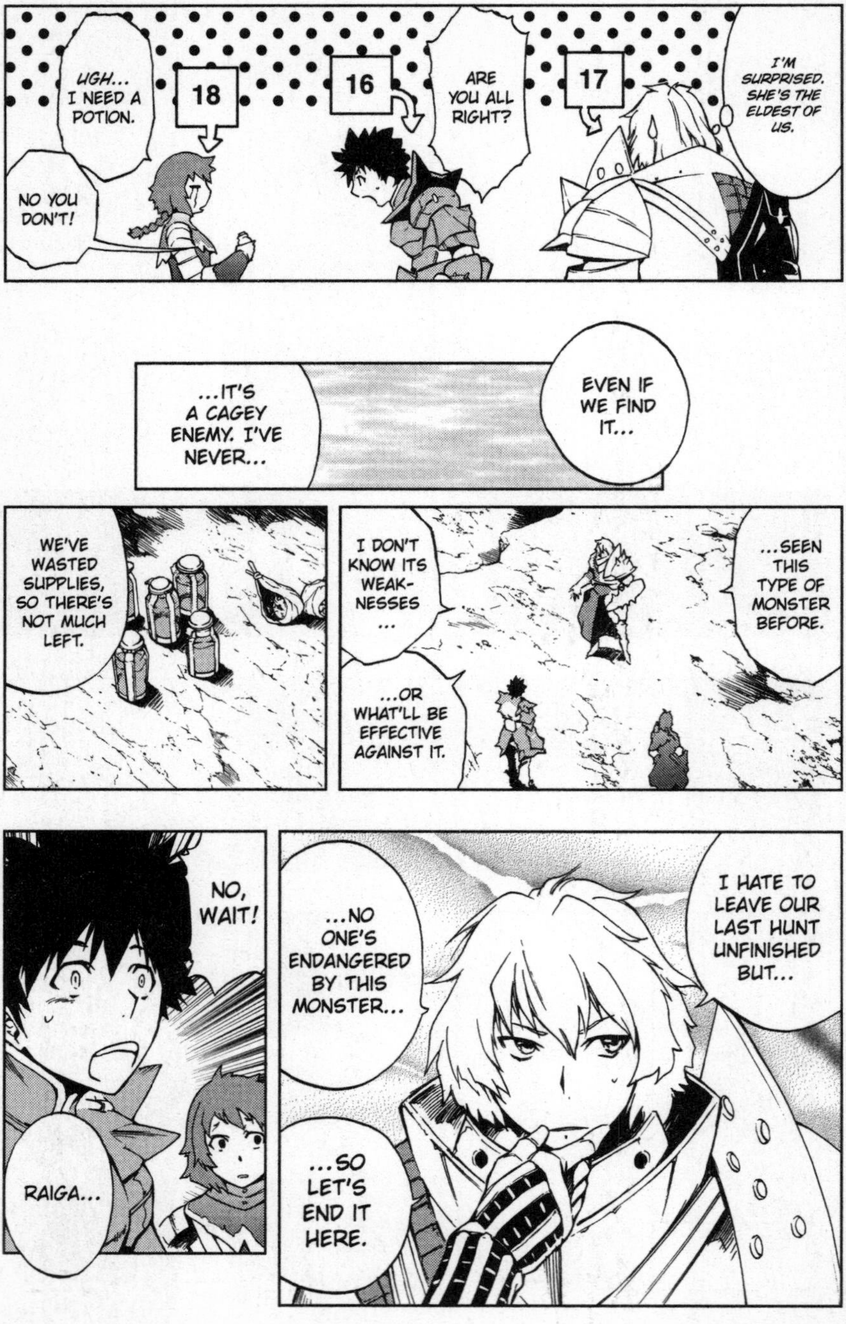
I'M SURPRISED. SHE'S THE ELDEST OF US.
17
ARE YOU ALL RIGHT?
16
UGH... I NEED A POTION.
18
NO YOU DON'T!
EVEN IF WE FIND IT...
...IT'S A CAGEY ENEMY. I'VE NEVER...
...SEEN THIS TYPE OF MONSTER BEFORE.
I DON'T KNOW ITS WEAK-NESSES...
...OR WHAT'LL BE EFFECTIVE AGAINST IT.
WE'VE WASTED SUPPLIES, SO THERE'S NOT MUCH LEFT.
I HATE TO LEAVE OUR LAST HUNT UNFINISHED BUT...
...NO ONE'S ENDANGERED BY THIS MONSTER...
...SO LET'S END IT HERE.
NO, WAIT!
RAIGA...

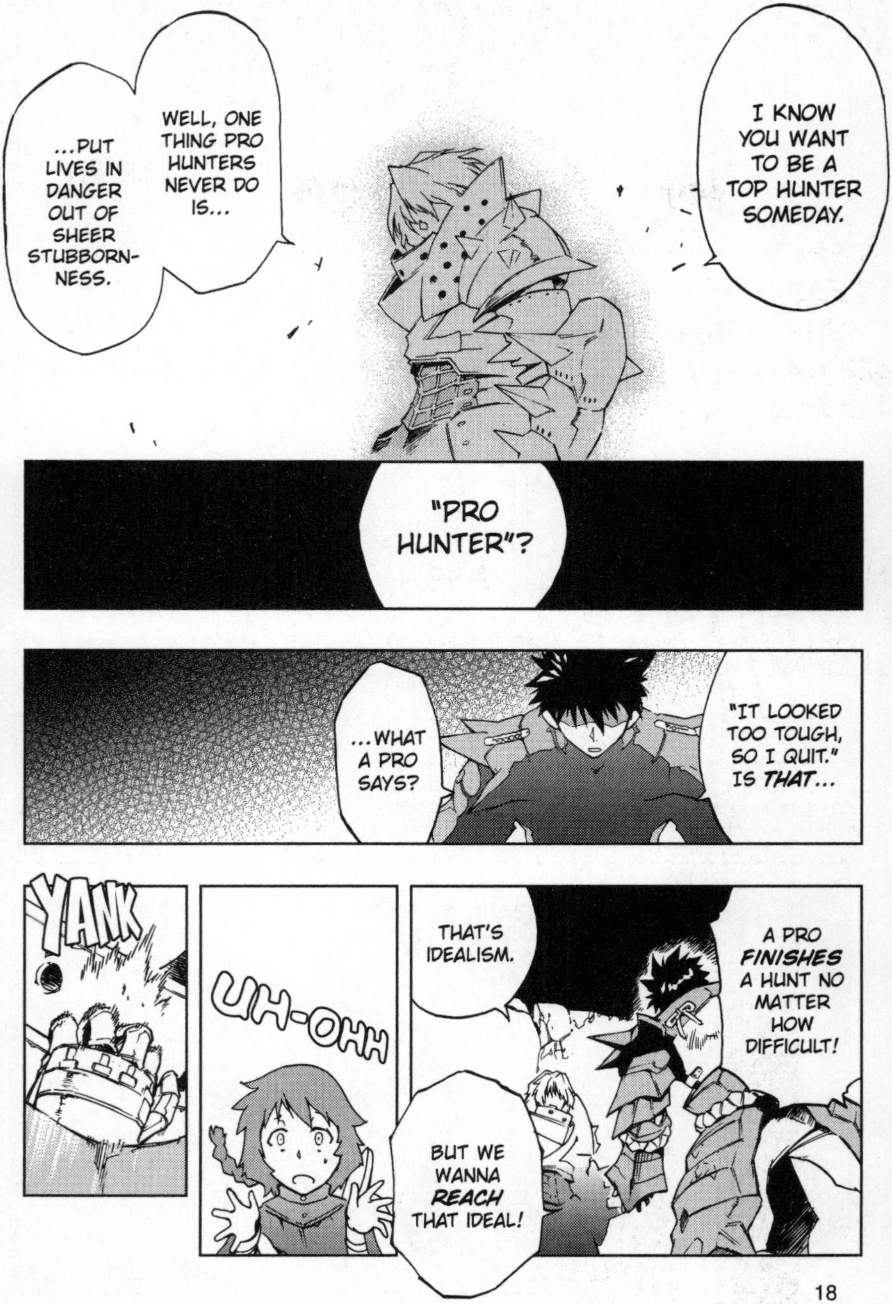
I KNOW YOU WANT TO BE A TOP HUNTER SOMEDAY.
WELL, ONE THING PRO HUNTERS NEVER DO IS...
...PUT LIVES IN DANGER OUT OF SHEER STUBBORN-NESS.
"PRO HUNTER"?
"IT LOOKED TOO TOUGH, SO I QUIT." IS *THAT*...
...WHAT A PRO SAYS?
A PRO *FINISHES* A HUNT NO MATTER HOW DIFFICULT!
THAT'S IDEALISM.
BUT WE WANNA *REACH* THAT IDEAL!
UH-OHH
YANK

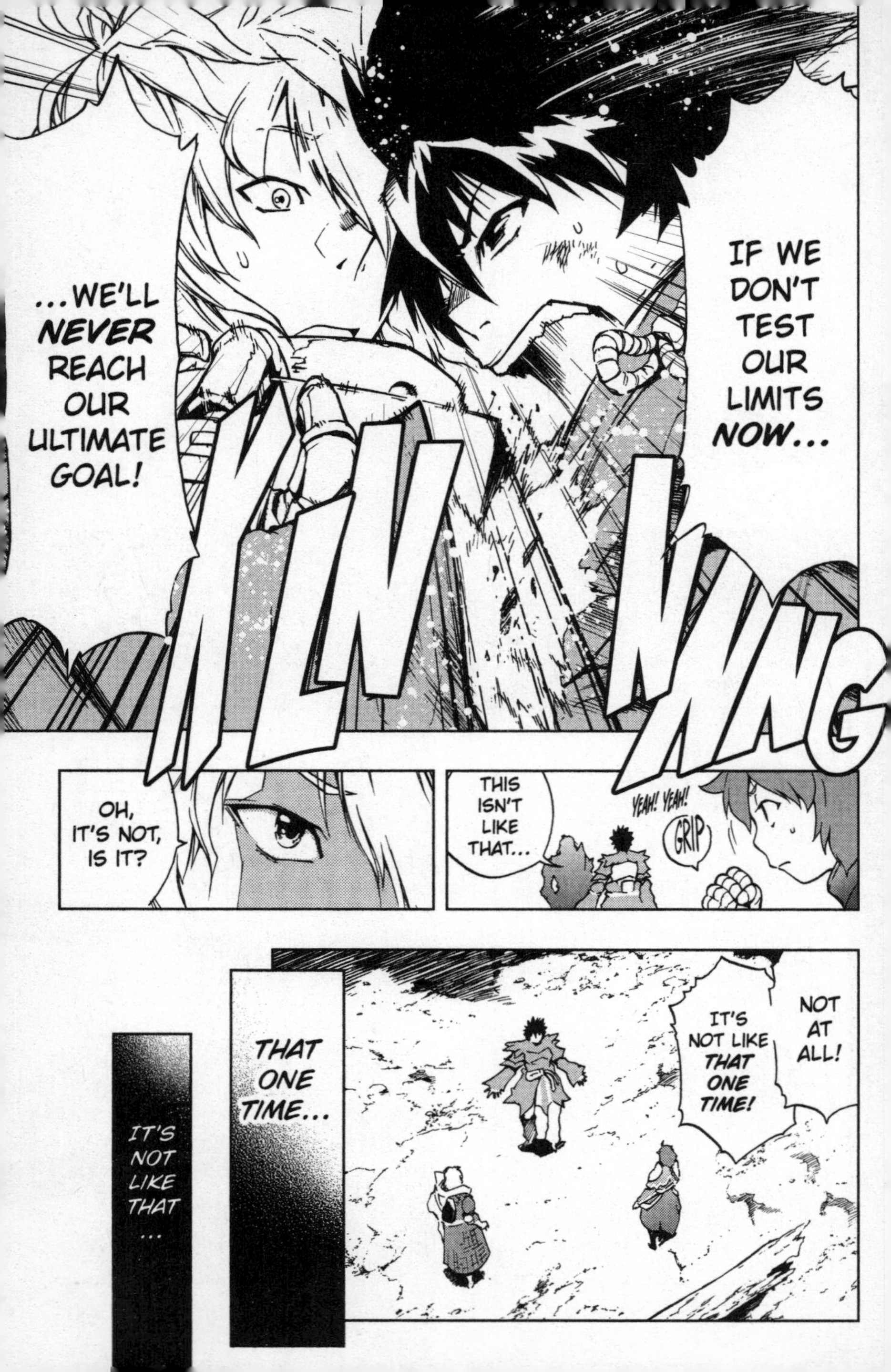
IF WE DON'T TEST OUR LIMITS *NOW*...
...WE'LL *NEVER* REACH OUR ULTIMATE GOAL!
THIS ISN'T LIKE THAT...
YEAH! YEAH!
GRIP
OH, IT'S NOT, IS IT?
NOT AT ALL!
IT'S NOT LIKE *THAT ONE TIME!*
THAT ONE TIME...
IT'S NOT LIKE THAT ...

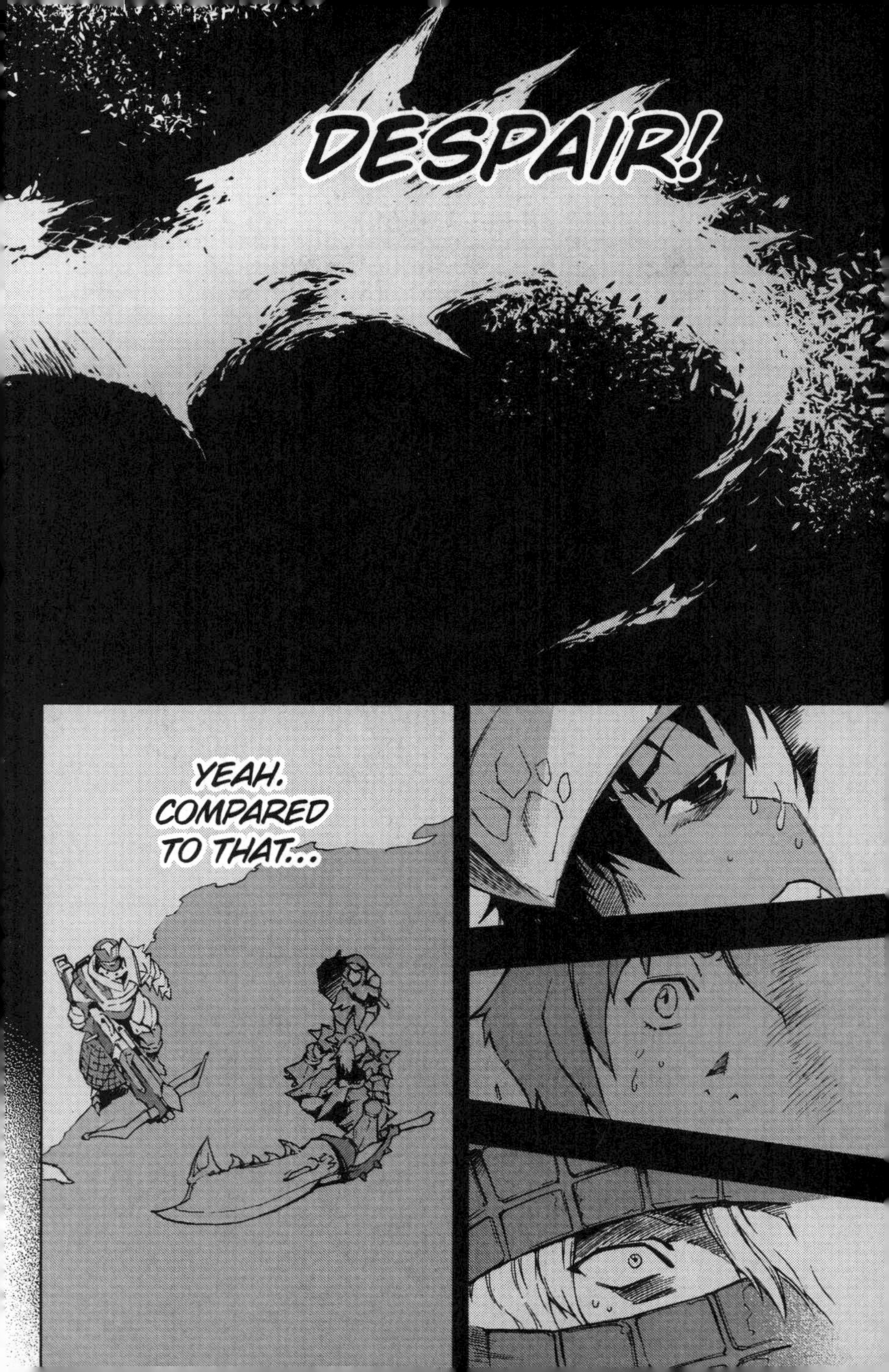
DESPAIR!
YEAH. COMPARED TO THAT...

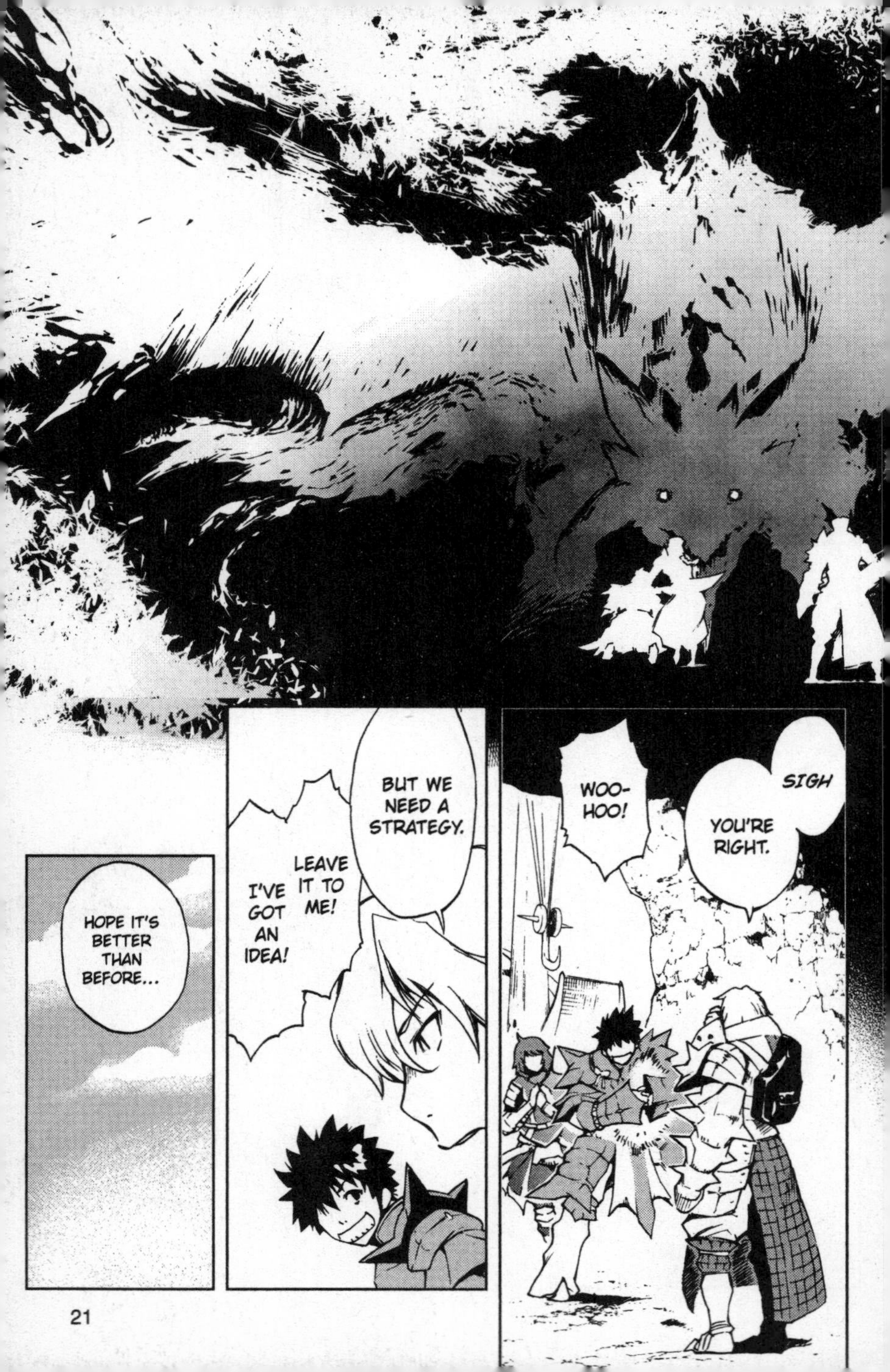
SIGH
YOU'RE RIGHT.
WOO-HOO!
BUT WE NEED A STRATEGY.
LEAVE IT TO ME!
I'VE GOT AN IDEA!
HOPE IT'S BETTER THAN BEFORE...

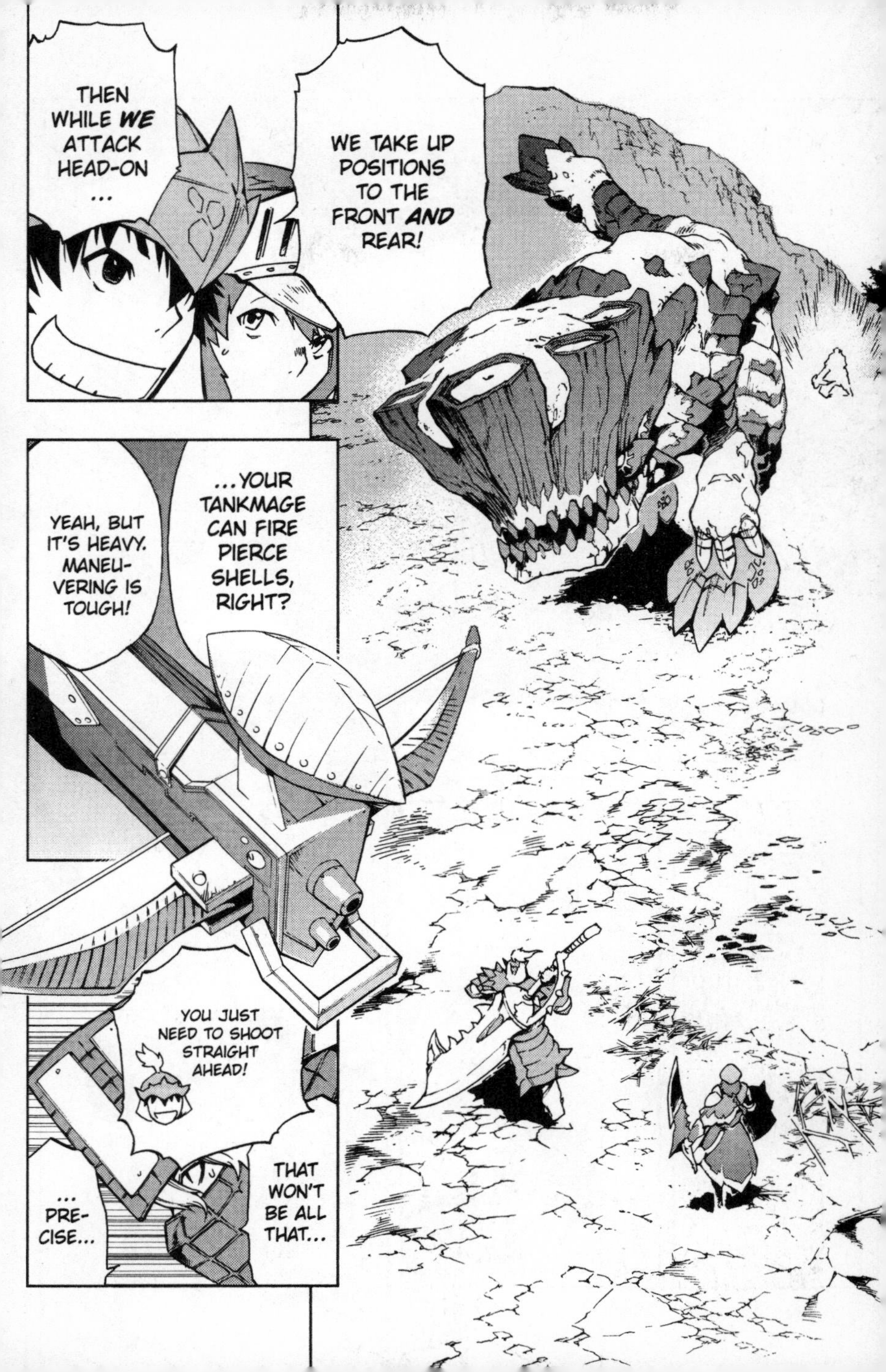
WE TAKE UP POSITIONS TO THE FRONT *AND* REAR!
THEN WHILE *WE* ATTACK HEAD-ON ...
...YOUR TANKMAGE CAN FIRE PIERCE SHELLS, RIGHT?
YEAH, BUT IT'S HEAVY. MANEU-VERING IS TOUGH!
YOU JUST NEED TO SHOOT STRAIGHT AHEAD!
THAT WON'T BE ALL THAT...
... PRE-CISE...

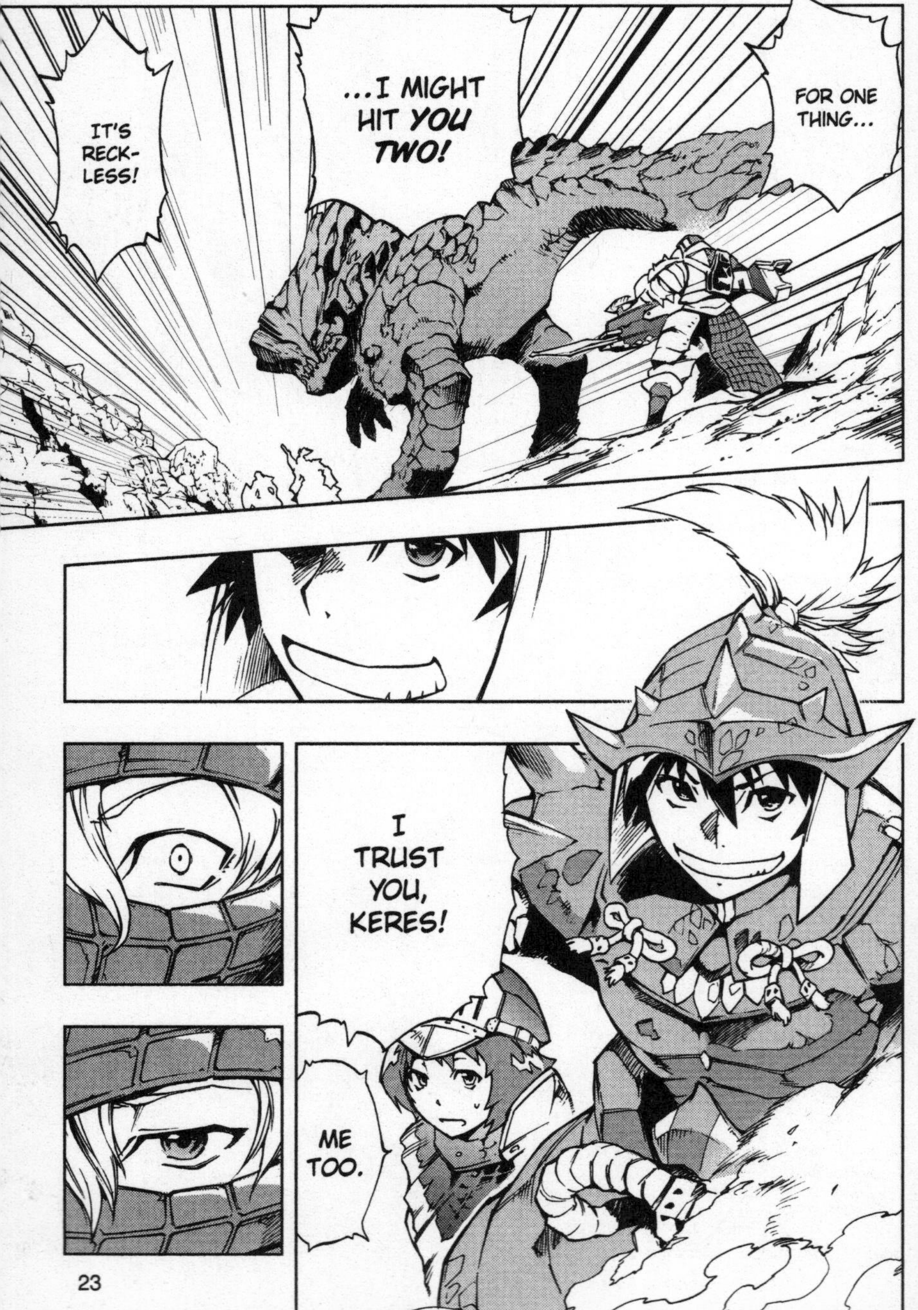
FOR ONE THING...
...I MIGHT HIT YOU TWO!
IT'S RECK-LESS!
I TRUST YOU, KERES!
ME TOO.

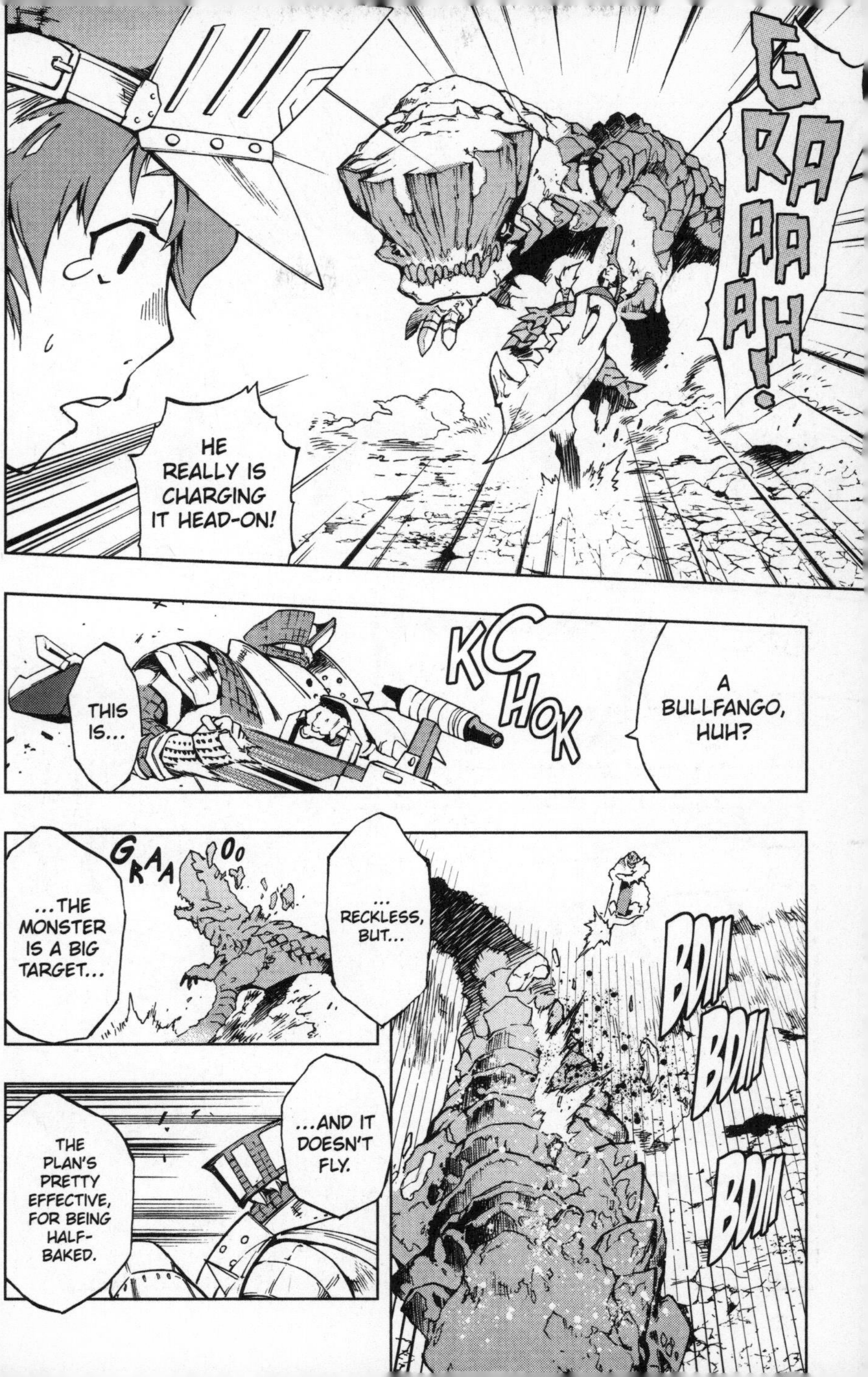
GRAAAAH!
HE REALLY IS CHARGING IT HEAD-ON!
A BULLFANGO, HUH?
KCHOK
THIS IS...
BOM
BOM
BOM
...RECKLESS, BUT...
GRAAOO
...THE MONSTER IS A BIG TARGET...
...AND IT DOESN'T FLY.
THE PLAN'S PRETTY EFFECTIVE, FOR BEING HALF-BAKED.

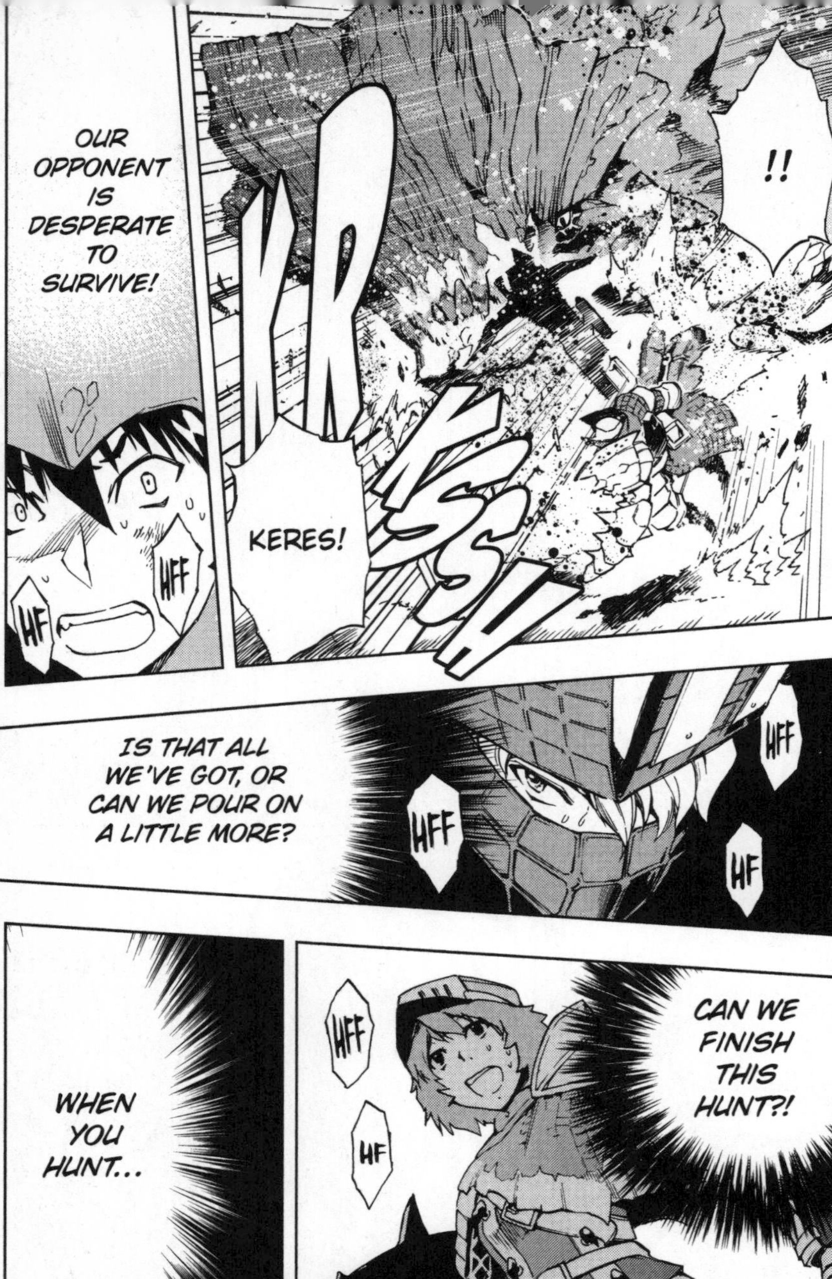
!!
KERES!
OUR OPPONENT IS DESPERATE TO SURVIVE!
HFF
HF
HFF
HF
IS THAT ALL WE'VE GOT, OR CAN WE POUR ON A LITTLE MORE?
HFF
CAN WE FINISH THIS HUNT?!
HFF
HF
WHEN YOU HUNT...

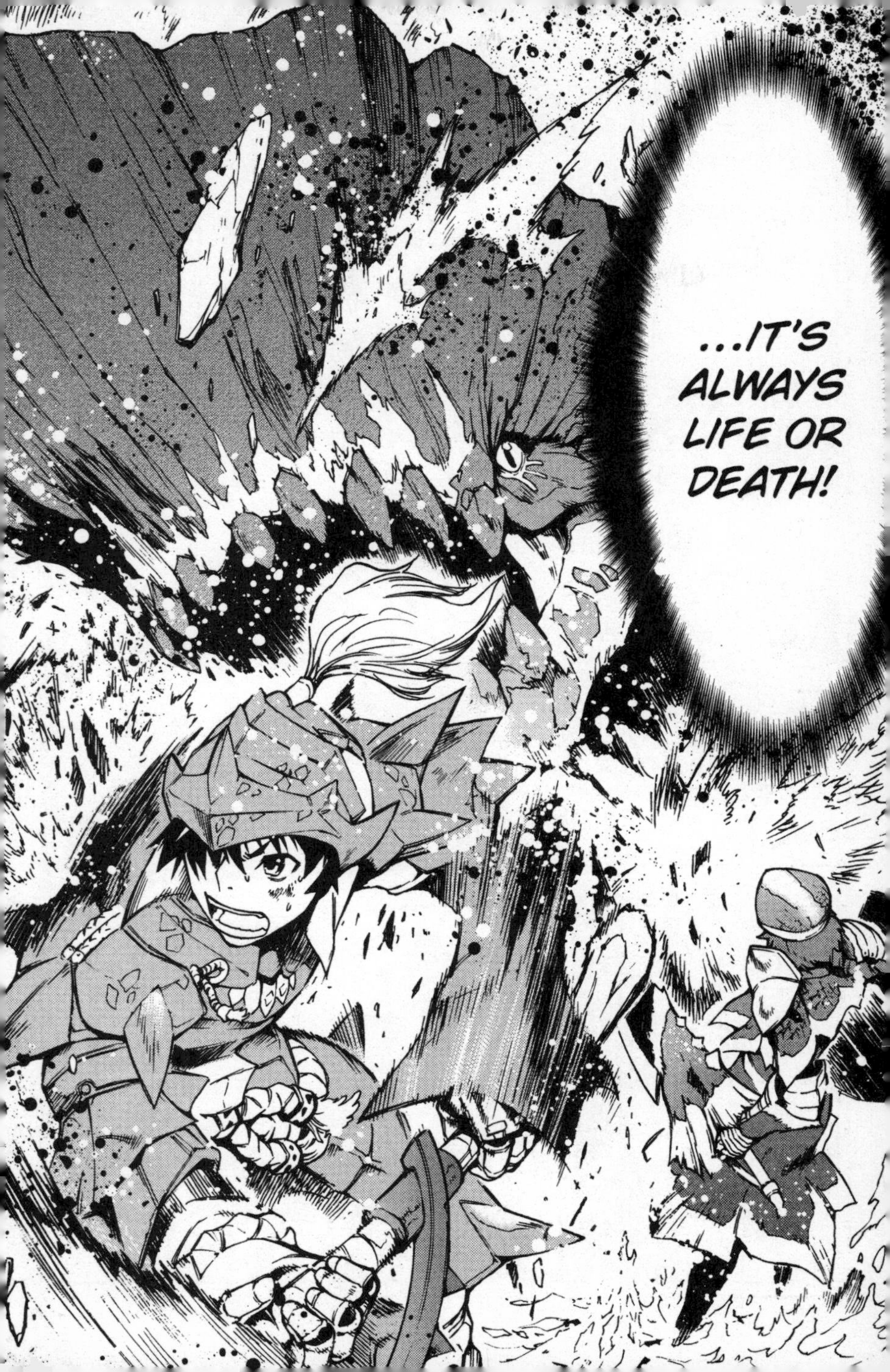
...IT'S ALWAYS LIFE OR DEATH!

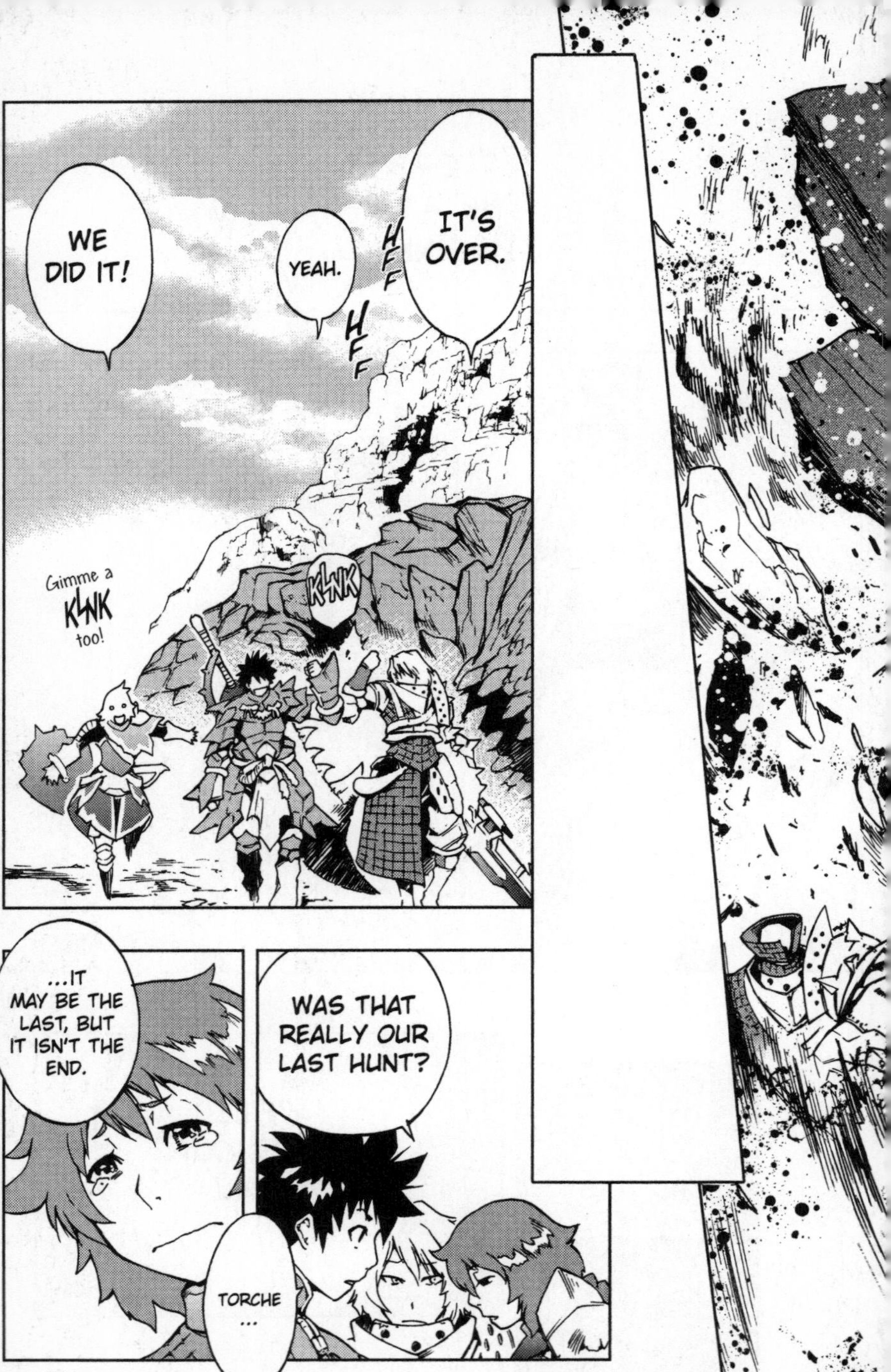
IT'S OVER.
HFF HFF
YEAH.
WE DID IT!
KLINK
Gimme a KLINK too!
WAS THAT REALLY OUR LAST HUNT?
TORCHE ...
...IT MAY BE THE LAST, BUT IT ISN'T THE END.

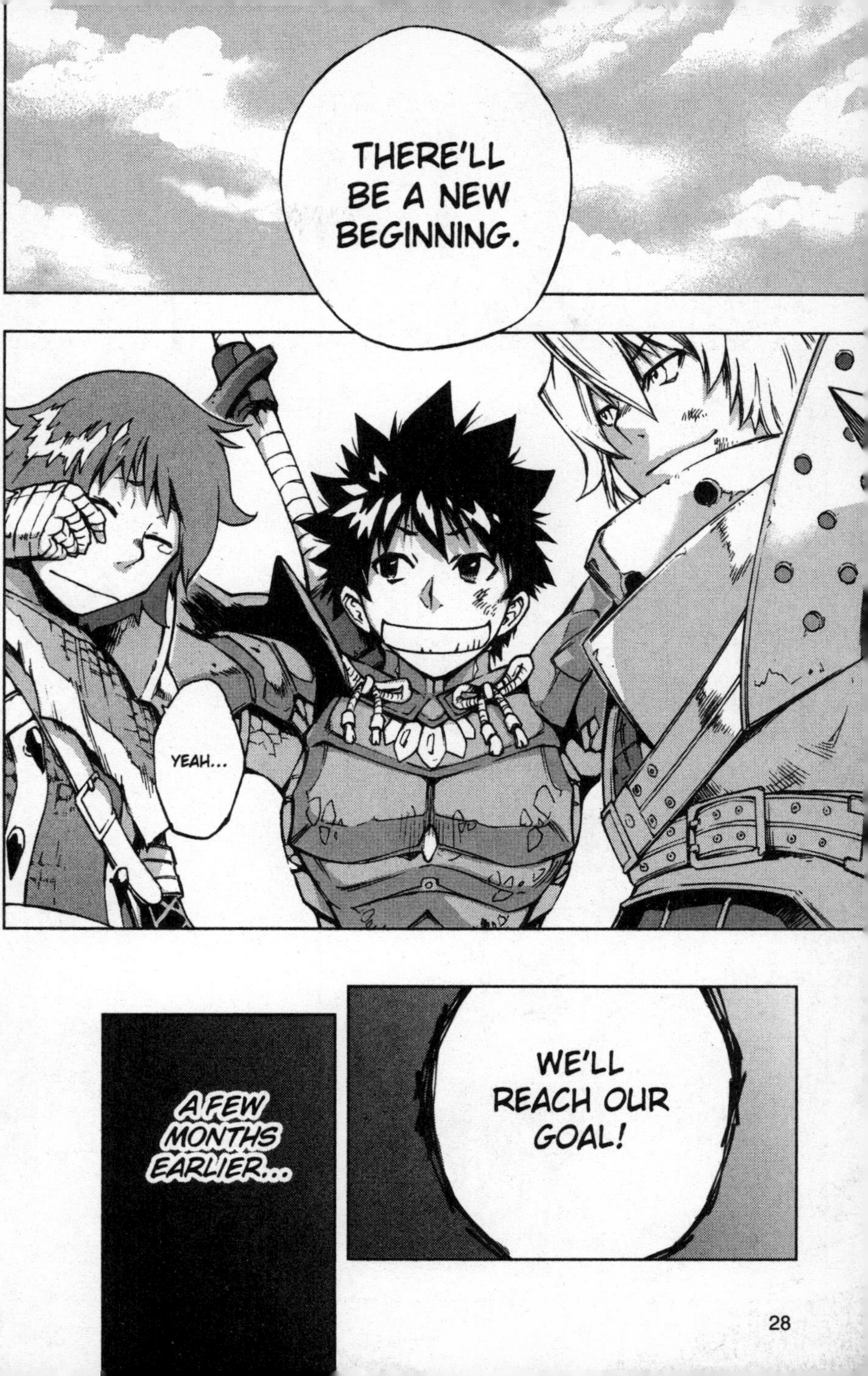
THERE'LL BE A NEW BEGINNING.
YEAH...
WE'LL REACH OUR GOAL!
A FEW MONTHS EARLIER...

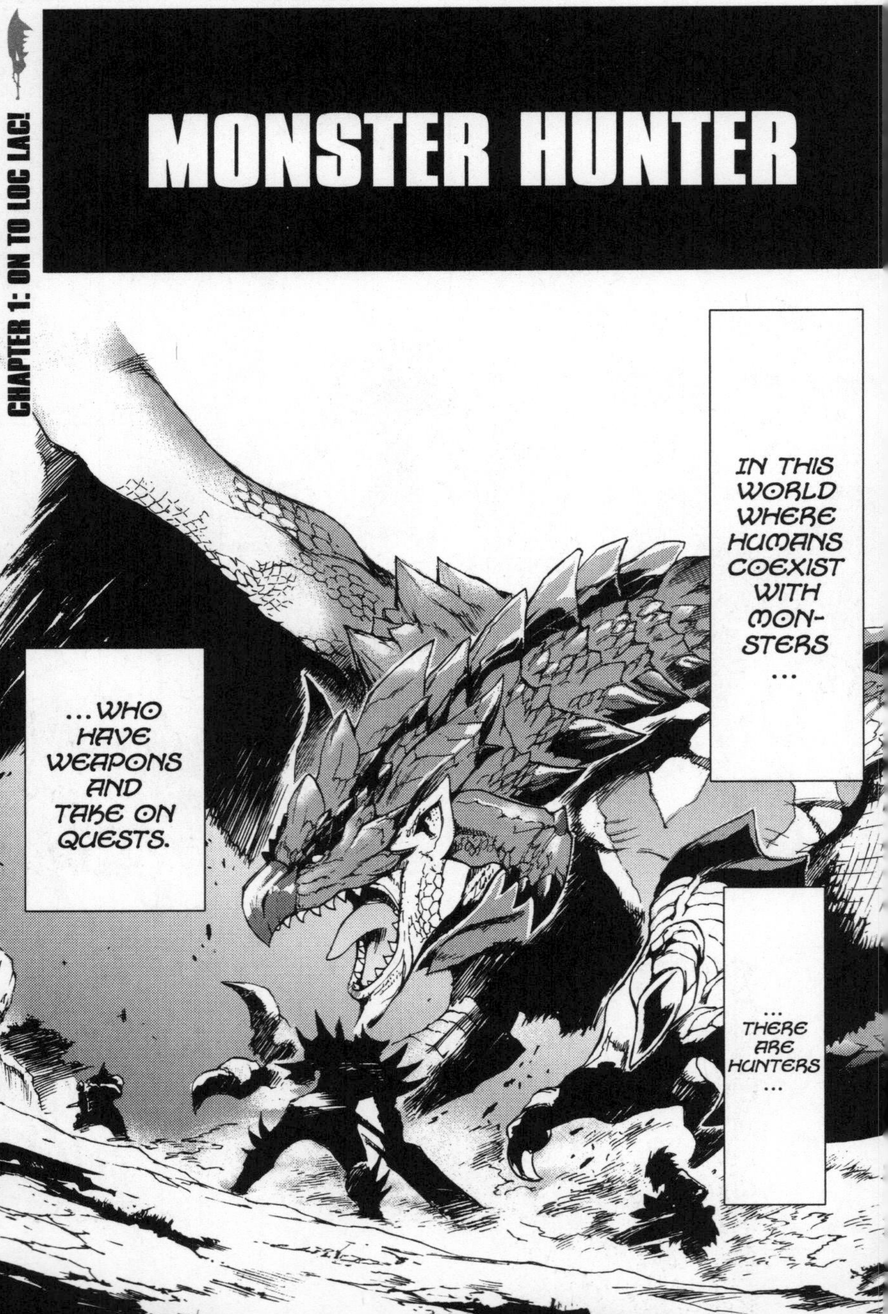
MONSTER HUNTER
CHAPTER 1: ON TO LOC LAC!
IN THIS WORLD WHERE HUMANS COEXIST WITH MON-STERS ...
... THERE ARE HUNTERS ...
...WHO HAVE WEAPONS AND TAKE ON QUESTS.

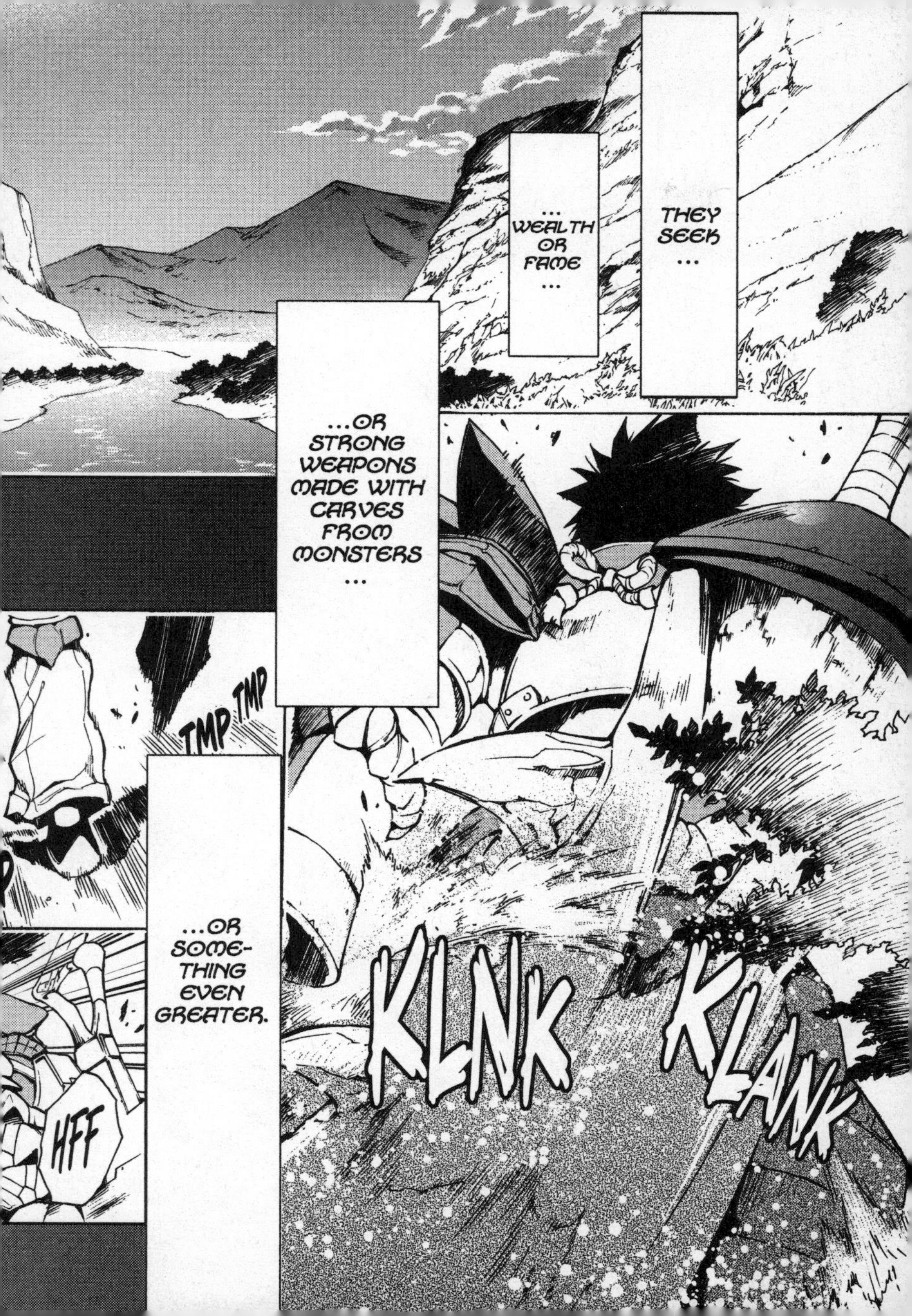
THEY SEEK ...
... WEALTH OR FAME ...
...OR STRONG WEAPONS MADE WITH CARVES FROM MONSTERS ...
KLNK
KLANK
TMP TMP
...OR SOME-THING EVEN GREATER.
HFF

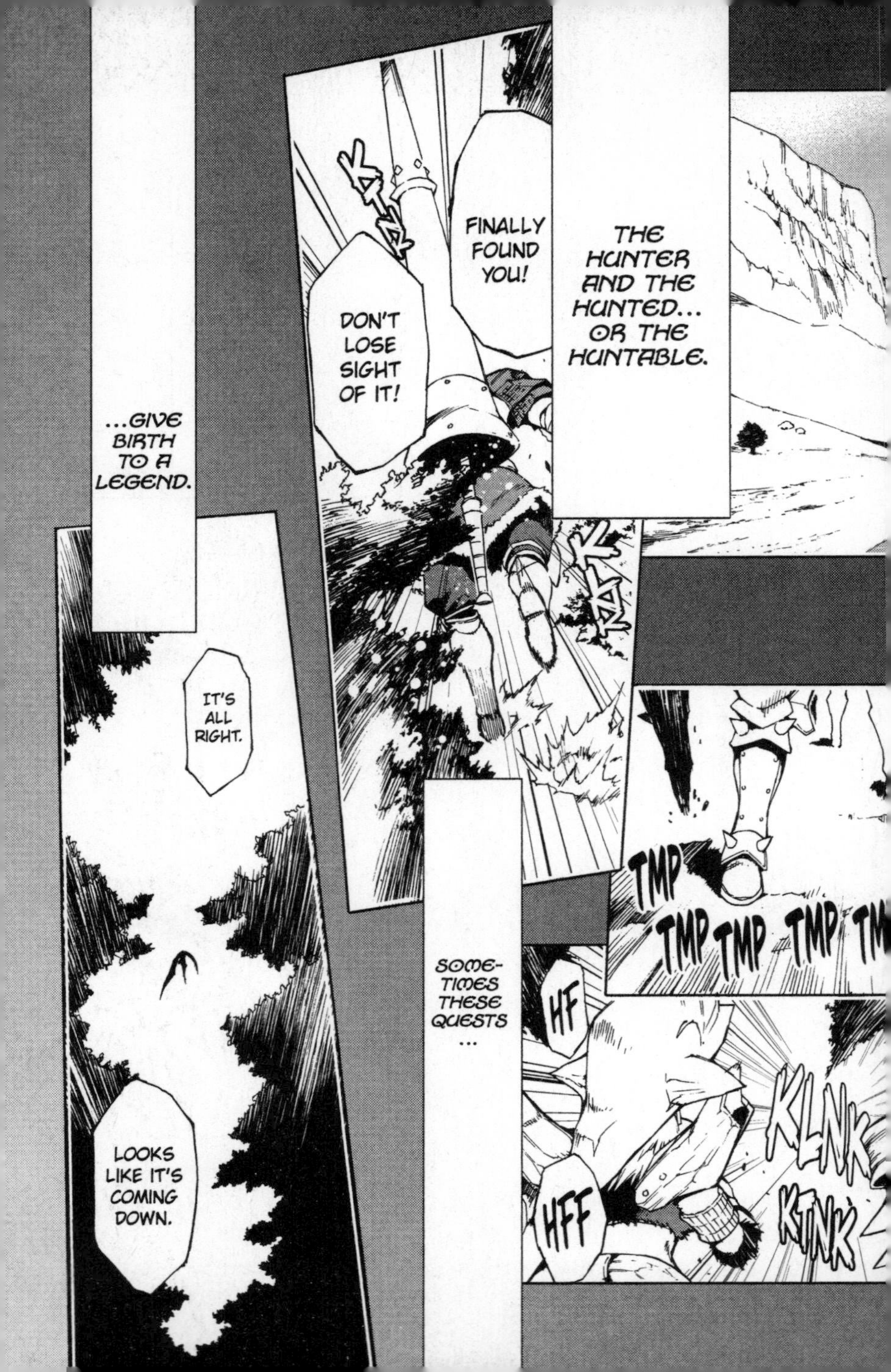
THE HUNTER AND THE HUNTED... OR THE HUNTABLE.
FINALLY FOUND YOU!
DON'T LOSE SIGHT OF IT!
TMP
TMP TMP TMP
SOMETIMES THESE QUESTS...
HF
KLNK
KTNK
HFF
...GIVE BIRTH TO A LEGEND.
IT'S ALL RIGHT.
LOOKS LIKE IT'S COMING DOWN.

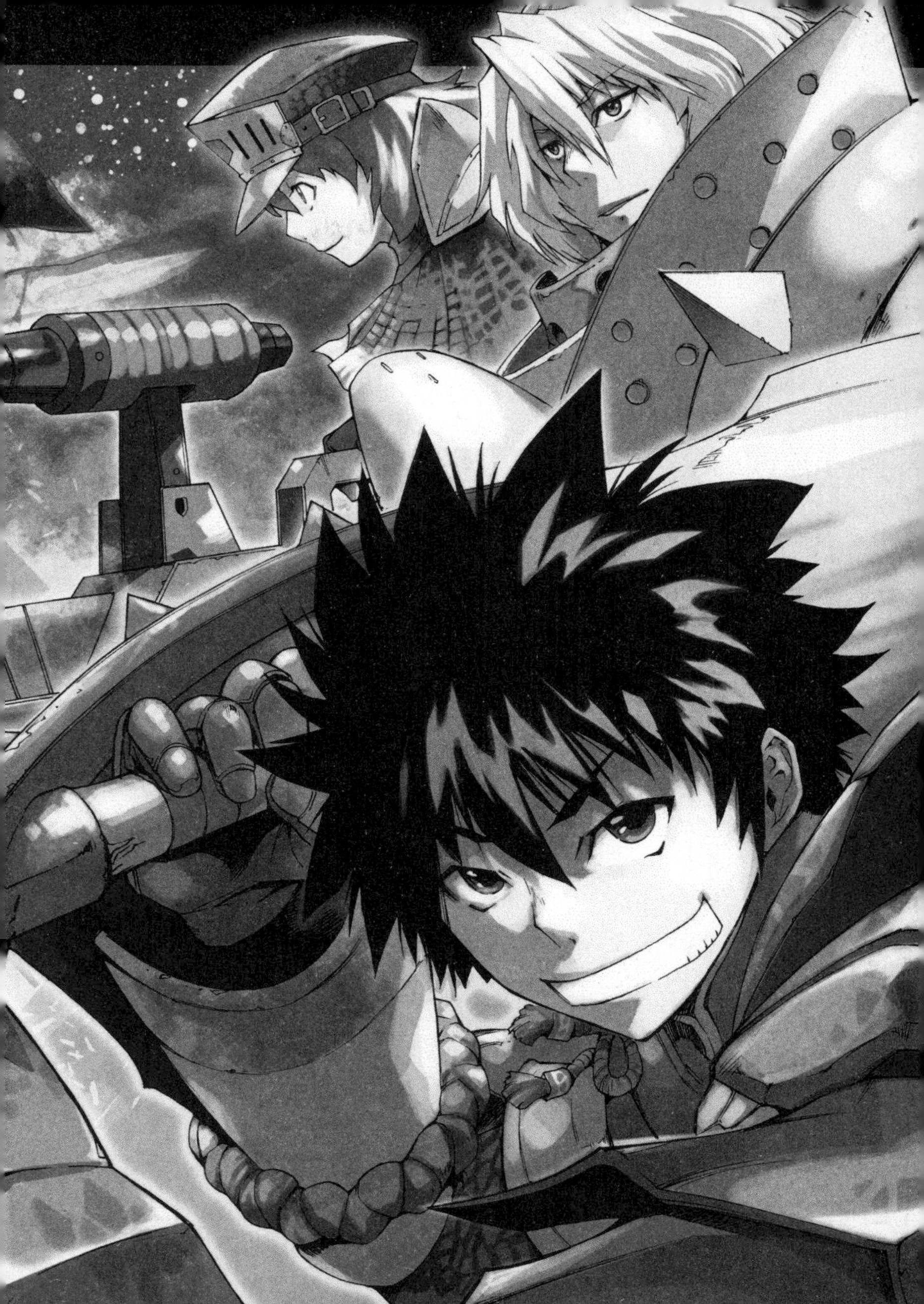

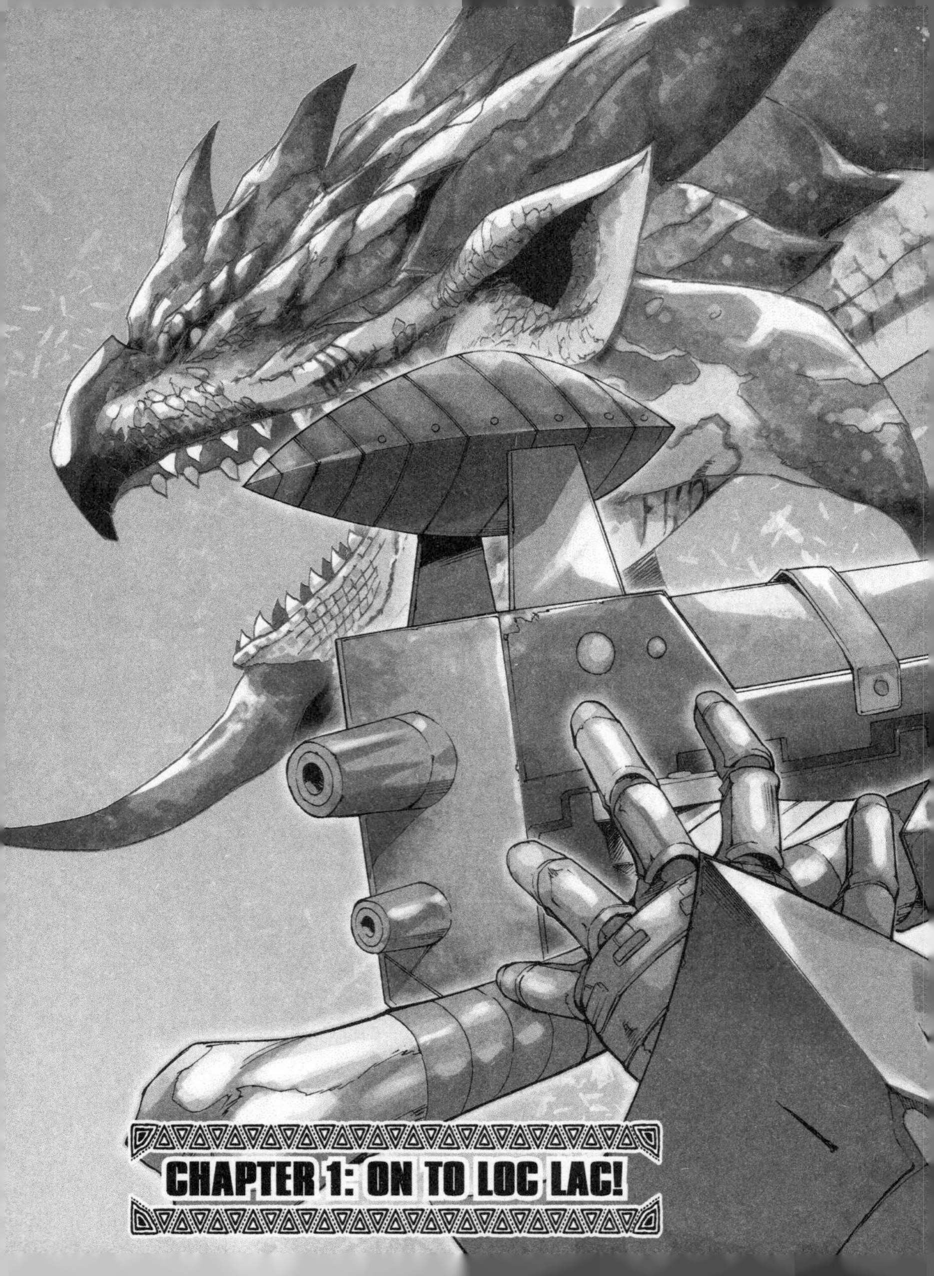
CHAPTER 1: ON TO LOC LAC!

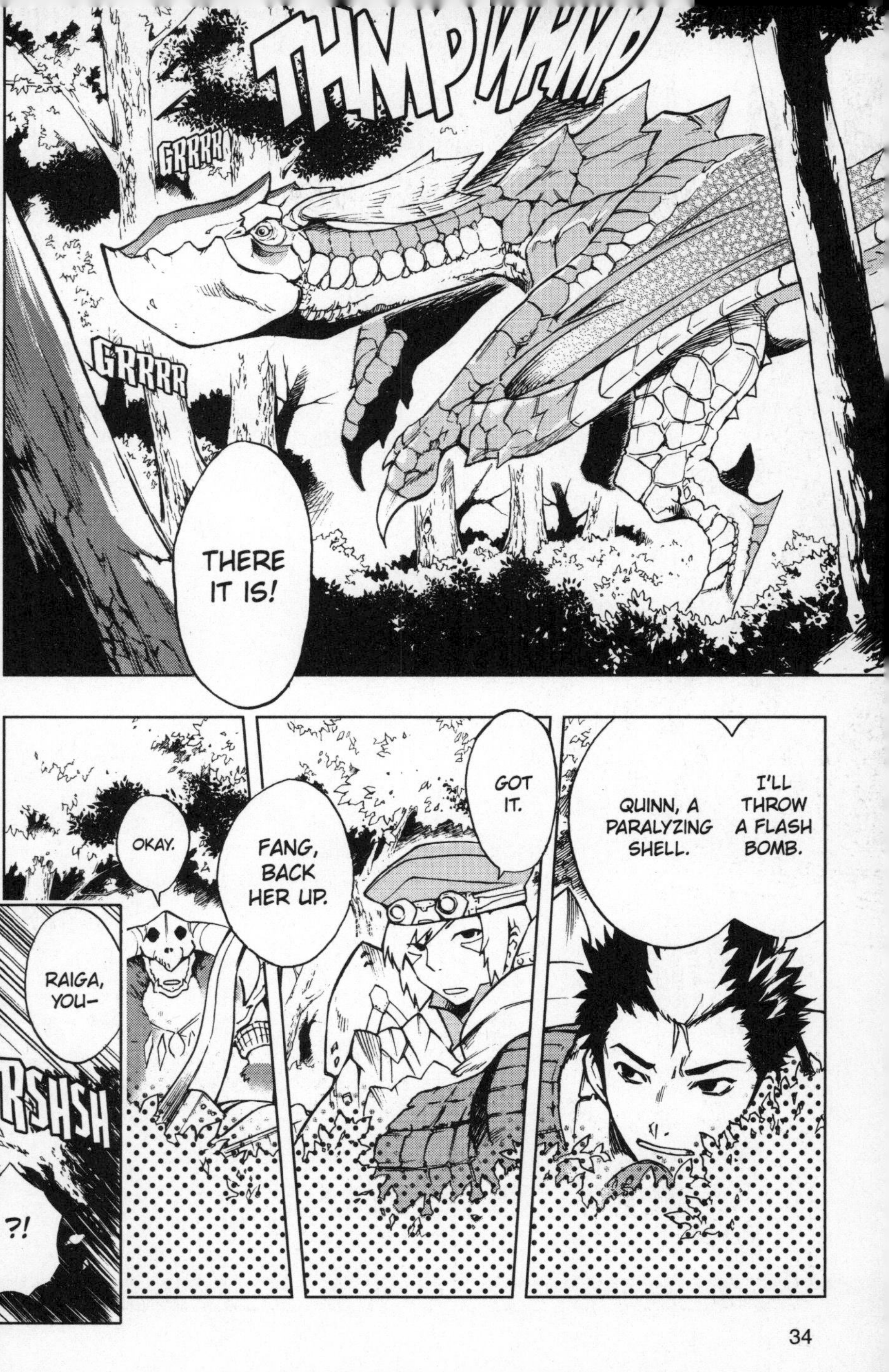
THMP WAMP
GRRRR
GRRRR
THERE IT IS!
I'LL THROW A FLASH BOMB.
QUINN, A PARALYZING SHELL.
GOT IT.
FANG, BACK HER UP.
OKAY.
RAIGA, YOU-
RSHSH
?!

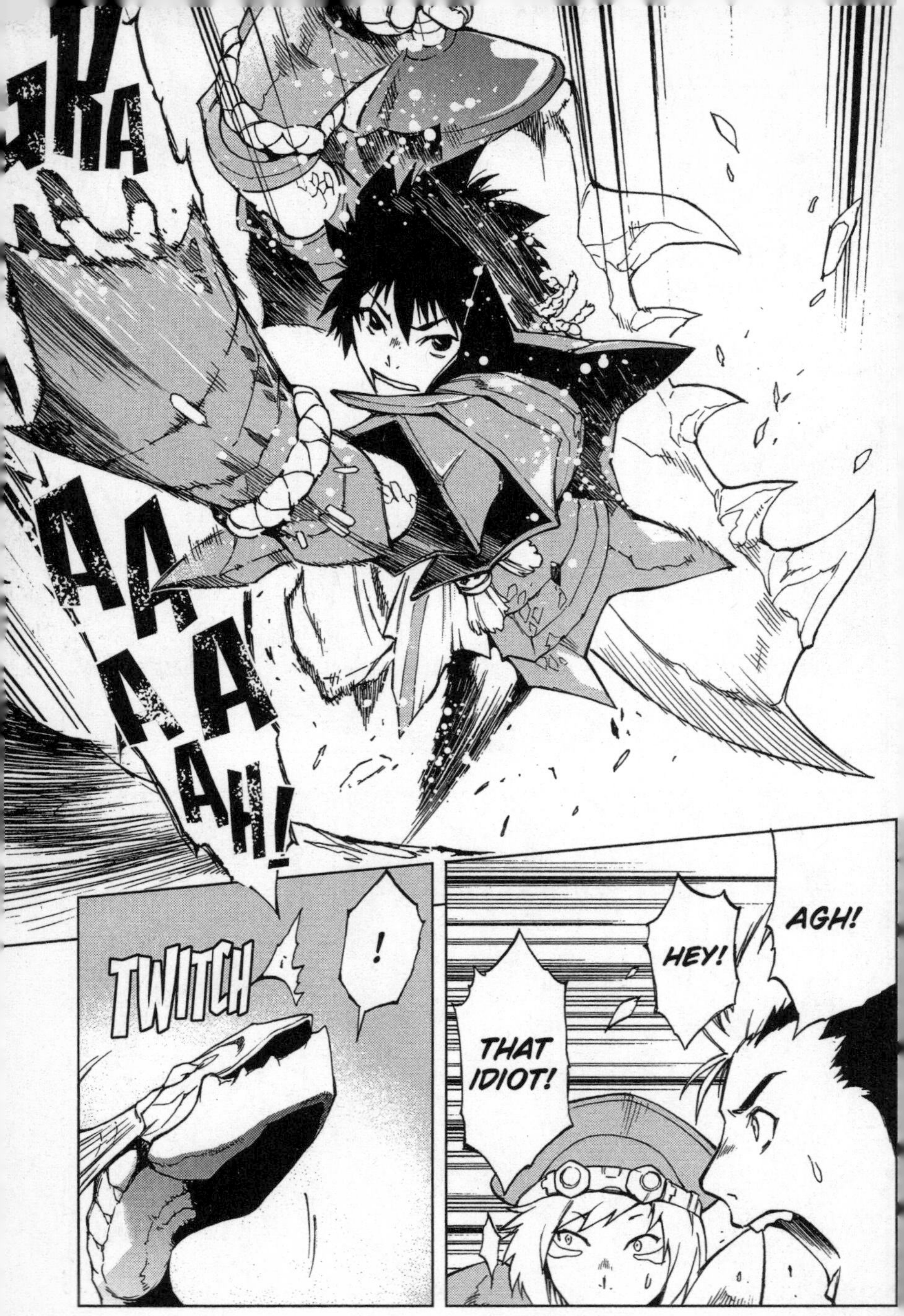
KA
AAAAAH!
AGH!
HEY!
THAT IDIOT!
!
TWITCH

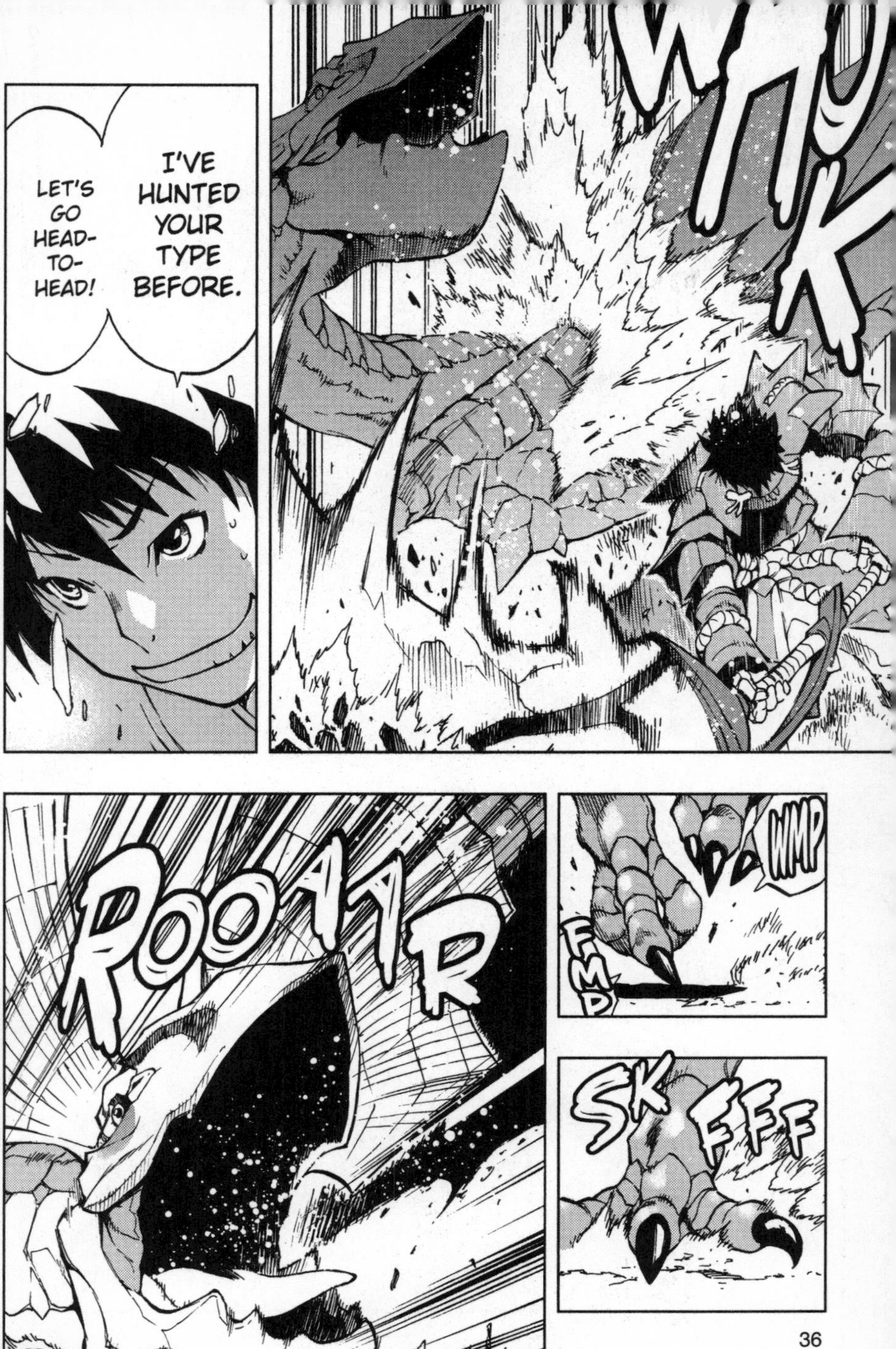
WHUK
I'VE HUNTED YOUR TYPE BEFORE.
LET'S GO HEAD-TO-HEAD!
WMP
FMP
SK FFF
ROOAAR

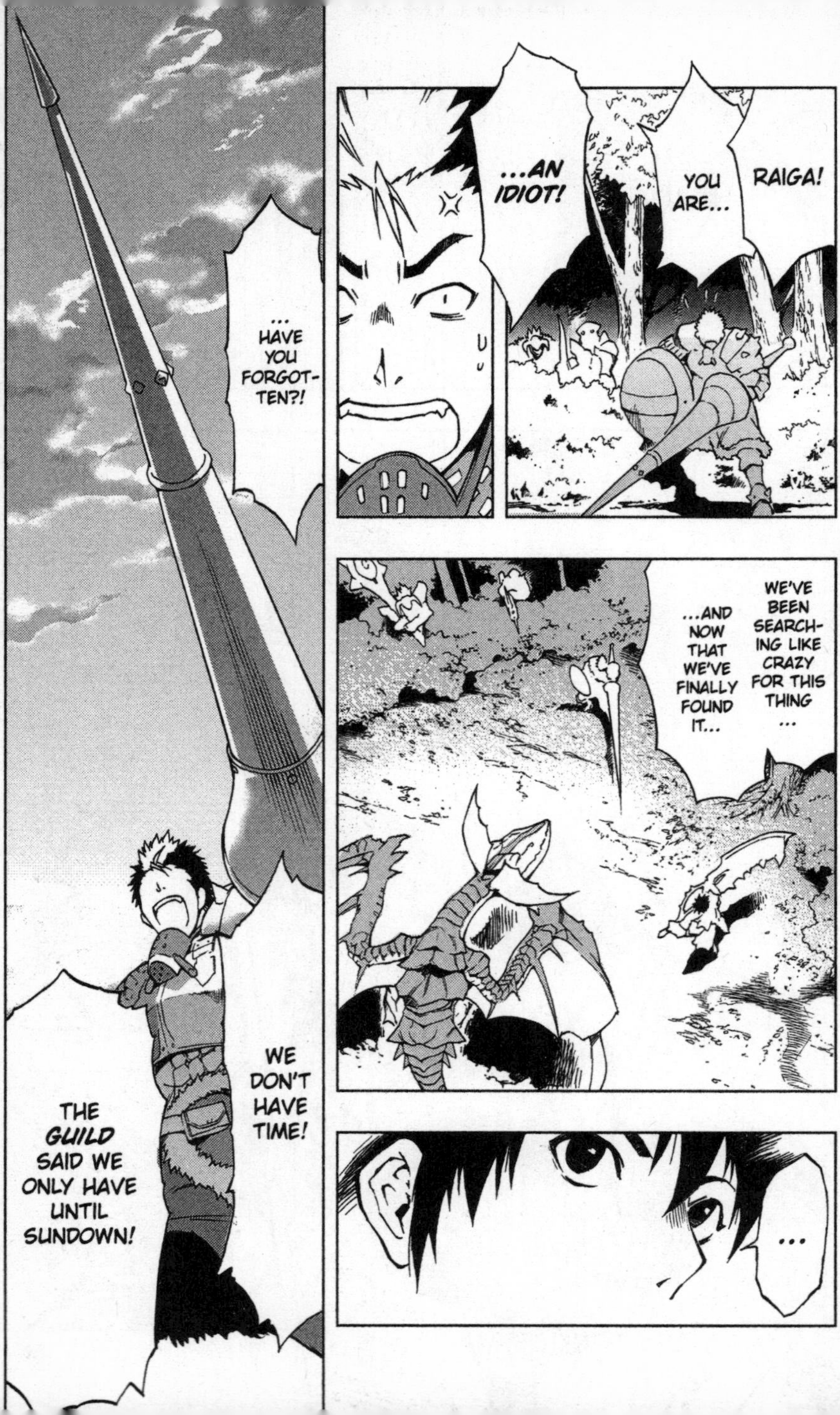
RAIGA!
YOU ARE...
...AN IDIOT!
WE'VE BEEN SEARCHING LIKE CRAZY FOR THIS THING ...
...AND NOW THAT WE'VE FINALLY FOUND IT...
...
... HAVE YOU FORGOTTEN?!
WE DON'T HAVE TIME!
THE GUILD SAID WE ONLY HAVE UNTIL SUNDOWN!

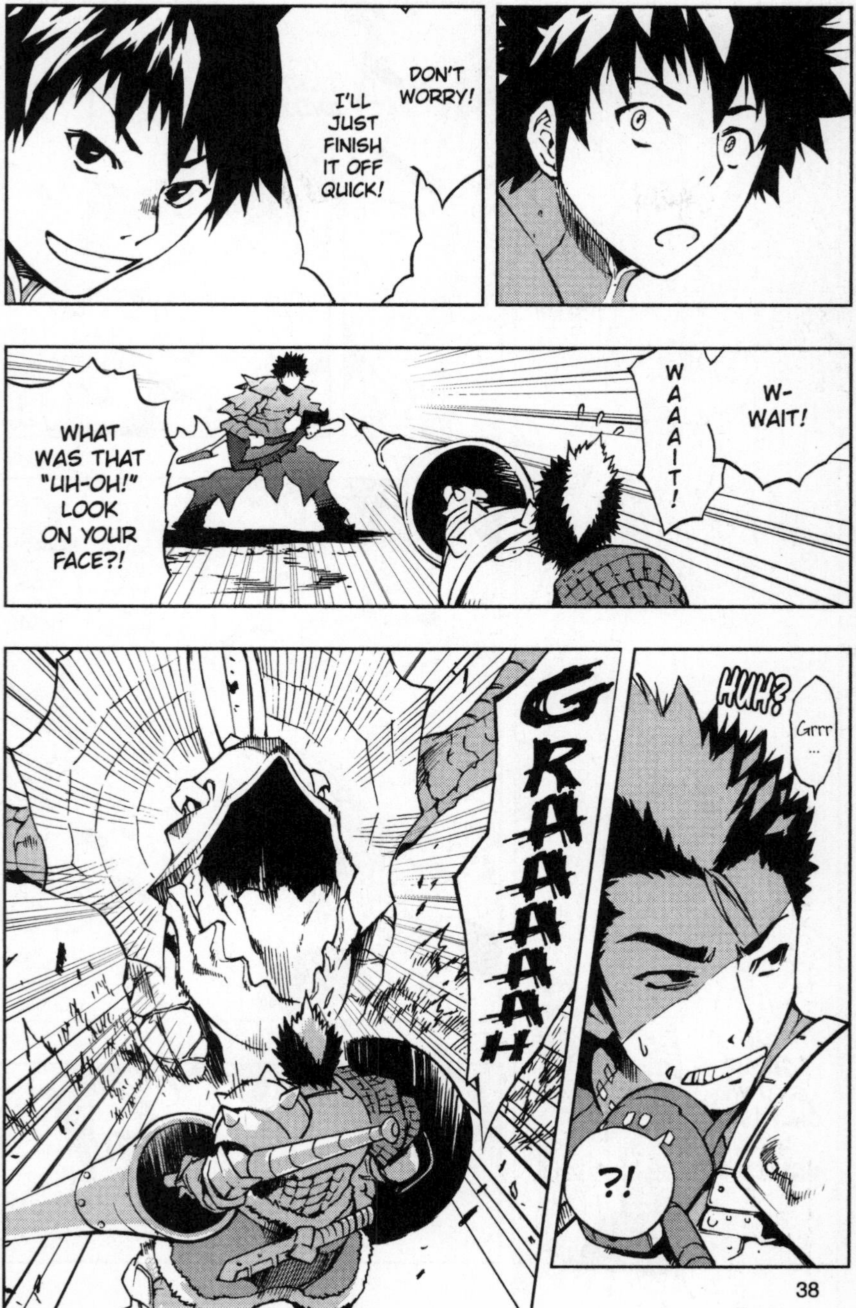
DON'T WORRY!
I'LL JUST FINISH IT OFF QUICK!
W- WAIT!
WAAAAIT!
WHAT WAS THAT "UH-OH!" LOOK ON YOUR FACE?!
HUH?
Grrr ...
?!
GRAAAAAAAH

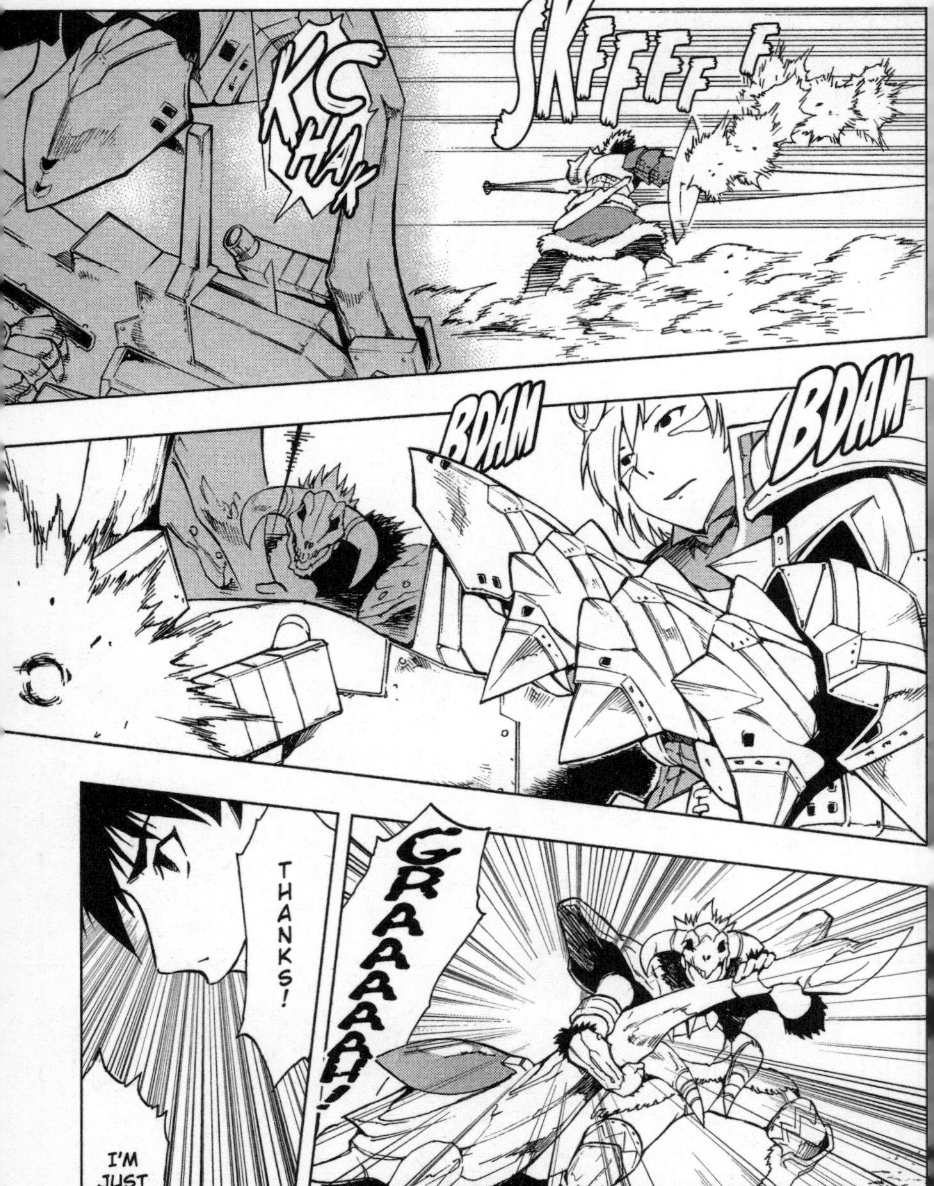
SKFFFF F
KC HAK
BDAM
BDAM
GRAAAAAAH!
THANKS!
I'M JUST WARMING-UP!

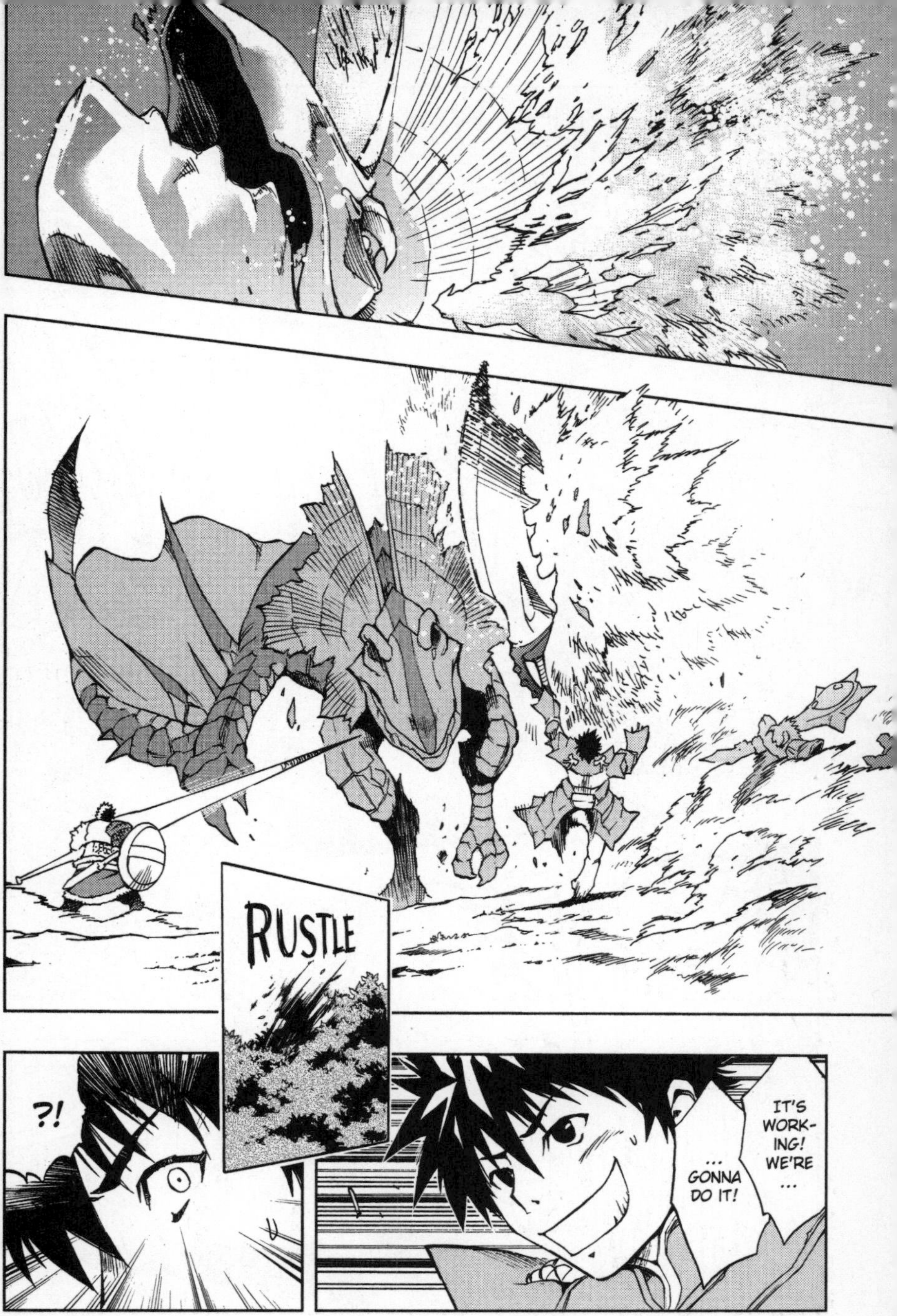
RUSTLE
IT'S WORKING! WE'RE ...
... GONNA DO IT!
?!

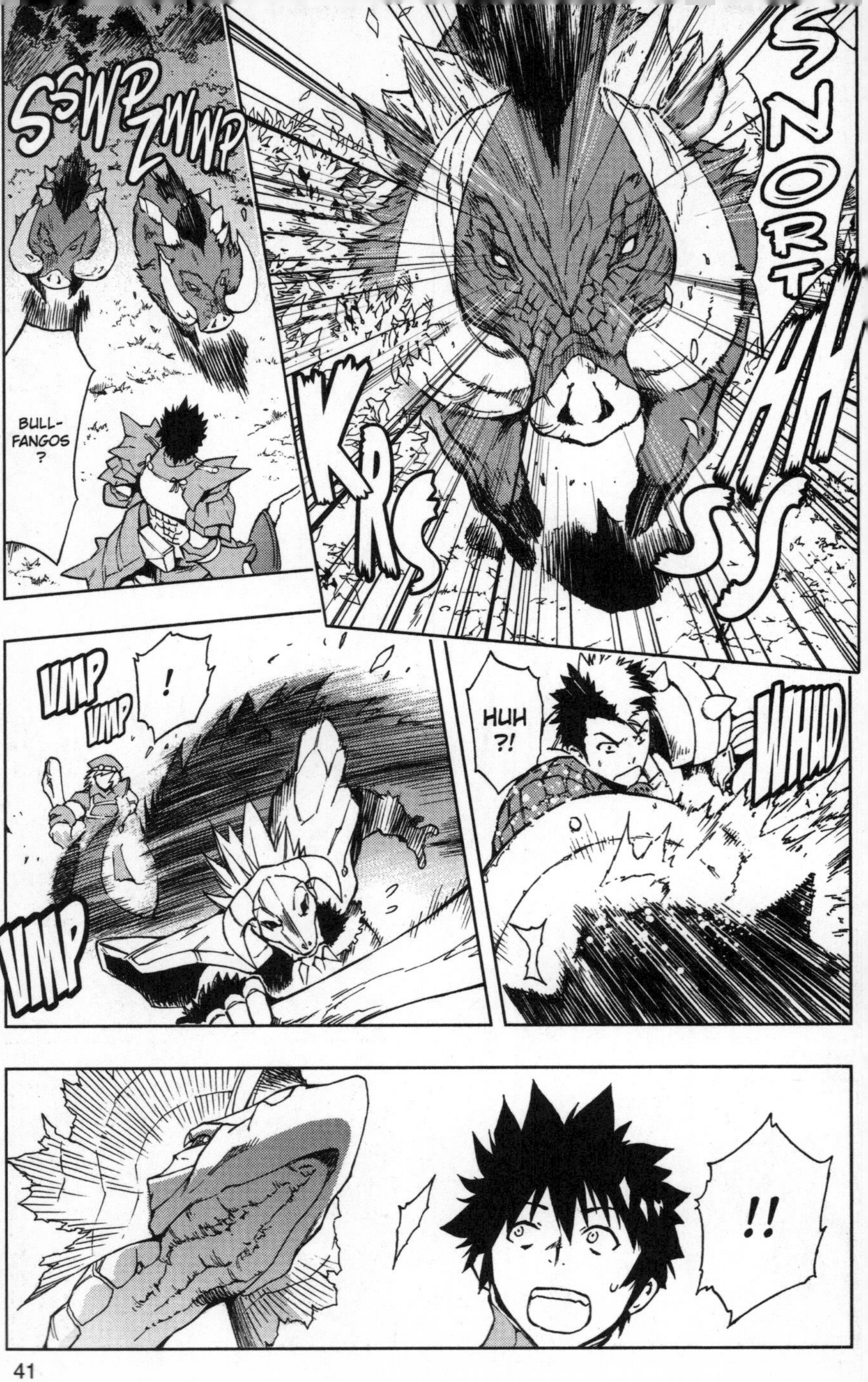
SNORT
HH
KRSSS
SSWP
ZWWP
BULL-FANGOS?
HUH?!
WHUD
!
VMP VMP
VMP
!!

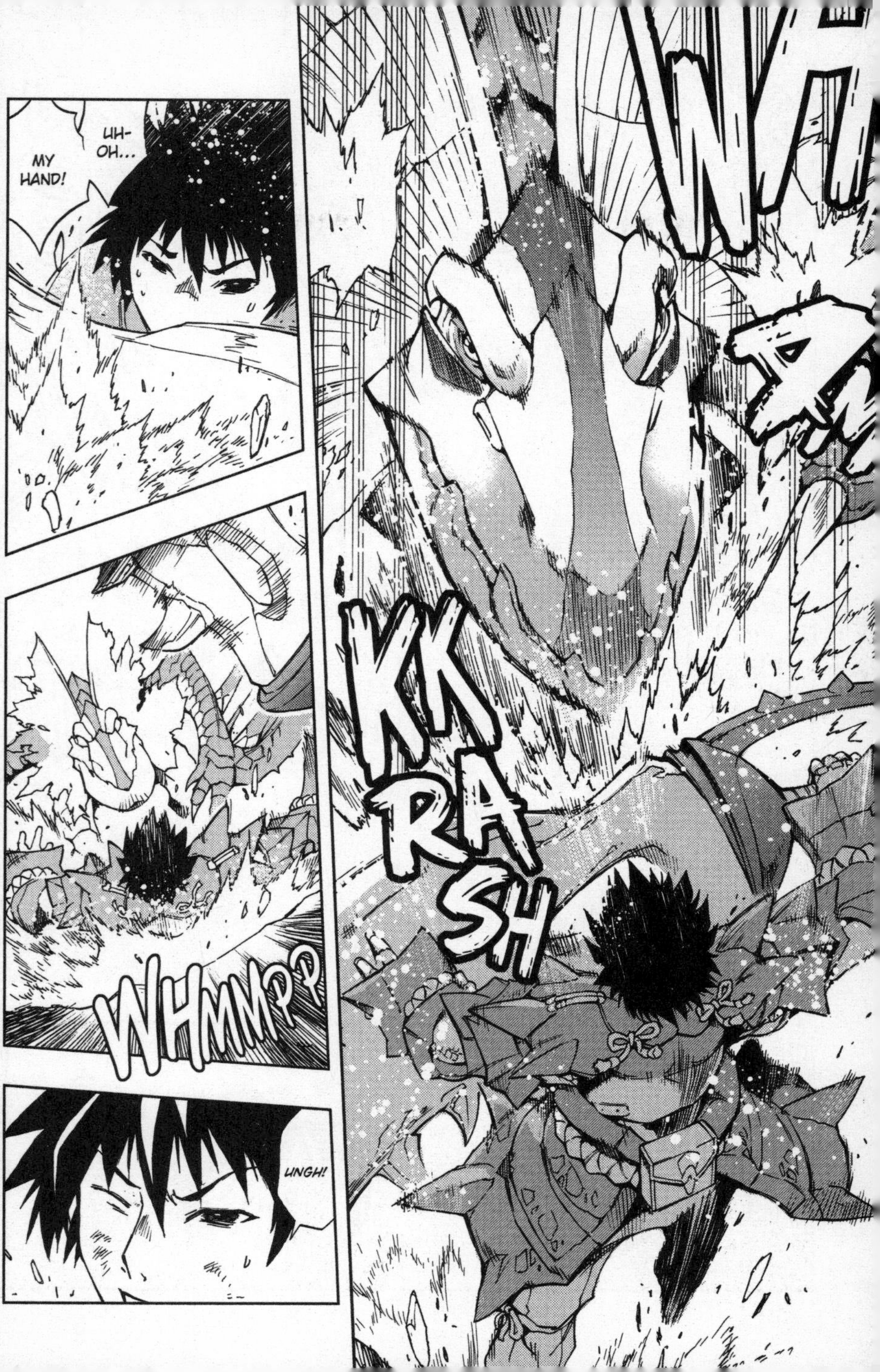
KKRASH
UH-OH...
MY HAND!
WHMMP
UNGH!

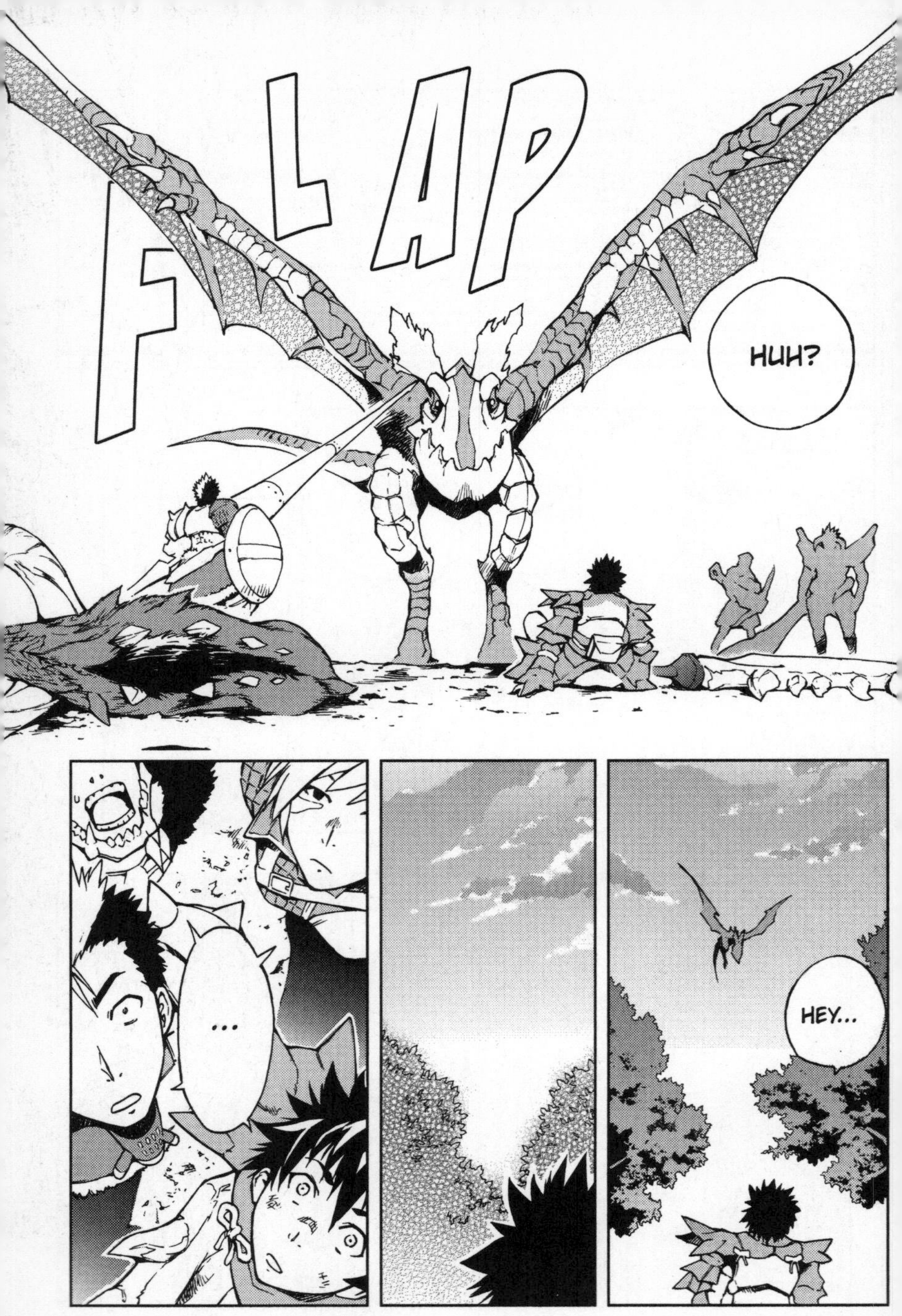
FLAP
HUH?
HEY...
...

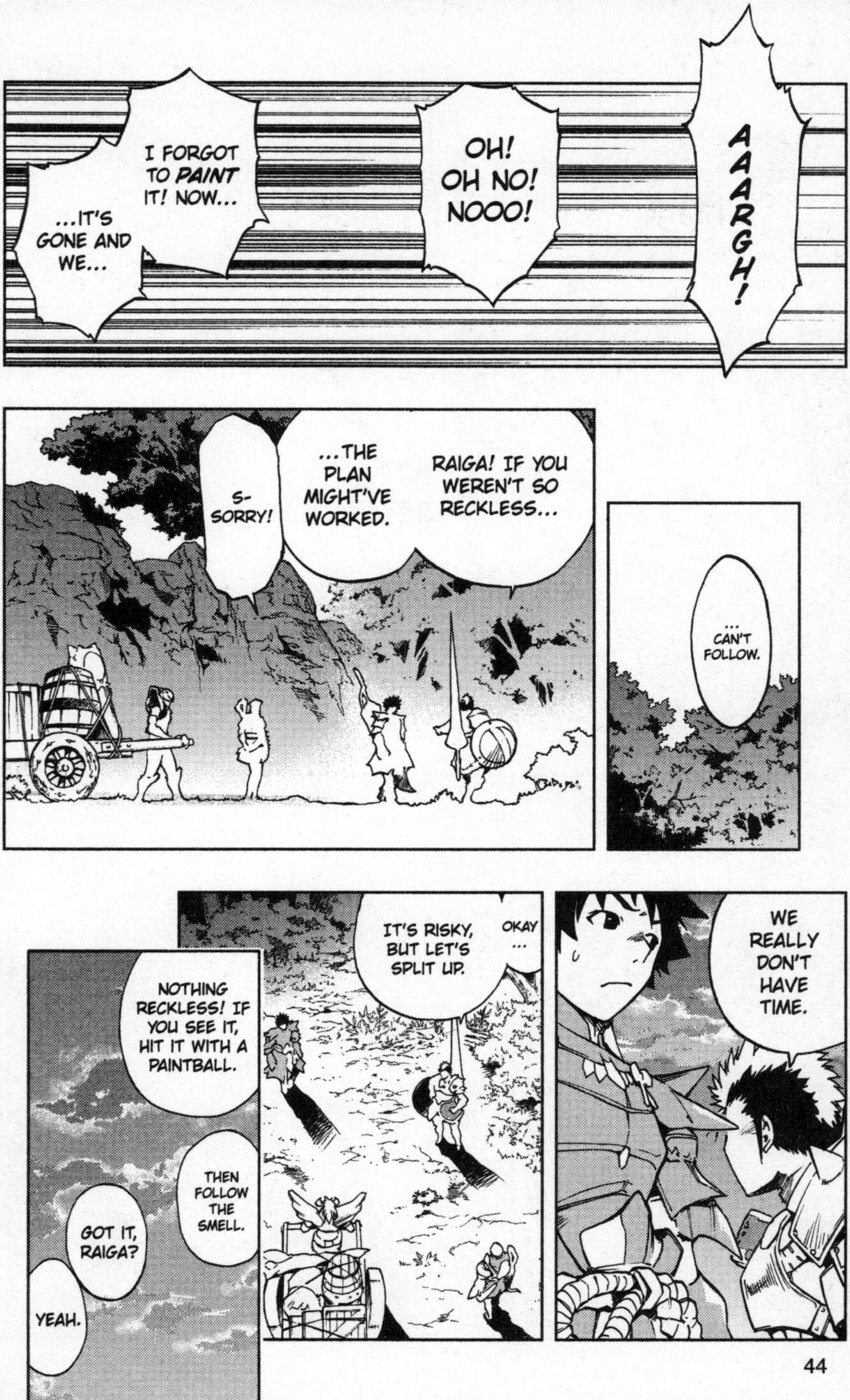
AAARGH!
OH! OH NO! NOOO!
I FORGOT TO PAINT IT! NOW...
...IT'S GONE AND WE...
...CAN'T FOLLOW.
RAIGA! IF YOU WEREN'T SO RECKLESS...
...THE PLAN MIGHT'VE WORKED.
S-SORRY!
WE REALLY DON'T HAVE TIME.
OKAY...
IT'S RISKY, BUT LET'S SPLIT UP.
NOTHING RECKLESS! IF YOU SEE IT, HIT IT WITH A PAINTBALL.
THEN FOLLOW THE SMELL.
GOT IT, RAIGA?
YEAH.

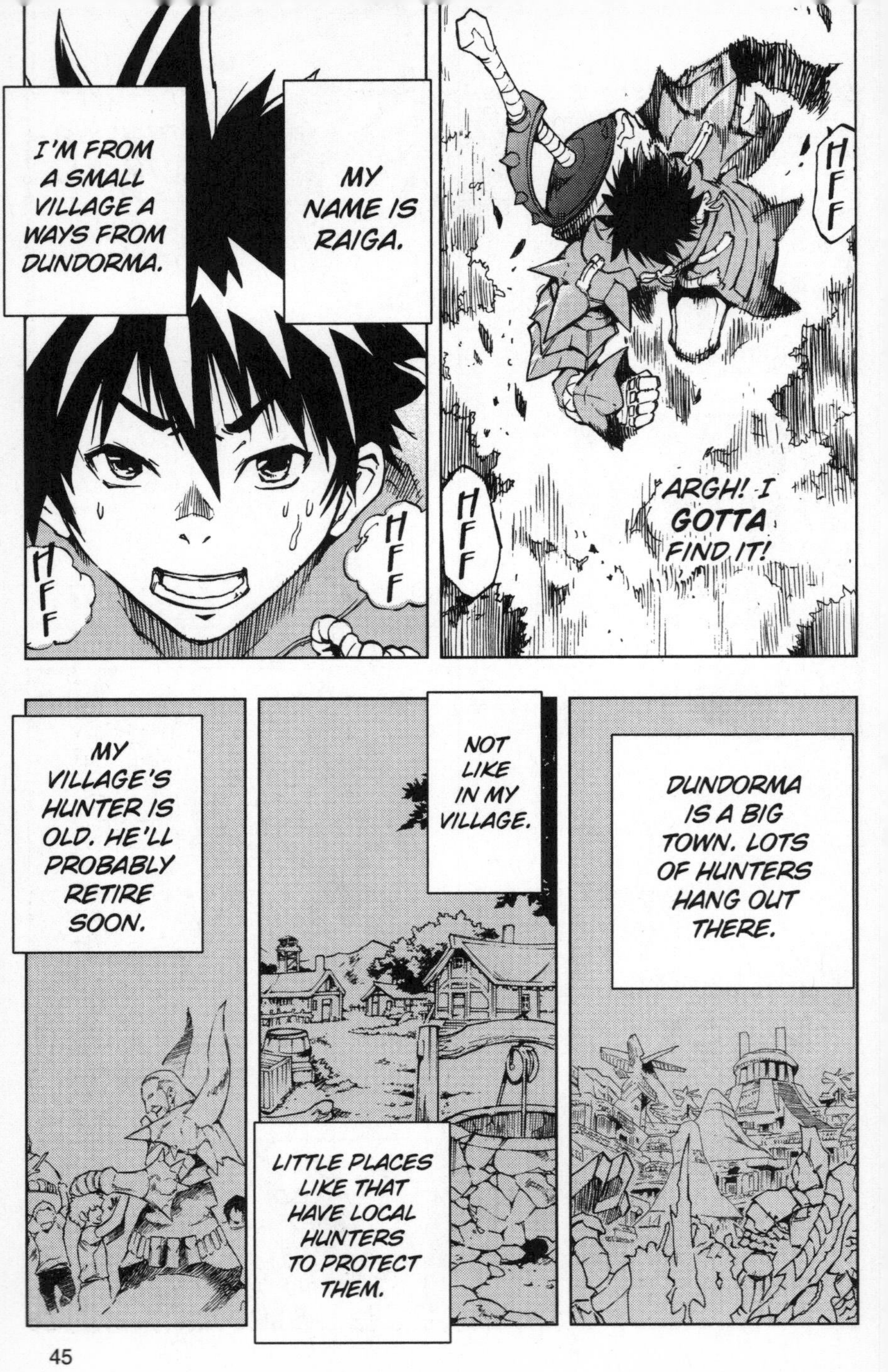
HFF
ARGH! I GOTTA FIND IT!
HFF
MY NAME IS RAIGA.
I'M FROM A SMALL VILLAGE A WAYS FROM DUNDORMA.
HFF
HFF
DUNDORMA IS A BIG TOWN. LOTS OF HUNTERS HANG OUT THERE.
NOT LIKE IN MY VILLAGE.
LITTLE PLACES LIKE THAT HAVE LOCAL HUNTERS TO PROTECT THEM.
MY VILLAGE'S HUNTER IS OLD. HE'LL PROBABLY RETIRE SOON.

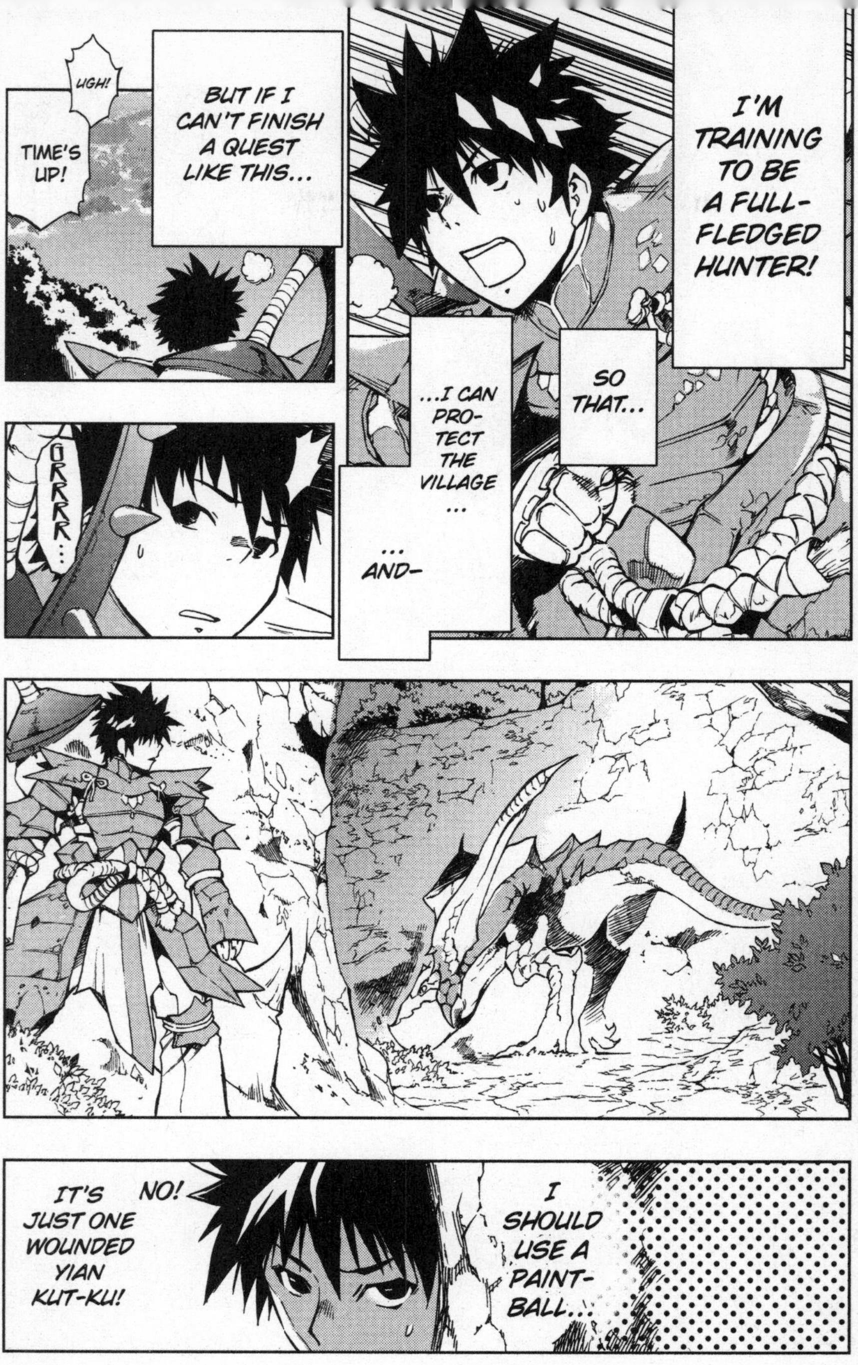
I'M TRAINING TO BE A FULL-FLEDGED HUNTER!
SO THAT...
...I CAN PROTECT THE VILLAGE...
...AND-
BUT IF I CAN'T FINISH A QUEST LIKE THIS...
UGH!
TIME'S UP!
GRRRR...
I SHOULD USE A PAINT-BALL...
NO!
IT'S JUST ONE WOUNDED YIAN KUT-KU!

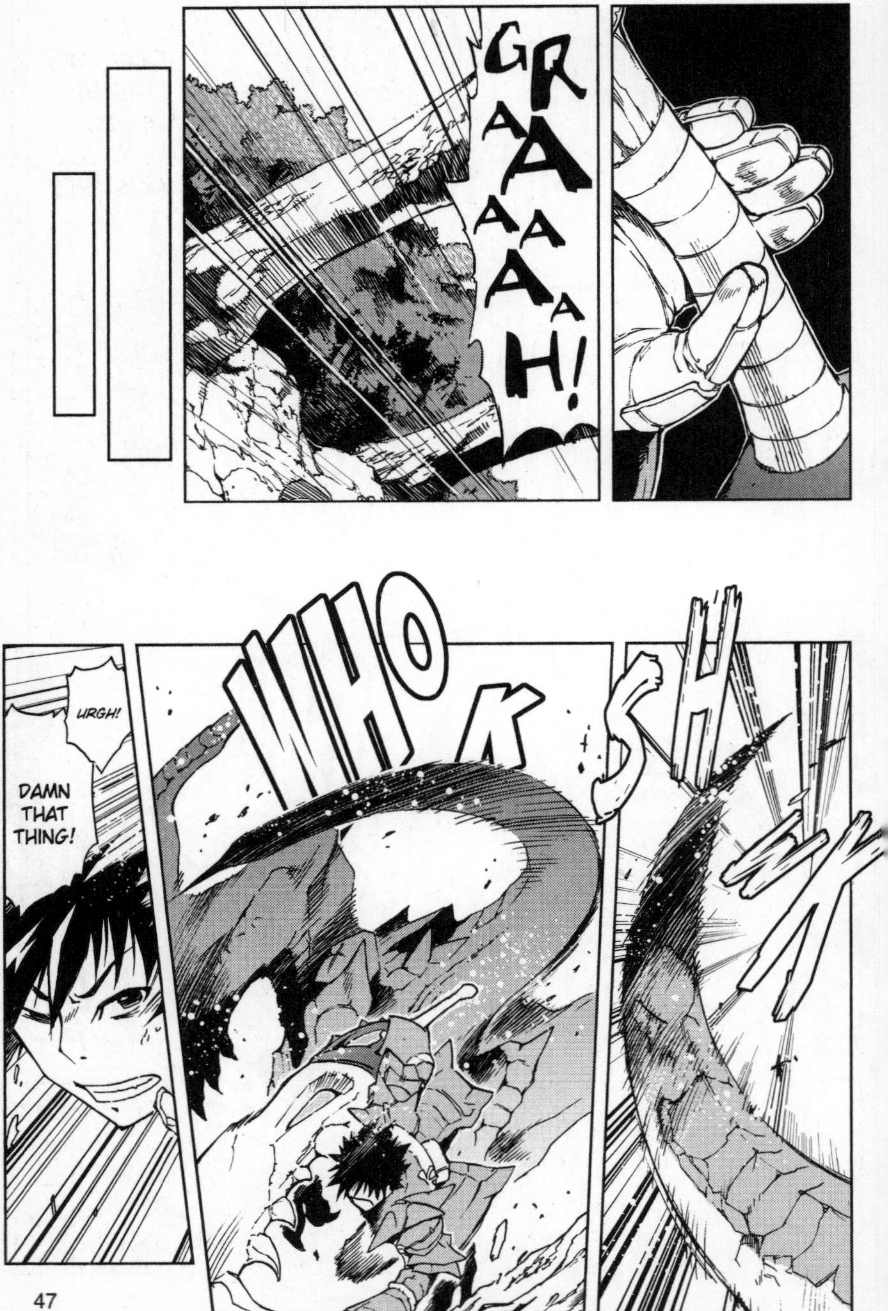
GRAAAAAAH!
WHOKSH
URGH!
DAMN THAT THING!

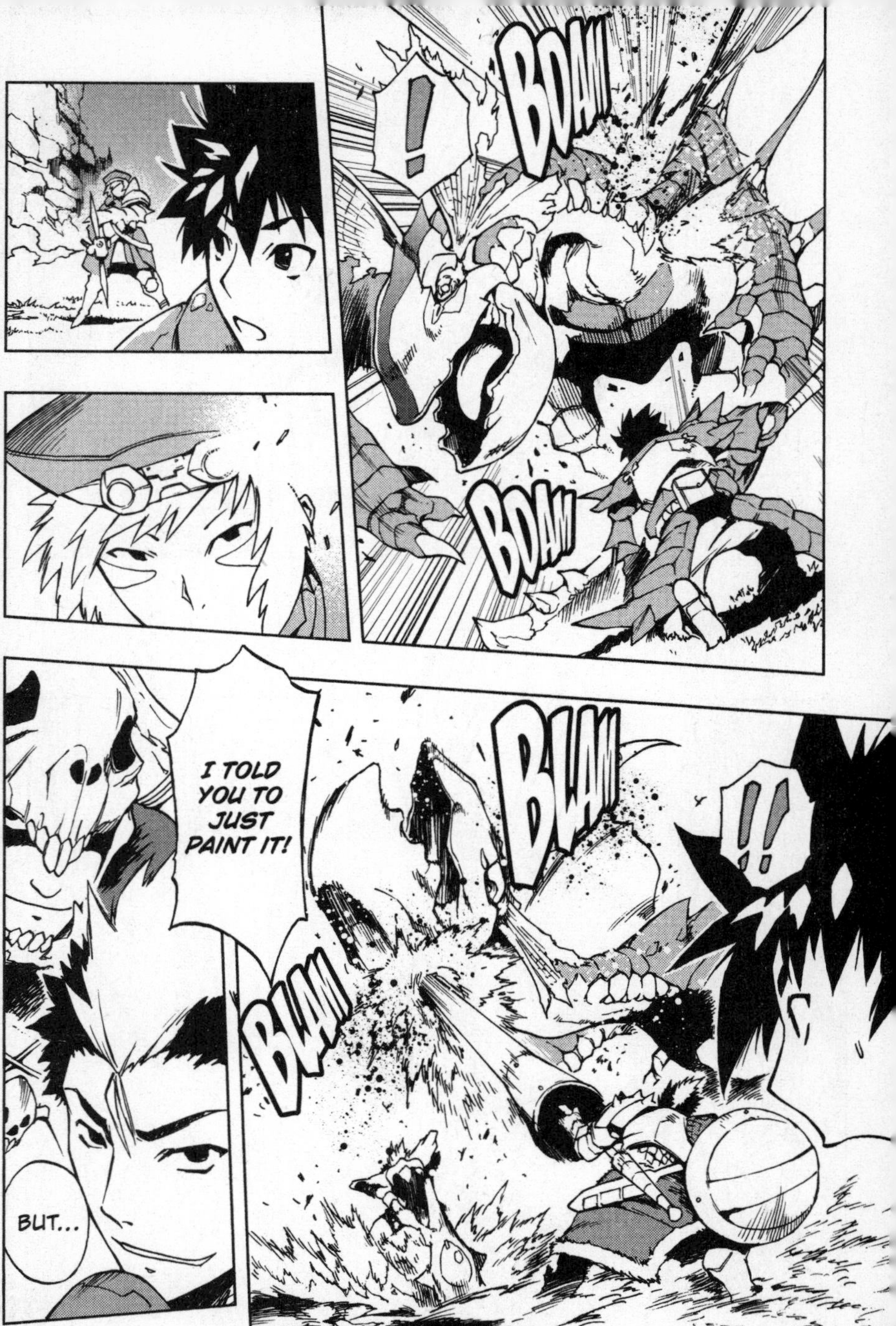
BOAM
!
BOAM
BLAM
!!
BLAM
I TOLD YOU TO JUST PAINT IT!
BUT...

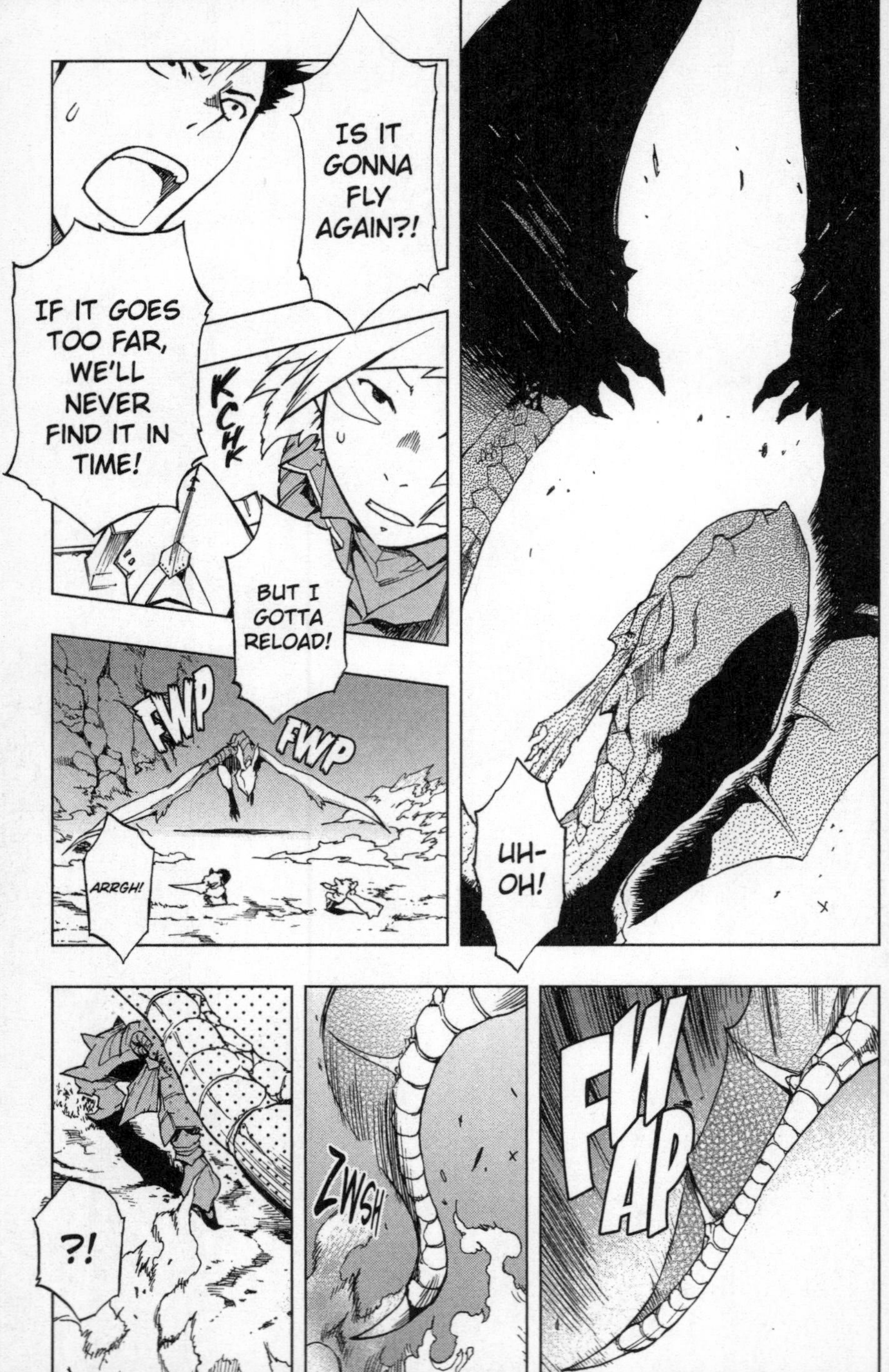
UH-OH!
IS IT GONNA FLY AGAIN?!
IF IT GOES TOO FAR, WE'LL NEVER FIND IT IN TIME!
KCHK
BUT I GOTTA RELOAD!
FWP
FWP
ARRGH!
FWAP
ZWSH
?!

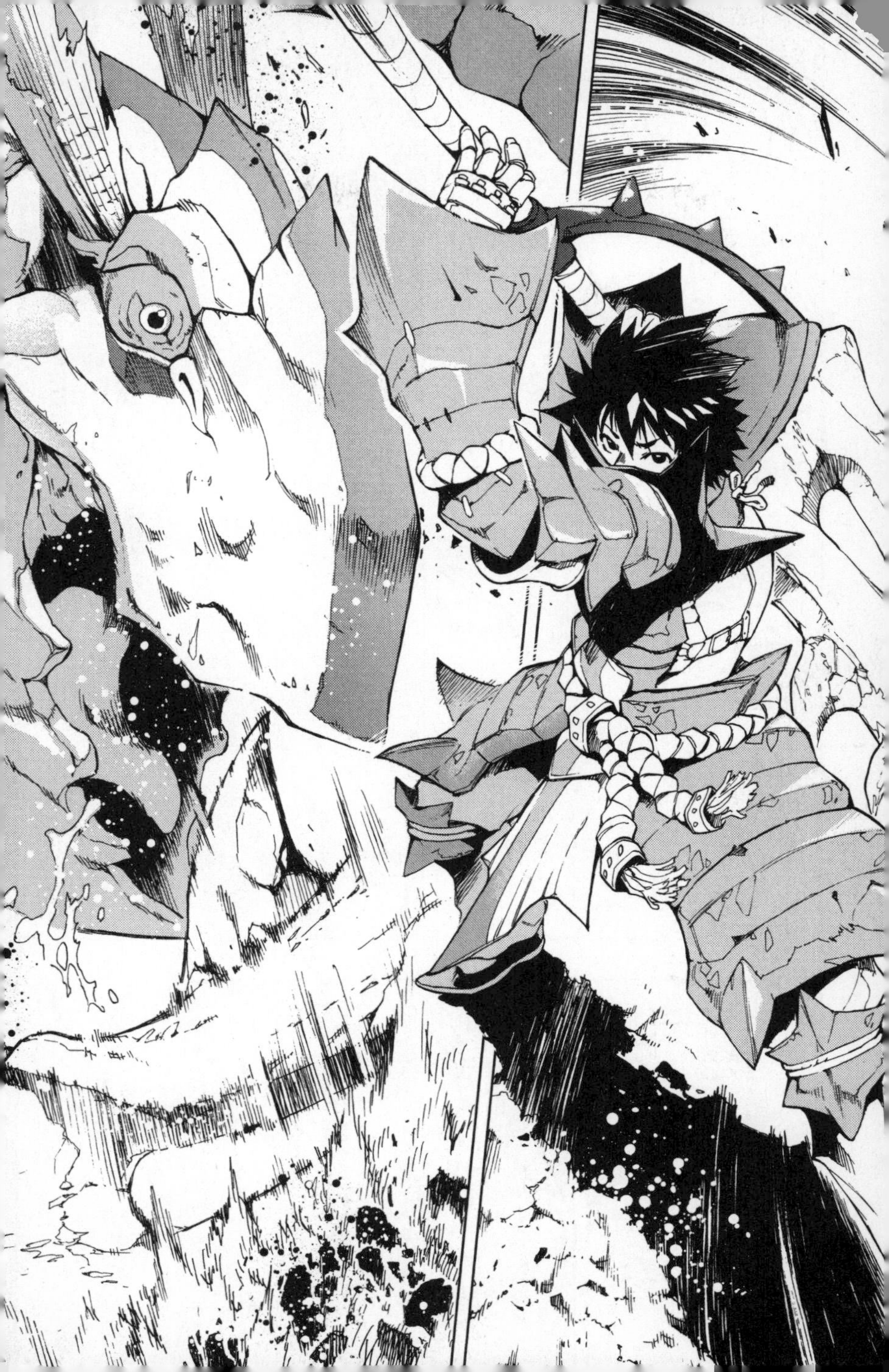

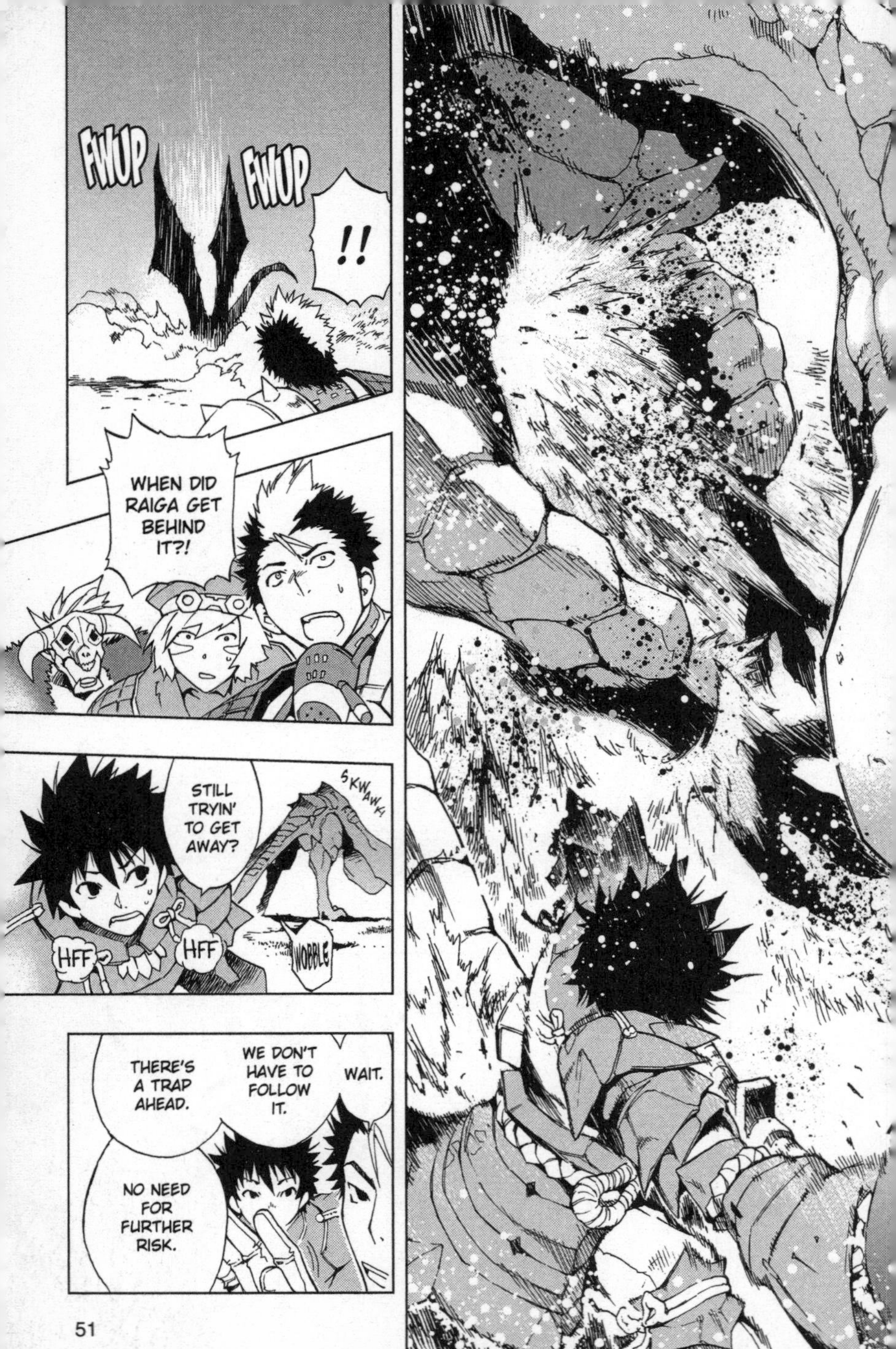
!!
FWUP
FWUP
WHEN DID RAIGA GET BEHIND IT?!
SKWAWK
STILL TRYIN' TO GET AWAY?
WOBBLE
HFF
HFF
WAIT.
WE DON'T HAVE TO FOLLOW IT.
THERE'S A TRAP AHEAD.
NO NEED FOR FURTHER RISK.

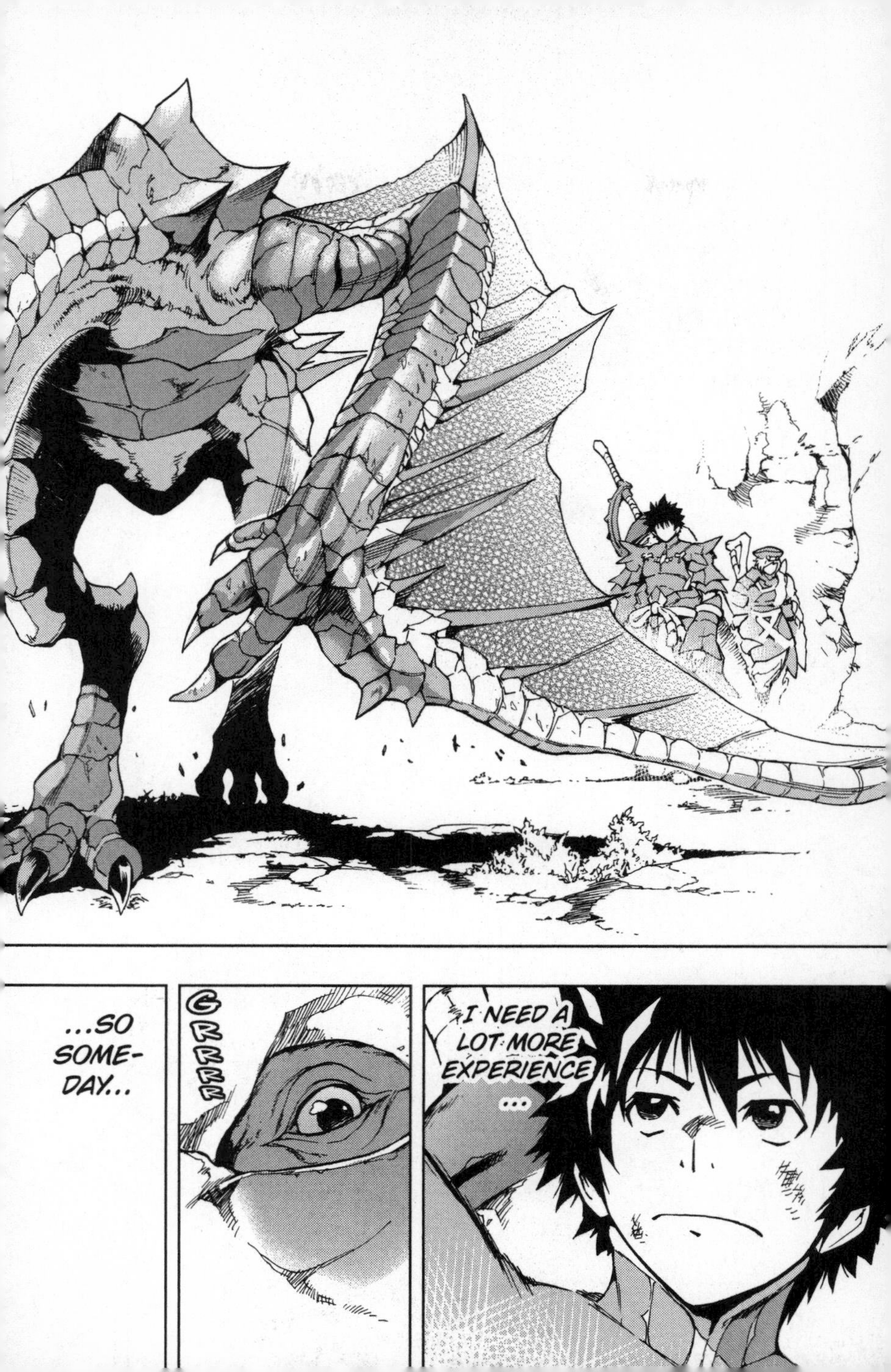
I NEED A LOT MORE EXPERIENCE
...
GRRRR
...SO SOME-DAY...

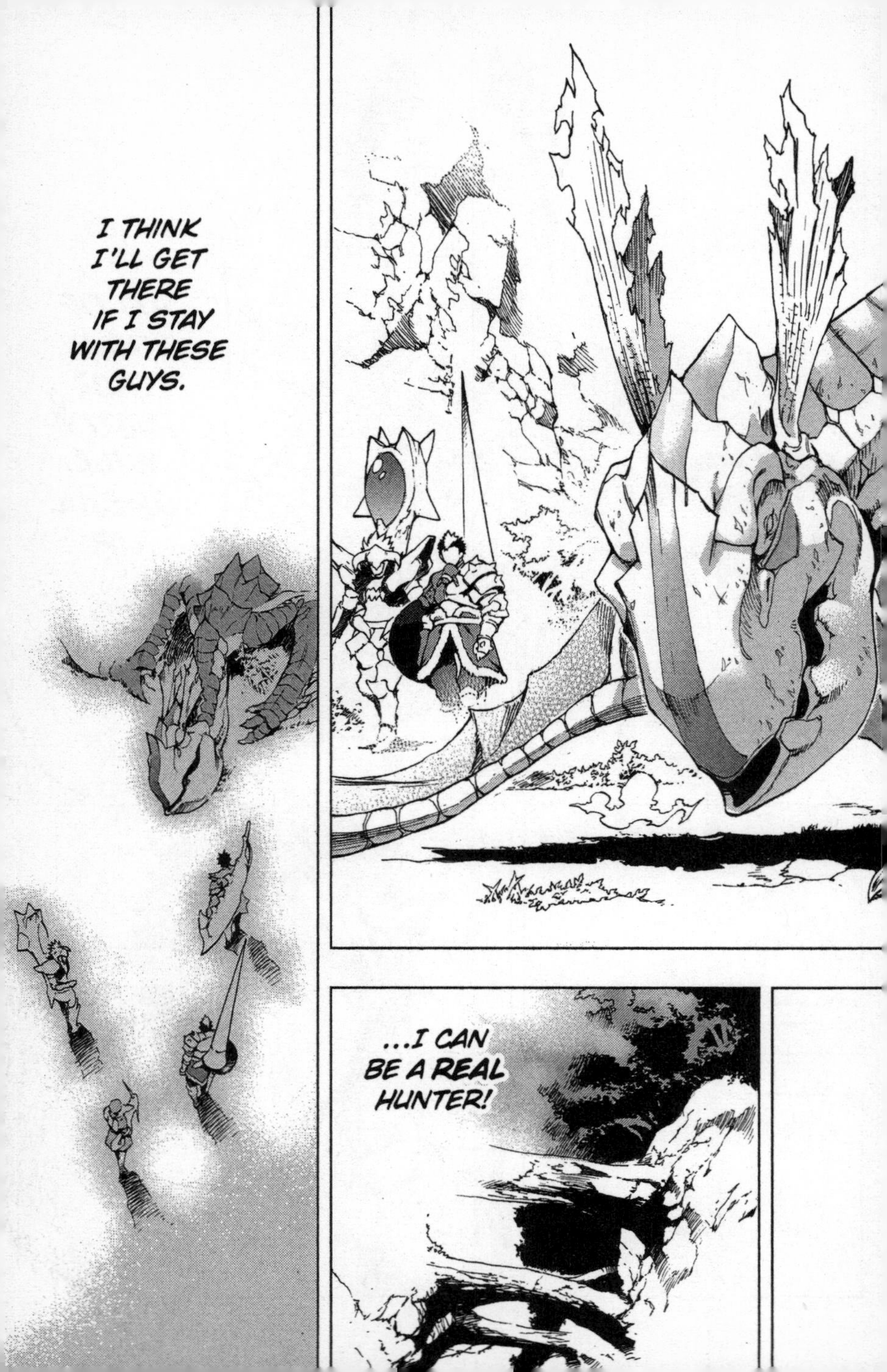
I THINK I'LL GET THERE IF I STAY WITH THESE GUYS.
...I CAN BE A REAL HUNTER!

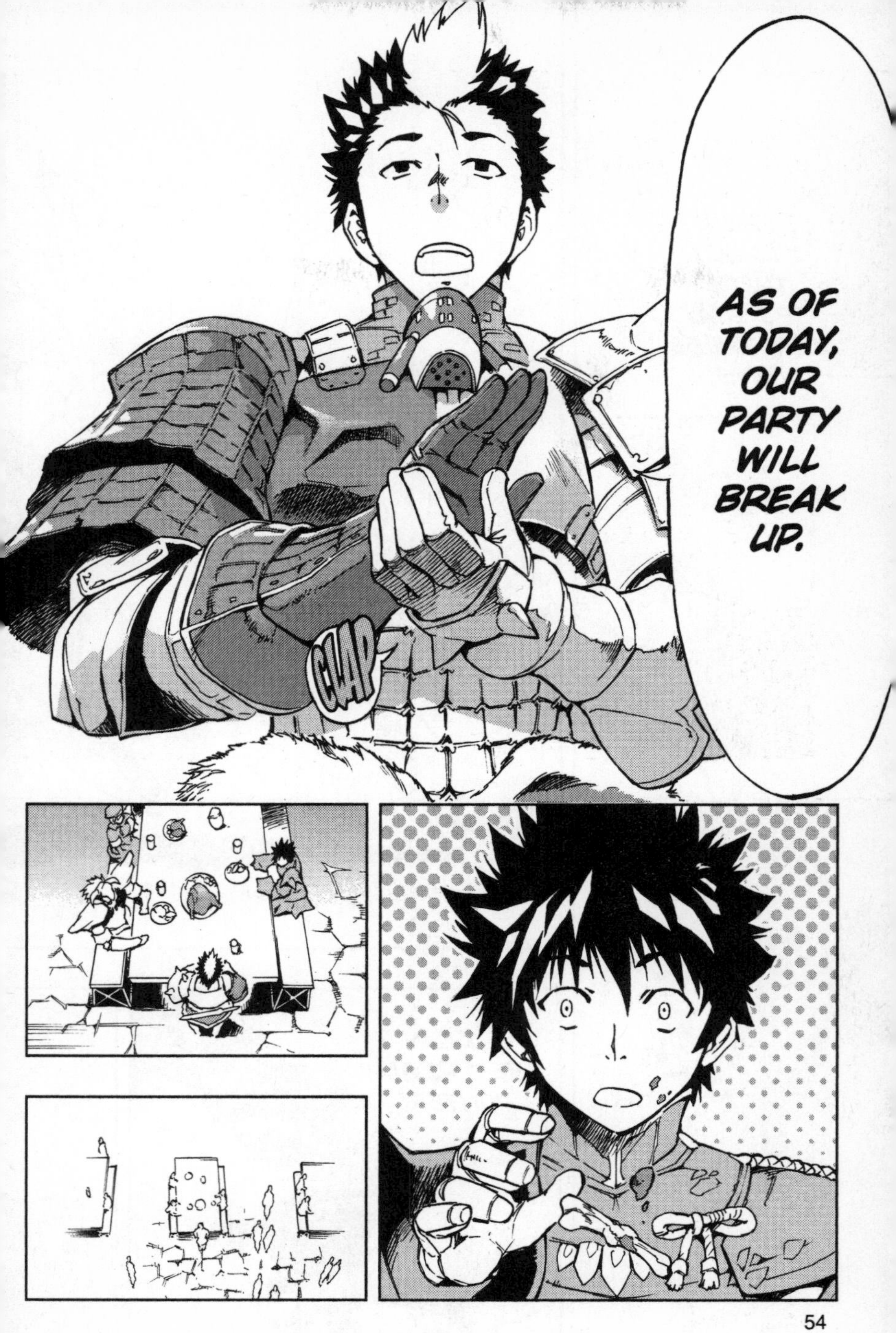
AS OF TODAY, OUR PARTY WILL BREAK UP.
CLAP

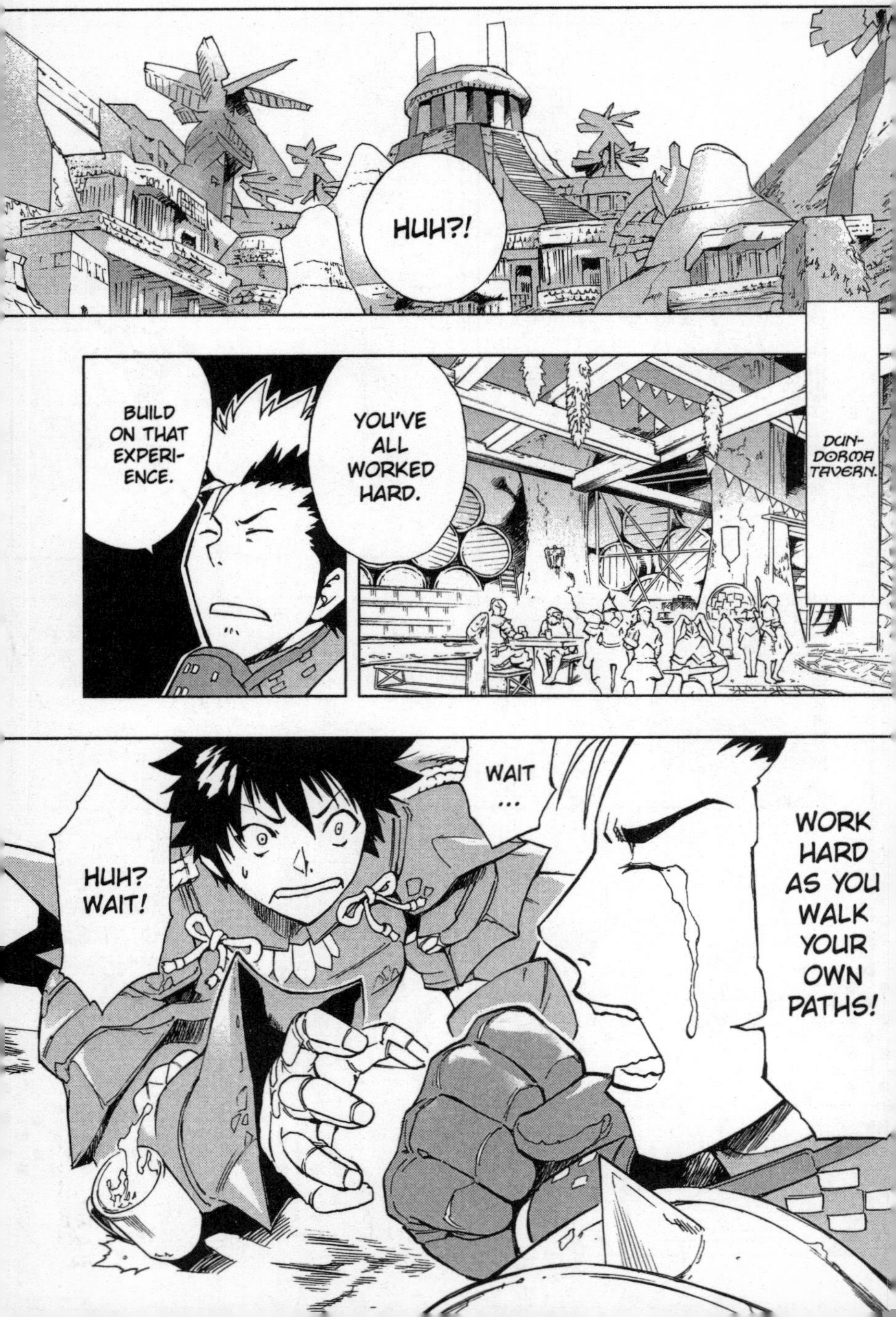
HUH?!
DUN-DORMA TAVERN.
YOU'VE ALL WORKED HARD.
BUILD ON THAT EXPERI-ENCE.
WORK HARD AS YOU WALK YOUR OWN PATHS!
WAIT...
HUH? WAIT!

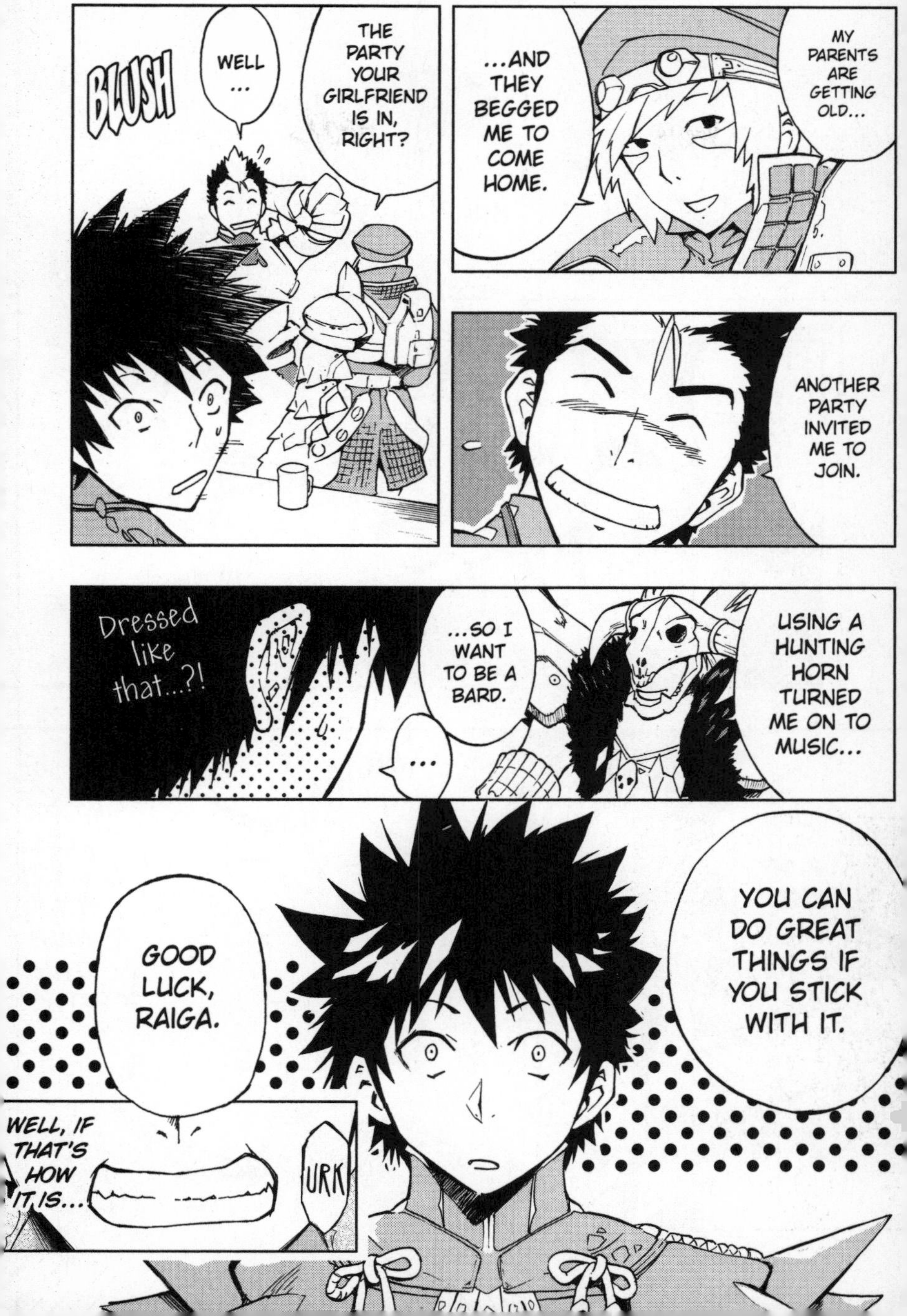
MY PARENTS ARE GETTING OLD...
...AND THEY BEGGED ME TO COME HOME.
ANOTHER PARTY INVITED ME TO JOIN.
THE PARTY YOUR GIRLFRIEND IS IN, RIGHT?
WELL ...
BLUSH
USING A HUNTING HORN TURNED ME ON TO MUSIC...
...SO I WANT TO BE A BARD.
...
Dressed like that...?!
YOU CAN DO GREAT THINGS IF YOU STICK WITH IT.
GOOD LUCK, RAIGA.
URK
WELL, IF THAT'S HOW IT IS...

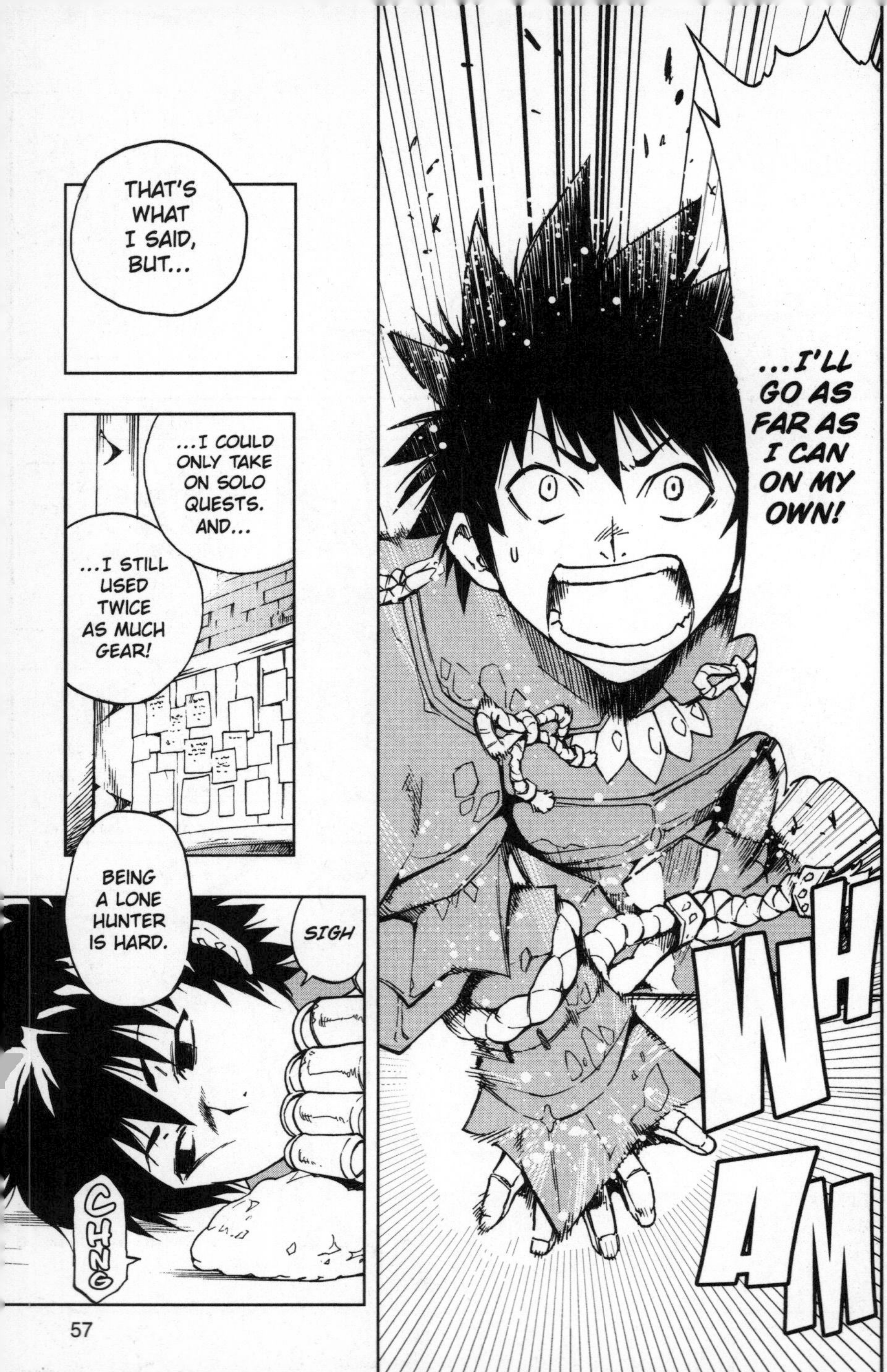
...I'LL GO AS FAR AS I CAN ON MY OWN!
WHAM
THAT'S WHAT I SAID, BUT...
...I COULD ONLY TAKE ON SOLO QUESTS. AND...
...I STILL USED TWICE AS MUCH GEAR!
SIGH
BEING A LONE HUNTER IS HARD.
CHNG

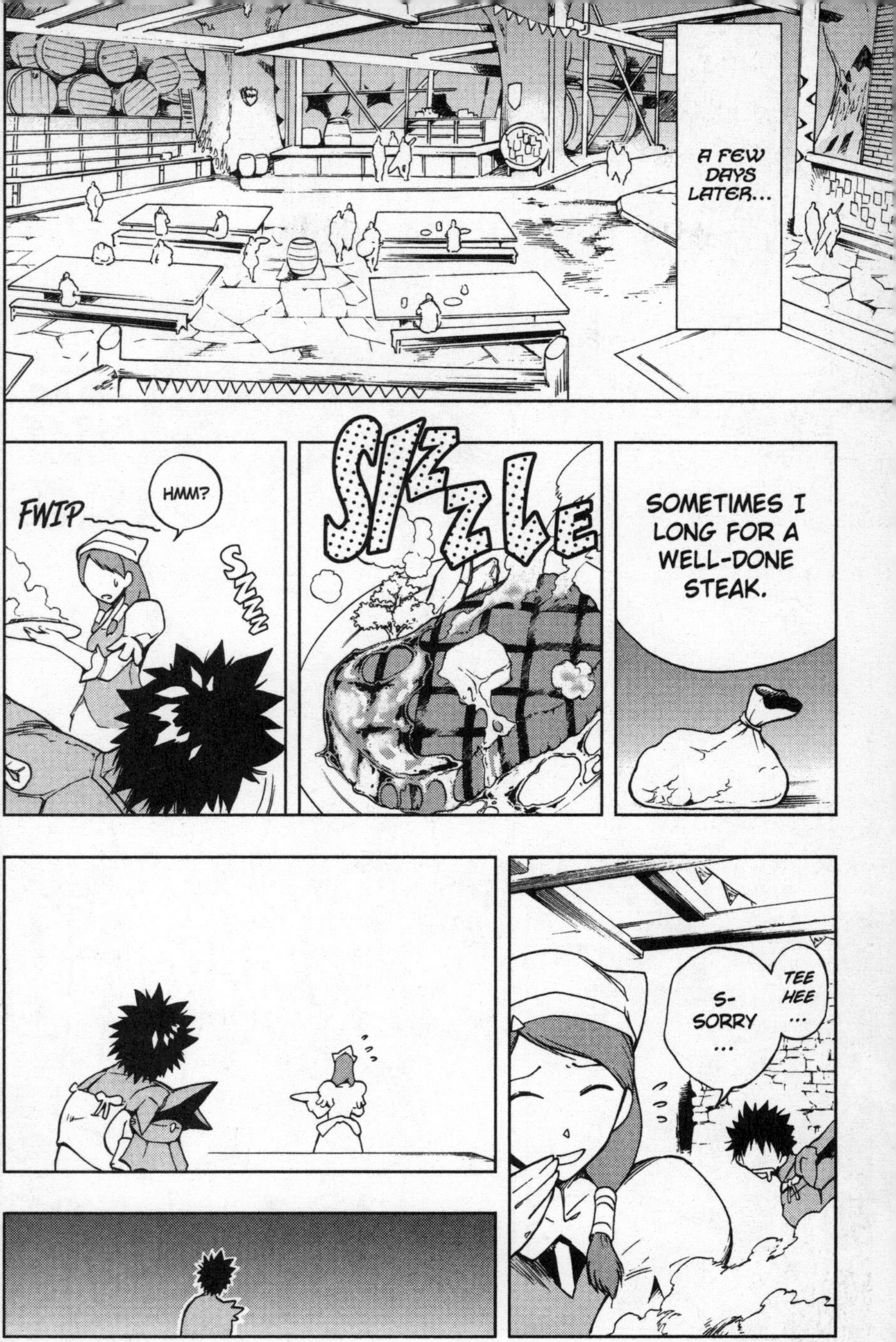
A FEW DAYS LATER...
SOMETIMES I LONG FOR A WELL-DONE STEAK.
SIZZLE
HMM?
FWIP
SNNN
TEE HEE ...
S- SORRY ...

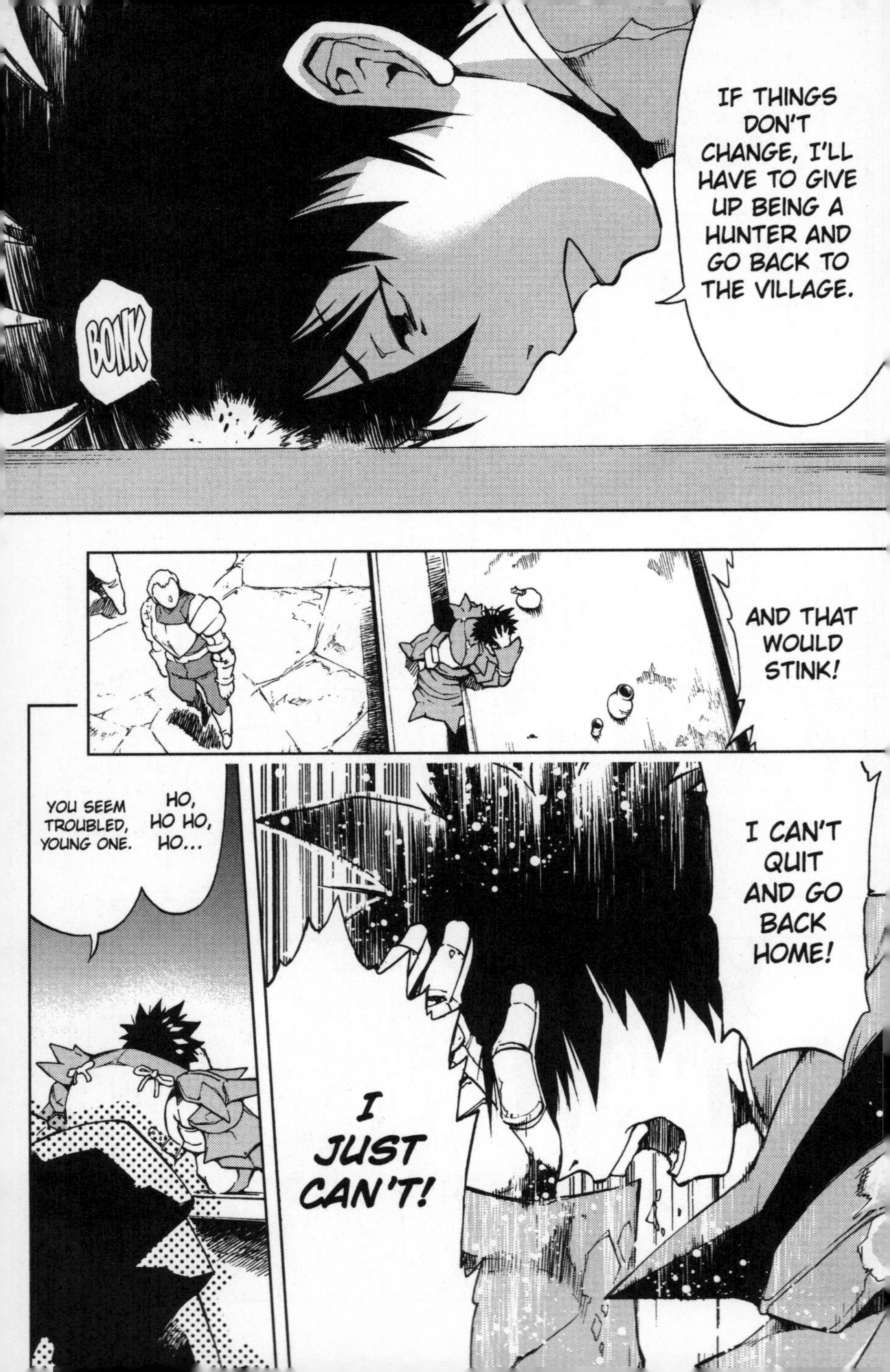
IF THINGS DON'T CHANGE, I'LL HAVE TO GIVE UP BEING A HUNTER AND GO BACK TO THE VILLAGE.
BONK
AND THAT WOULD STINK!
I CAN'T QUIT AND GO BACK HOME!
I JUST CAN'T!
HO, HO HO, HO...
YOU SEEM TROUBLED, YOUNG ONE.

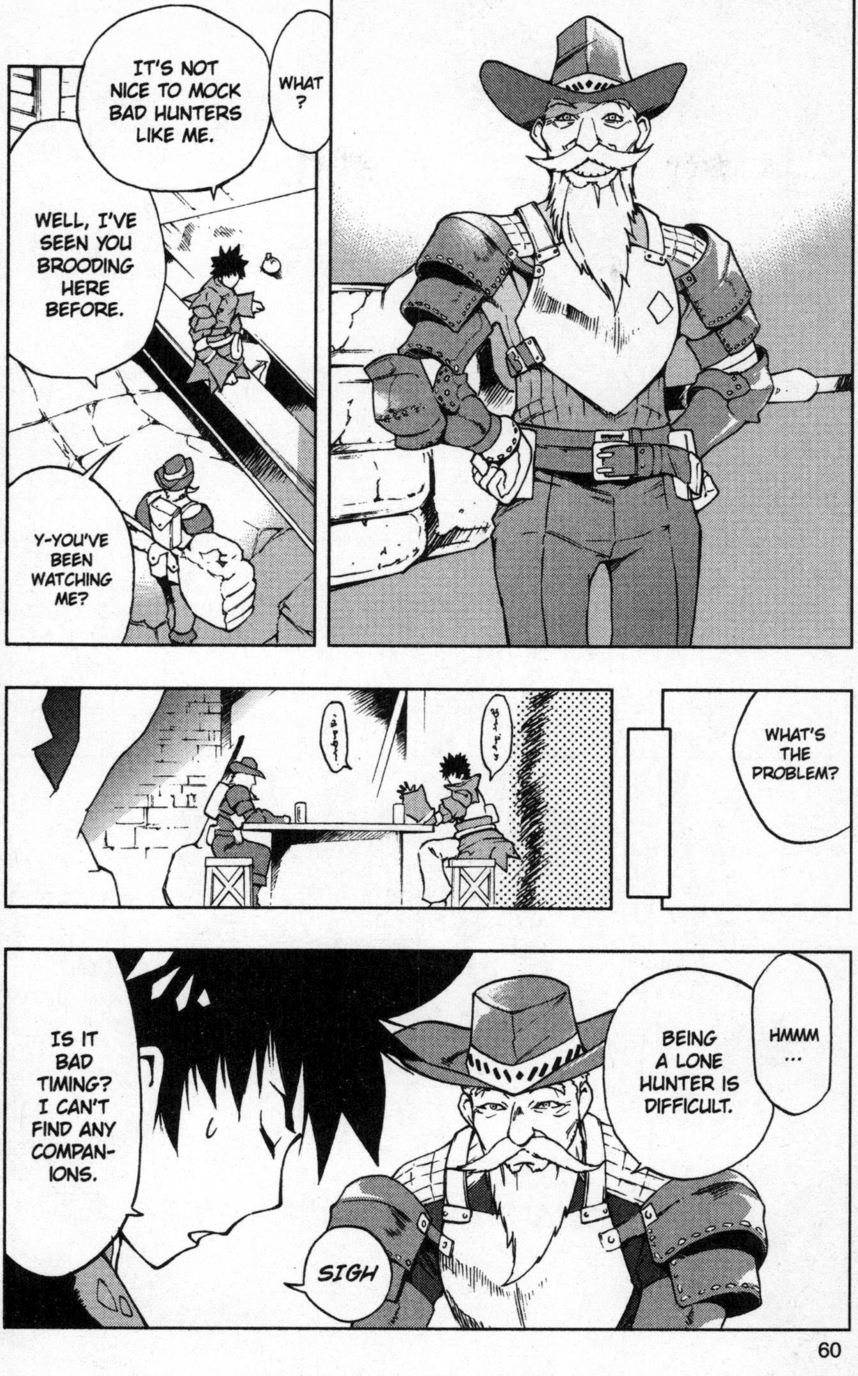
WHAT?
IT'S NOT NICE TO MOCK BAD HUNTERS LIKE ME.
WELL, I'VE SEEN YOU BROODING HERE BEFORE.
Y-YOU'VE BEEN WATCHING ME?
WHAT'S THE PROBLEM?
HMMM ...
BEING A LONE HUNTER IS DIFFICULT.
IS IT BAD TIMING? I CAN'T FIND ANY COMPANIONS.
SIGH

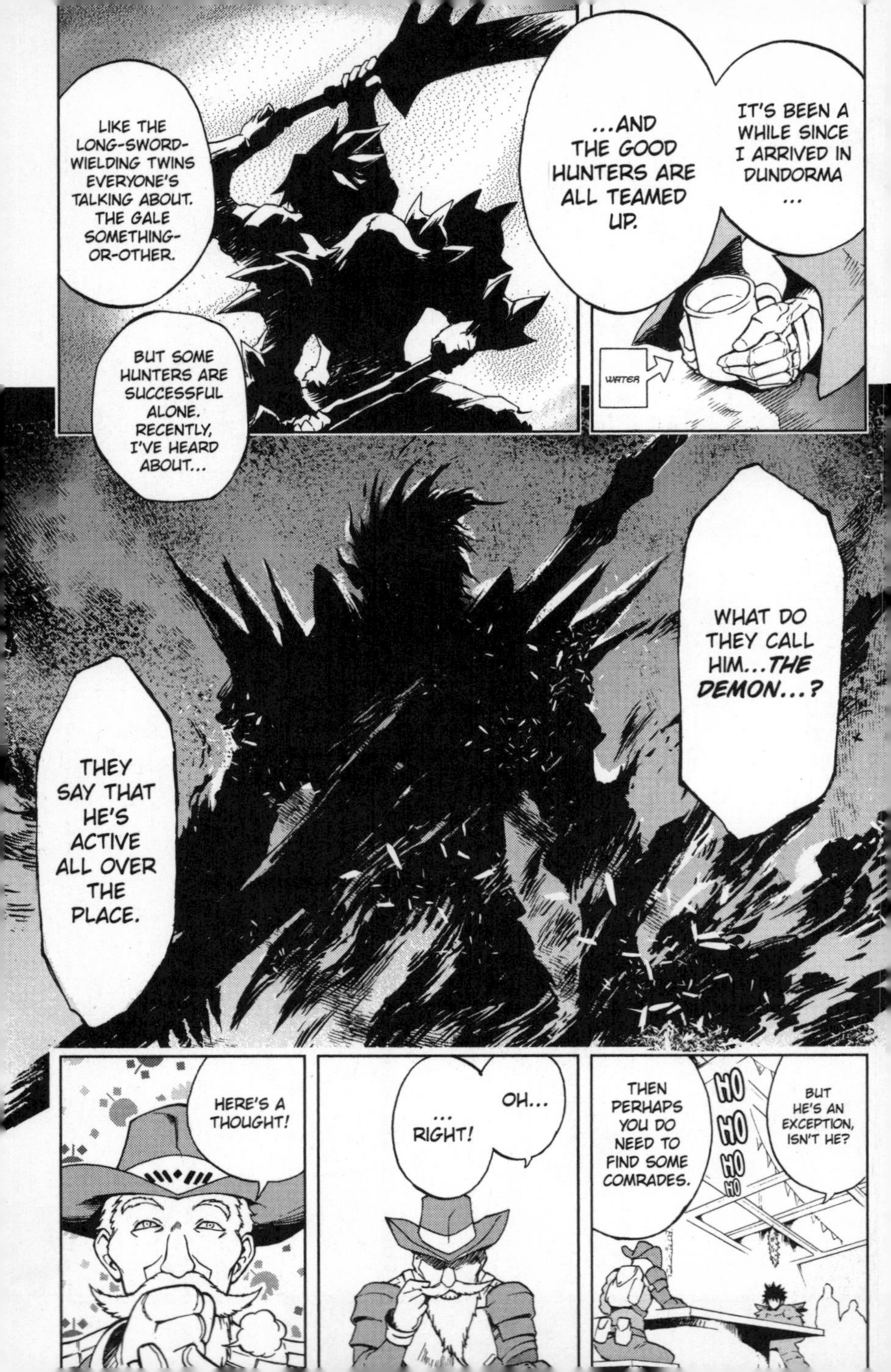
IT'S BEEN A WHILE SINCE I ARRIVED IN DUNDORMA ...
...AND THE GOOD HUNTERS ARE ALL TEAMED UP.
WATER
LIKE THE LONG-SWORD-WIELDING TWINS EVERYONE'S TALKING ABOUT. THE GALE SOMETHING-OR-OTHER.
BUT SOME HUNTERS ARE SUCCESSFUL ALONE. RECENTLY, I'VE HEARD ABOUT...
WHAT DO THEY CALL HIM...*THE DEMON...?*
THEY SAY THAT HE'S ACTIVE ALL OVER THE PLACE.
BUT HE'S AN EXCEPTION, ISN'T HE?
HO HO HO HO
THEN PERHAPS YOU DO NEED TO FIND SOME COMRADES.
OH...
... RIGHT!
HERE'S A THOUGHT!

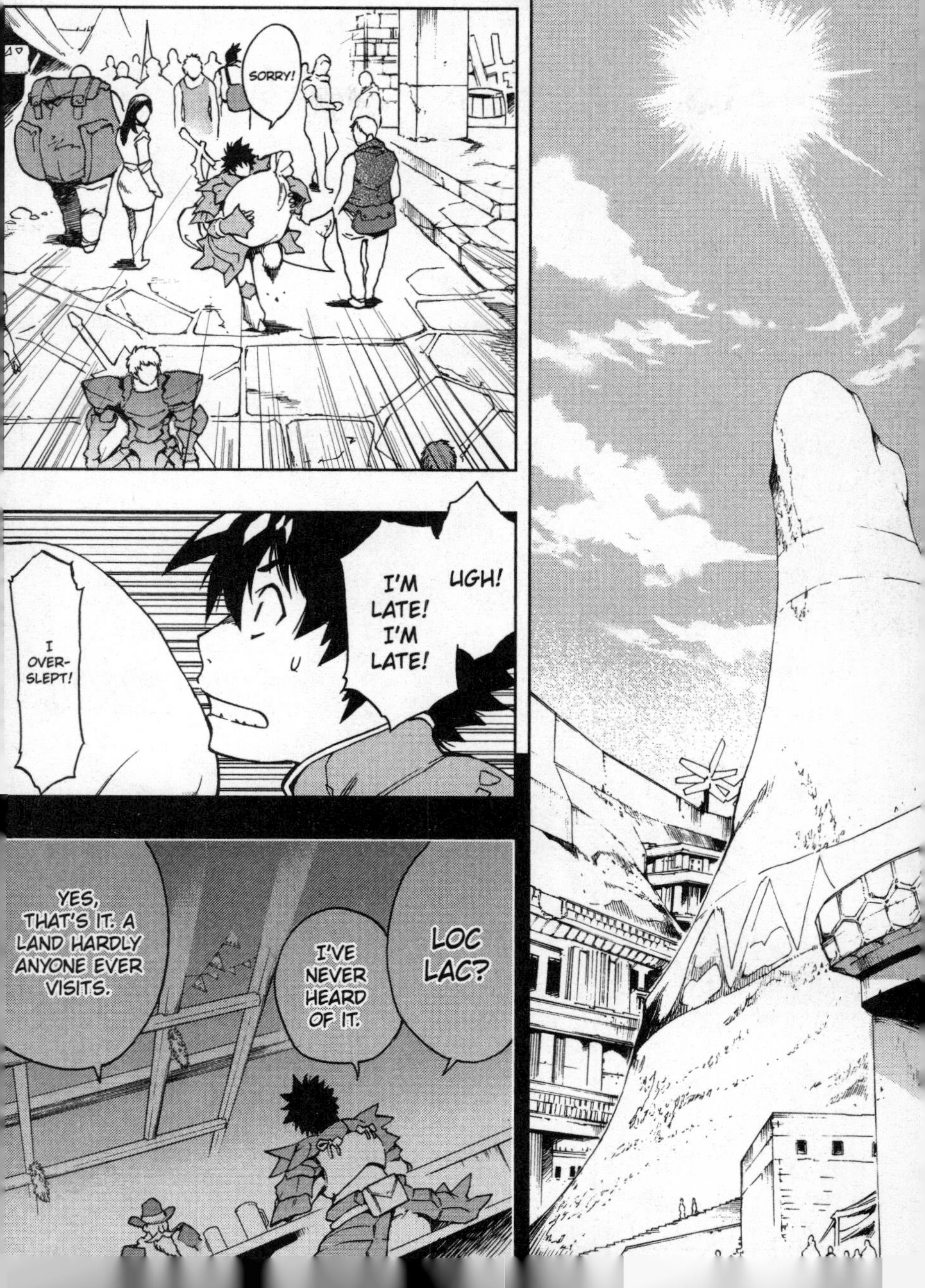
SORRY!
UGH!
I'M LATE! I'M LATE!
I OVER-SLEPT!
LOC LAC?
I'VE NEVER HEARD OF IT.
YES, THAT'S IT. A LAND HARDLY ANYONE EVER VISITS.

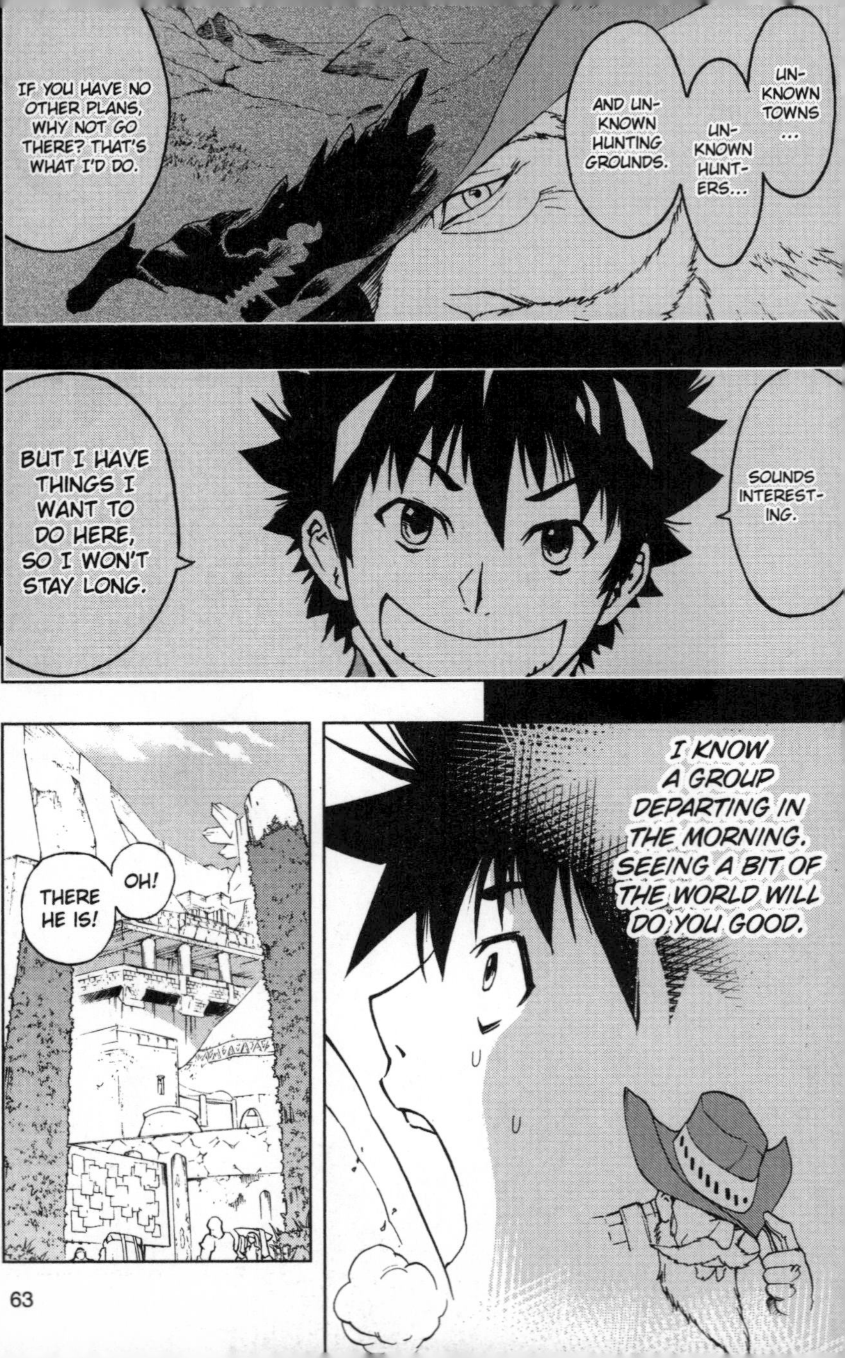
UN-KNOWN TOWNS...
UN-KNOWN HUNT-ERS...
AND UN-KNOWN HUNTING GROUNDS.
IF YOU HAVE NO OTHER PLANS, WHY NOT GO THERE? THAT'S WHAT I'D DO.
SOUNDS INTEREST-ING.
BUT I HAVE THINGS I WANT TO DO HERE, SO I WON'T STAY LONG.
I KNOW A GROUP DEPARTING IN THE MORNING. SEEING A BIT OF THE WORLD WILL DO YOU GOOD.
OH!
THERE HE IS!

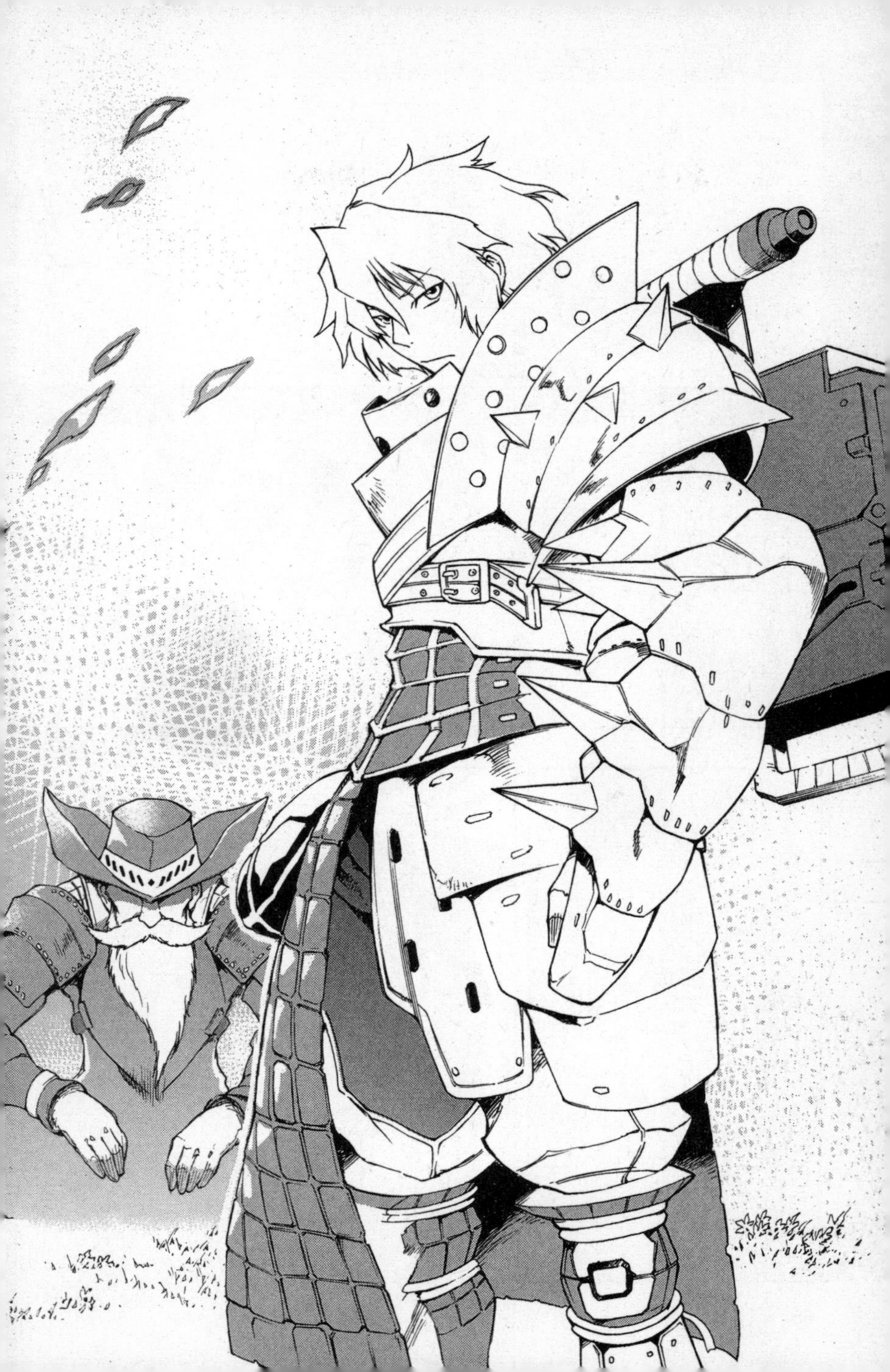

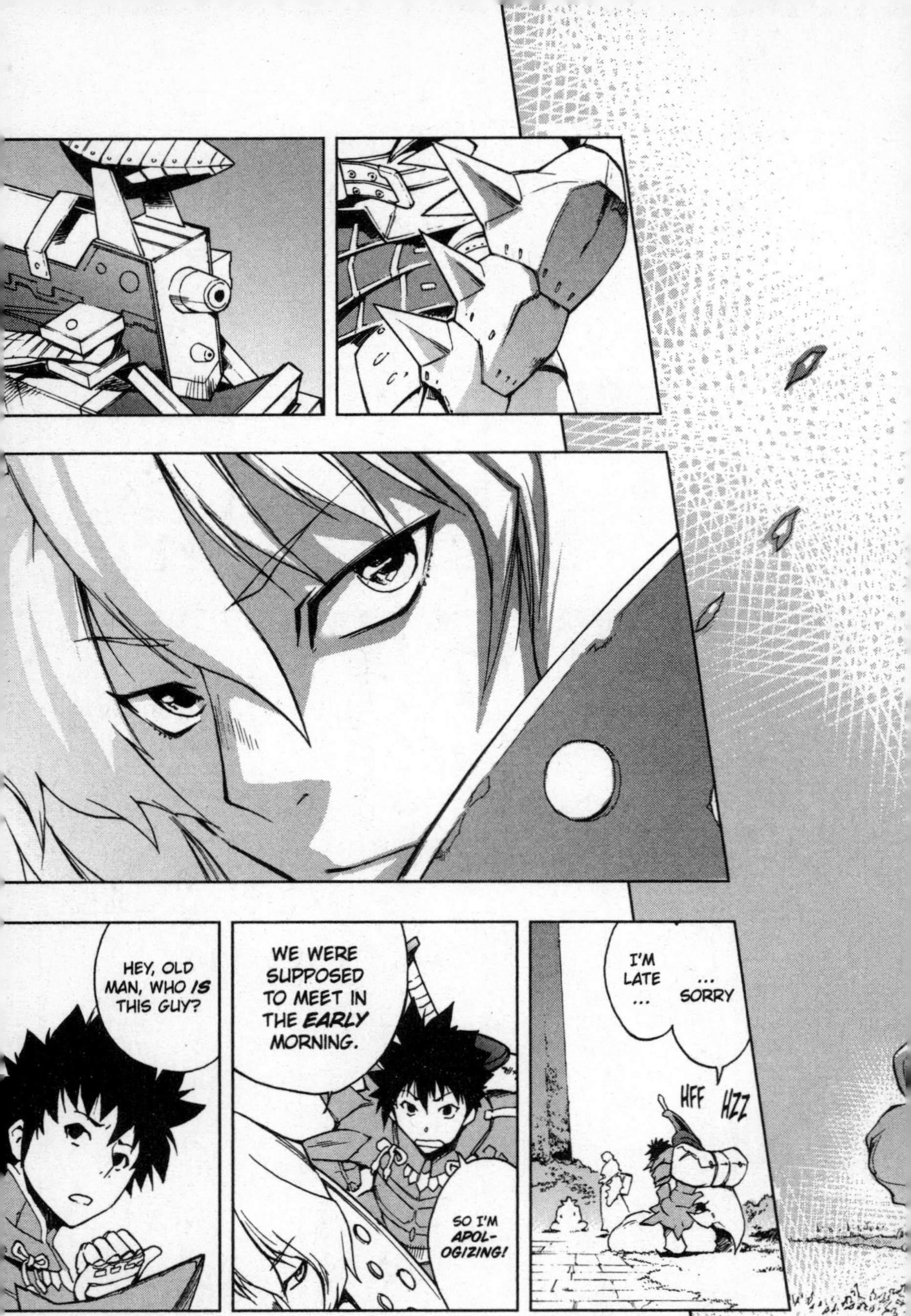
I'M LATE ...
... SORRY
HFF
HZZ
WE WERE SUPPOSED TO MEET IN THE *EARLY* MORNING.
SO I'M *APOLOGIZING!*
HEY, OLD MAN, WHO *IS* THIS GUY?

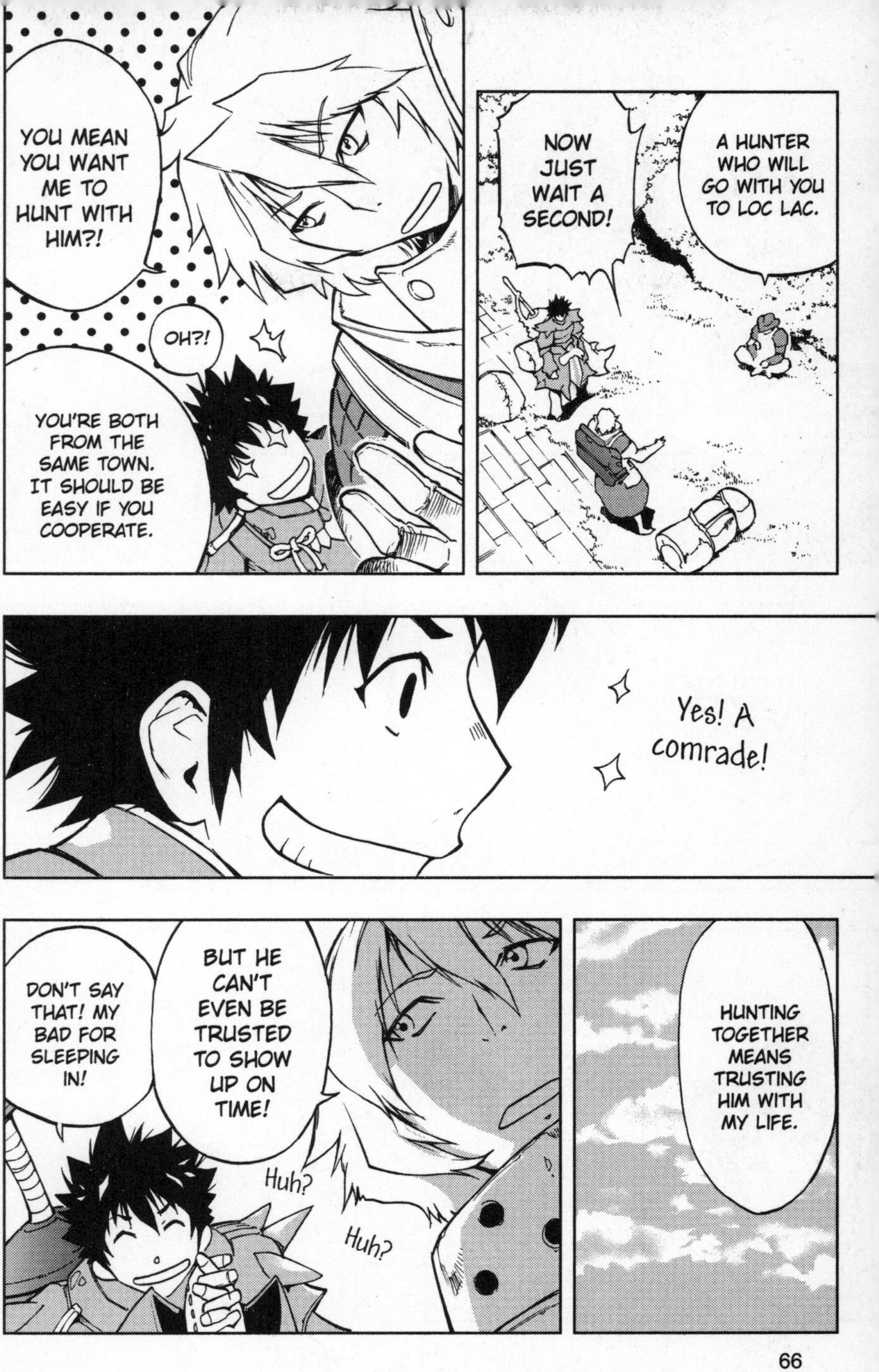
A HUNTER WHO WILL GO WITH YOU TO LOC LAC.
NOW JUST WAIT A SECOND!
YOU MEAN YOU WANT ME TO HUNT WITH HIM?!
OH?!
YOU'RE BOTH FROM THE SAME TOWN. IT SHOULD BE EASY IF YOU COOPERATE.
Yes! A comrade!
HUNTING TOGETHER MEANS TRUSTING HIM WITH MY LIFE.
BUT HE CAN'T EVEN BE TRUSTED TO SHOW UP ON TIME!
Huh?
Huh?
DON'T SAY THAT! MY BAD FOR SLEEPING IN!

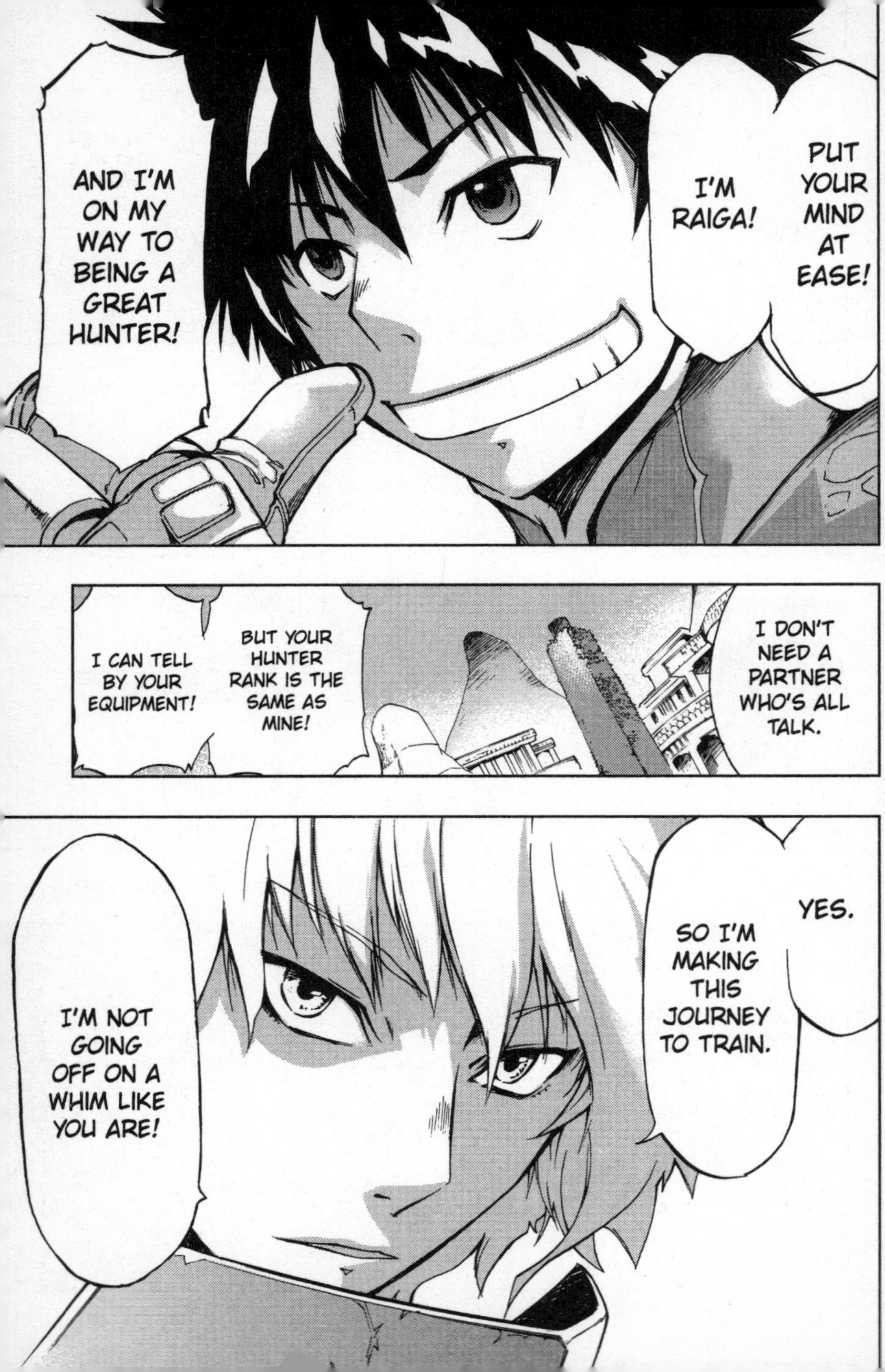
PUT YOUR MIND AT EASE!
I'M RAIGA!
AND I'M ON MY WAY TO BEING A GREAT HUNTER!
I DON'T NEED A PARTNER WHO'S ALL TALK.
BUT YOUR HUNTER RANK IS THE SAME AS MINE!
I CAN TELL BY YOUR EQUIPMENT!
YES.
SO I'M MAKING THIS JOURNEY TO TRAIN.
I'M NOT GOING OFF ON A WHIM LIKE YOU ARE!

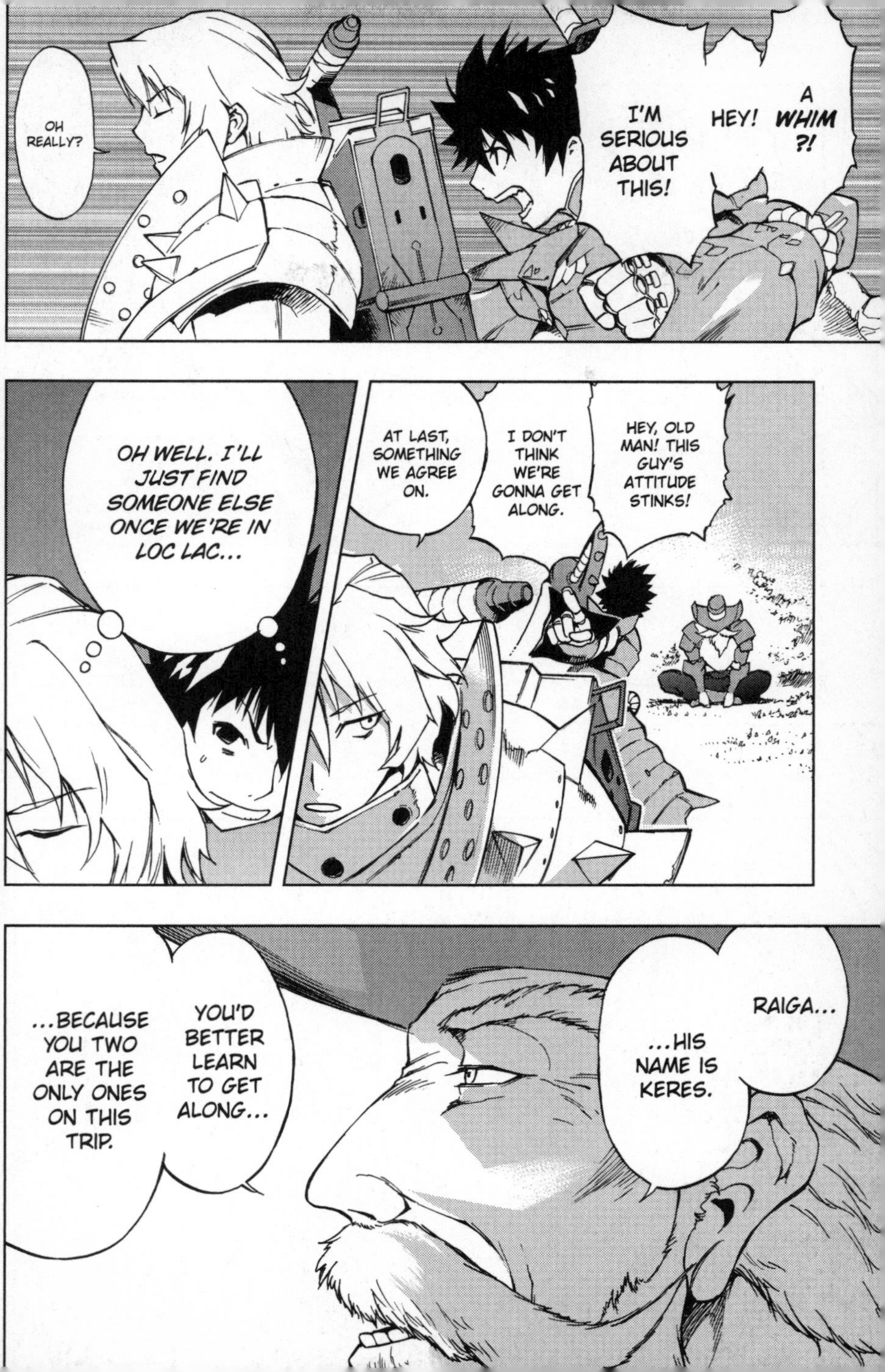
A WHIM ?!
HEY!
I'M SERIOUS ABOUT THIS!
OH REALLY?
HEY, OLD MAN! THIS GUY'S ATTITUDE STINKS!
I DON'T THINK WE'RE GONNA GET ALONG.
AT LAST, SOMETHING WE AGREE ON.
OH WELL. I'LL JUST FIND SOMEONE ELSE ONCE WE'RE IN LOC LAC...
RAIGA...
...HIS NAME IS KERES.
YOU'D BETTER LEARN TO GET ALONG...
...BECAUSE YOU TWO ARE THE ONLY ONES ON THIS TRIP.

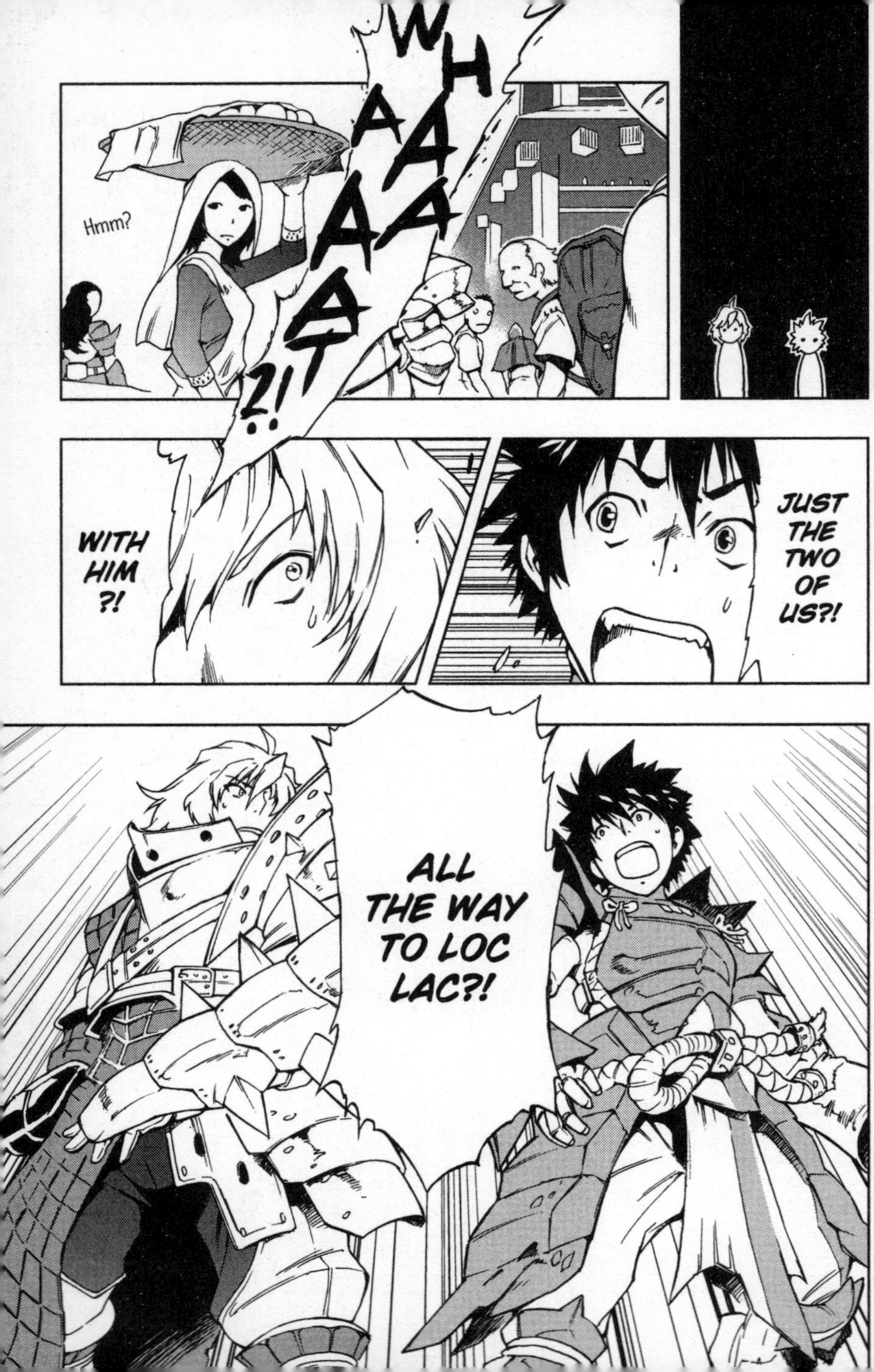

Hmm?
WHAAAAAT?!
JUST THE TWO OF US?!
WITH HIM?!
ALL THE WAY TO LOC LAC?!

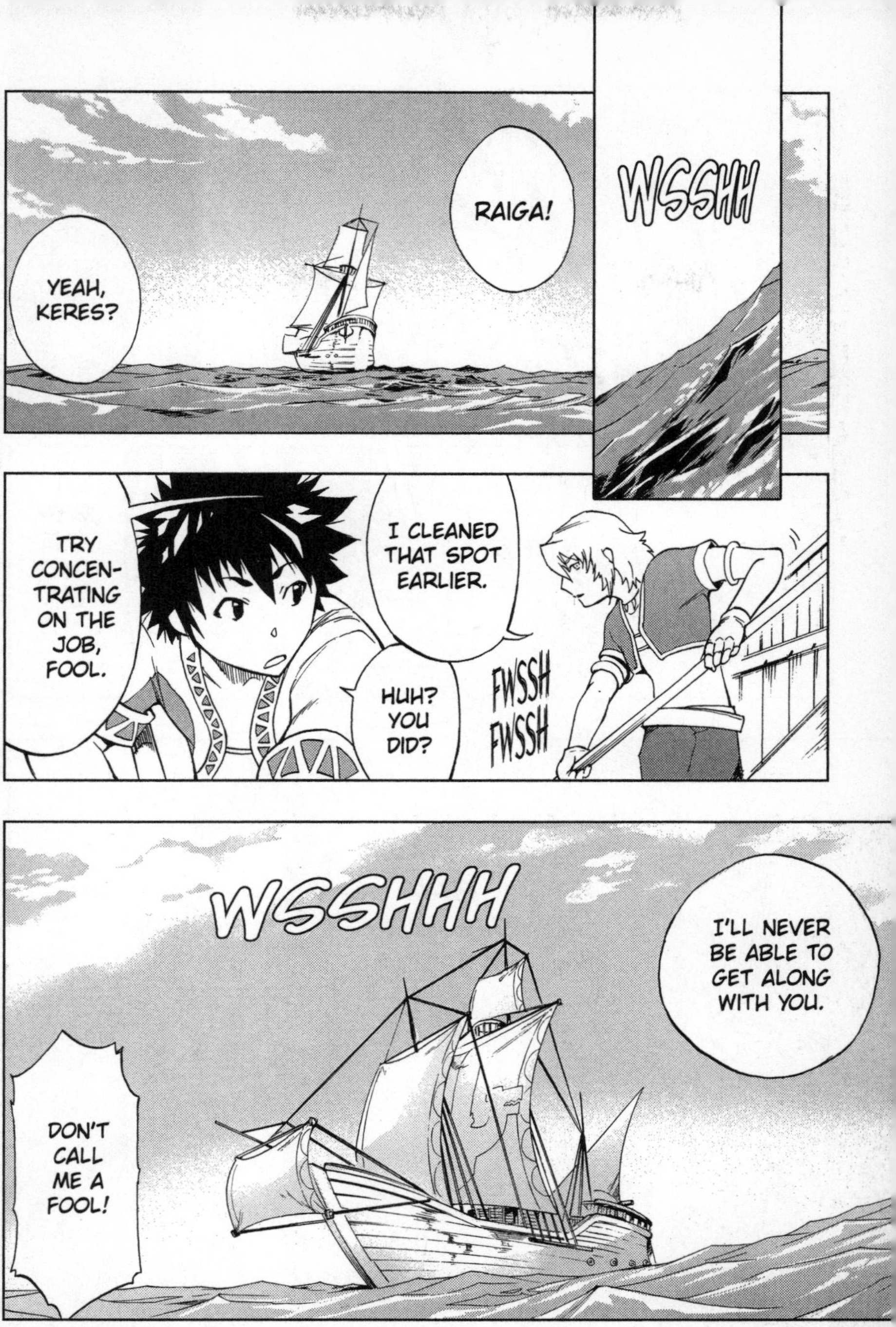
WSSHH
RAIGA!
YEAH, KERES?
I CLEANED THAT SPOT EARLIER.
HUH? YOU DID?
FWSSH FWSSH
TRY CONCEN-TRATING ON THE JOB, FOOL.
WSSHHH
I'LL NEVER BE ABLE TO GET ALONG WITH YOU.
DON'T CALL ME A FOOL!

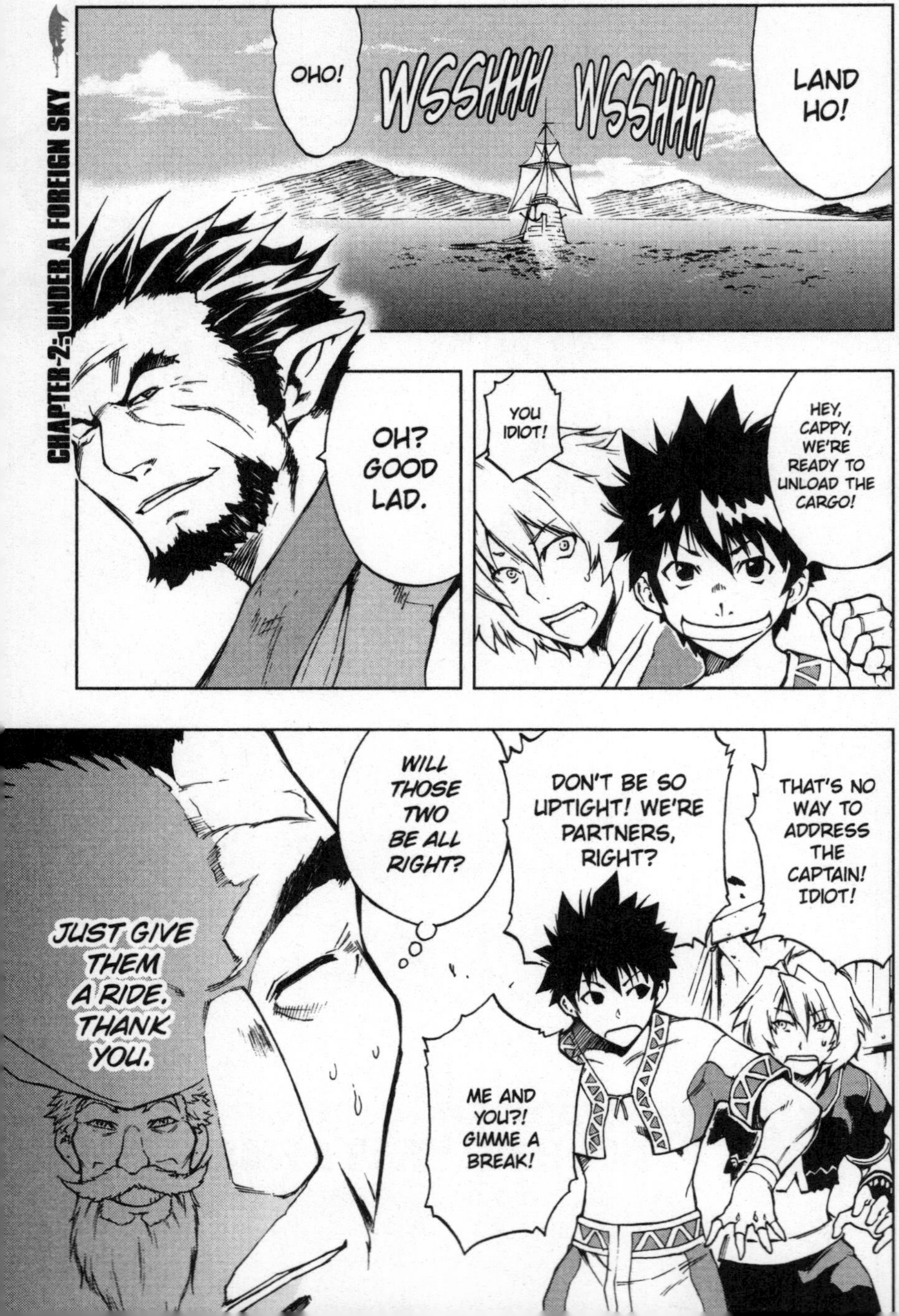
CHAPTER 2: UNDER A FOREIGN SKY
LAND HO!
WSSHHH WSSHHH
OHO!
HEY, CAPPY, WE'RE READY TO UNLOAD THE CARGO!
YOU IDIOT!
OH? GOOD LAD.
THAT'S NO WAY TO ADDRESS THE CAPTAIN! IDIOT!
DON'T BE SO UPTIGHT! WE'RE PARTNERS, RIGHT?
ME AND YOU?! GIMME A BREAK!
WILL THOSE TWO BE ALL RIGHT?
JUST GIVE THEM A RIDE. THANK YOU.

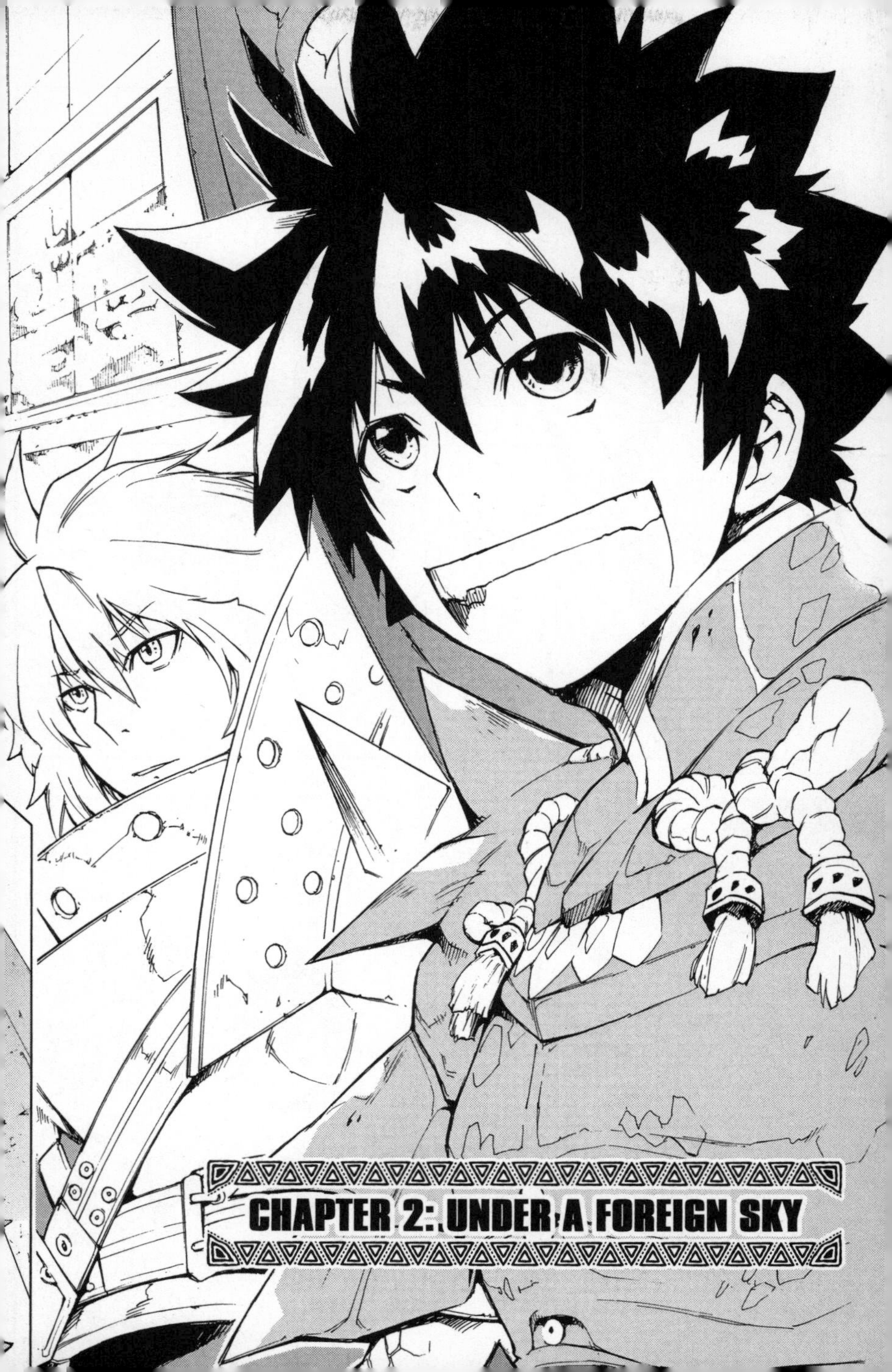
CHAPTER 2: UNDER A FOREIGN SKY

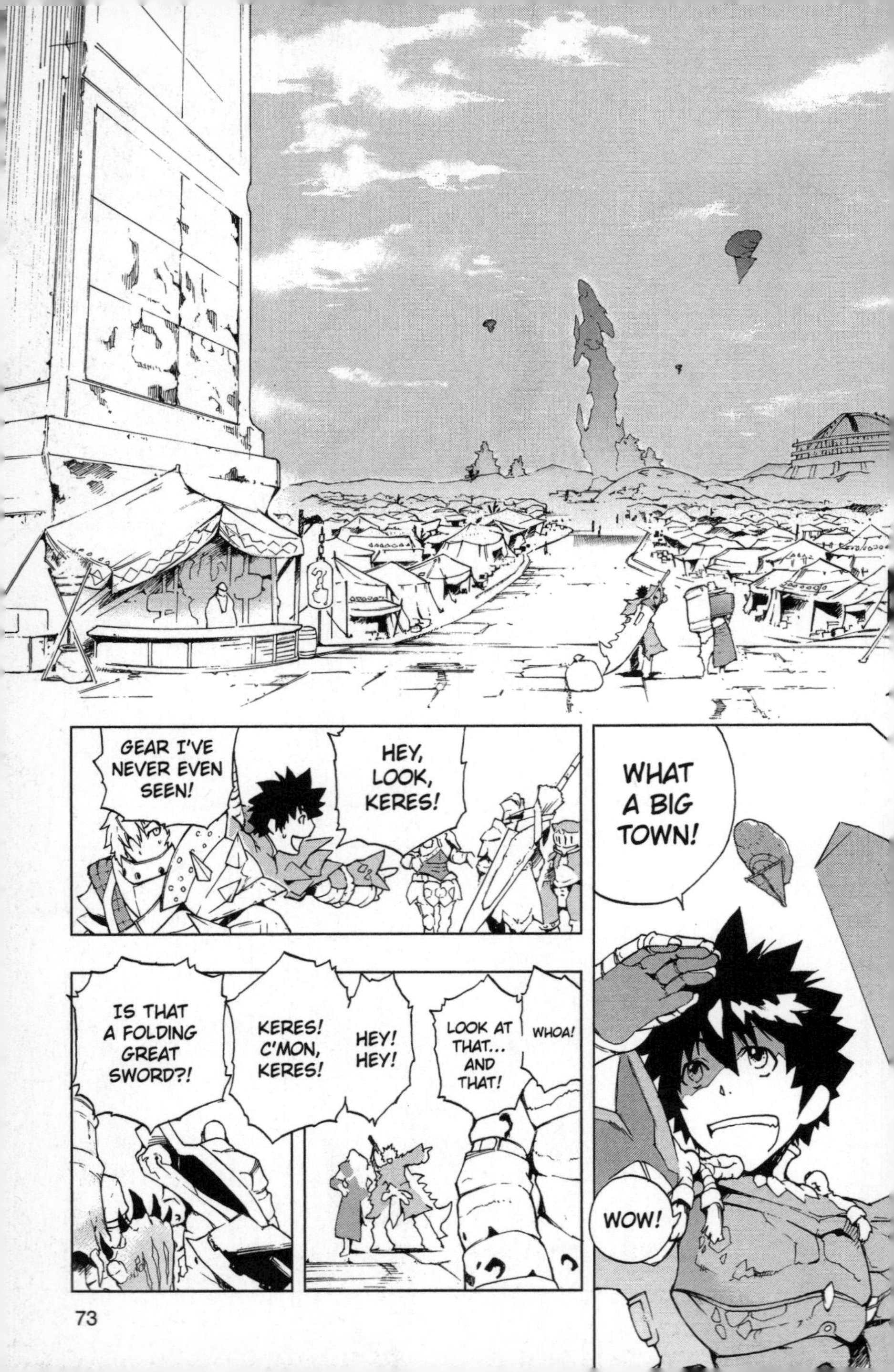
WHAT A BIG TOWN!
WOW!
HEY, LOOK, KERES!
GEAR I'VE NEVER EVEN SEEN!
WHOA!
LOOK AT THAT... AND THAT!
HEY! HEY!
KERES! C'MON, KERES!
IS THAT A FOLDING GREAT SWORD?!

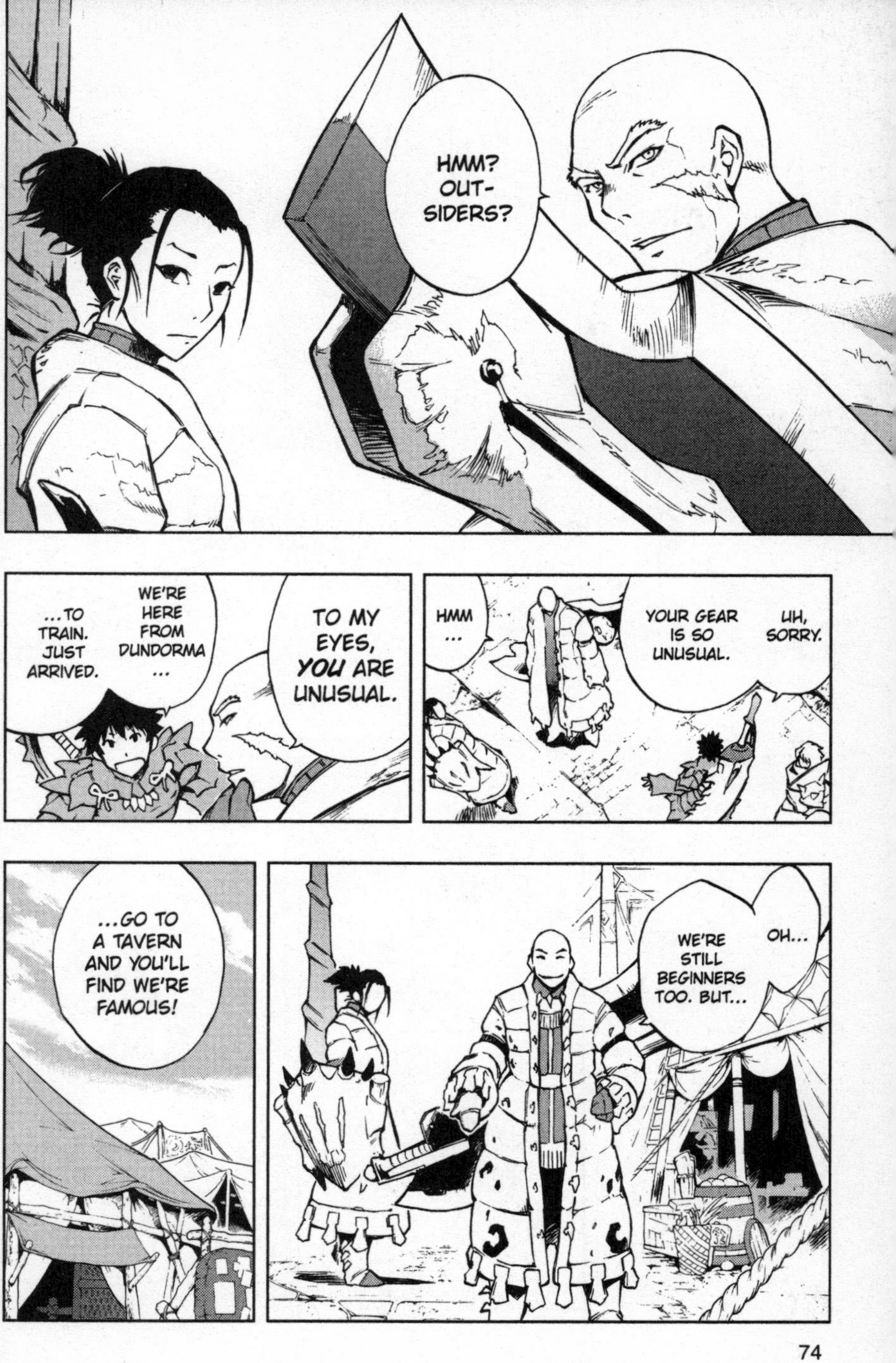
HMM? OUT-SIDERS?
UH, SORRY.
YOUR GEAR IS SO UNUSUAL.
HMM ...
TO MY EYES, *YOU* ARE UNUSUAL.
WE'RE HERE FROM DUNDORMA ...
...TO TRAIN. JUST ARRIVED.
OH...
WE'RE STILL BEGINNERS TOO. BUT...
...GO TO A TAVERN AND YOU'LL FIND WE'RE FAMOUS!

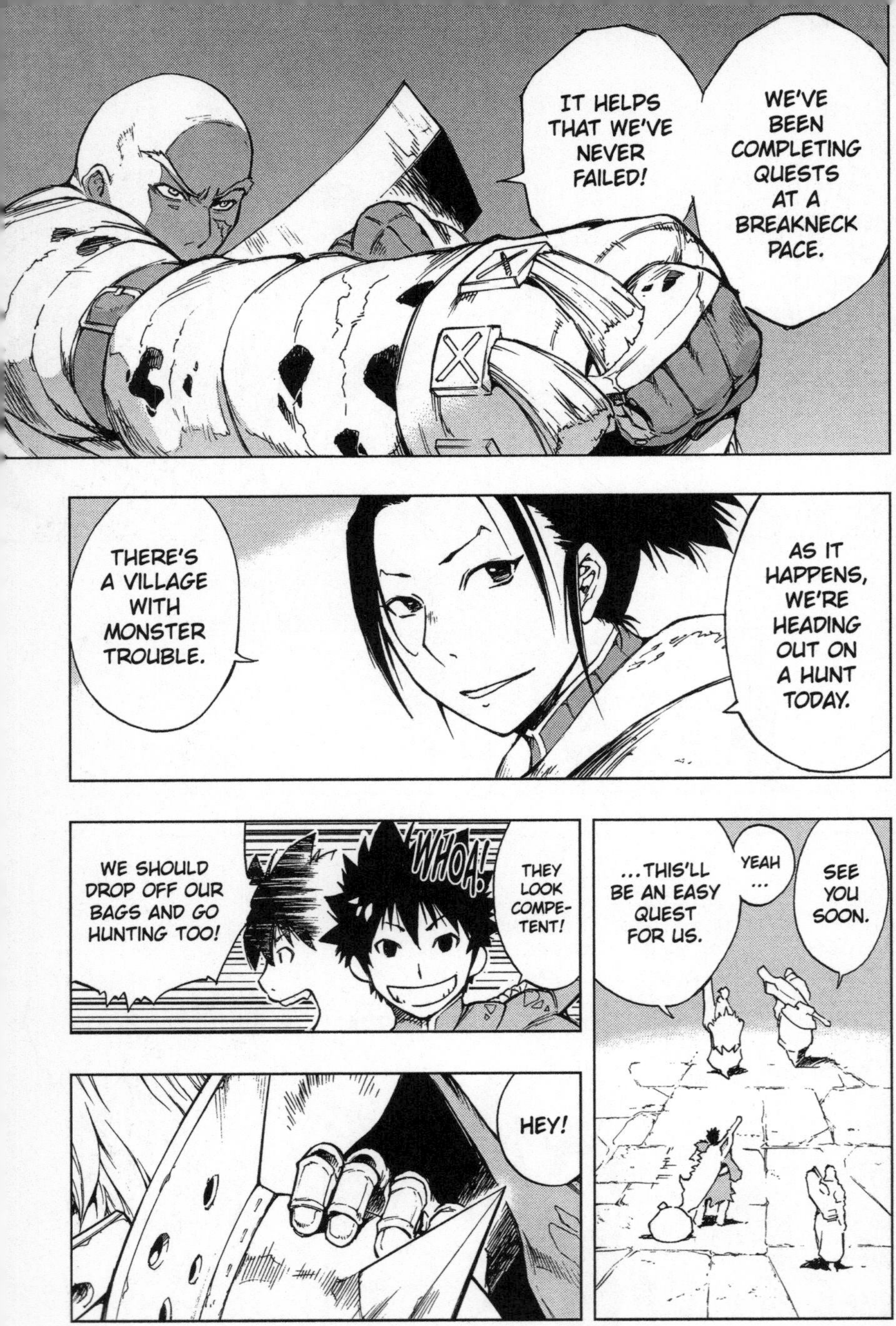

WE'VE BEEN COMPLETING QUESTS AT A BREAKNECK PACE.
IT HELPS THAT WE'VE NEVER FAILED!
AS IT HAPPENS, WE'RE HEADING OUT ON A HUNT TODAY.
THERE'S A VILLAGE WITH MONSTER TROUBLE.
SEE YOU SOON.
YEAH...
...THIS'LL BE AN EASY QUEST FOR US.
WHOA!
THEY LOOK COMPETENT!
WE SHOULD DROP OFF OUR BAGS AND GO HUNTING TOO!
HEY!

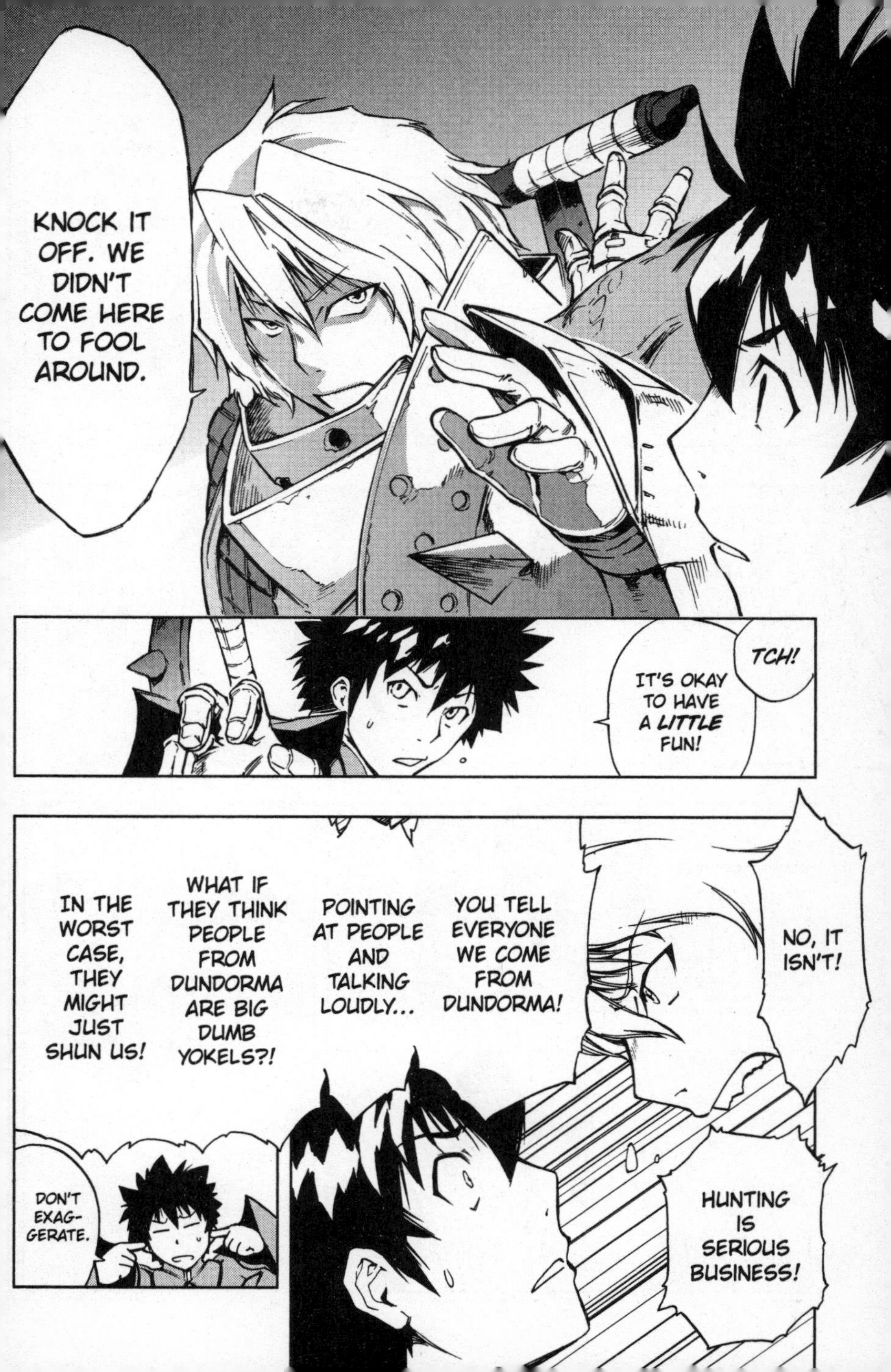
KNOCK IT OFF. WE DIDN'T COME HERE TO FOOL AROUND.
TCH!
IT'S OKAY TO HAVE A *LITTLE* FUN!
NO, IT ISN'T!
HUNTING IS SERIOUS BUSINESS!
YOU TELL EVERYONE WE COME FROM DUNDORMA!
POINTING AT PEOPLE AND TALKING LOUDLY...
WHAT IF THEY THINK PEOPLE FROM DUNDORMA ARE BIG DUMB YOKELS?!
IN THE WORST CASE, THEY MIGHT JUST SHUN US!
DON'T EXAG-GERATE.

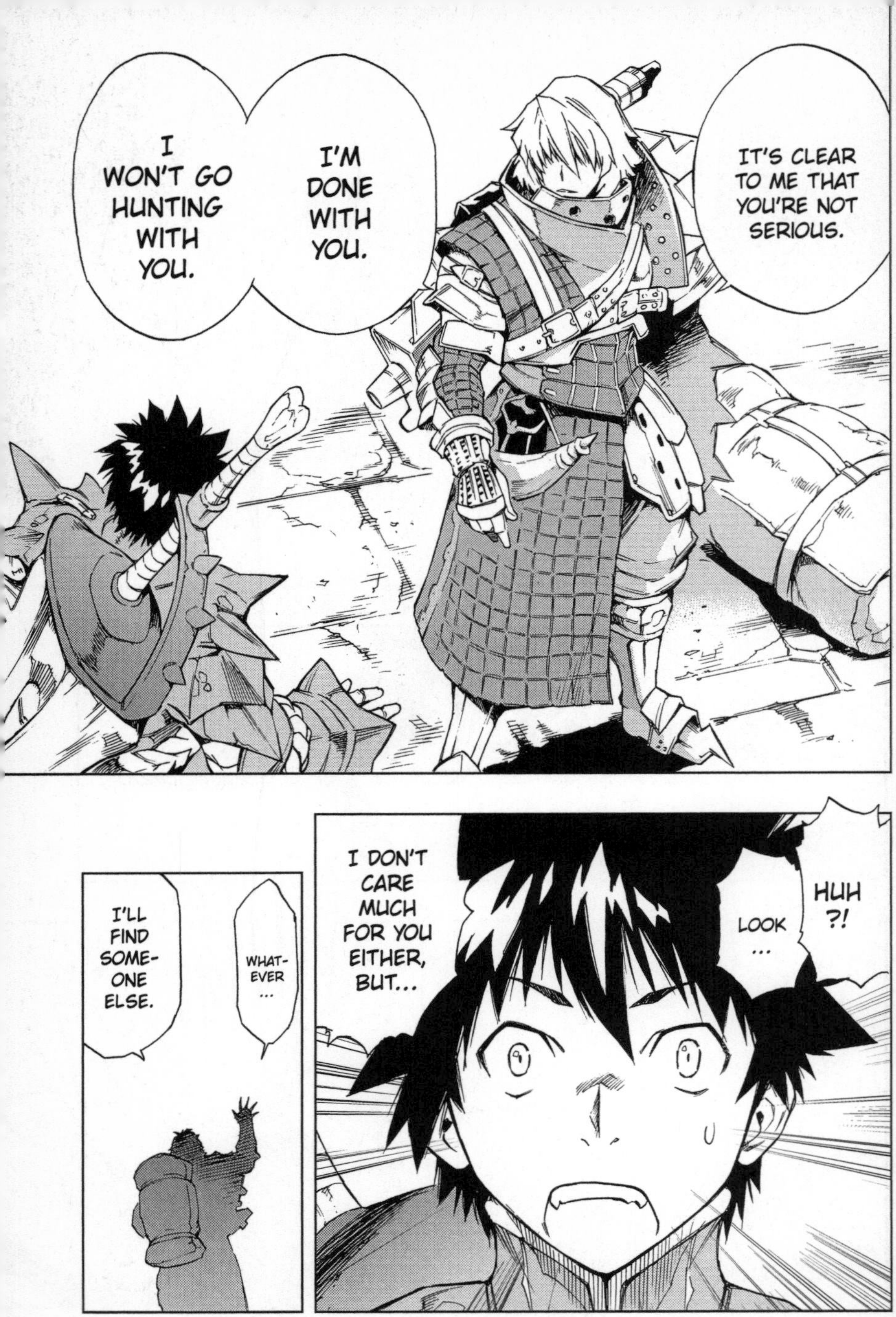
IT'S CLEAR TO ME THAT YOU'RE NOT SERIOUS.
I'M DONE WITH YOU.
I WON'T GO HUNTING WITH YOU.
HUH ?!
LOOK ...
I DON'T CARE MUCH FOR YOU EITHER, BUT...
WHAT-EVER ...
I'LL FIND SOME-ONE ELSE.

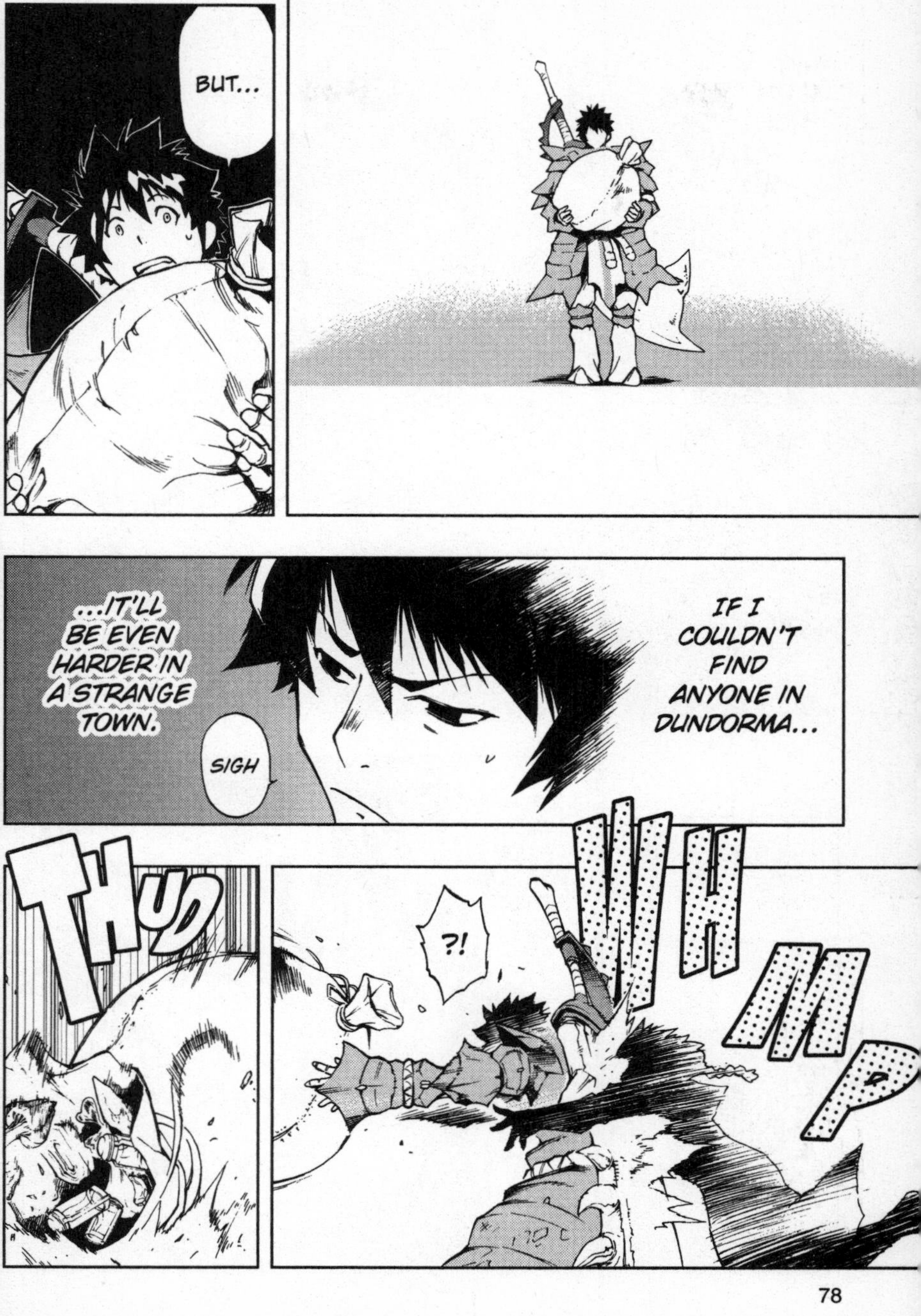
BUT...
IF I COULDN'T FIND ANYONE IN DUNDORMA...
...IT'LL BE EVEN HARDER IN A STRANGE TOWN.
SIGH
WHMP
?!
THUD

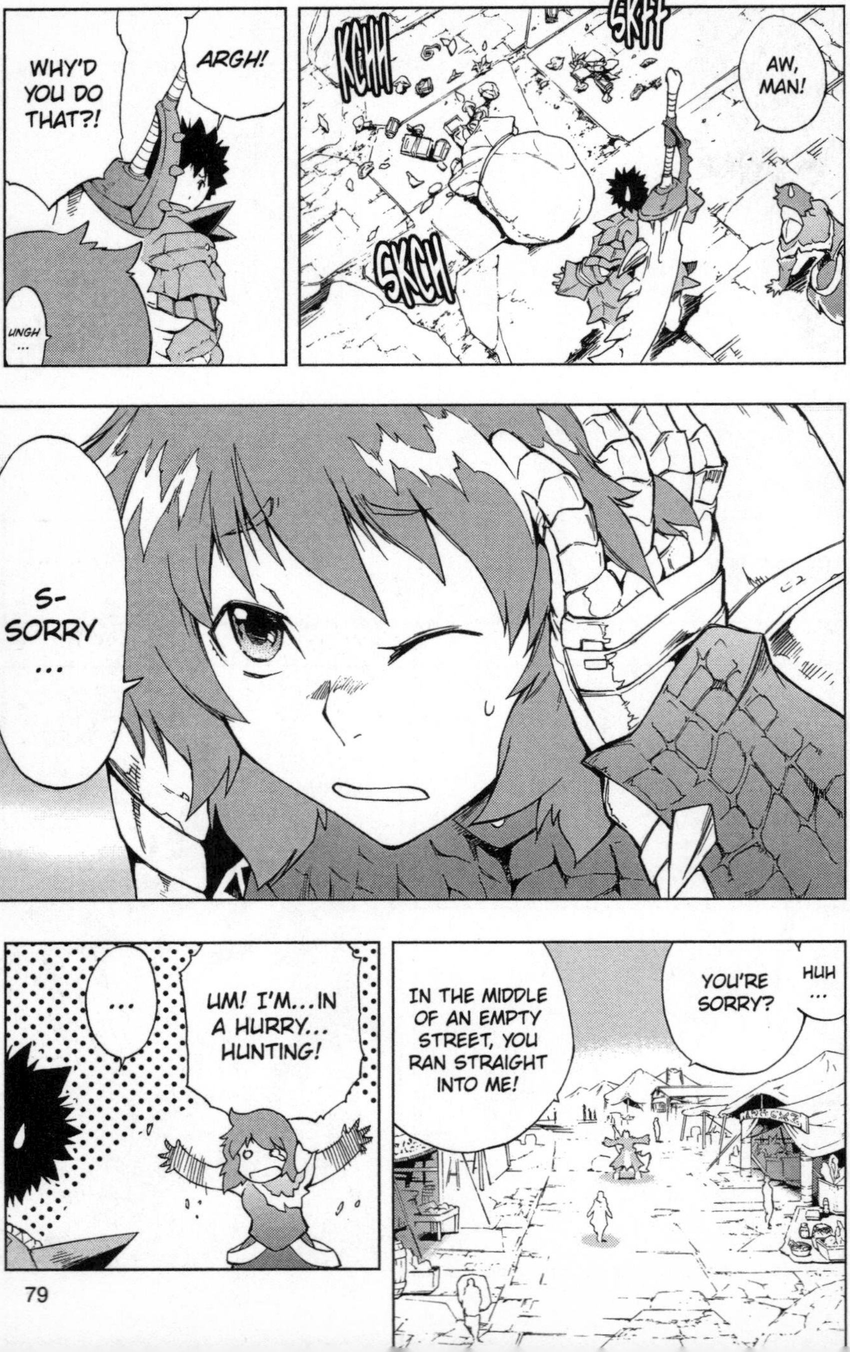
SKFF
AW, MAN!
KCHH
SKCH
ARGH!
WHY'D YOU DO THAT?!
UNGH ...
S-SORRY ...
HUH ...
YOU'RE SORRY?
IN THE MIDDLE OF AN EMPTY STREET, YOU RAN STRAIGHT INTO ME!
UM! I'M...IN A HURRY... HUNTING!
...

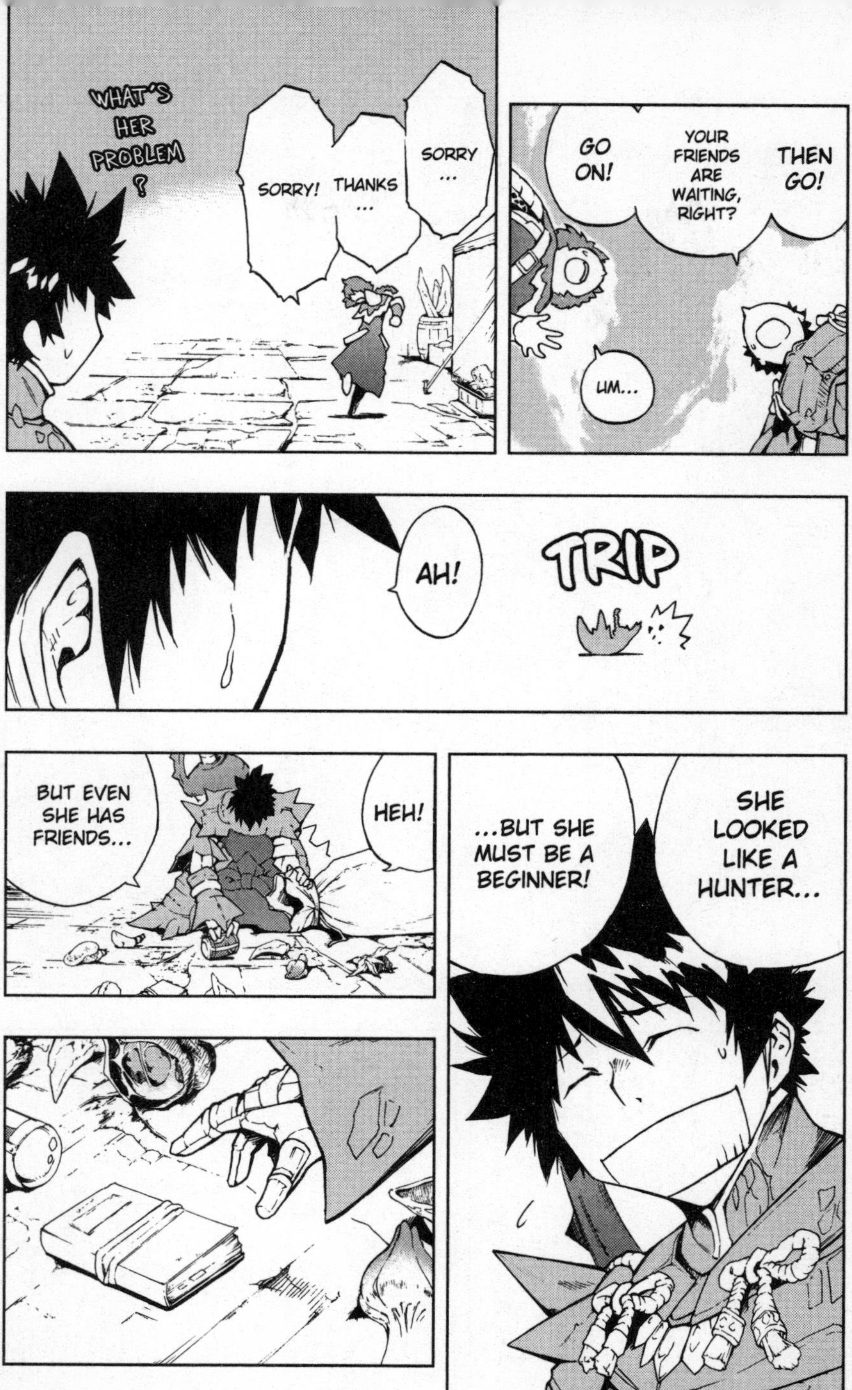
THEN GO!
YOUR FRIENDS ARE WAITING, RIGHT?
GO ON!
UM...
SORRY ...
THANKS ...
SORRY!
WHAT'S HER PROBLEM ?
TRIP
AH!
SHE LOOKED LIKE A HUNTER...
...BUT SHE MUST BE A BEGINNER!
HEH!
BUT EVEN SHE HAS FRIENDS...

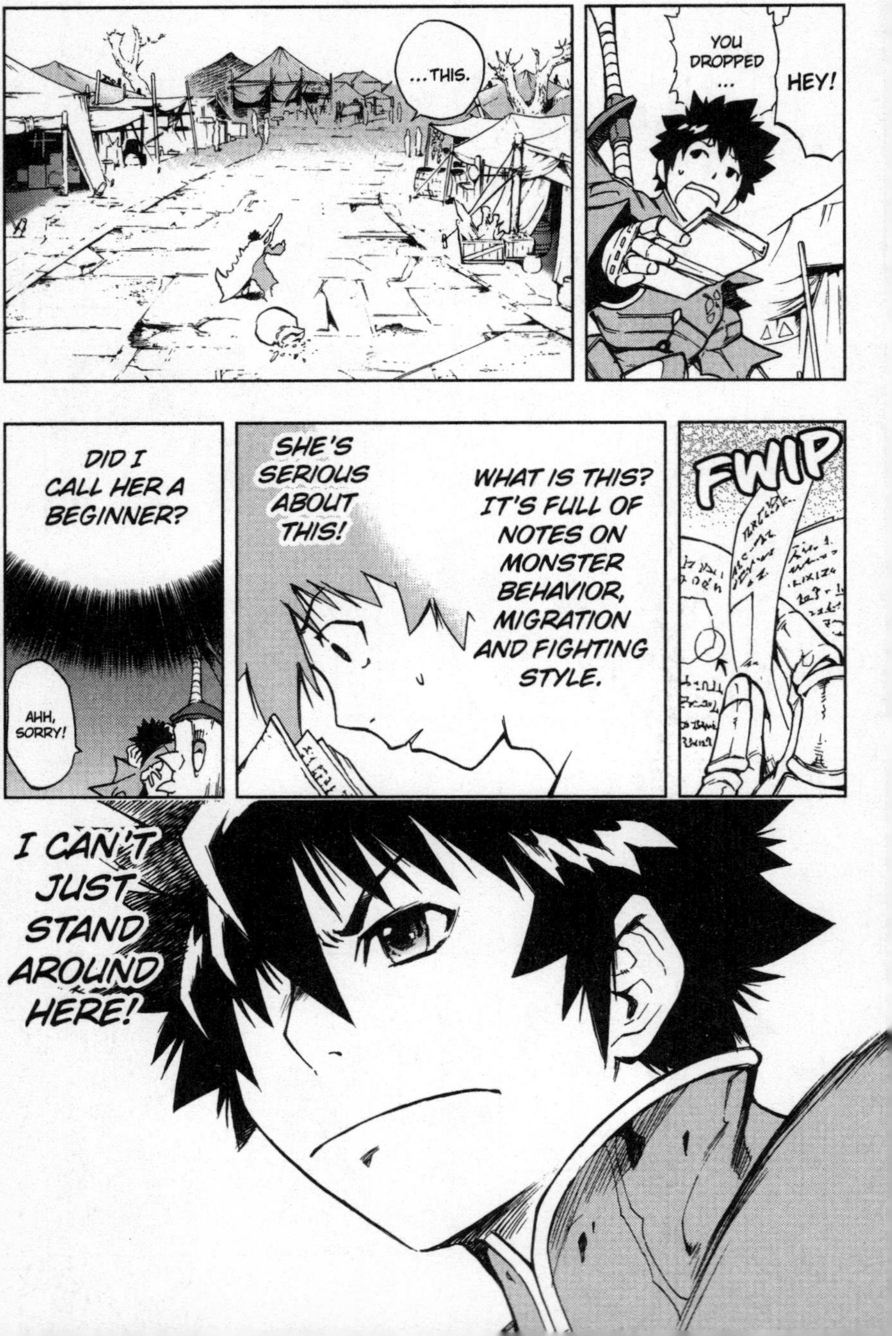
HEY!
YOU DROPPED ...
...THIS.
FWIP
WHAT IS THIS? IT'S FULL OF NOTES ON MONSTER BEHAVIOR, MIGRATION AND FIGHTING STYLE.
SHE'S SERIOUS ABOUT THIS!
DID I CALL HER A BEGINNER?
AHH, SORRY!
I CAN'T JUST STAND AROUND HERE!

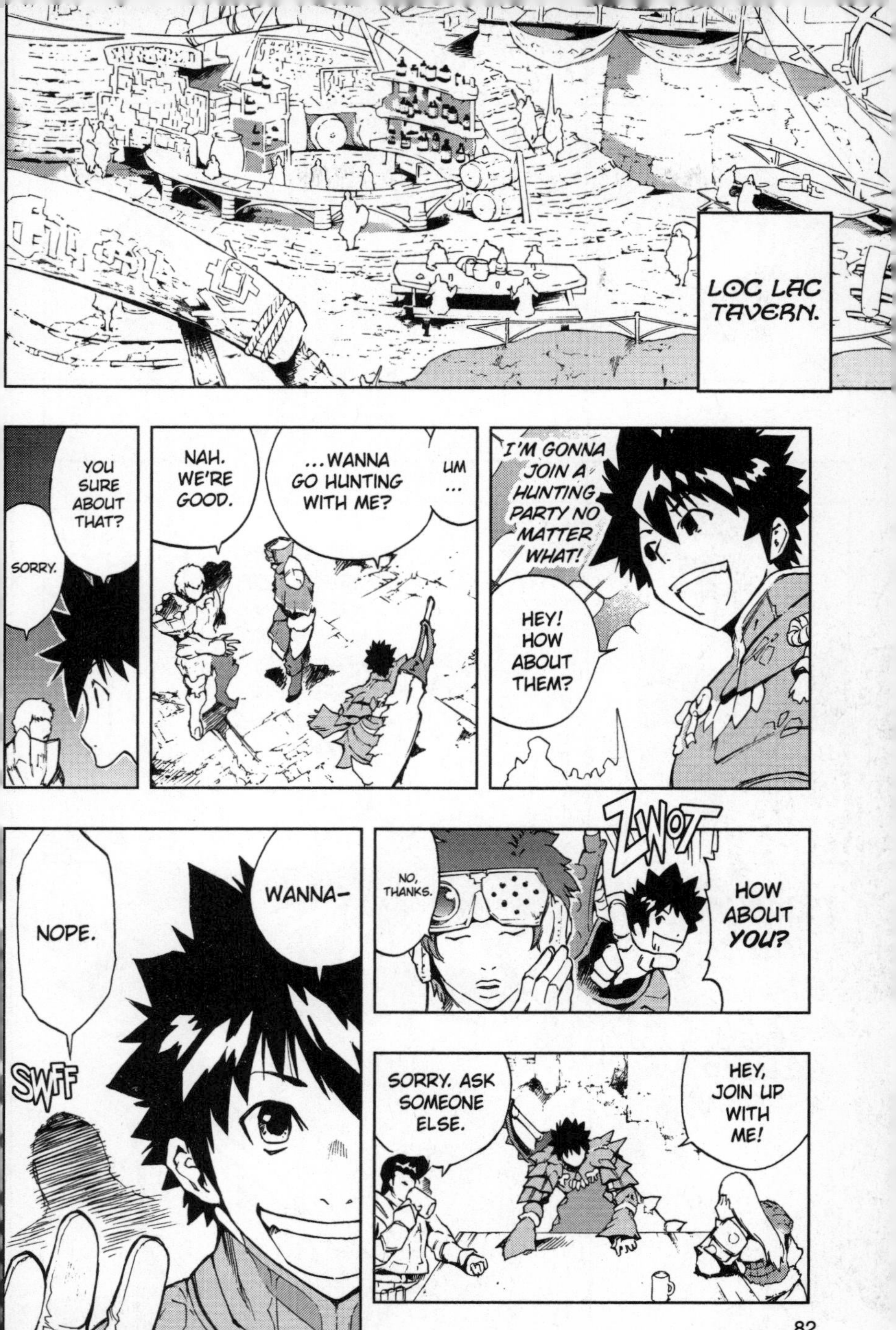
LOC LAC TAVERN.
I'M GONNA JOIN A HUNTING PARTY NO MATTER WHAT!
HEY! HOW ABOUT THEM?
UM ...
...WANNA GO HUNTING WITH ME?
NAH. WE'RE GOOD.
YOU SURE ABOUT THAT?
SORRY.
HOW ABOUT YOU?
ZWOT
NO, THANKS.
HEY, JOIN UP WITH ME!
SORRY. ASK SOMEONE ELSE.
WANNA-
NOPE.
SWFF

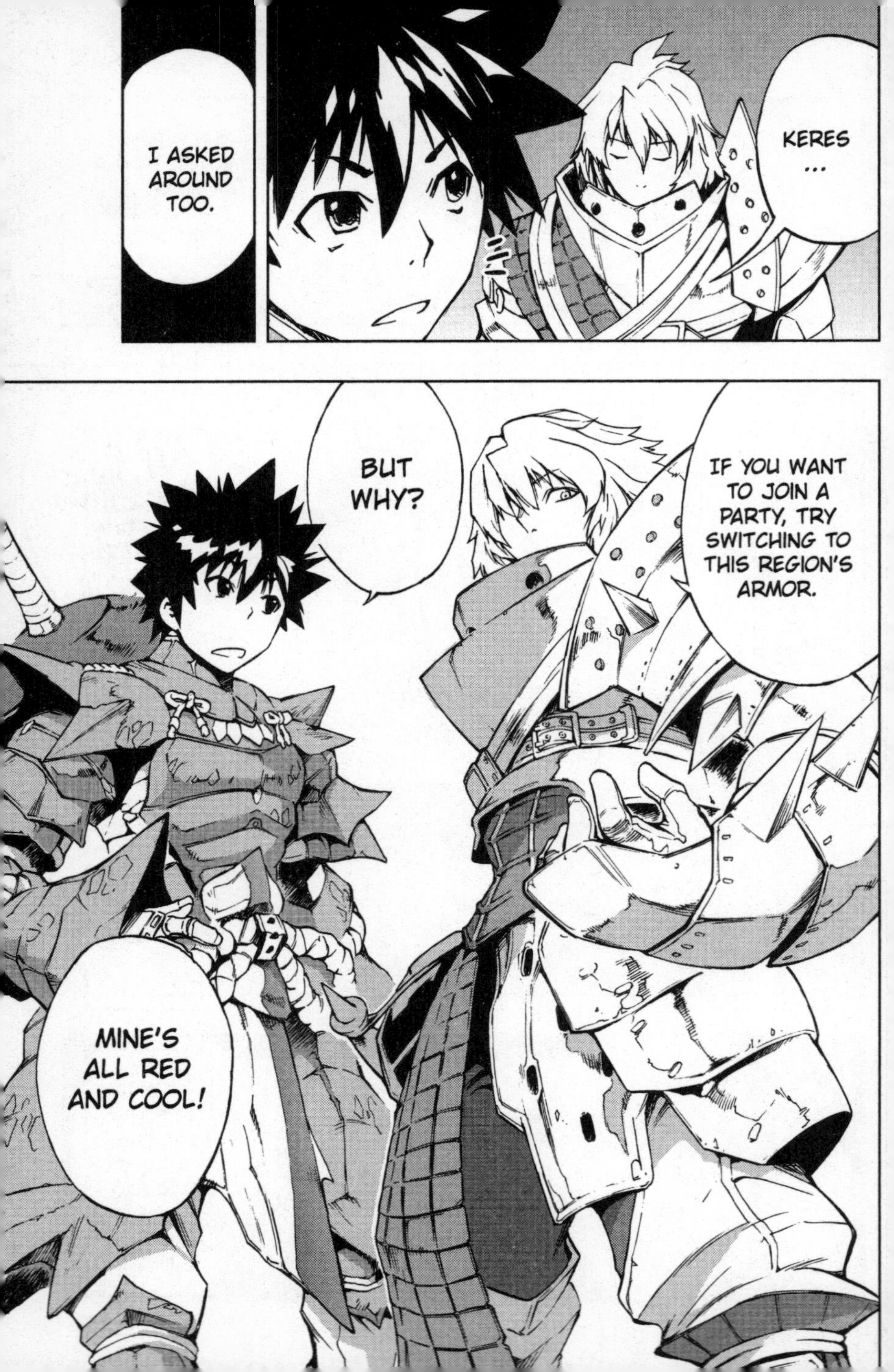
KERES ...
I ASKED AROUND TOO.
IF YOU WANT TO JOIN A PARTY, TRY SWITCHING TO THIS REGION'S ARMOR.
BUT WHY?
MINE'S ALL RED AND COOL!

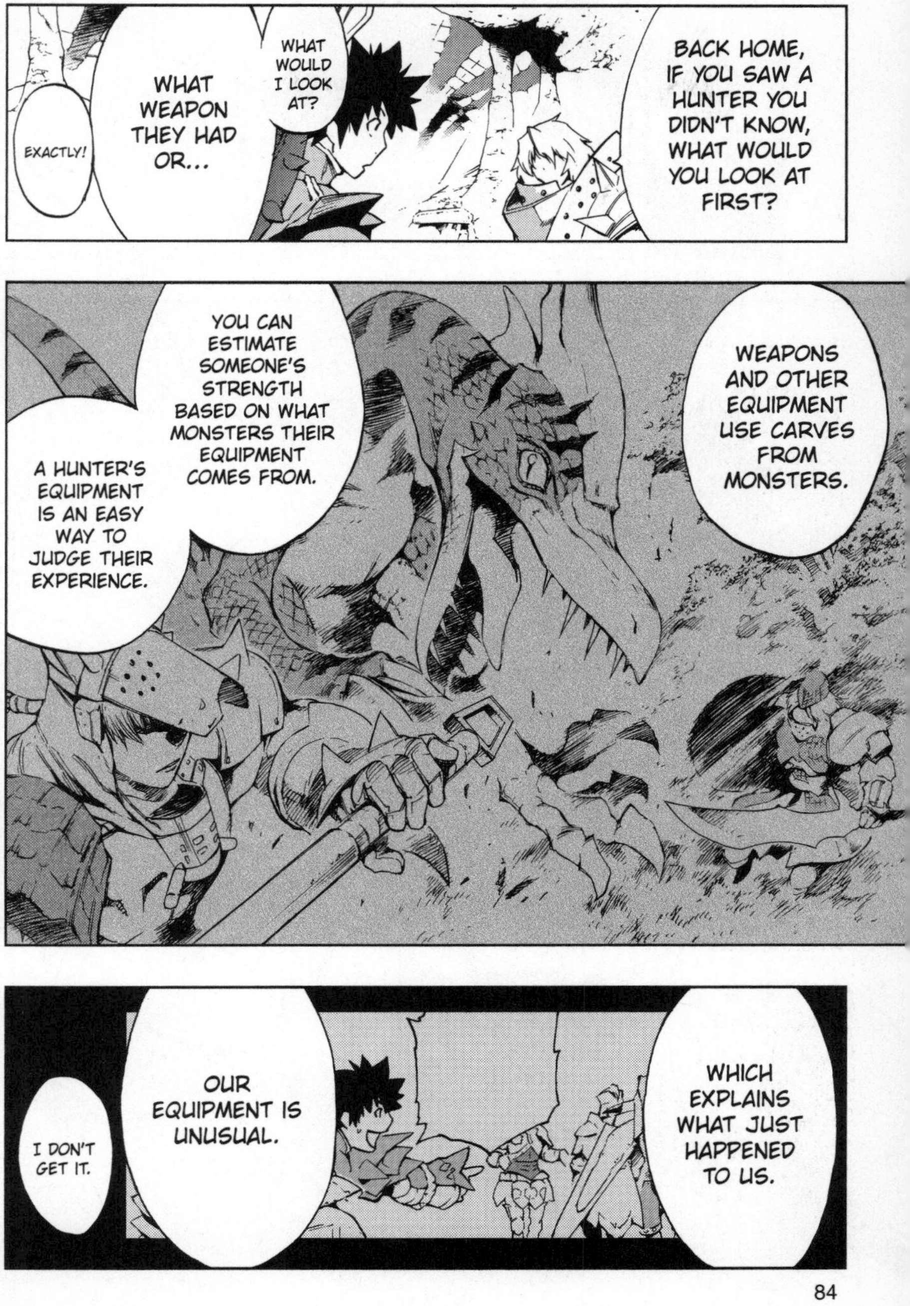
BACK HOME, IF YOU SAW A HUNTER YOU DIDN'T KNOW, WHAT WOULD YOU LOOK AT FIRST?
WHAT WOULD I LOOK AT?
WHAT WEAPON THEY HAD OR...
EXACTLY!
WEAPONS AND OTHER EQUIPMENT USE CARVES FROM MONSTERS.
YOU CAN ESTIMATE SOMEONE'S STRENGTH BASED ON WHAT MONSTERS THEIR EQUIPMENT COMES FROM.
A HUNTER'S EQUIPMENT IS AN EASY WAY TO JUDGE THEIR EXPERIENCE.
WHICH EXPLAINS WHAT JUST HAPPENED TO US.
OUR EQUIPMENT IS UNUSUAL.
I DON'T GET IT.

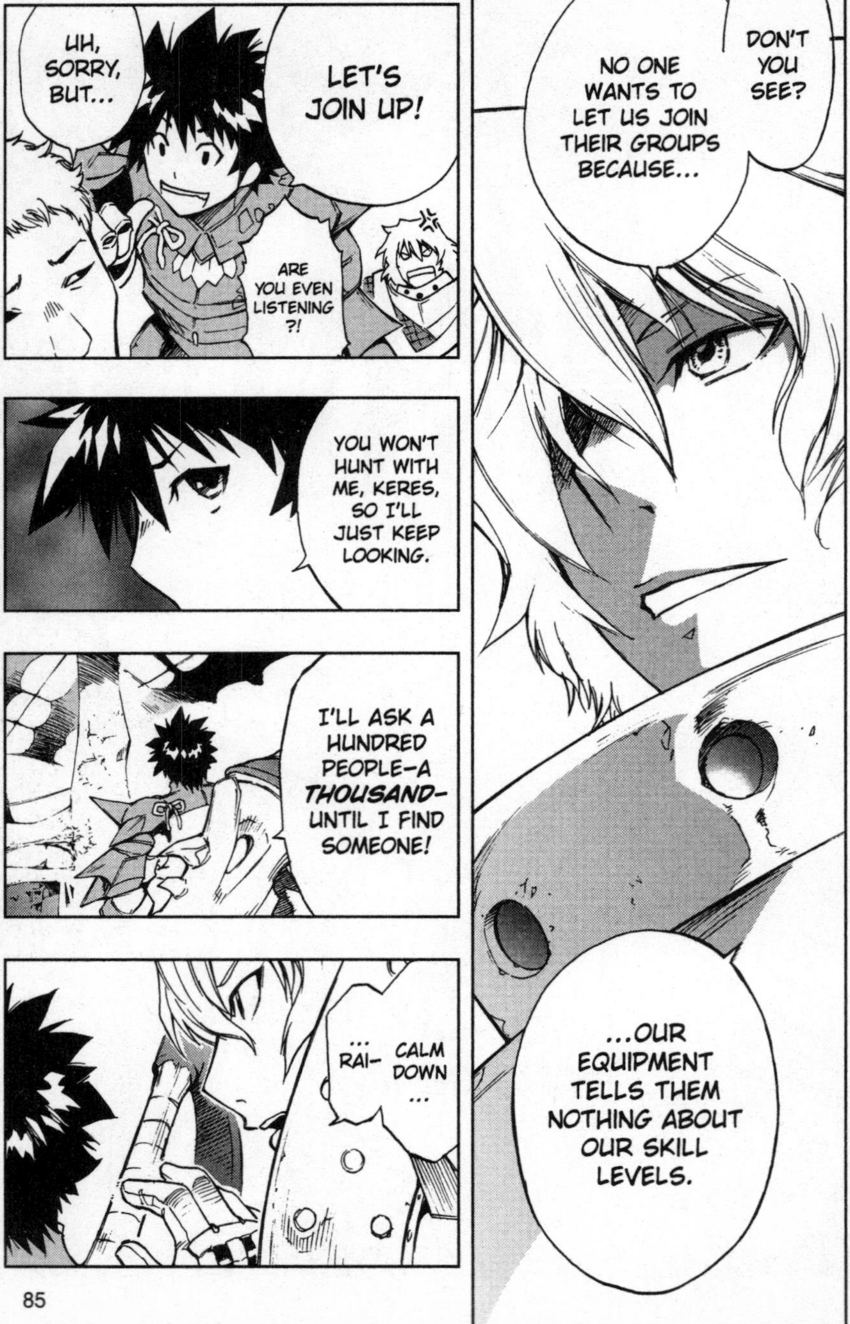
LET'S JOIN UP!
UH, SORRY, BUT...
ARE YOU EVEN LISTENING ?!
YOU WON'T HUNT WITH ME, KERES, SO I'LL JUST KEEP LOOKING.
I'LL ASK A HUNDRED PEOPLE—A *THOUSAND*—UNTIL I FIND SOMEONE!
CALM DOWN ...
... RAI-
DON'T YOU SEE?
NO ONE WANTS TO LET US JOIN THEIR GROUPS BECAUSE...
...OUR EQUIPMENT TELLS THEM NOTHING ABOUT OUR SKILL LEVELS.

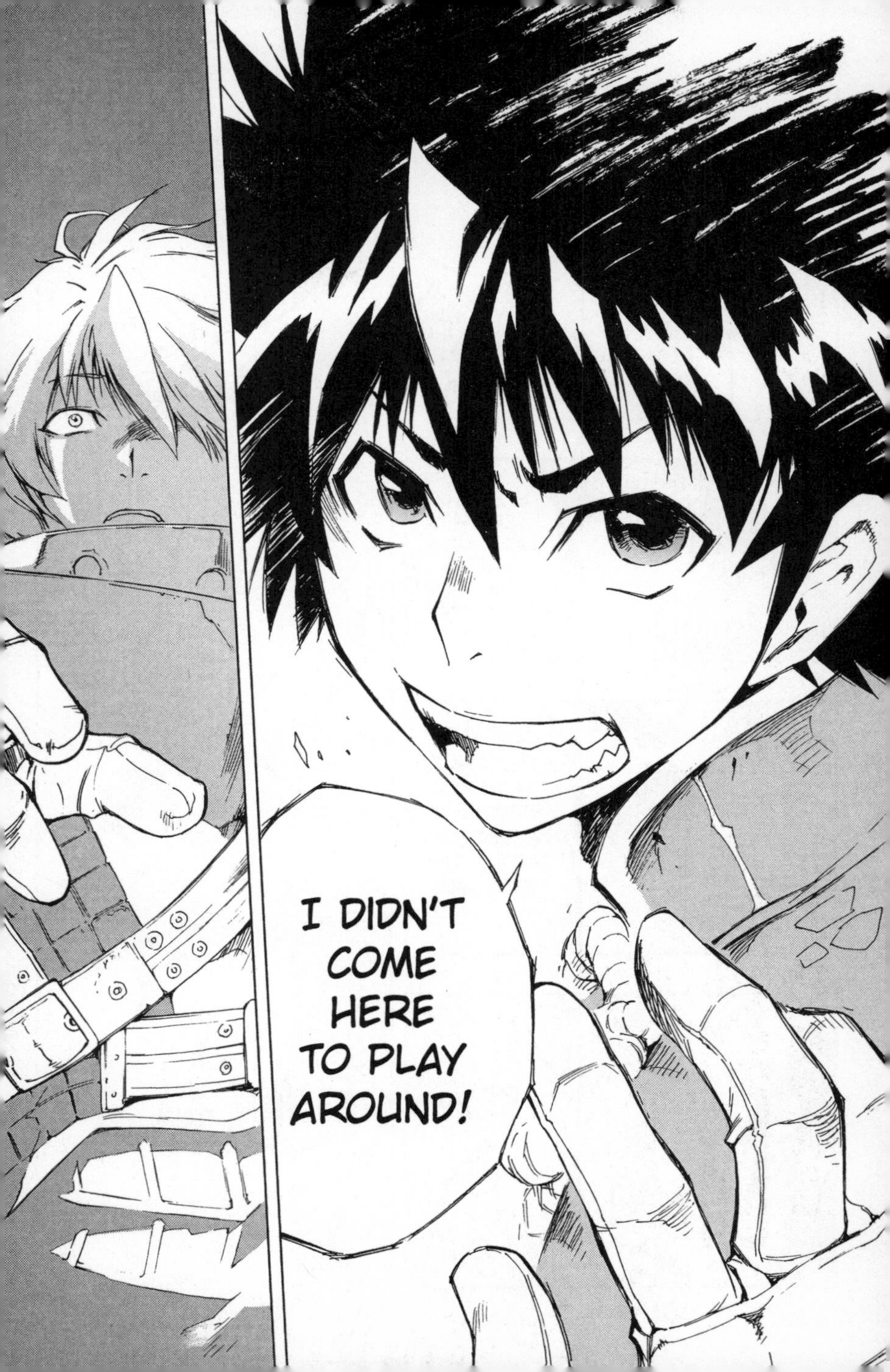
I DIDN'T COME HERE TO PLAY AROUND!

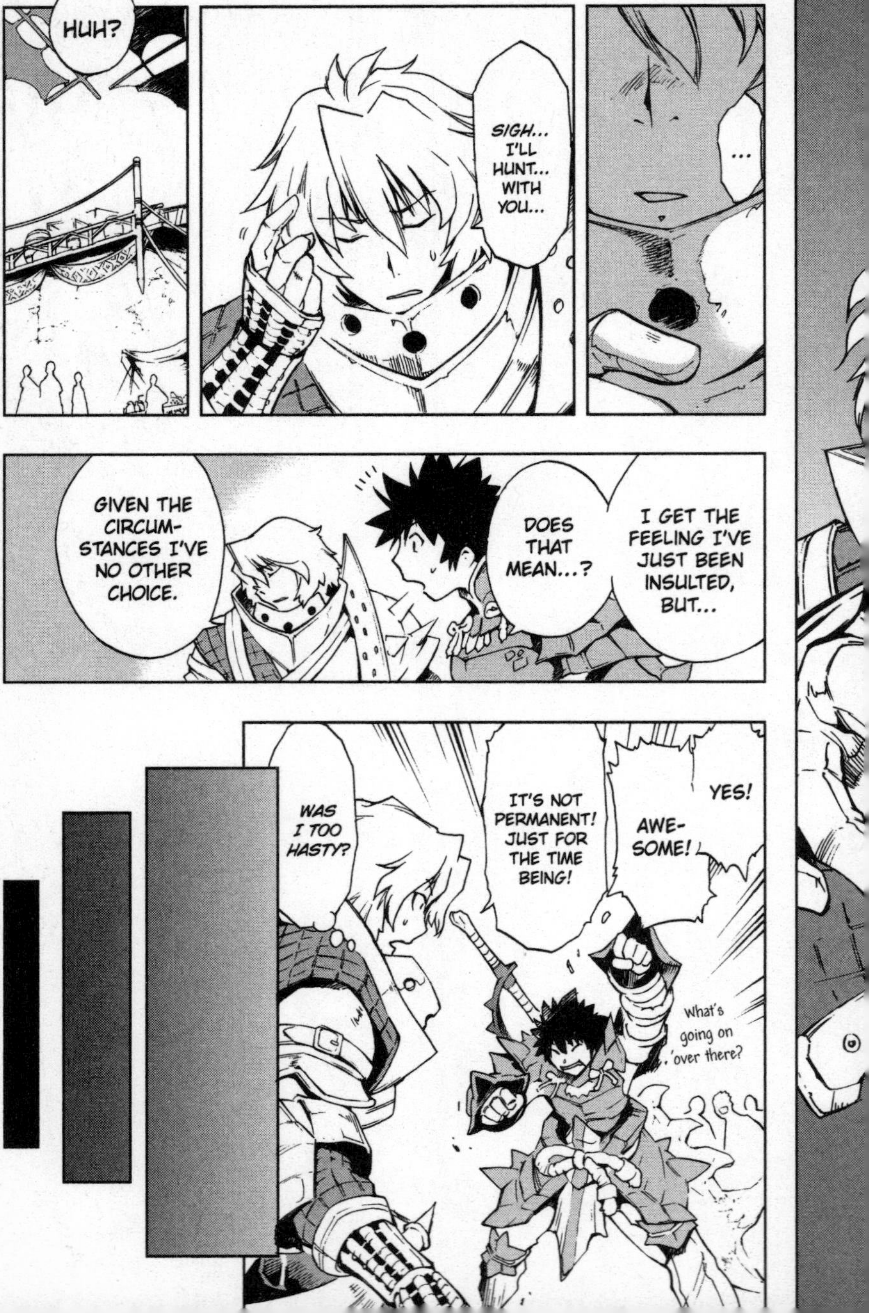
...
SIGH... I'LL HUNT... WITH YOU...
HUH?
I GET THE FEELING I'VE JUST BEEN INSULTED, BUT...
DOES THAT MEAN...?
GIVEN THE CIRCUM-STANCES I'VE NO OTHER CHOICE.
YES!
AWE-SOME!
IT'S NOT PERMANENT! JUST FOR THE TIME BEING!
WAS I TOO HASTY?
What's going on over there?

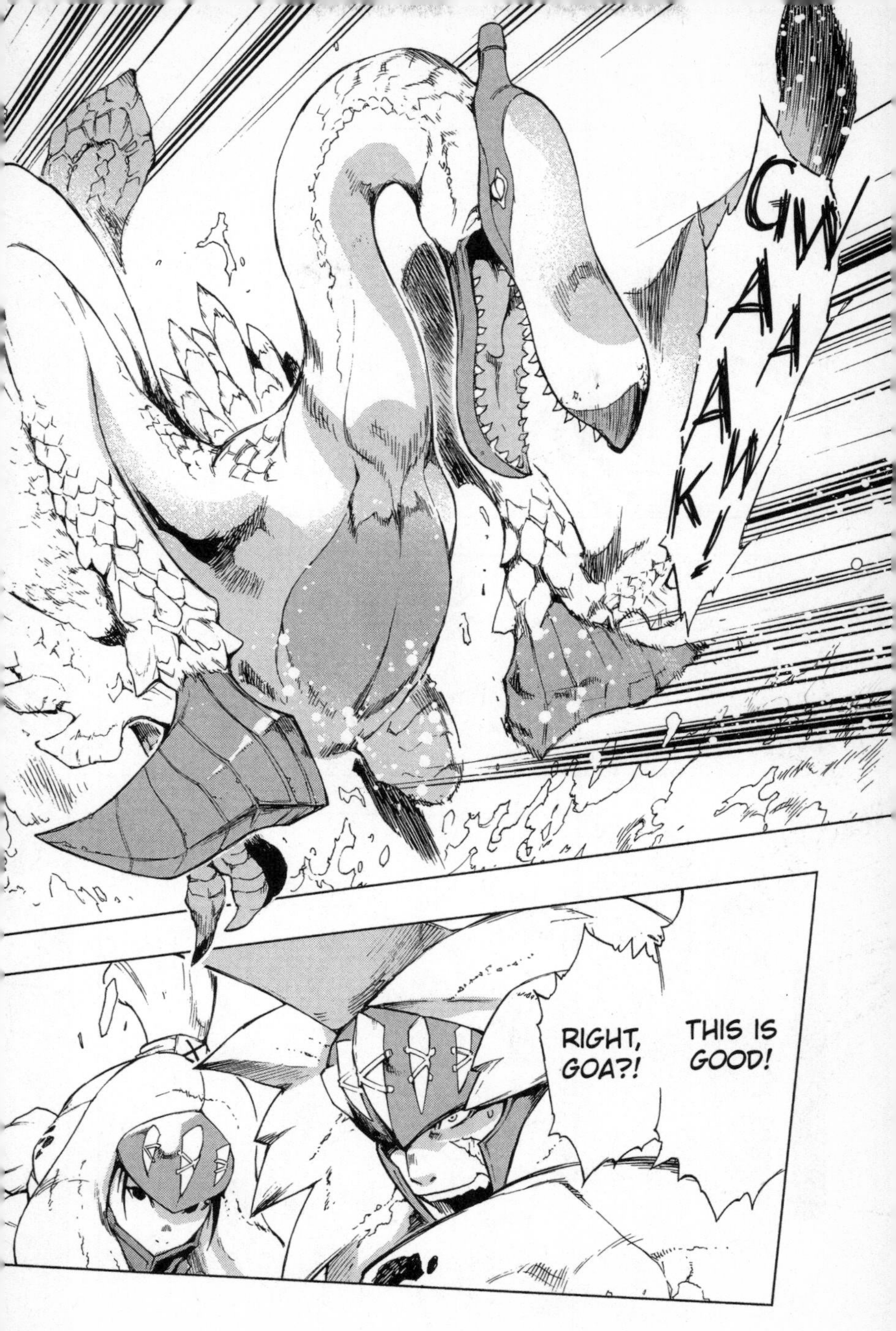
GWAAAWK!
THIS IS GOOD!
RIGHT, GOA?!

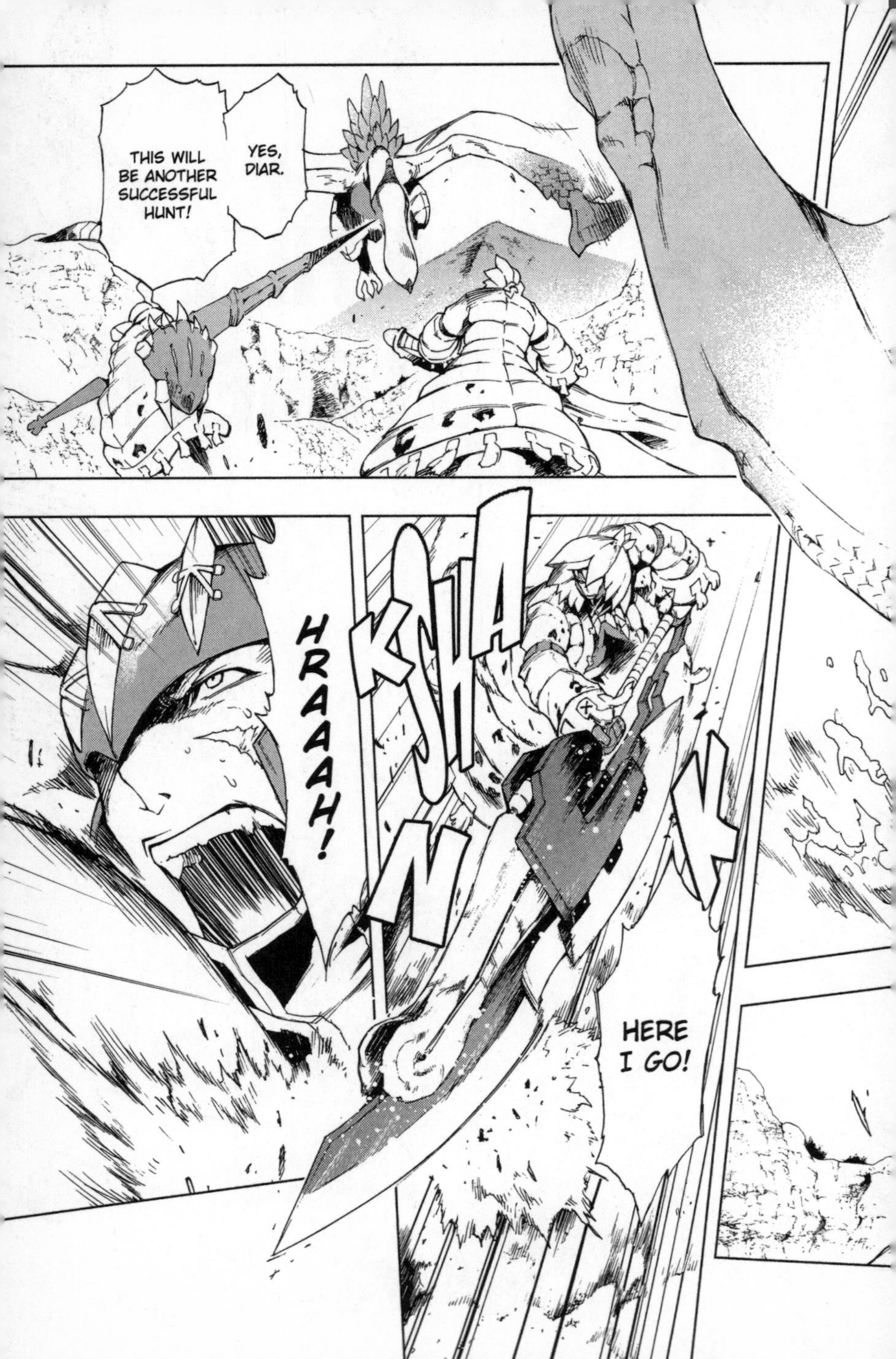
YES, DIAR.
THIS WILL BE ANOTHER SUCCESSFUL HUNT!
HERE I GO!
KSHANK
HRAAAAH!

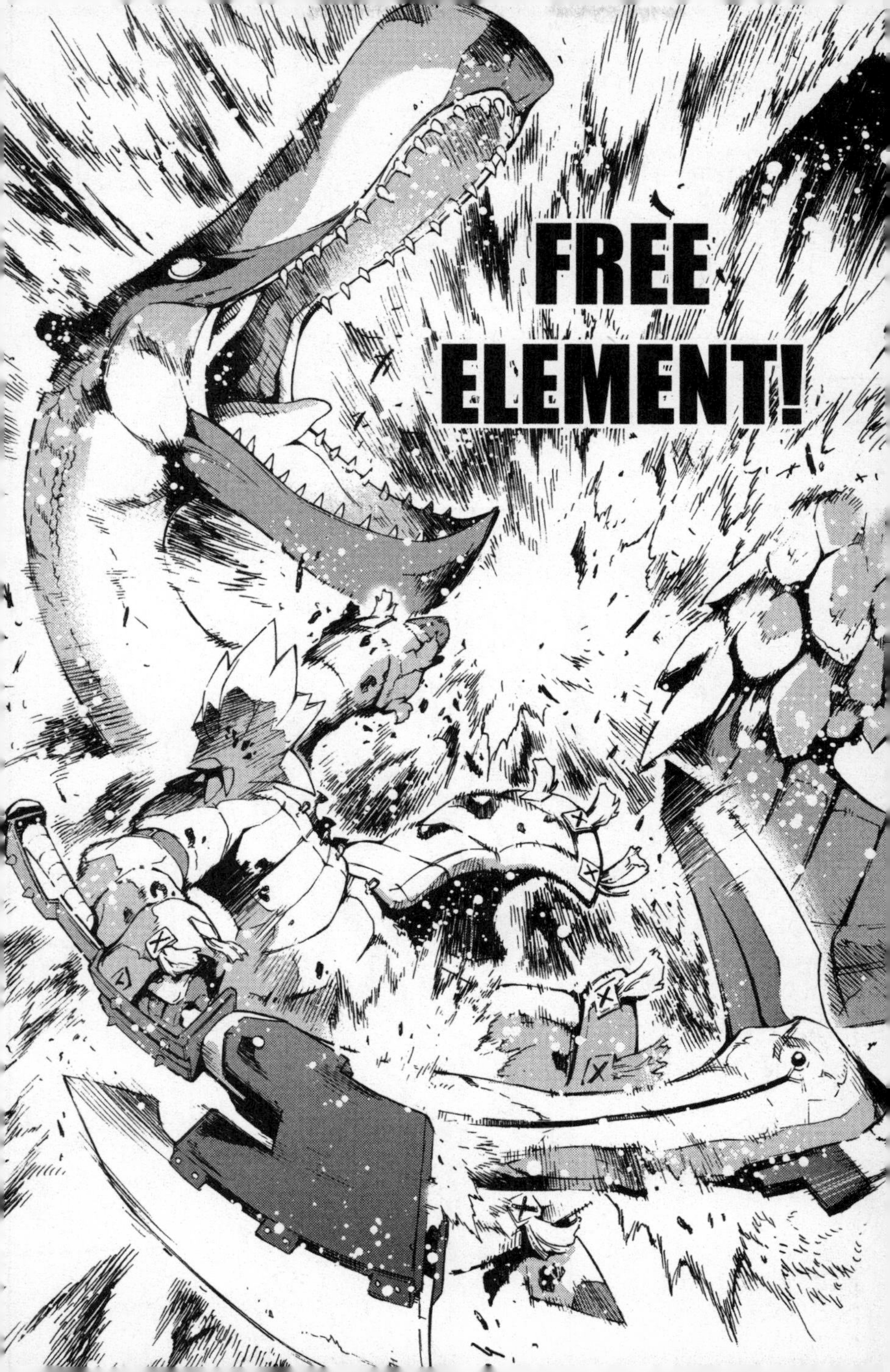
FREE
ELEMENT!

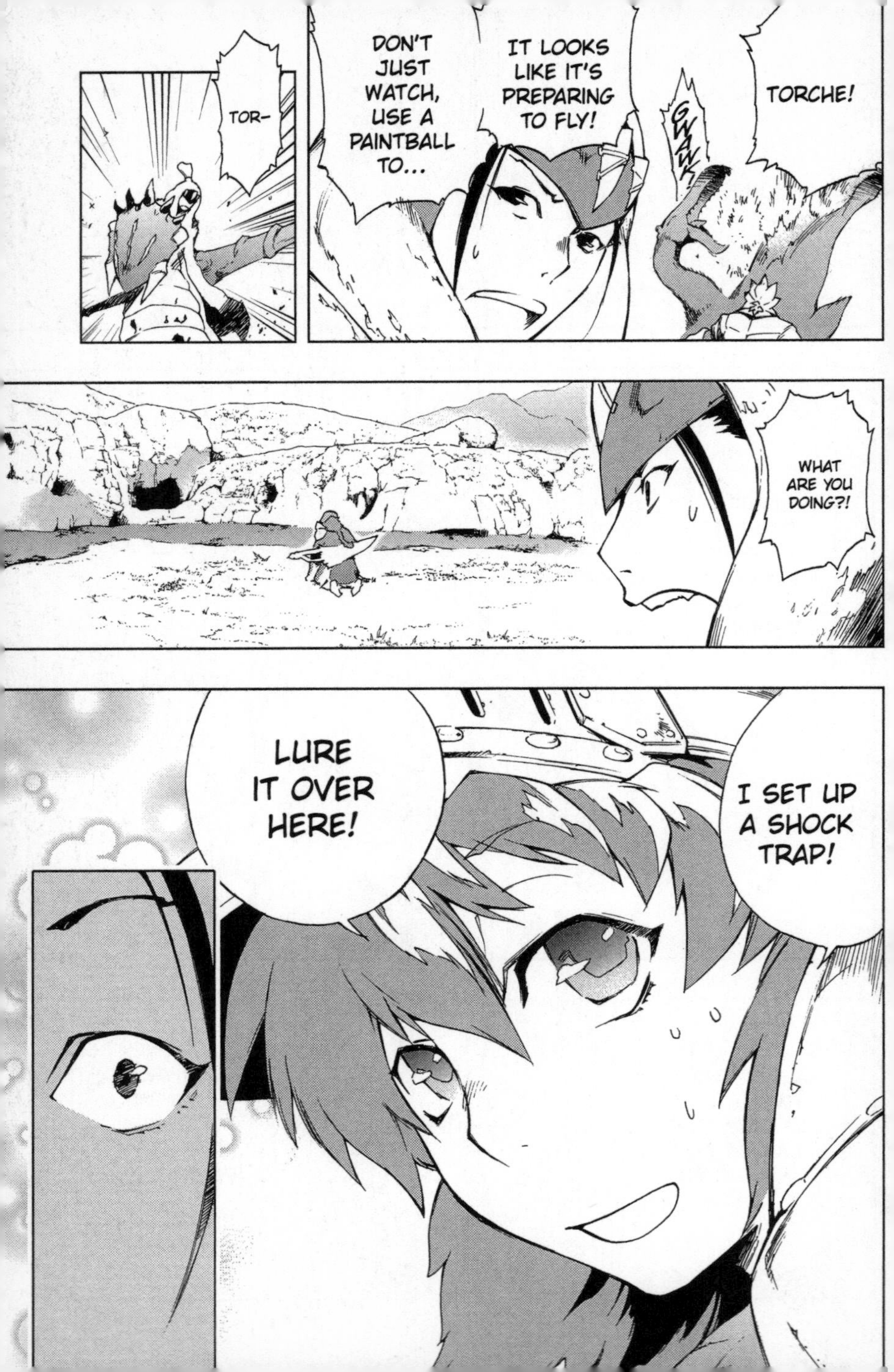
TORCHE!
GWAWK!
IT LOOKS LIKE IT'S PREPARING TO FLY!
DON'T JUST WATCH, USE A PAINTBALL TO...
TOR-
WHAT ARE YOU DOING?!
I SET UP A SHOCK TRAP!
LURE IT OVER HERE!

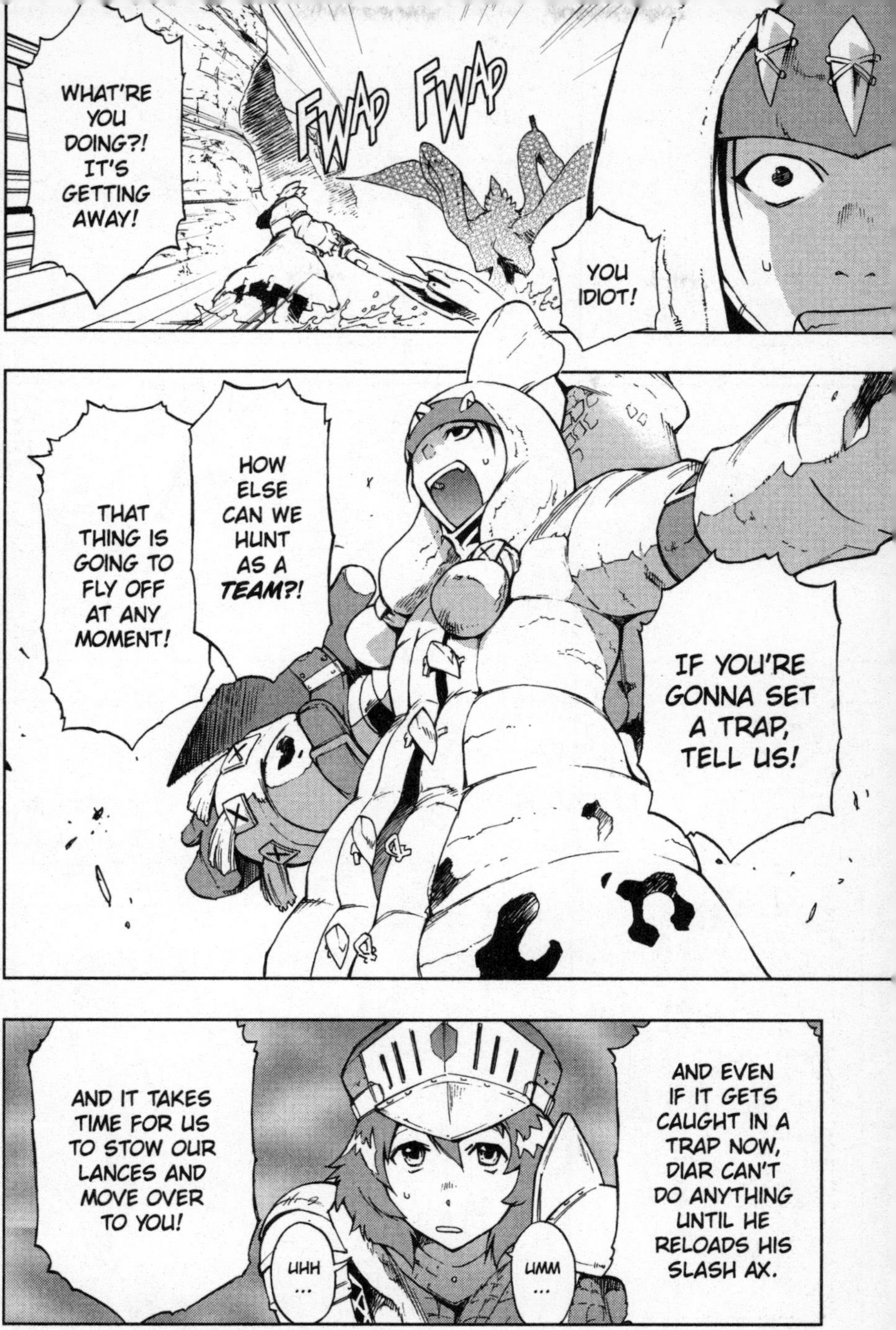
YOU IDIOT!
FWAP FWAP
WHAT'RE YOU DOING?! IT'S GETTING AWAY!
IF YOU'RE GONNA SET A TRAP, TELL US!
HOW ELSE CAN WE HUNT AS A *TEAM*?!
THAT THING IS GOING TO FLY OFF AT ANY MOMENT!
AND EVEN IF IT GETS CAUGHT IN A TRAP NOW, DIAR CAN'T DO ANYTHING UNTIL HE RELOADS HIS SLASH AX.
UMM ...
UHH ...
AND IT TAKES TIME FOR US TO STOW OUR LANCES AND MOVE OVER TO YOU!

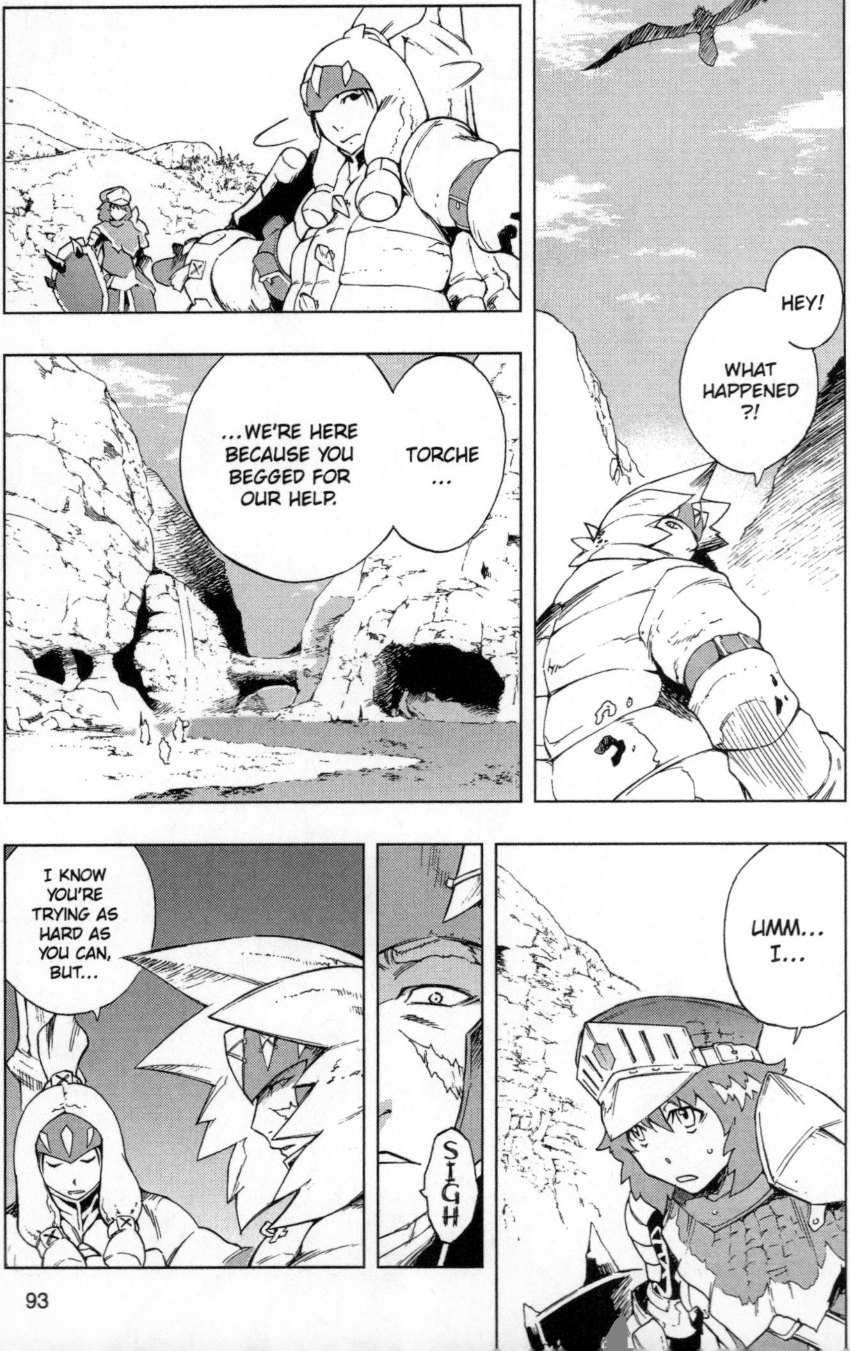
HEY!
WHAT HAPPENED?!
TORCHE ...
...WE'RE HERE BECAUSE YOU BEGGED FOR OUR HELP.
UMM... I...
SIGH
I KNOW YOU'RE TRYING AS HARD AS YOU CAN, BUT...

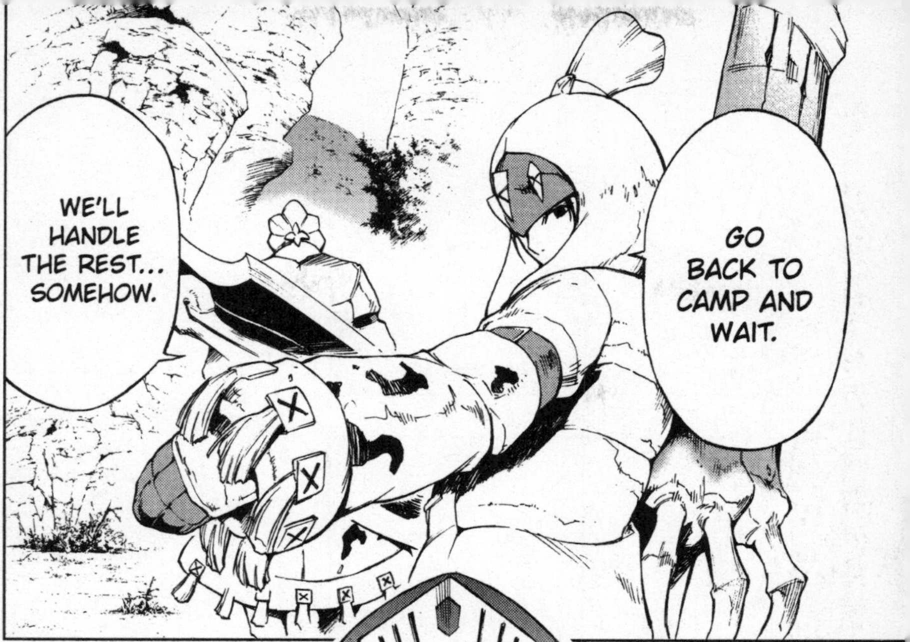
GO BACK TO CAMP AND WAIT.
WE'LL HANDLE THE REST... SOMEHOW.
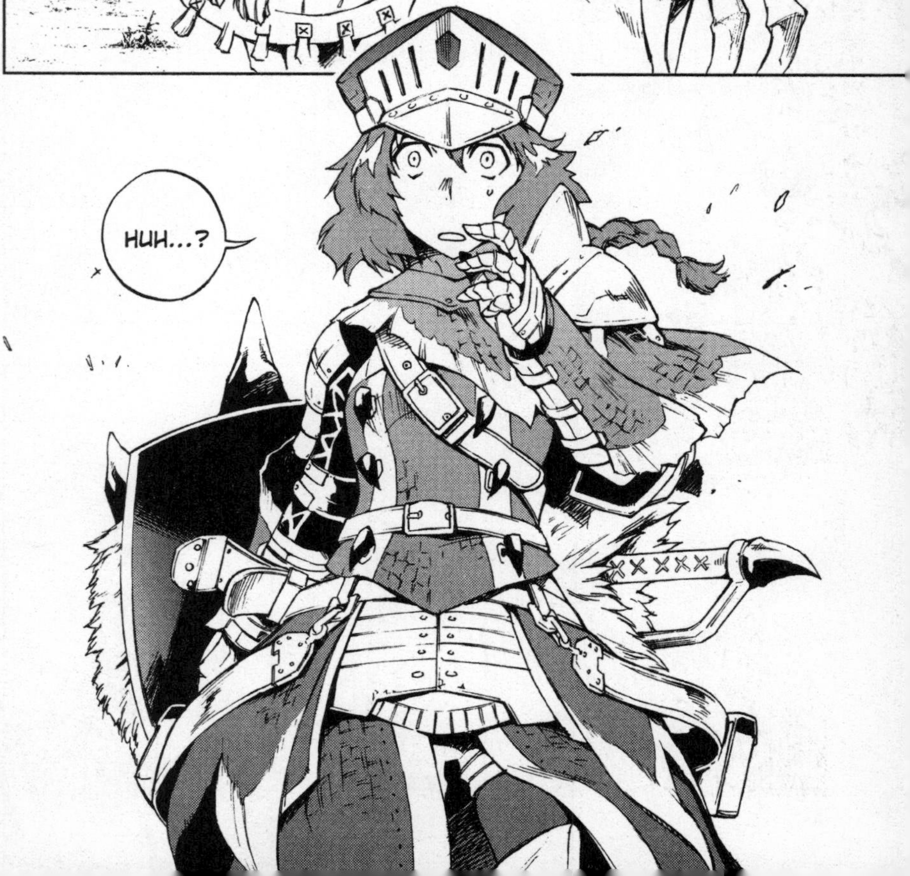
HUH...?

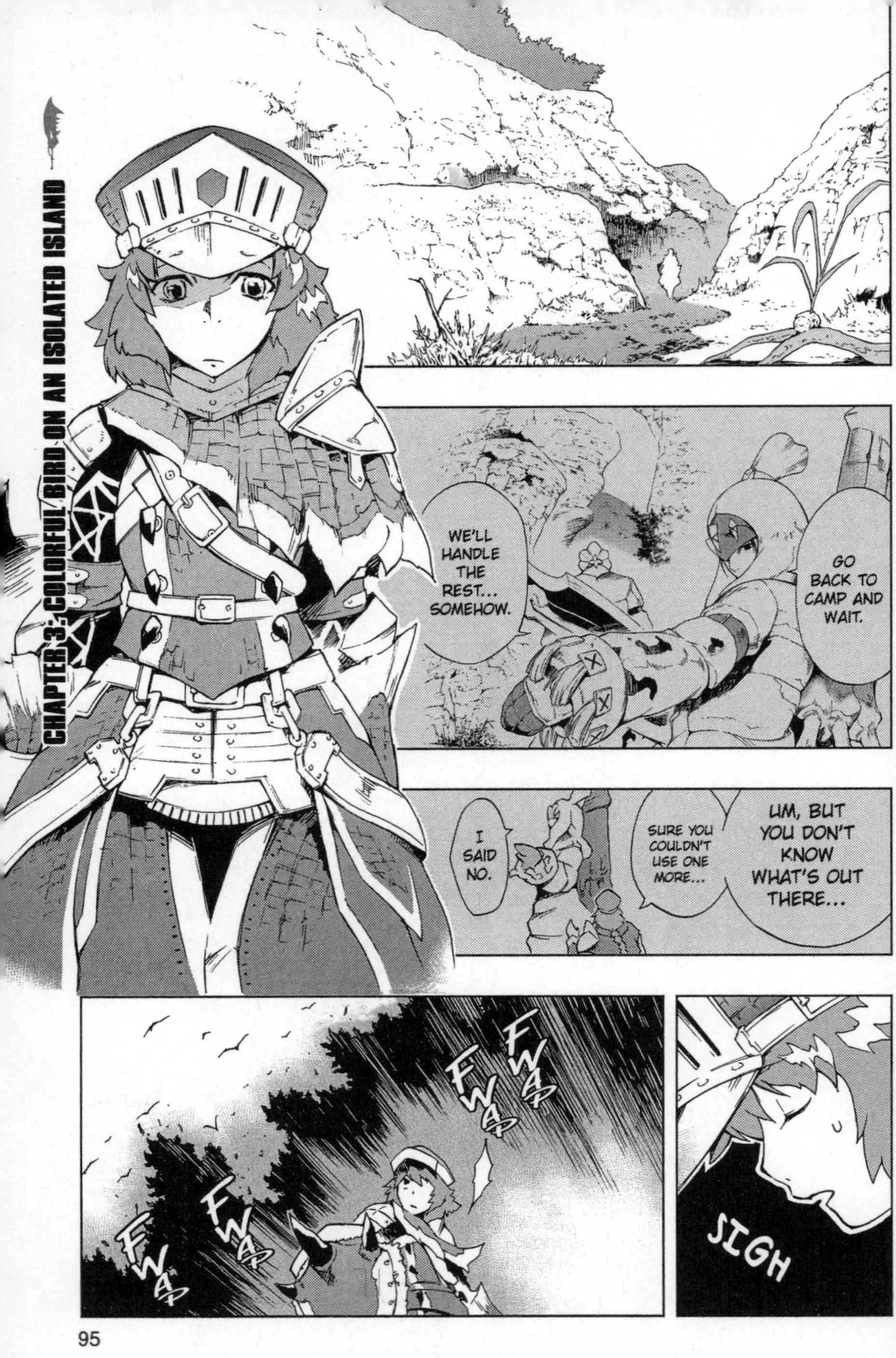
CHAPTER 3: COLORFUL BIRD ON AN ISOLATED ISLAND
GO BACK TO CAMP AND WAIT.
WE'LL HANDLE THE REST... SOMEHOW.
UM, BUT YOU DON'T KNOW WHAT'S OUT THERE...
SURE YOU COULDN'T USE ONE MORE...
I SAID NO.
SIGH
FWAP
FWAP
FWAP
FWAP

CHAPTER 3: COLORFUL BIRD ON AN ISOLATED ISLAND

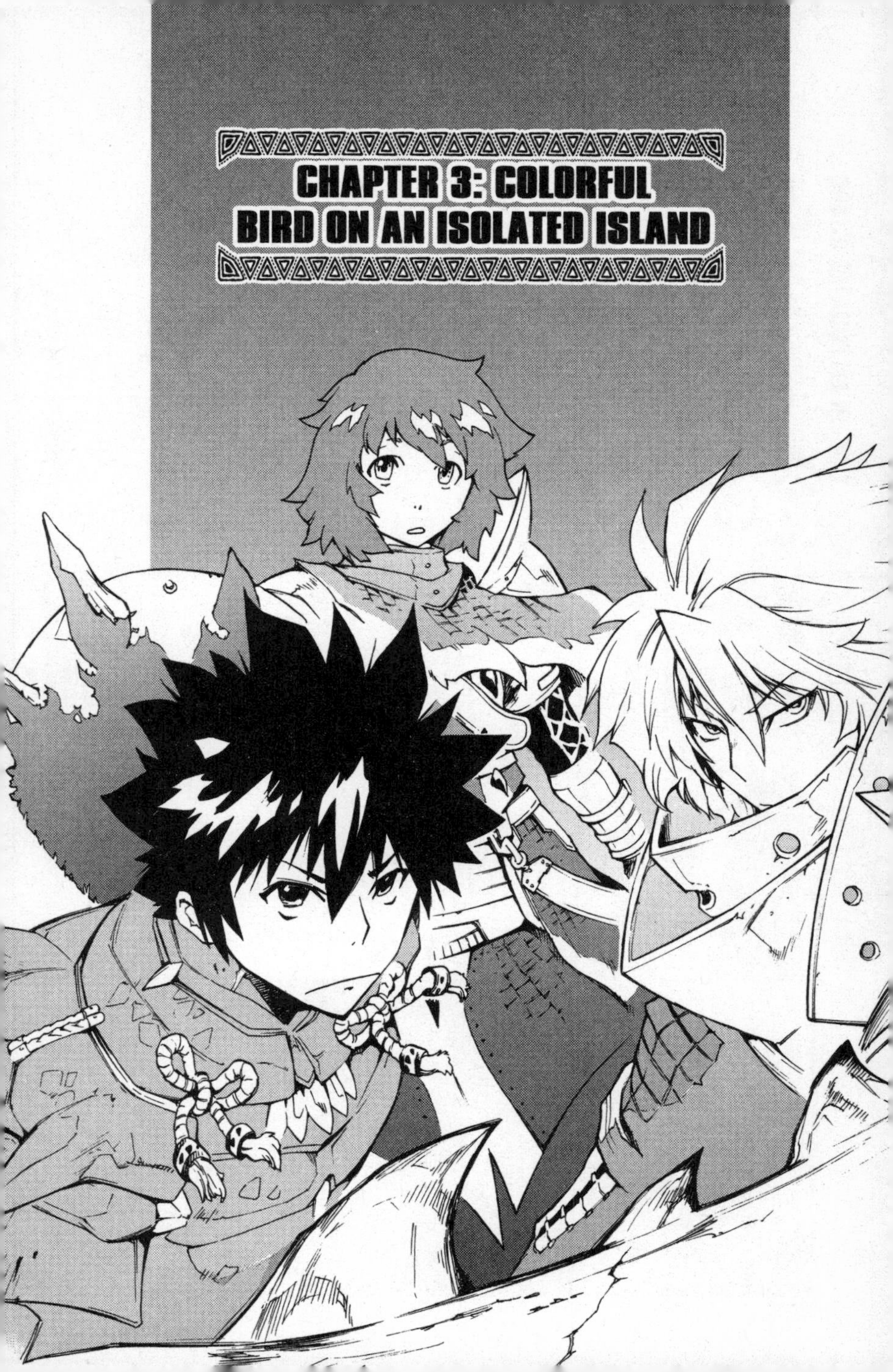

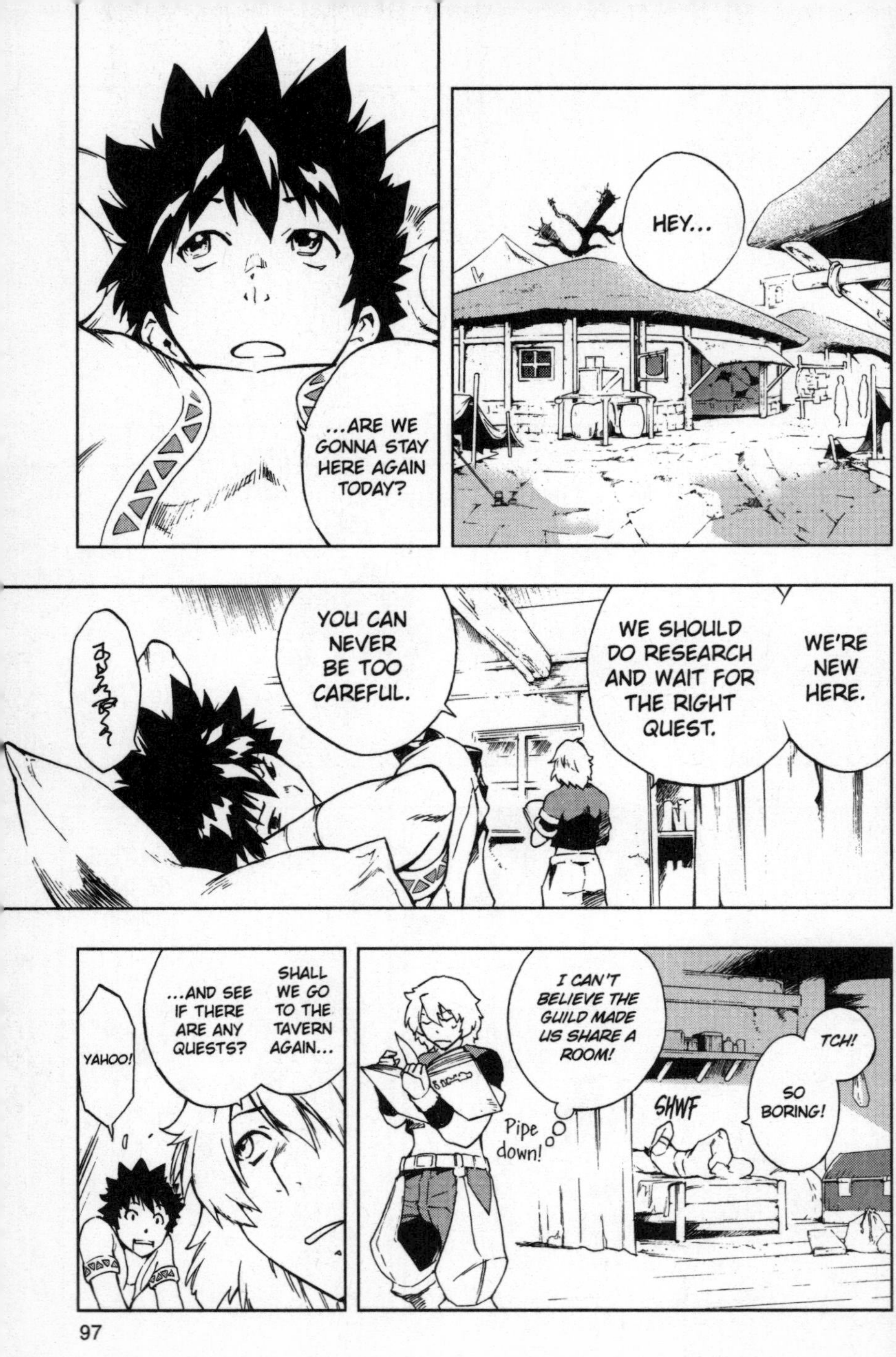
HEY...
...ARE WE GONNA STAY HERE AGAIN TODAY?
WE'RE NEW HERE.
WE SHOULD DO RESEARCH AND WAIT FOR THE RIGHT QUEST.
YOU CAN NEVER BE TOO CAREFUL.
TCH!
SO BORING!
SHWF
I CAN'T BELIEVE THE GUILD MADE US SHARE A ROOM!
Pipe down!
SHALL WE GO TO THE TAVERN AGAIN...
...AND SEE IF THERE ARE ANY QUESTS?
YAHOO!

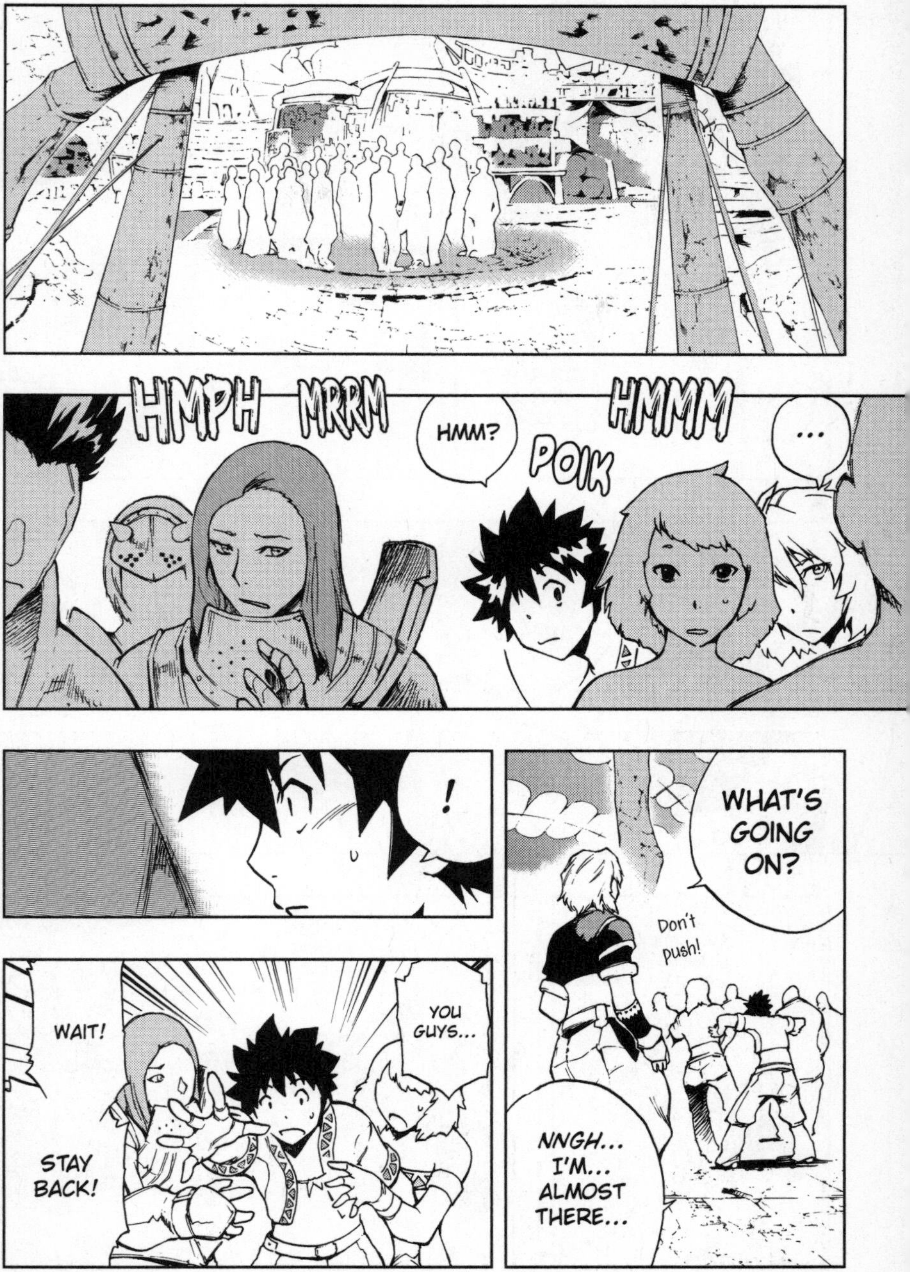
...
HMMM
POIK
HMM?
MRRM
HMPH
WHAT'S GOING ON?
Don't push!
NNGH... I'M... ALMOST THERE...
!
YOU GUYS...
WAIT!
STAY BACK!

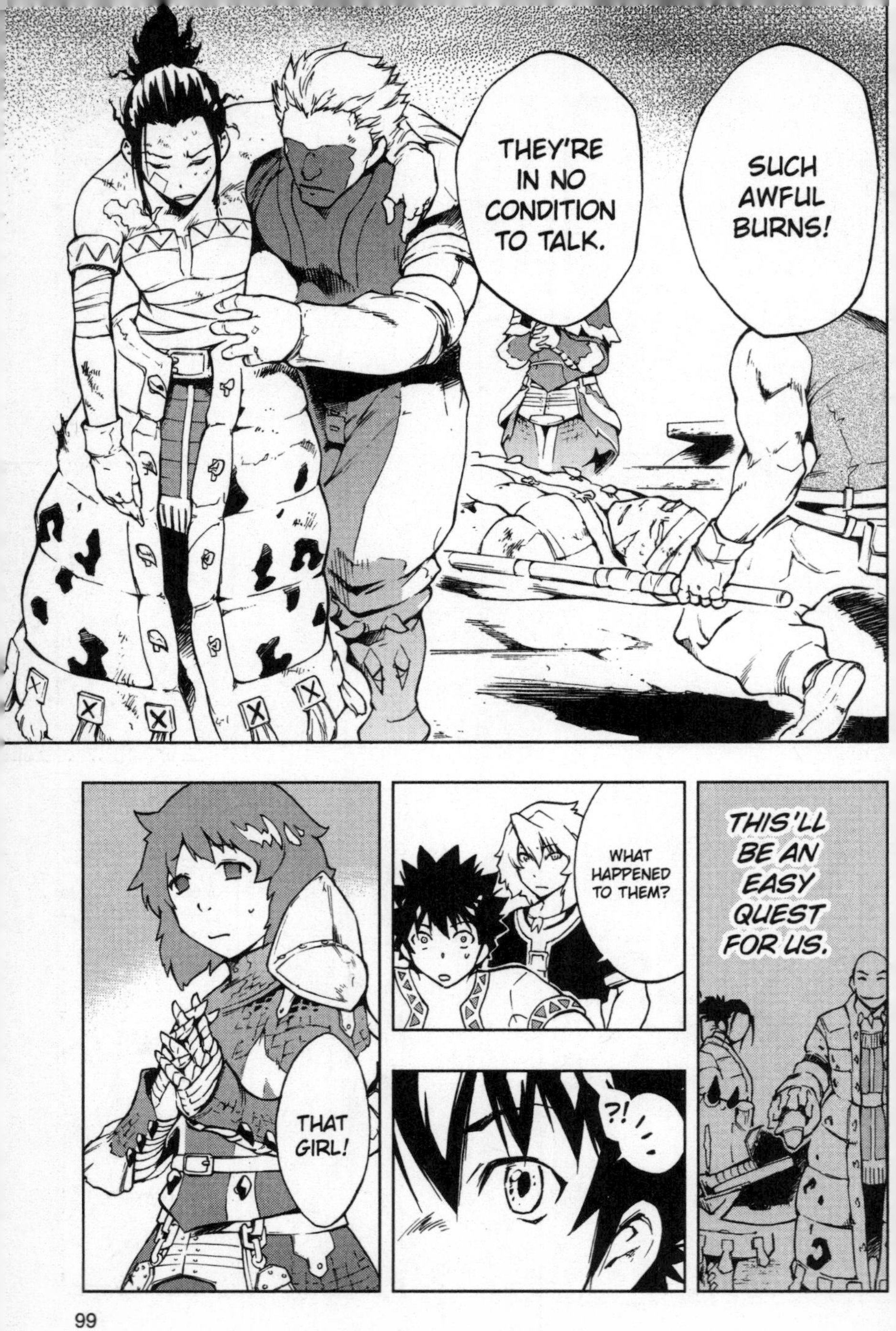
SUCH AWFUL BURNS!
THEY'RE IN NO CONDITION TO TALK.
THIS'LL BE AN EASY QUEST FOR US.
WHAT HAPPENED TO THEM?
?!
THAT GIRL!

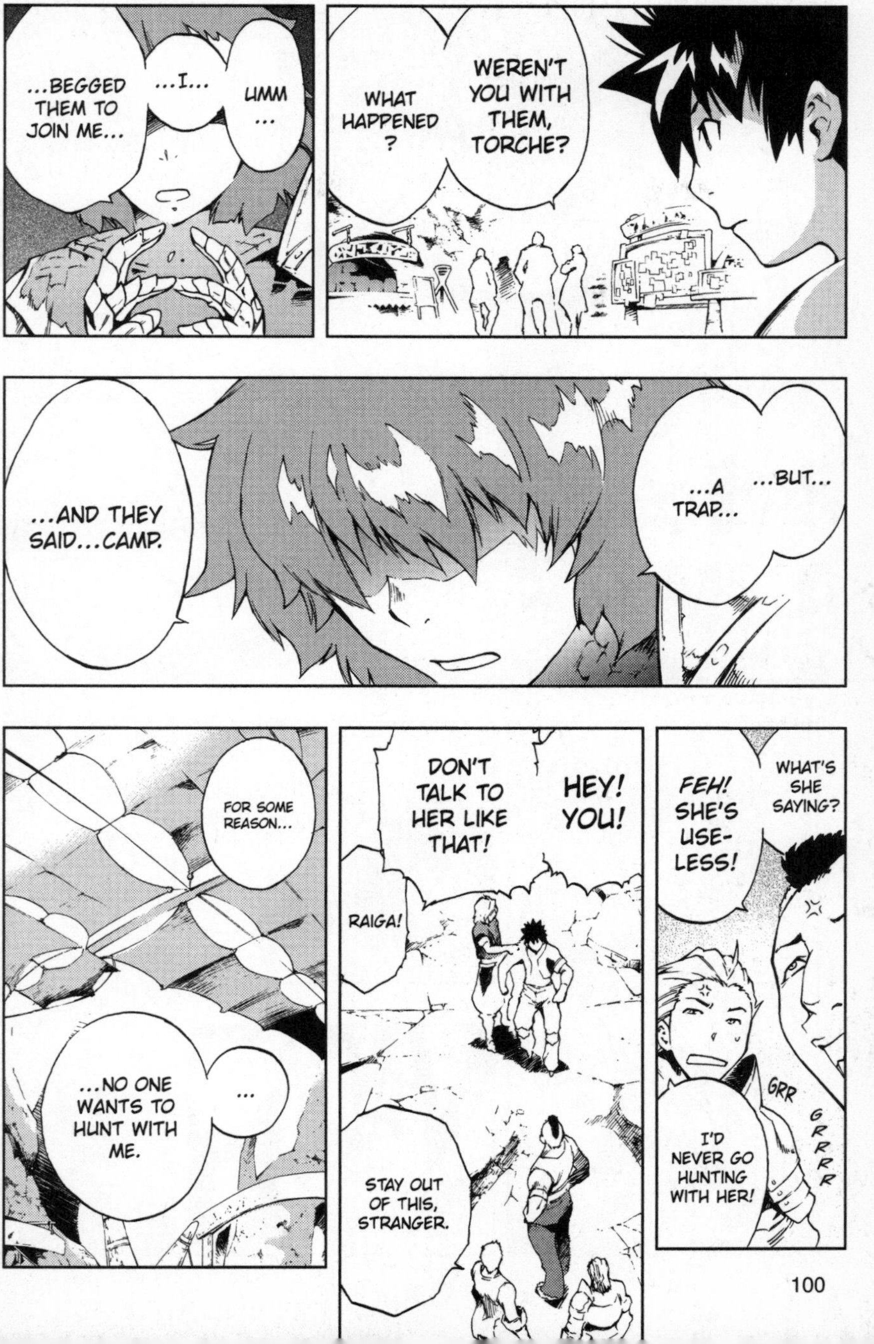
WEREN'T YOU WITH THEM, TORCHE?
WHAT HAPPENED?
UMM...
...I...
...BEGGED THEM TO JOIN ME...
...BUT...
...A TRAP...
...AND THEY SAID...CAMP.
WHAT'S SHE SAYING?
FEH! SHE'S USELESS!
GRR
GRRR
I'D NEVER GO HUNTING WITH HER!
HEY! YOU!
DON'T TALK TO HER LIKE THAT!
RAIGA!
STAY OUT OF THIS, STRANGER.
FOR SOME REASON...
...
...NO ONE WANTS TO HUNT WITH ME.

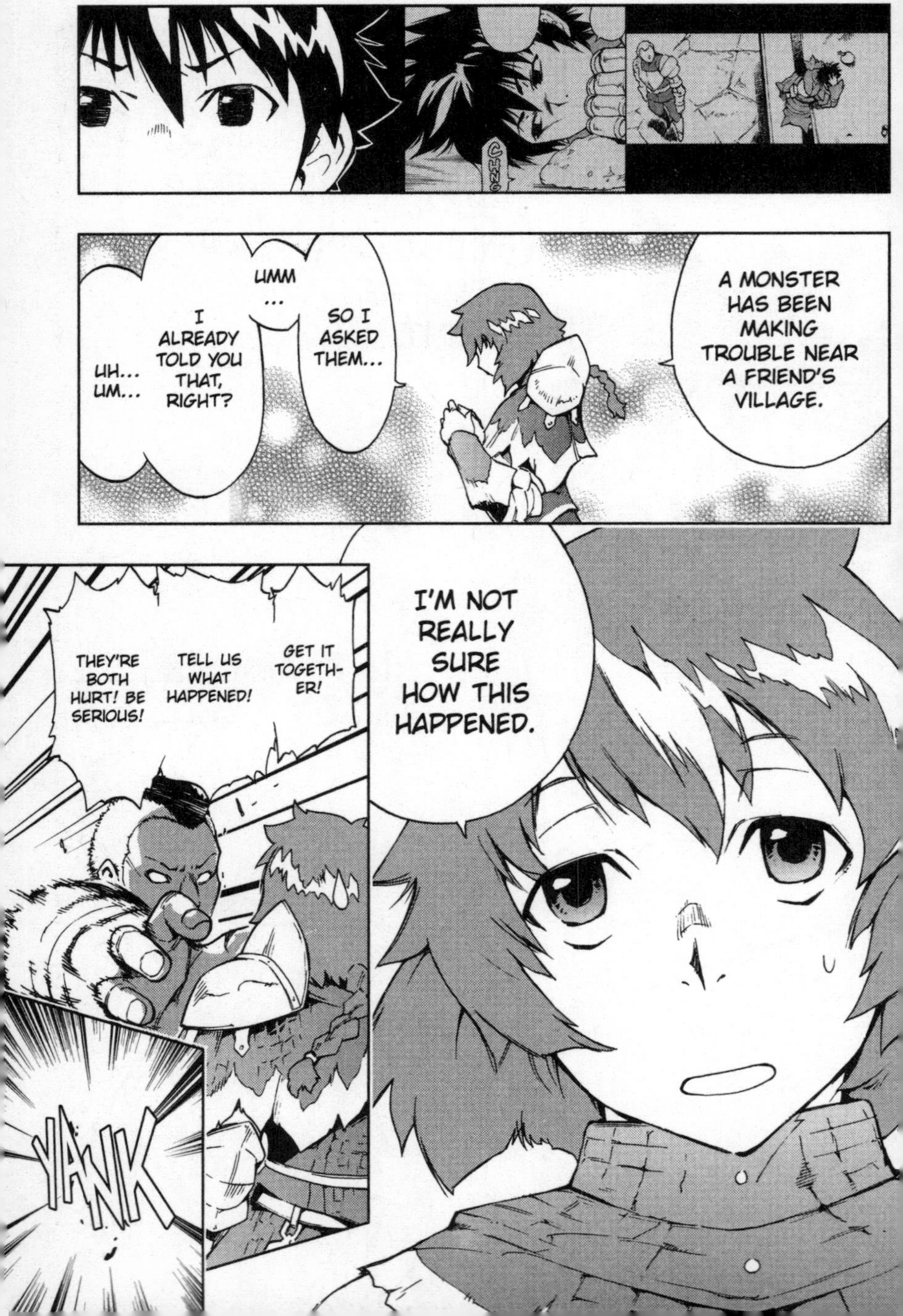
CHING
A MONSTER HAS BEEN MAKING TROUBLE NEAR A FRIEND'S VILLAGE.
SO I ASKED THEM...
UMM ...
I ALREADY TOLD YOU THAT, RIGHT?
UH... UM...
I'M NOT REALLY SURE HOW THIS HAPPENED.
GET IT TOGETHER!
TELL US WHAT HAPPENED!
THEY'RE BOTH HURT! BE SERIOUS!
YANK

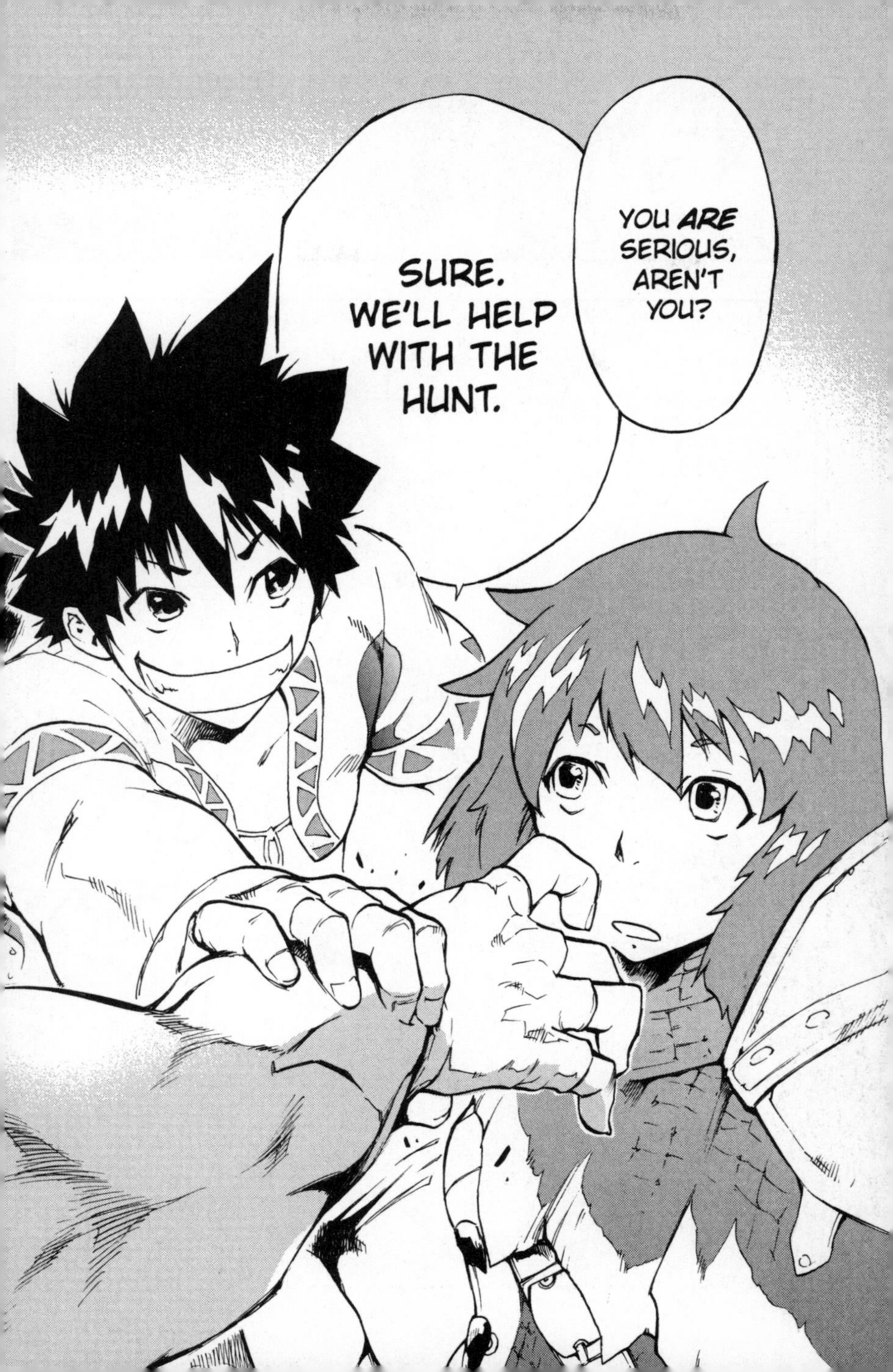
YOU **ARE** SERIOUS, AREN'T YOU?
SURE. WE'LL HELP WITH THE HUNT.

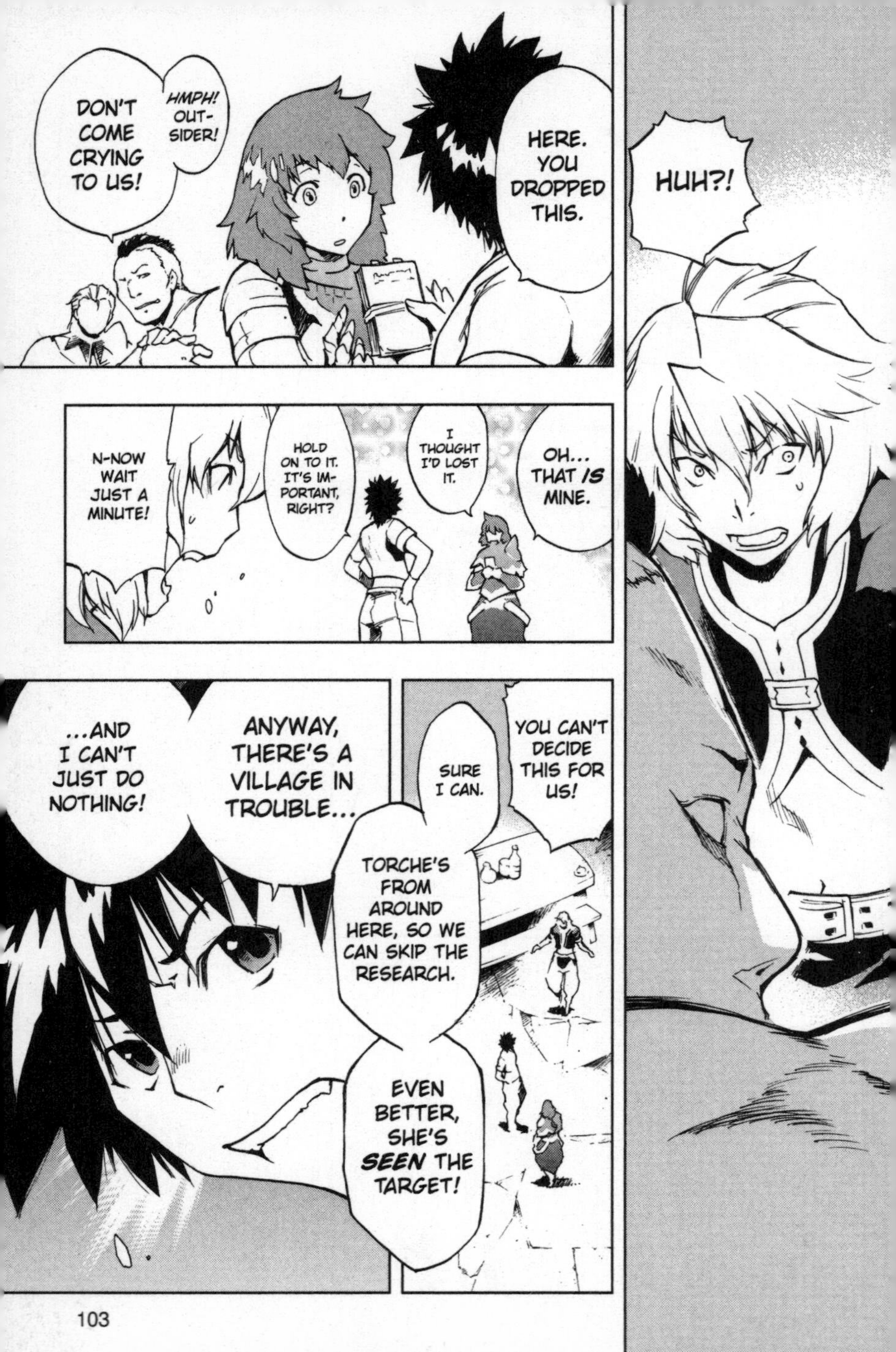
HUH?!
HERE. YOU DROPPED THIS.
HMPH! OUT-SIDER!
DON'T COME CRYING TO US!
OH... THAT *IS* MINE.
I THOUGHT I'D LOST IT.
HOLD ON TO IT. IT'S IM-PORTANT, RIGHT?
N-NOW WAIT JUST A MINUTE!
YOU CAN'T DECIDE THIS FOR US!
SURE I CAN.
TORCHE'S FROM AROUND HERE, SO WE CAN SKIP THE RESEARCH.
EVEN BETTER, SHE'S *SEEN* THE TARGET!
ANYWAY, THERE'S A VILLAGE IN TROUBLE...
...AND I CAN'T JUST DO NOTHING!

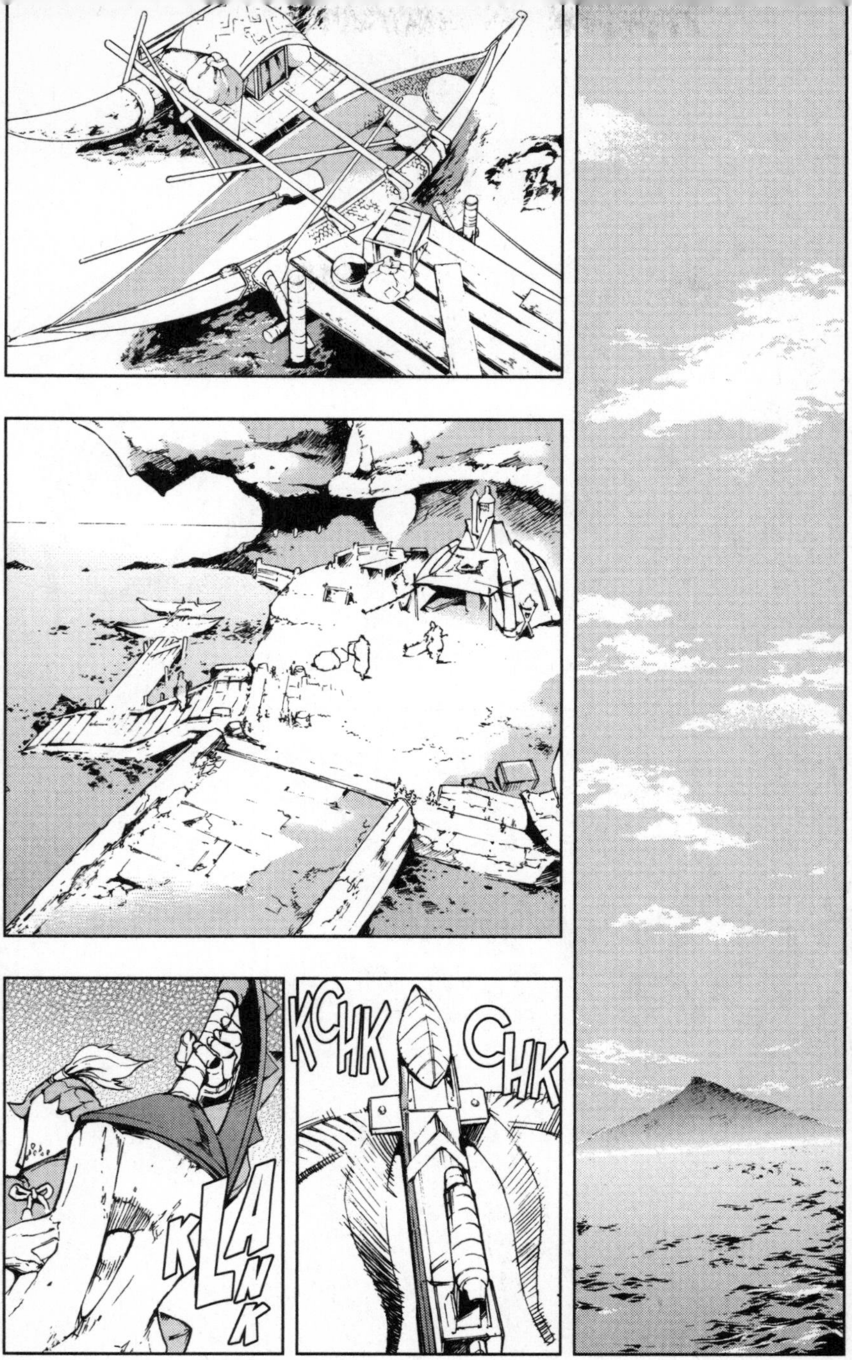
KCHK
CHK
KLANK

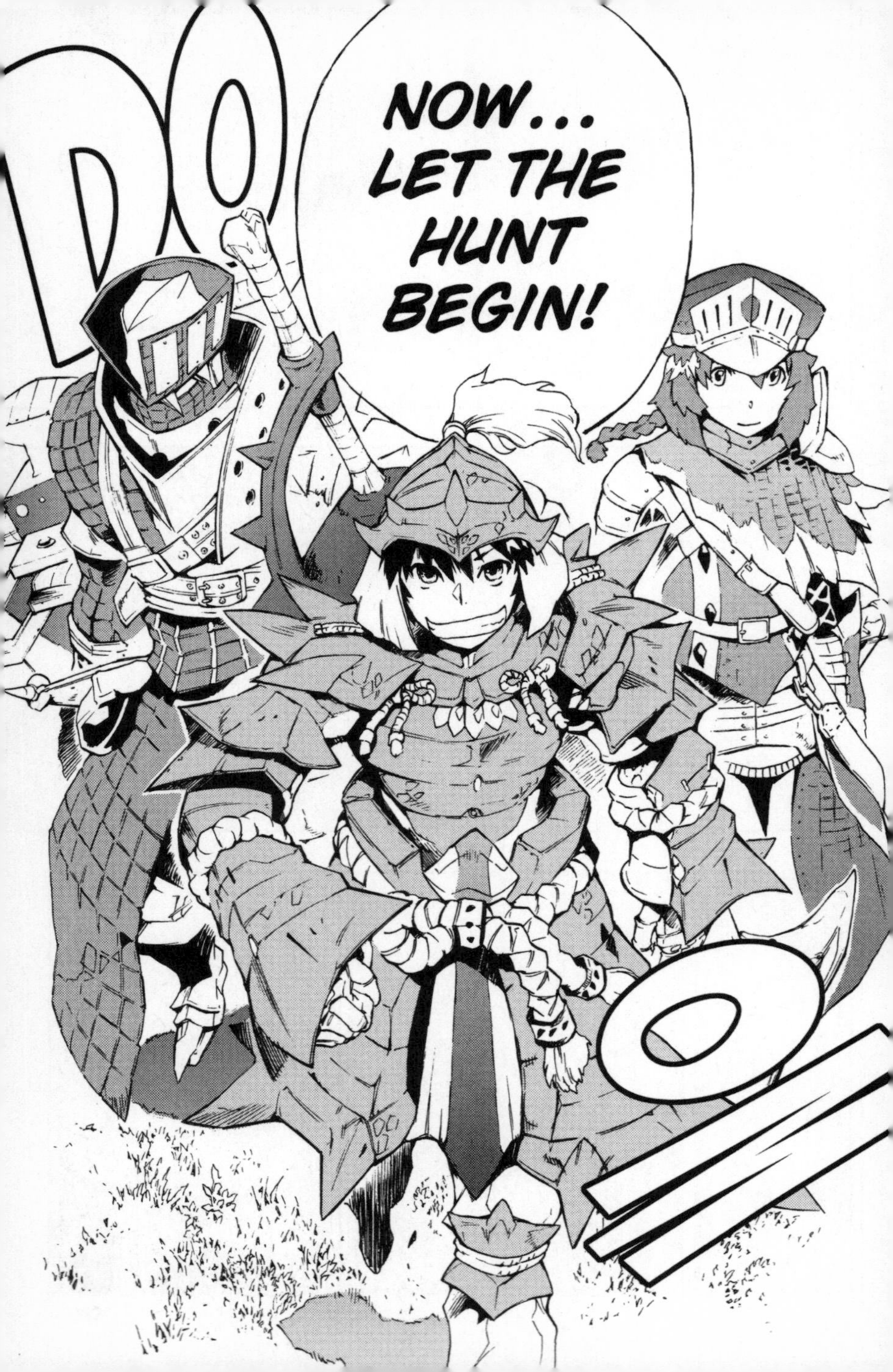
DO
NOW... LET THE HUNT BEGIN!
O

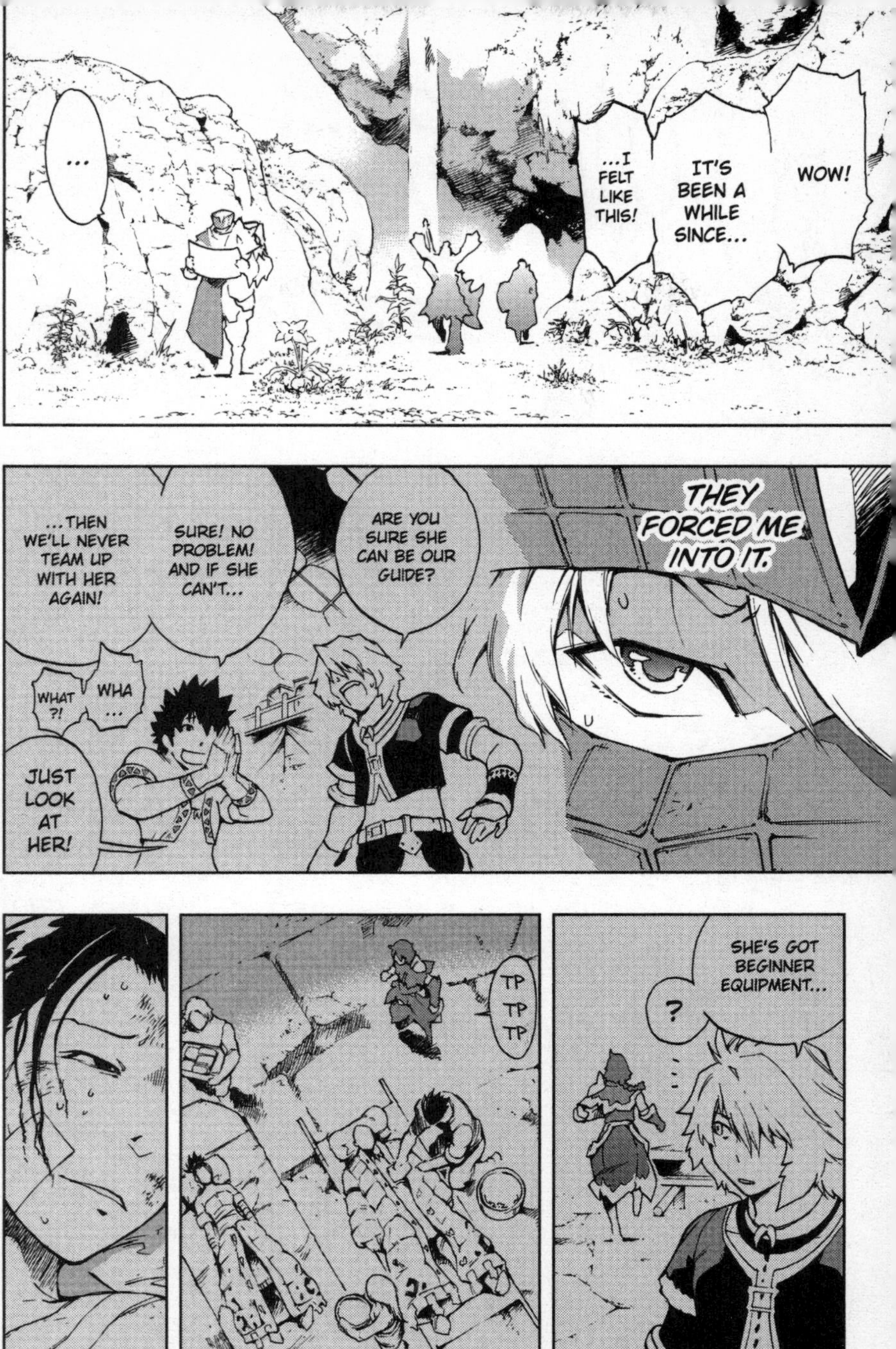
WOW!
IT'S BEEN A WHILE SINCE...
...I FELT LIKE THIS!
...
THEY FORCED ME INTO IT.
ARE YOU SURE SHE CAN BE OUR GUIDE?
SURE! NO PROBLEM! AND IF SHE CAN'T...
...THEN WE'LL NEVER TEAM UP WITH HER AGAIN!
WHA...
WHAT?!
JUST LOOK AT HER!
SHE'S GOT BEGINNER EQUIPMENT...
?
TP TP TP

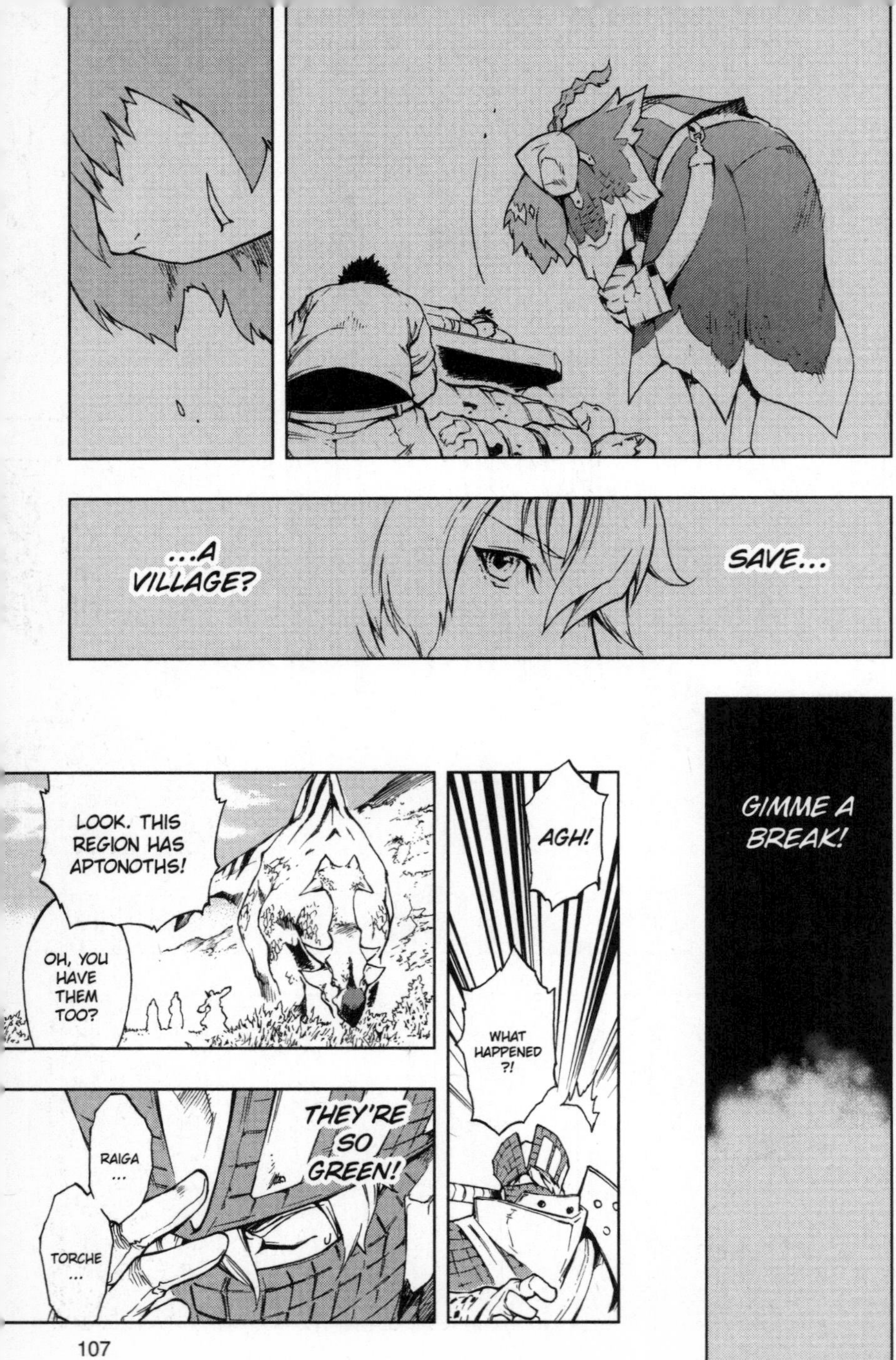
SAVE...
...A VILLAGE?
GIMME A BREAK!
AGH!
WHAT HAPPENED?!
LOOK. THIS REGION HAS APTONOTHS!
OH, YOU HAVE THEM TOO?
THEY'RE SO GREEN!
RAIGA...
TORCHE...

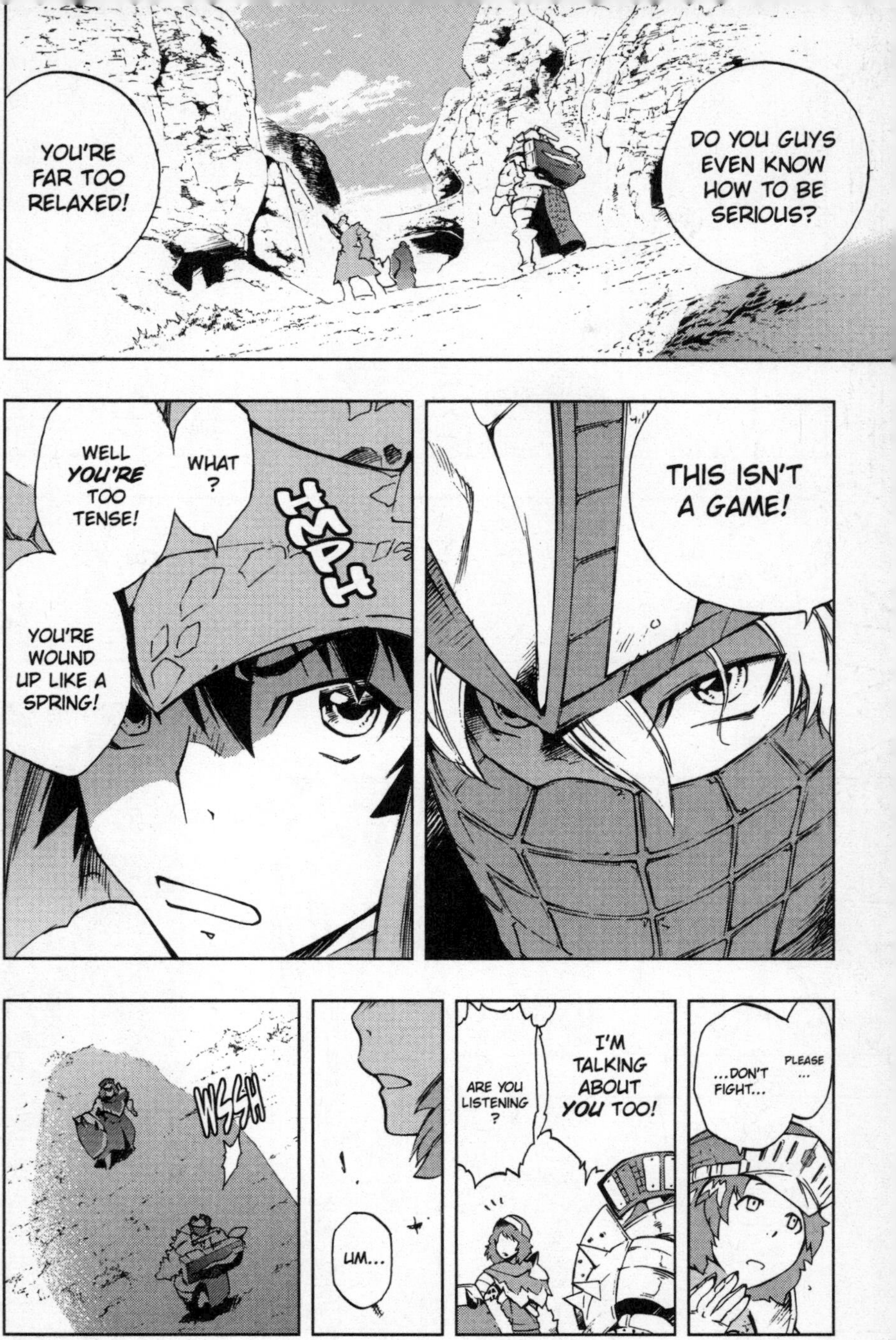
DO YOU GUYS EVEN KNOW HOW TO BE SERIOUS?
YOU'RE FAR TOO RELAXED!
THIS ISN'T A GAME!
WHAT?
HMPH
WELL *YOU'RE* TOO TENSE!
YOU'RE WOUND UP LIKE A SPRING!
PLEASE...
...DON'T FIGHT...
I'M TALKING ABOUT *YOU* TOO!
ARE YOU LISTENING?
!
UM...
WSSH

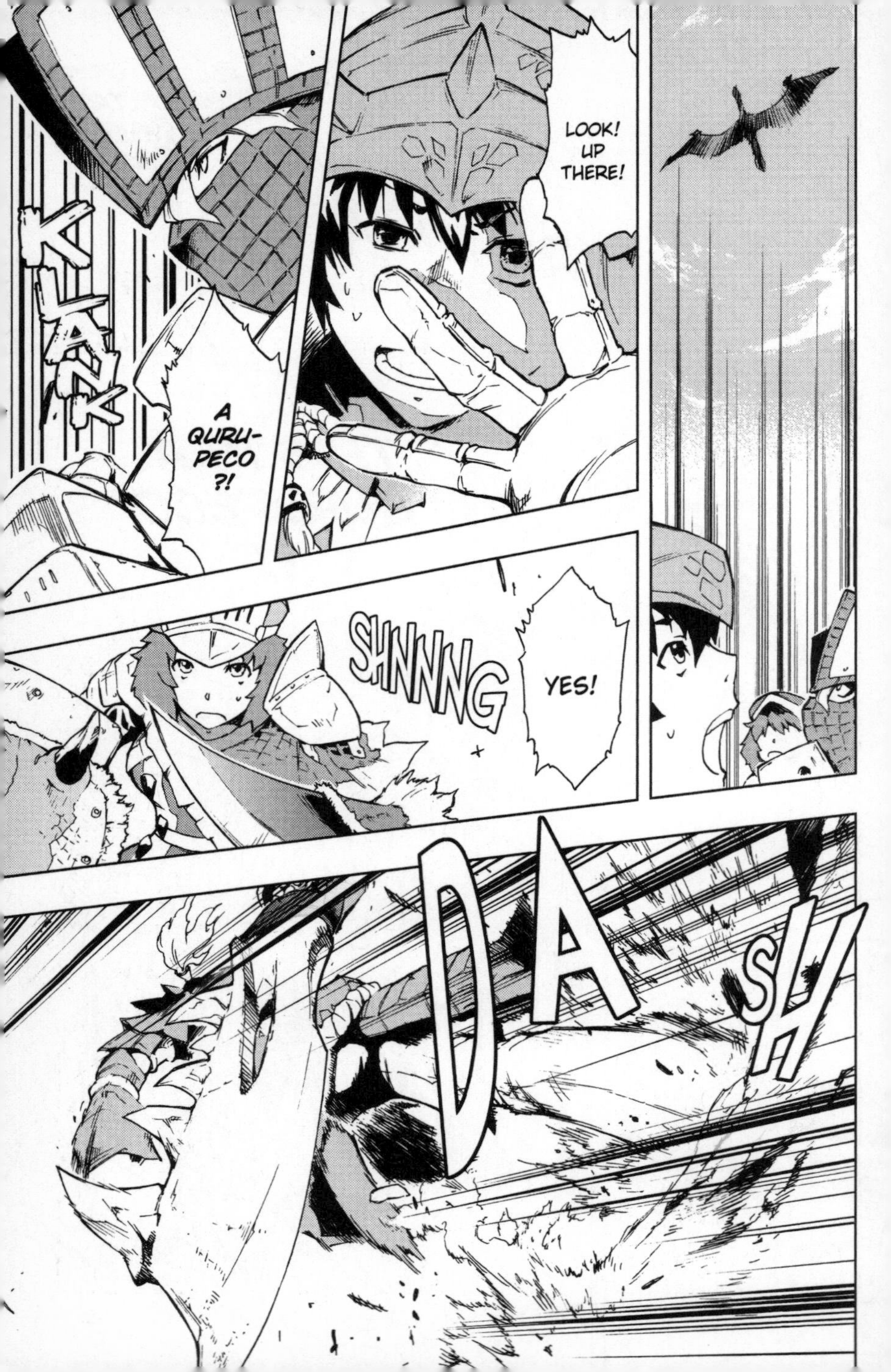
LOOK! UP THERE!
A QURU-PECO ?!
KLANK
YES!
SHNNNG
DASH

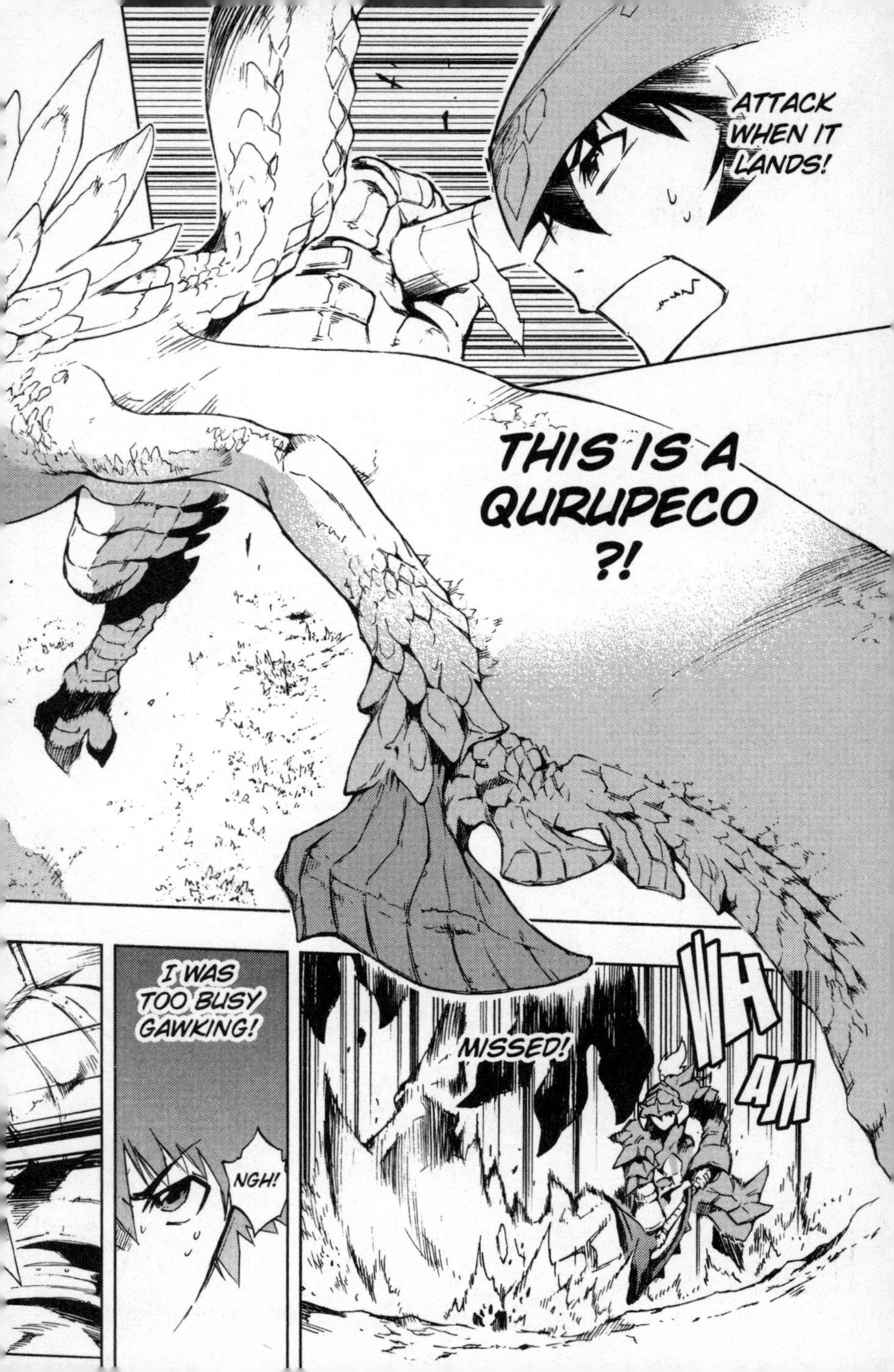
ATTACK WHEN IT LANDS!
THIS IS A QURUPECO ?!
WHAM
MISSED!
I WAS TOO BUSY GAWKING!
NGH!

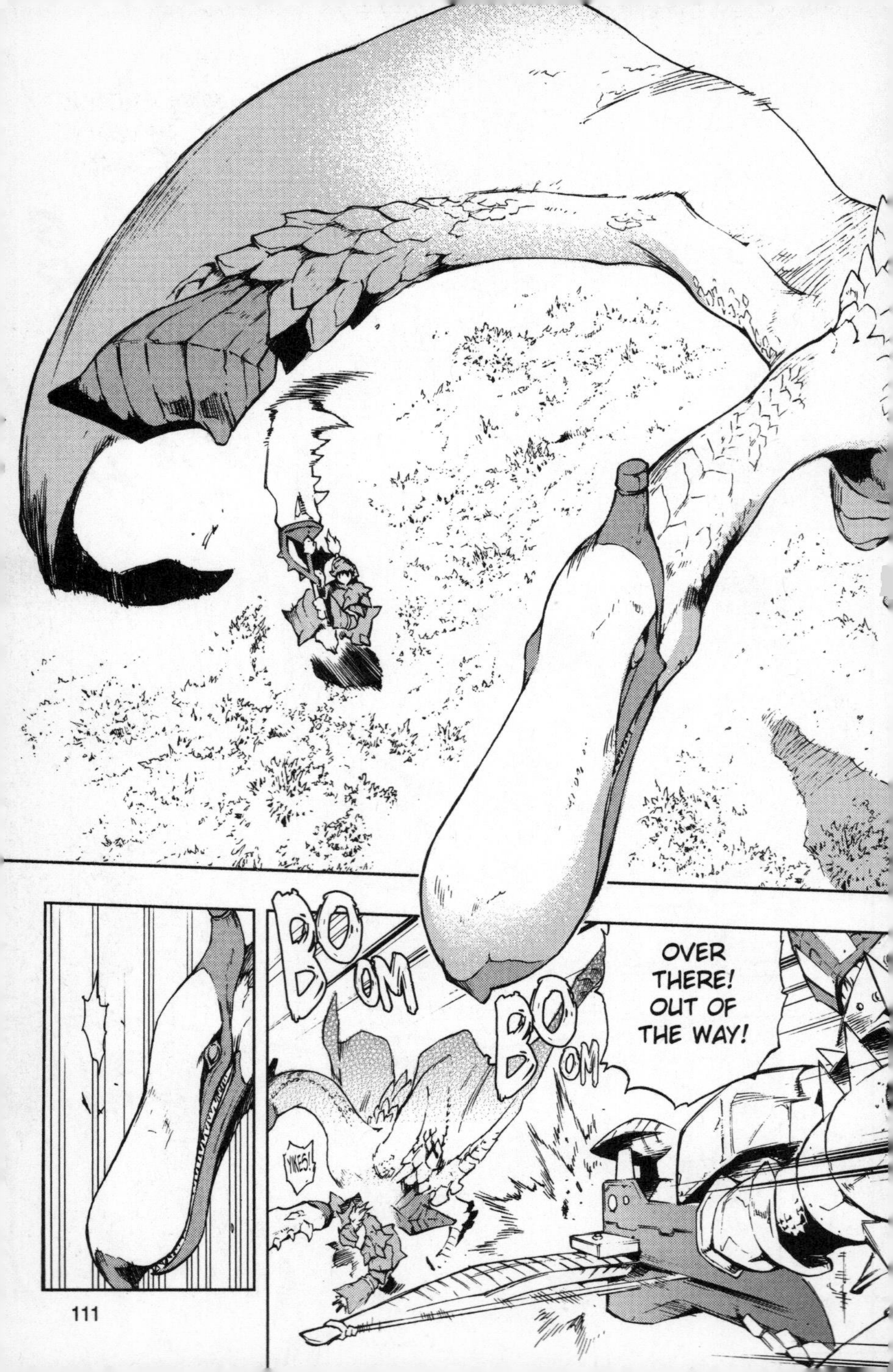
OVER THERE! OUT OF THE WAY!
BOOM
BOOM
YIKES!

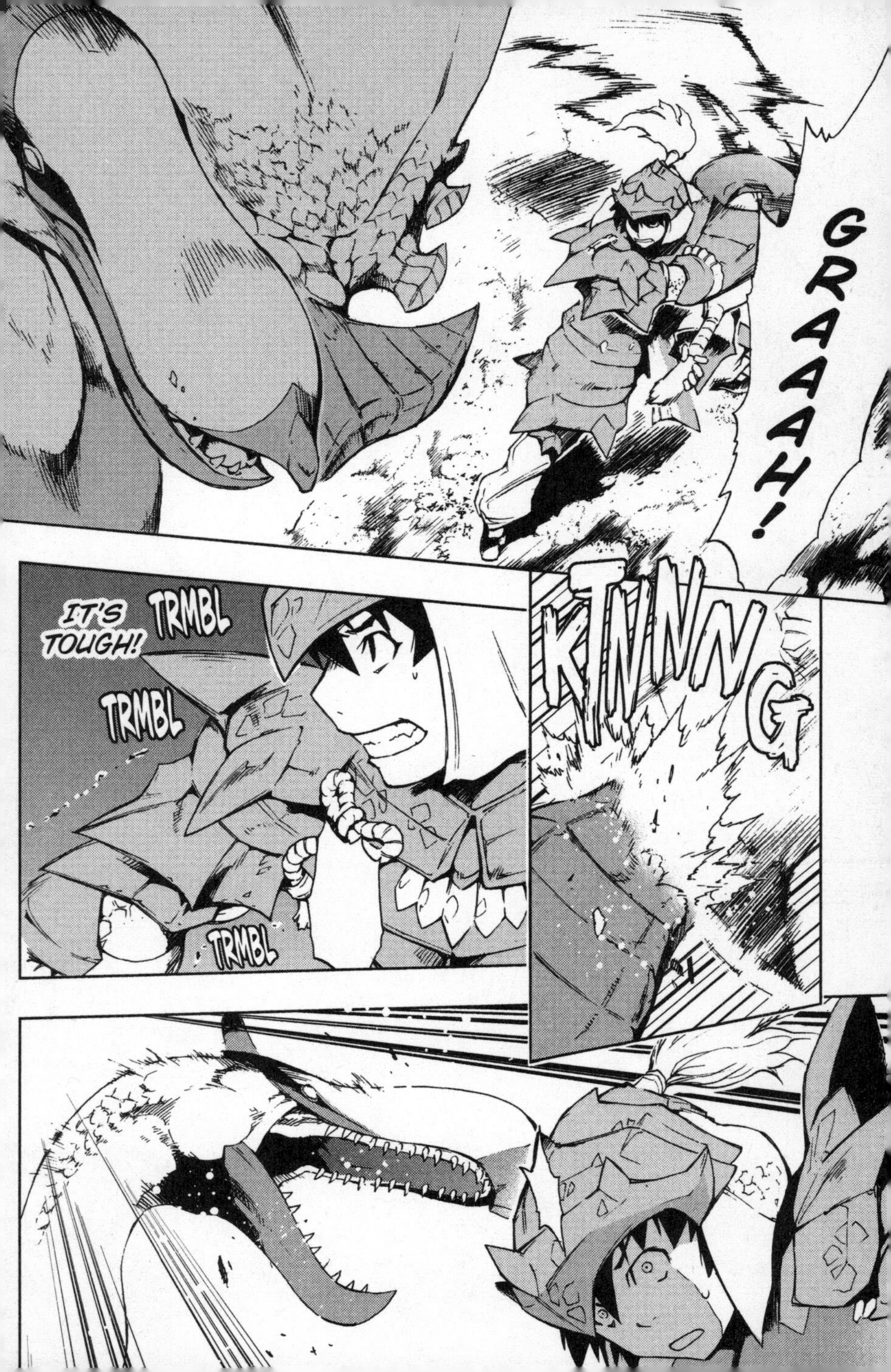
GRAAAAH!
KTNNNG
IT'S TOUGH!
TRMBL
TRMBL
TRMBL

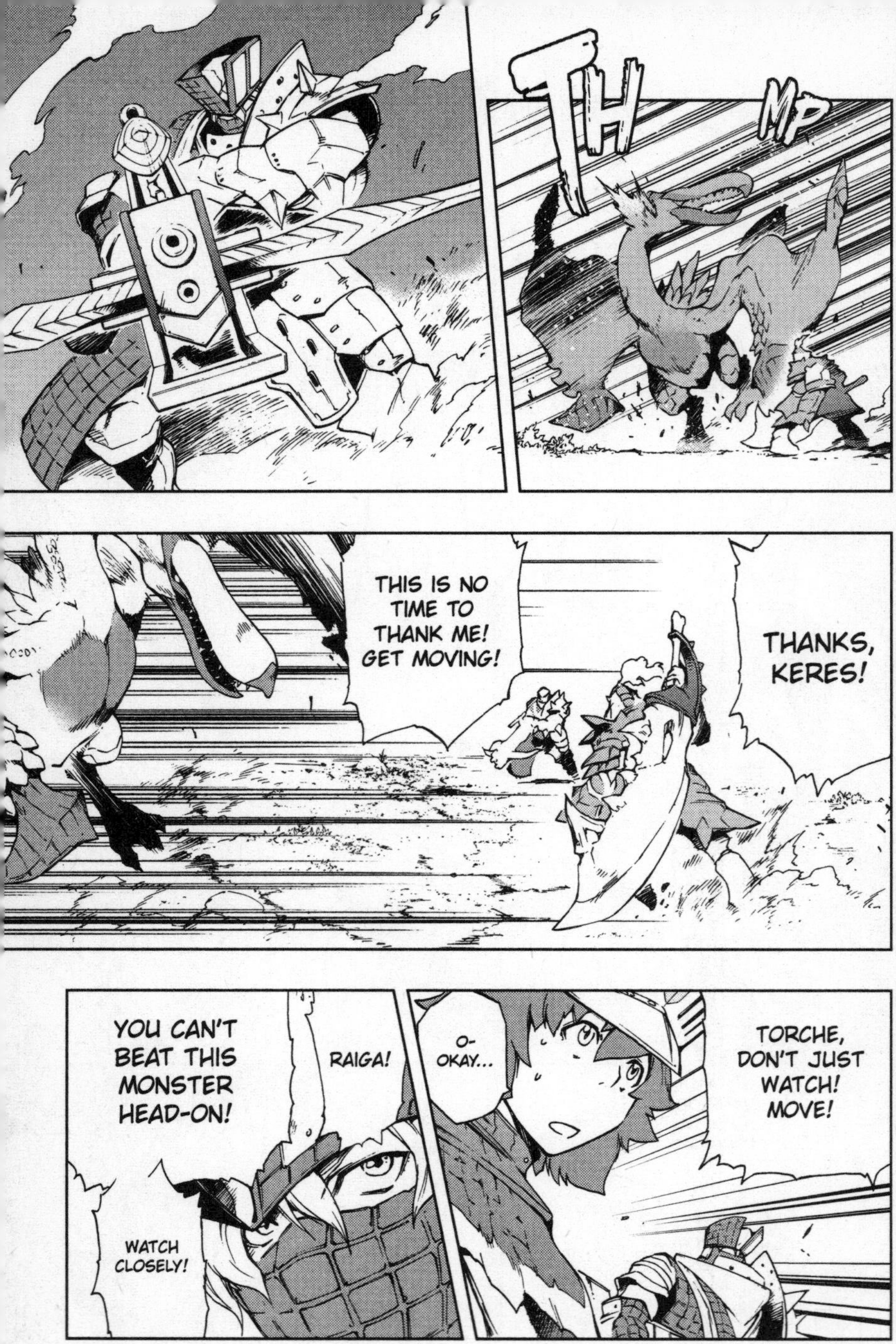

TH MP
THANKS, KERES!
THIS IS NO TIME TO THANK ME! GET MOVING!
TORCHE, DON'T JUST WATCH! MOVE!
O-OKAY...
RAIGA!
YOU CAN'T BEAT THIS MONSTER HEAD-ON!
WATCH CLOSELY!

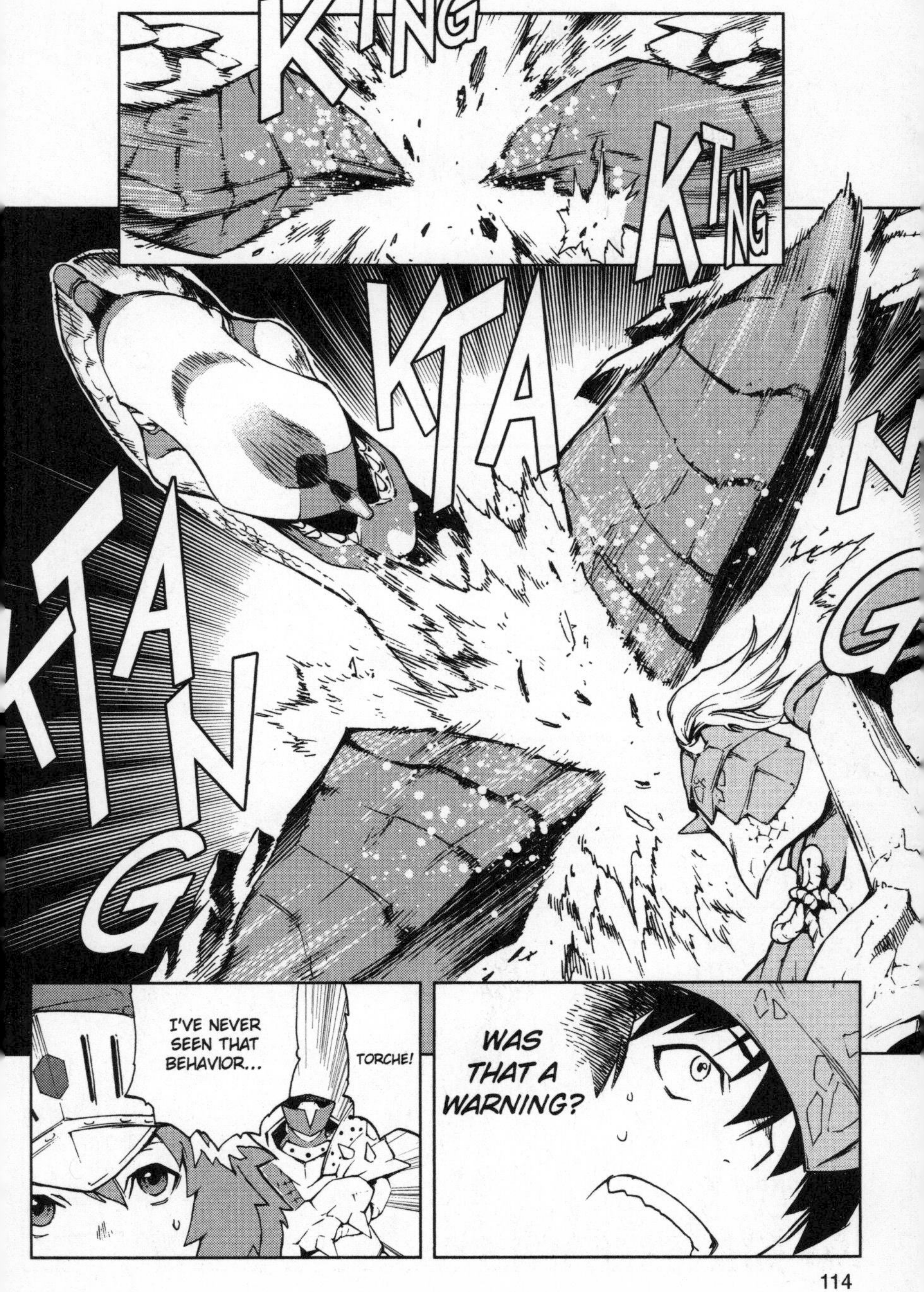
KTNG
KTNG
KTANG
KTANG
WAS THAT A WARNING?
TORCHE!
I'VE NEVER SEEN THAT BEHAVIOR...

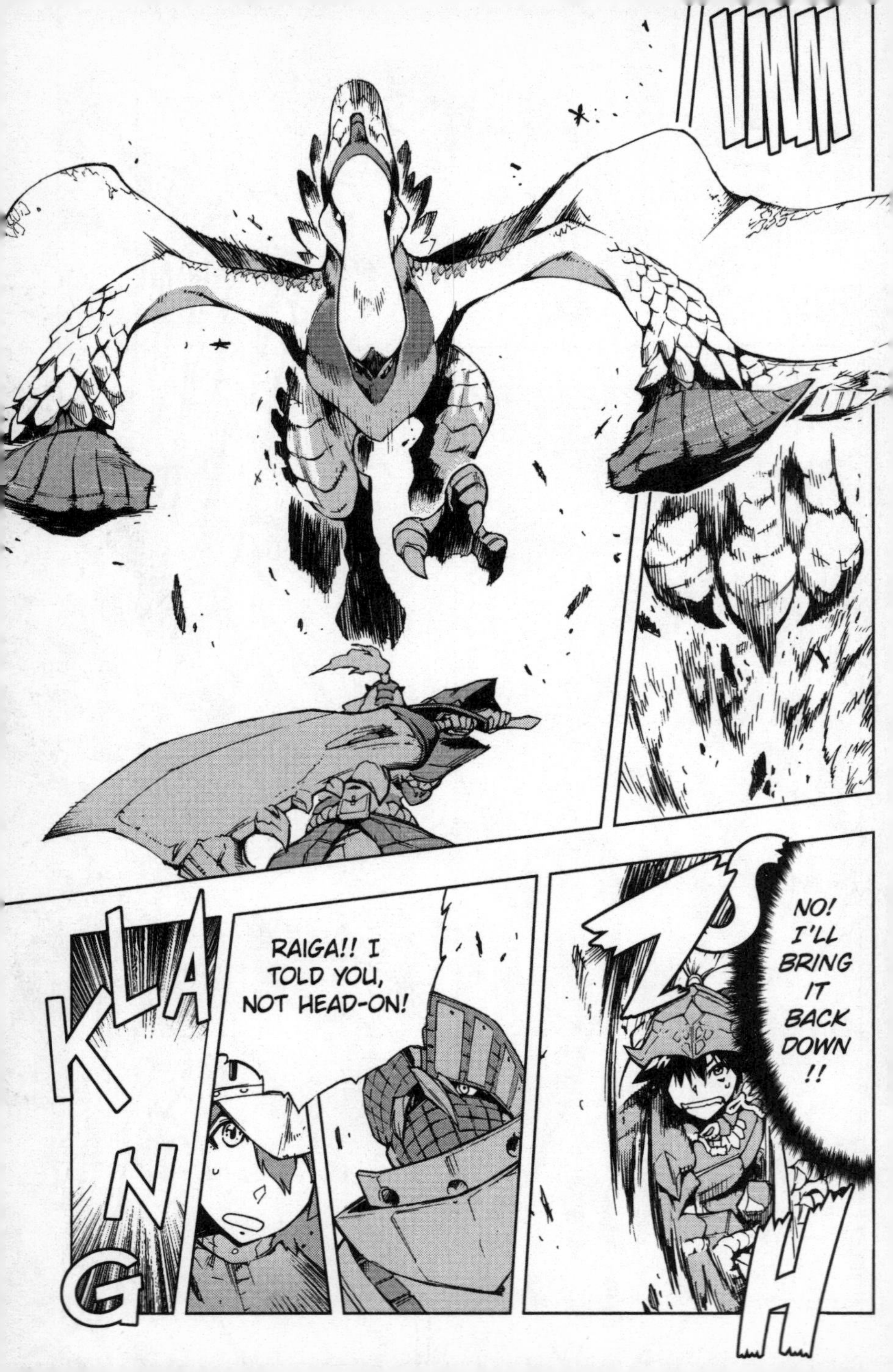

VMMM
ZSH
NO! I'LL BRING IT BACK DOWN!!
RAIGA!! I TOLD YOU, NOT HEAD-ON!
KLANG

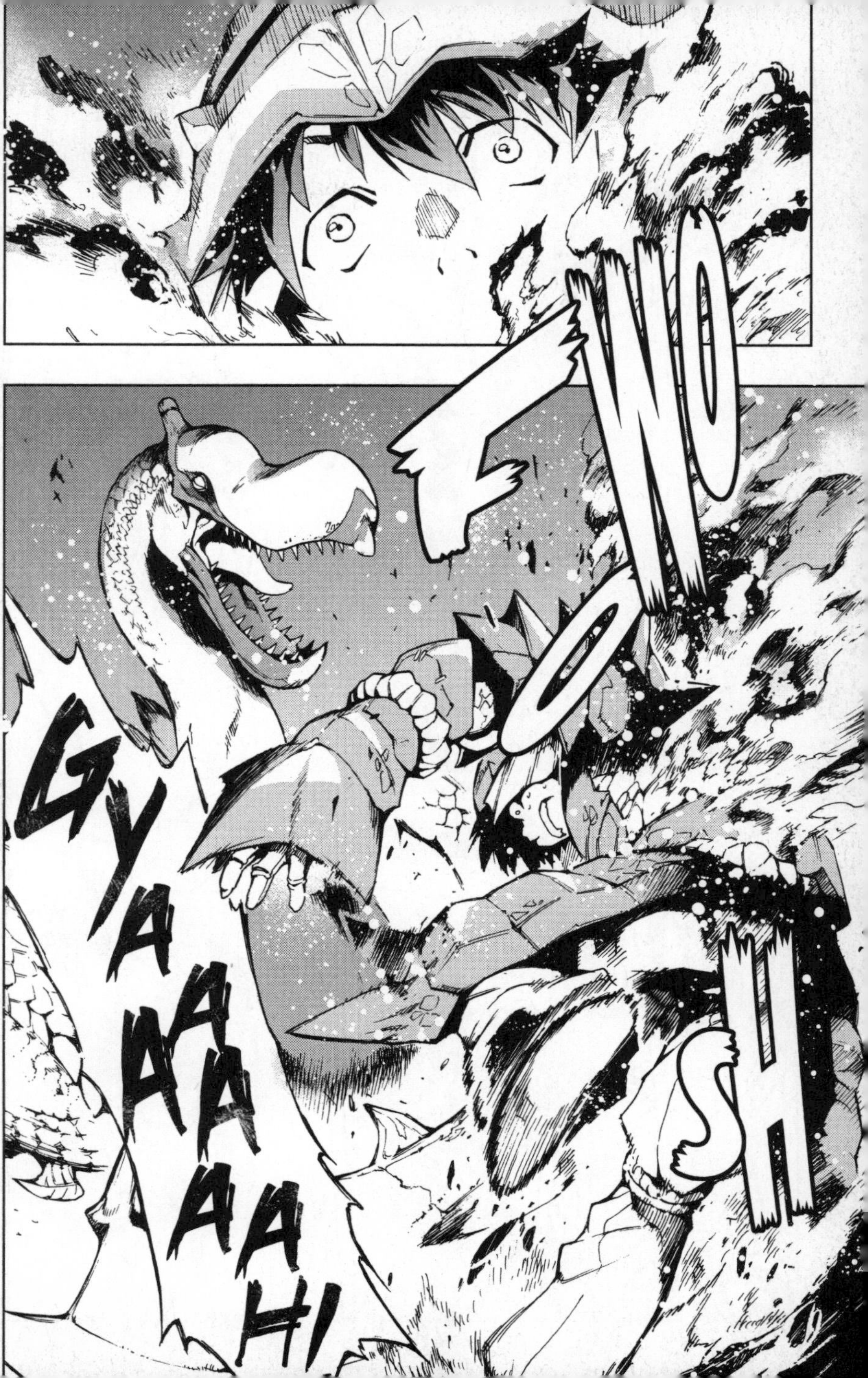
WOOSH
GYAAAAAAAHI

CHAPTER 4: DISCORD

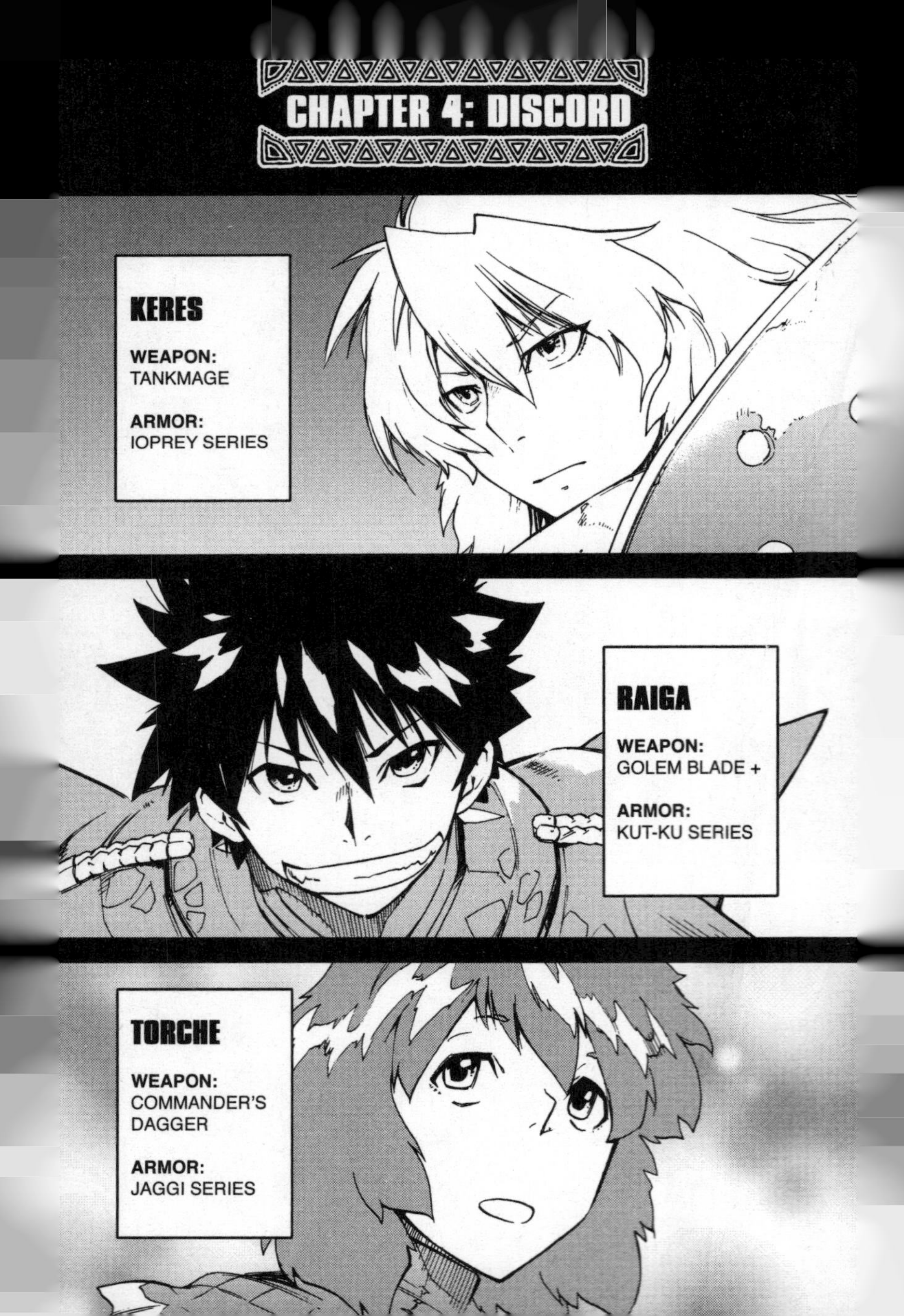
KERES
WEAPON: TANKMAGE
ARMOR: IOPREY SERIES
RAIGA
WEAPON: GOLEM BLADE +
ARMOR: KUT-KU SERIES
TORCHE
WEAPON: COMMANDER'S DAGGER
ARMOR: JAGGI SERIES

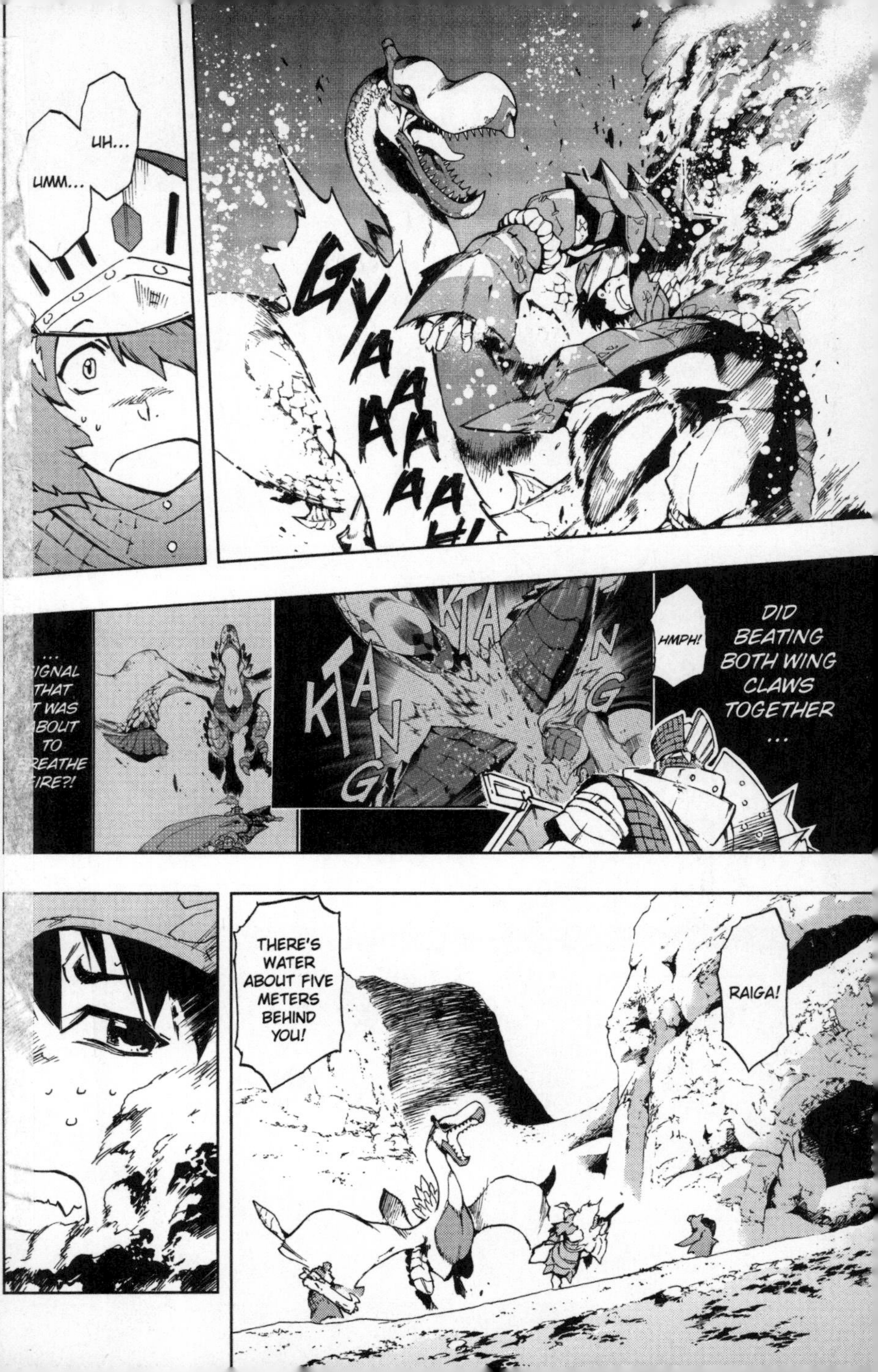
GYAAAAAAH!
UH...
UMM...
HMPH!
DID BEATING BOTH WING CLAWS TOGETHER...
KTANG
KTANG
...SIGNAL THAT IT WAS ABOUT TO BREATHE FIRE?!
RAIGA!
THERE'S WATER ABOUT FIVE METERS BEHIND YOU!

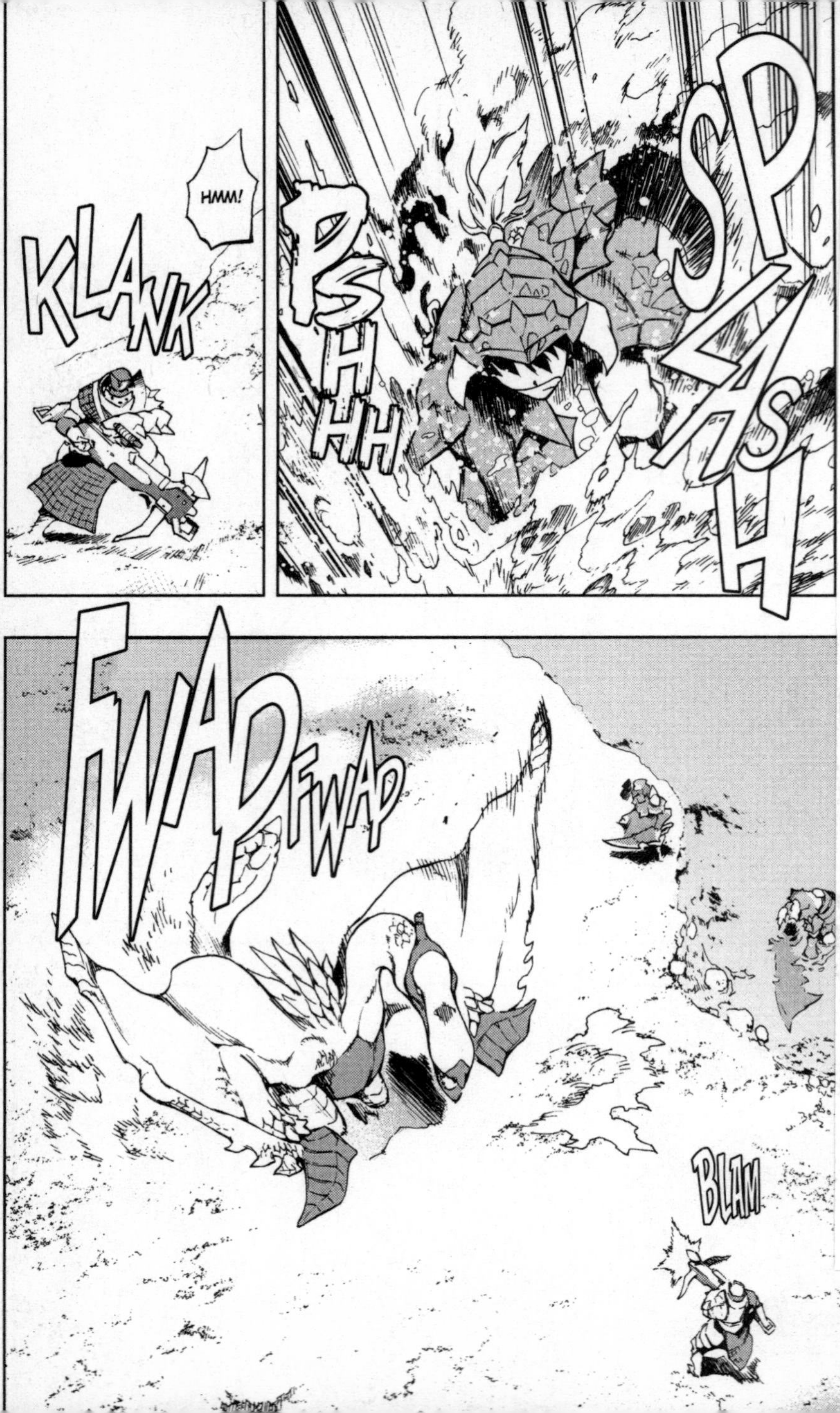
SPLASH
PSHHHH
HMM!
KLANK
FWAP
FWAP
BLAM

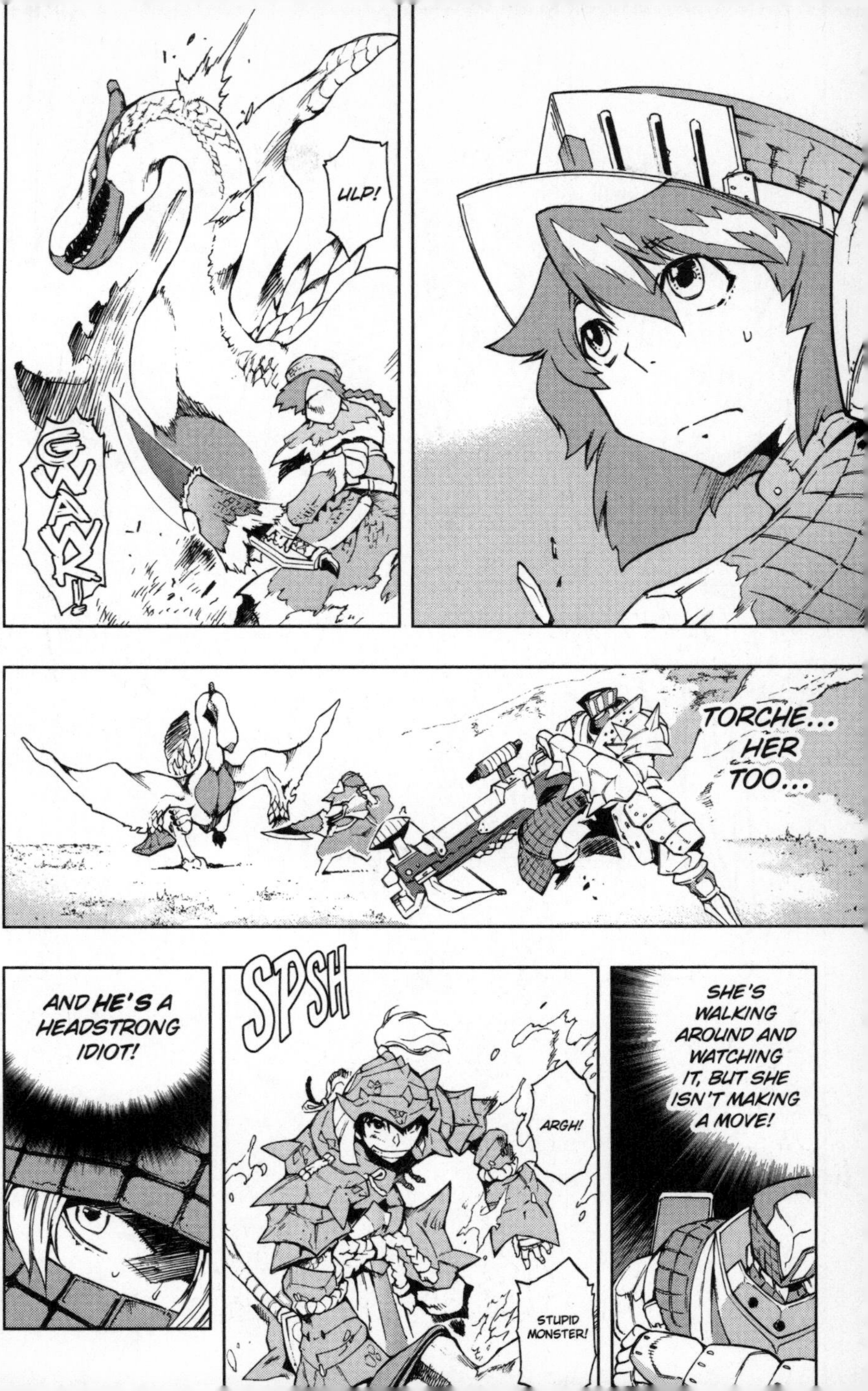
ULP!
GWAWK!
TORCHE... HER TOO...
SHE'S WALKING AROUND AND WATCHING IT, BUT SHE ISN'T MAKING A MOVE!
SPSH
ARGH!
STUPID MONSTER!
AND HE'S A HEADSTRONG IDIOT!

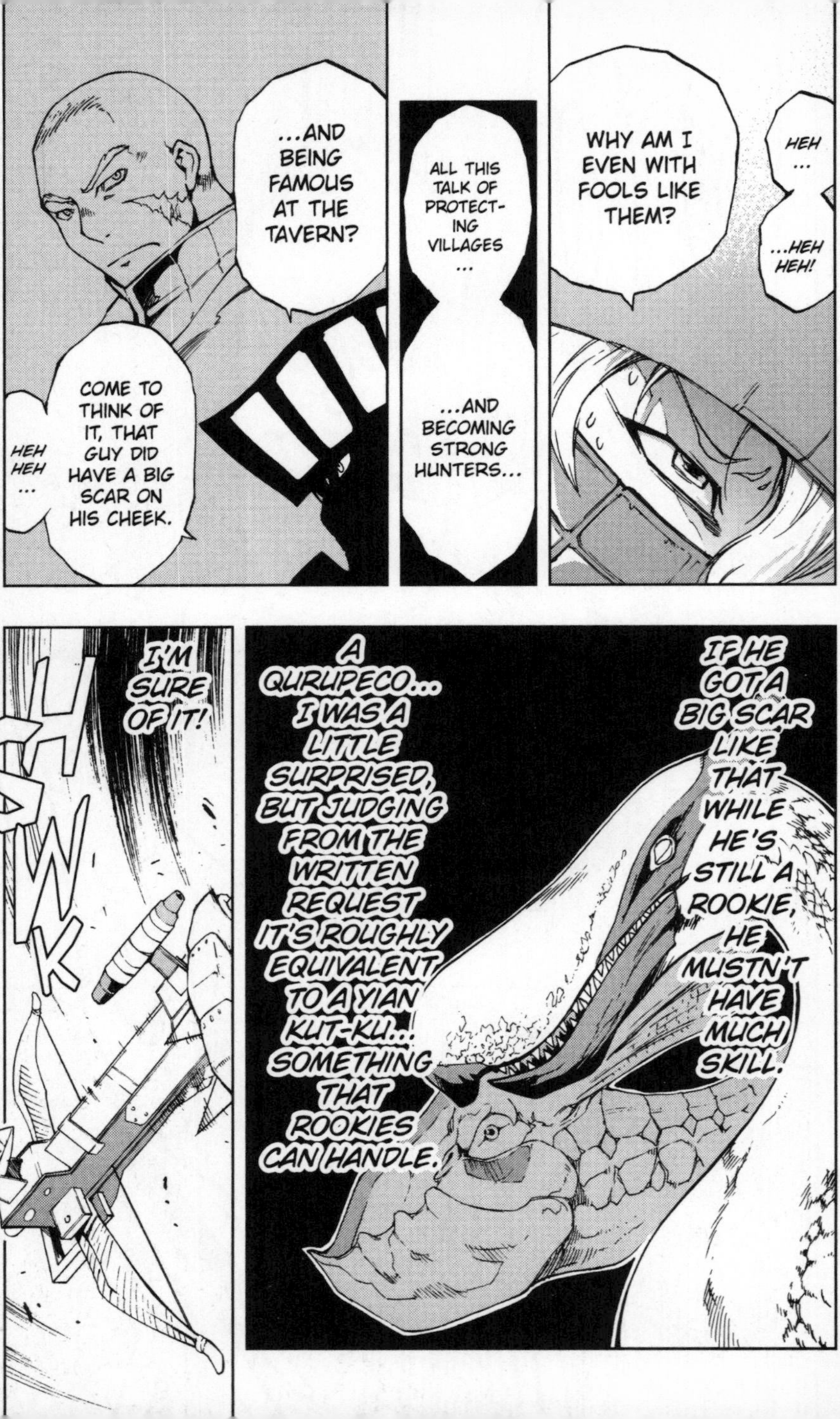
HEH... ...HEH HEH!
WHY AM I EVEN WITH FOOLS LIKE THEM?
ALL THIS TALK OF PROTECT-ING VILLAGES...
...AND BECOMING STRONG HUNTERS...
...AND BEING FAMOUS AT THE TAVERN?
COME TO THINK OF IT, THAT GUY DID HAVE A BIG SCAR ON HIS CHEEK.
HEH HEH...
IF HE GOT A BIG SCAR LIKE THAT WHILE HE'S STILL A ROOKIE, HE MUSTN'T HAVE MUCH SKILL.
A QURUPECO... I WAS A LITTLE SURPRISED, BUT JUDGING FROM THE WRITTEN REQUEST IT'S ROUGHLY EQUIVALENT TO A YIAN KUT-KU... SOMETHING THAT ROOKIES CAN HANDLE.
I'M SURE OF IT!
SHWK

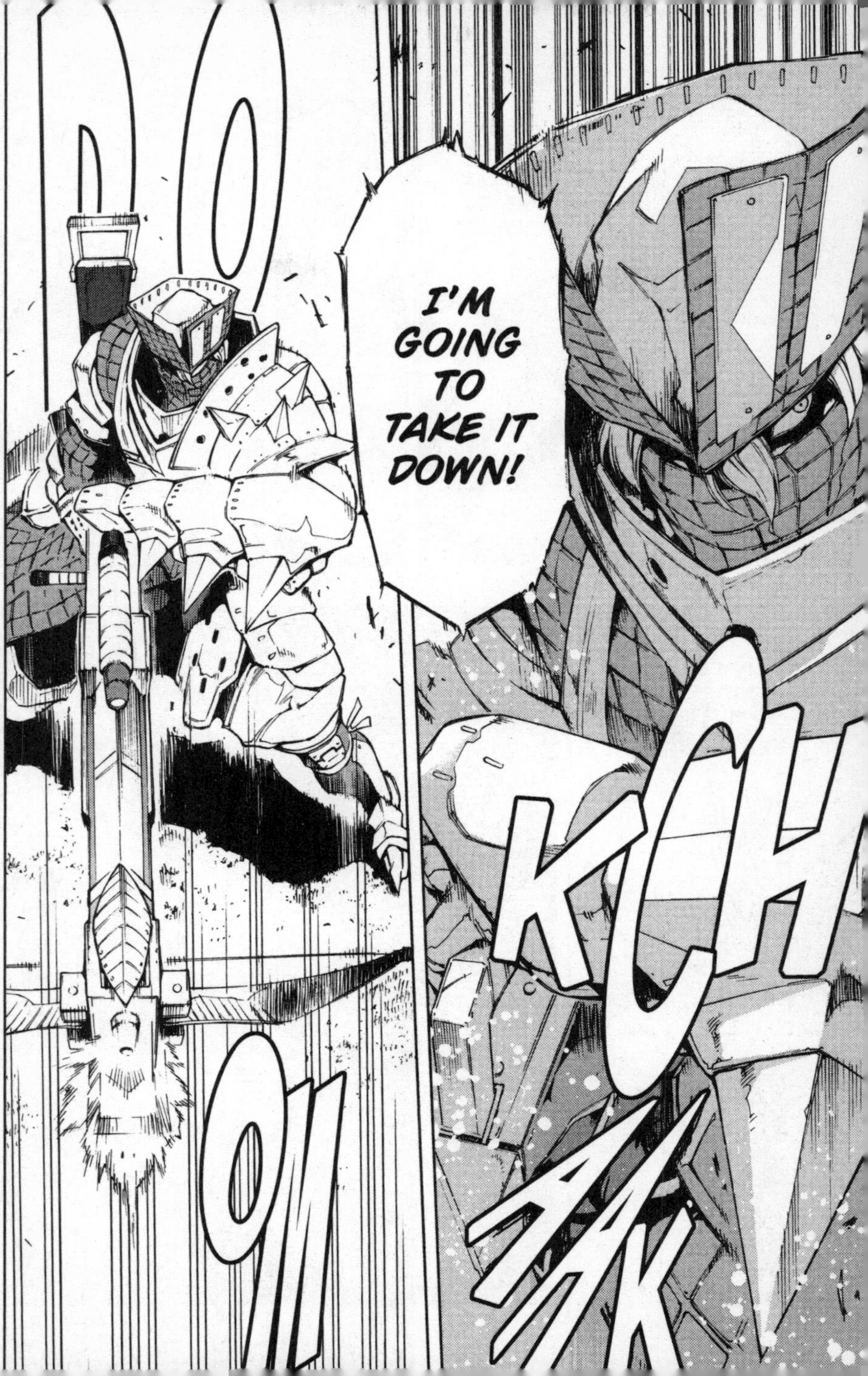
I'M GOING TO TAKE IT DOWN!
KCHAAAK
DO

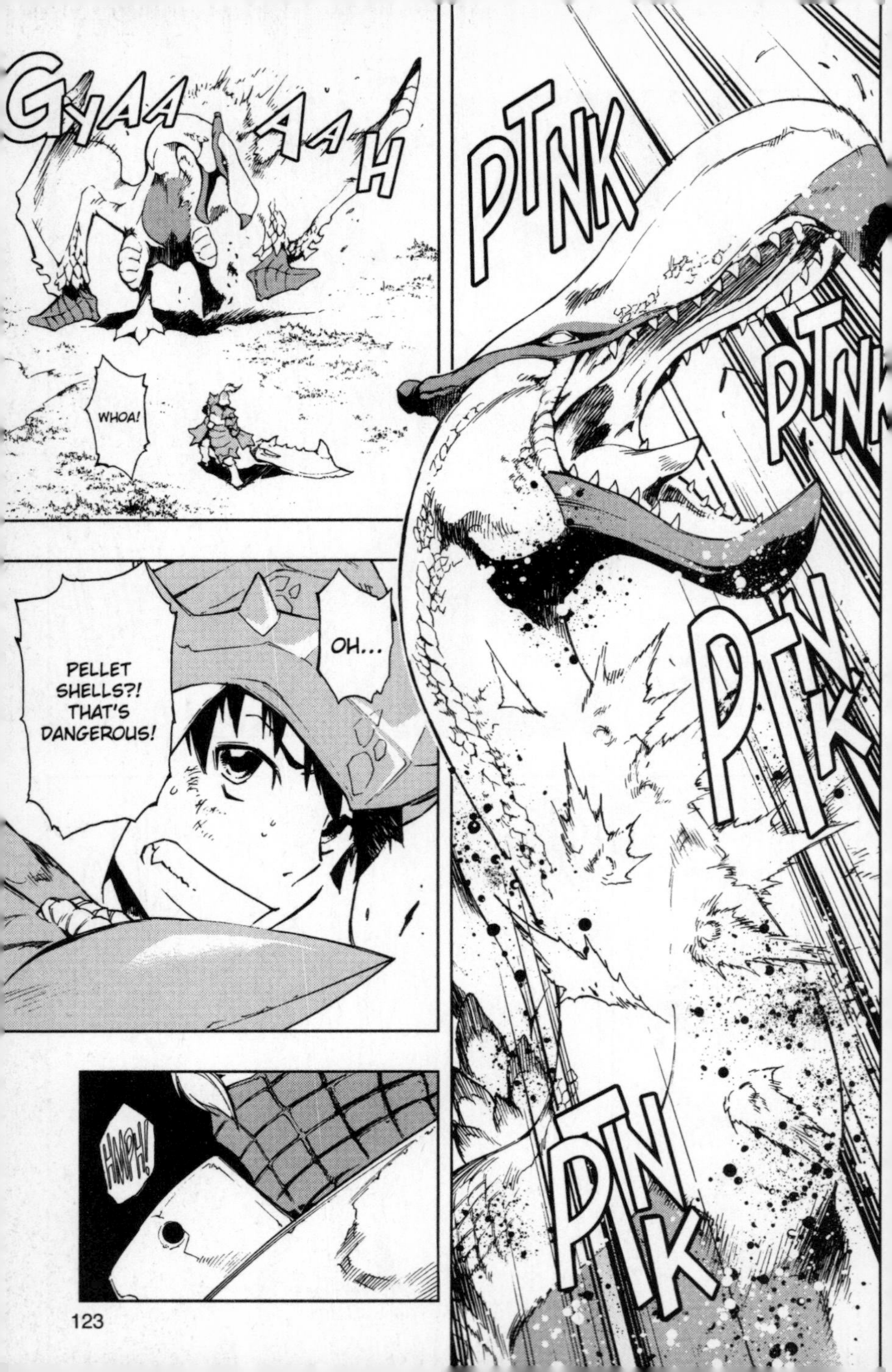
PTNK
PTNK
PTNK
PTNK
GYAAAAAH
WHOA!
OH...
PELLET SHELLS?! THAT'S DANGEROUS!
HMPH!

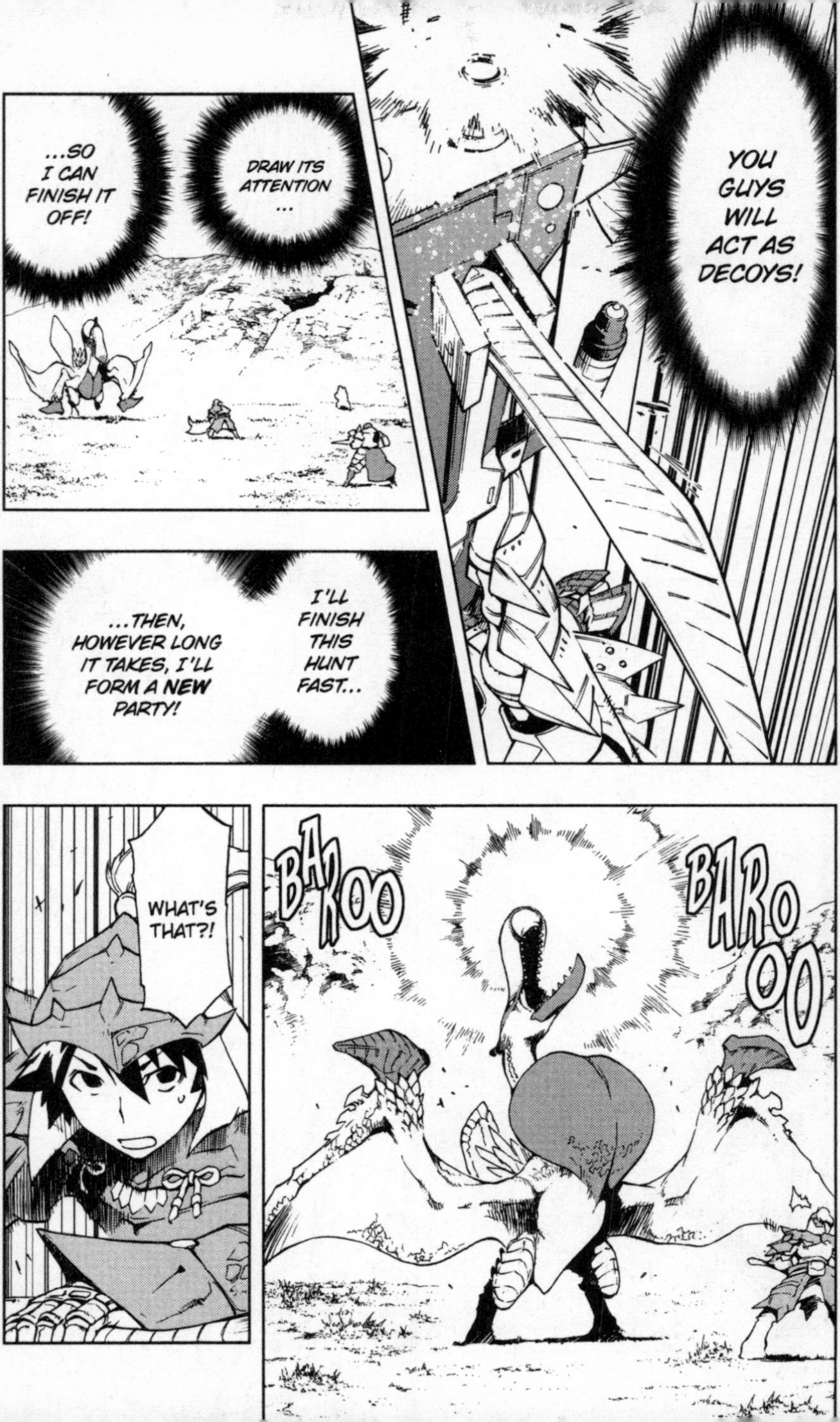
YOU GUYS WILL ACT AS DECOYS!
DRAW ITS ATTENTION...
...SO I CAN FINISH IT OFF!
I'LL FINISH THIS HUNT FAST...
...THEN, HOWEVER LONG IT TAKES, I'LL FORM A **NEW** PARTY!
BAROOO
BAROOO
WHAT'S THAT?!

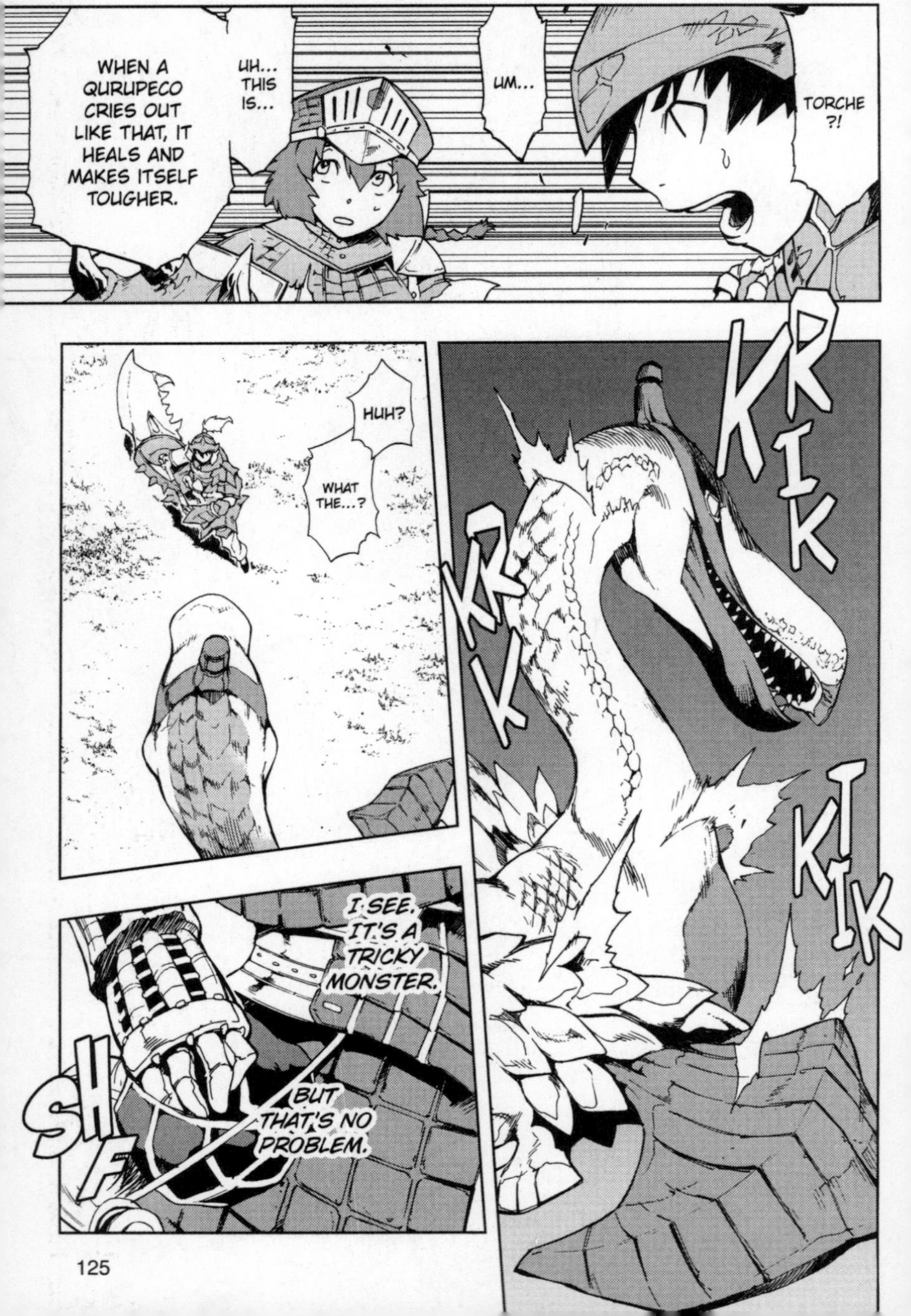
TORCHE ?!
UM...
UH... THIS IS...
WHEN A QURUPECO CRIES OUT LIKE THAT, IT HEALS AND MAKES ITSELF TOUGHER.
KRIK
KRIK
KTIK
HUH?
WHAT THE...?
I SEE. IT'S A TRICKY MONSTER.
BUT THAT'S NO PROBLEM.
SHF

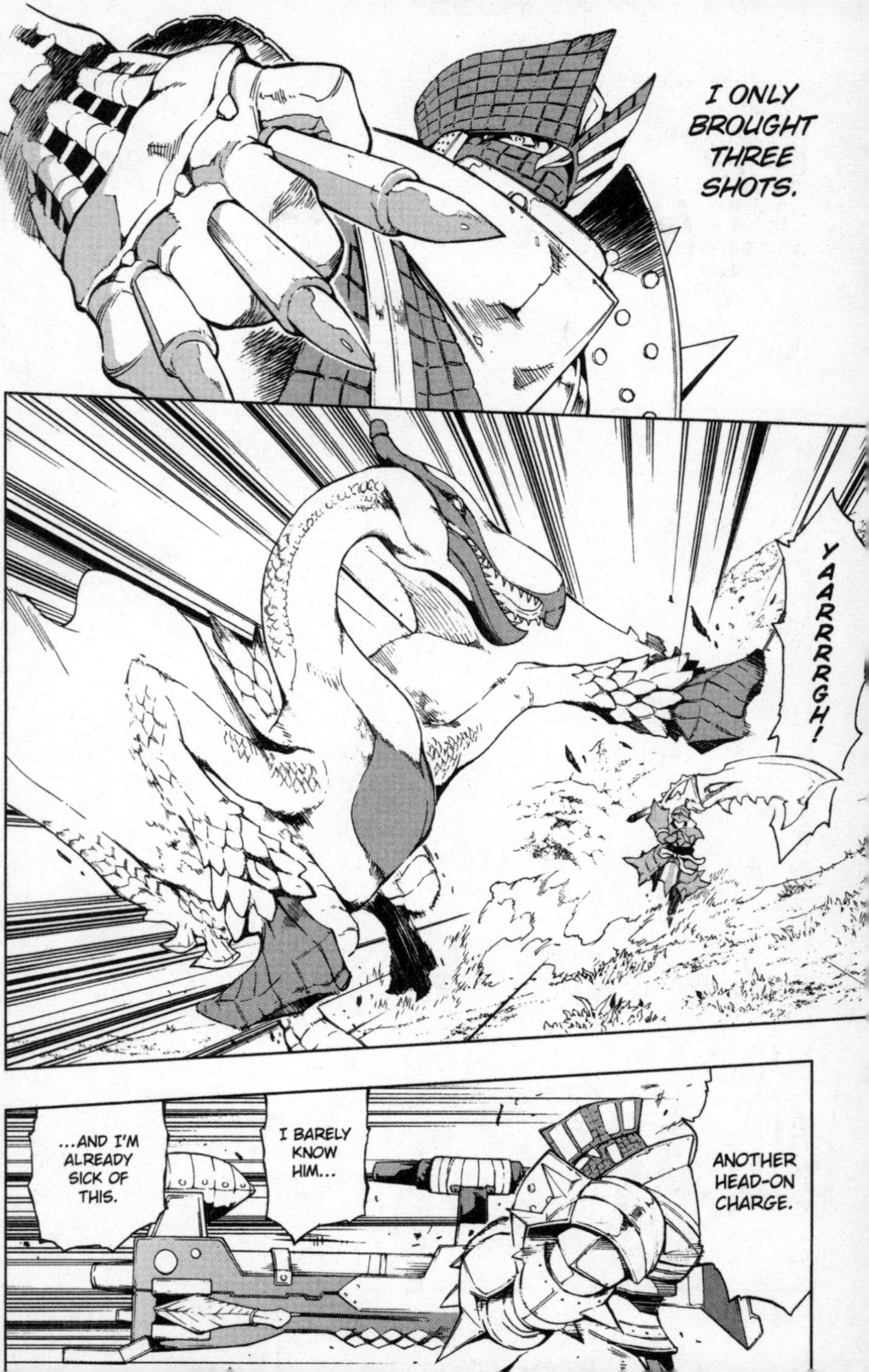
I ONLY BROUGHT THREE SHOTS.
YAARRRRGH!
ANOTHER HEAD-ON CHARGE.
I BARELY KNOW HIM...
...AND I'M ALREADY SICK OF THIS.

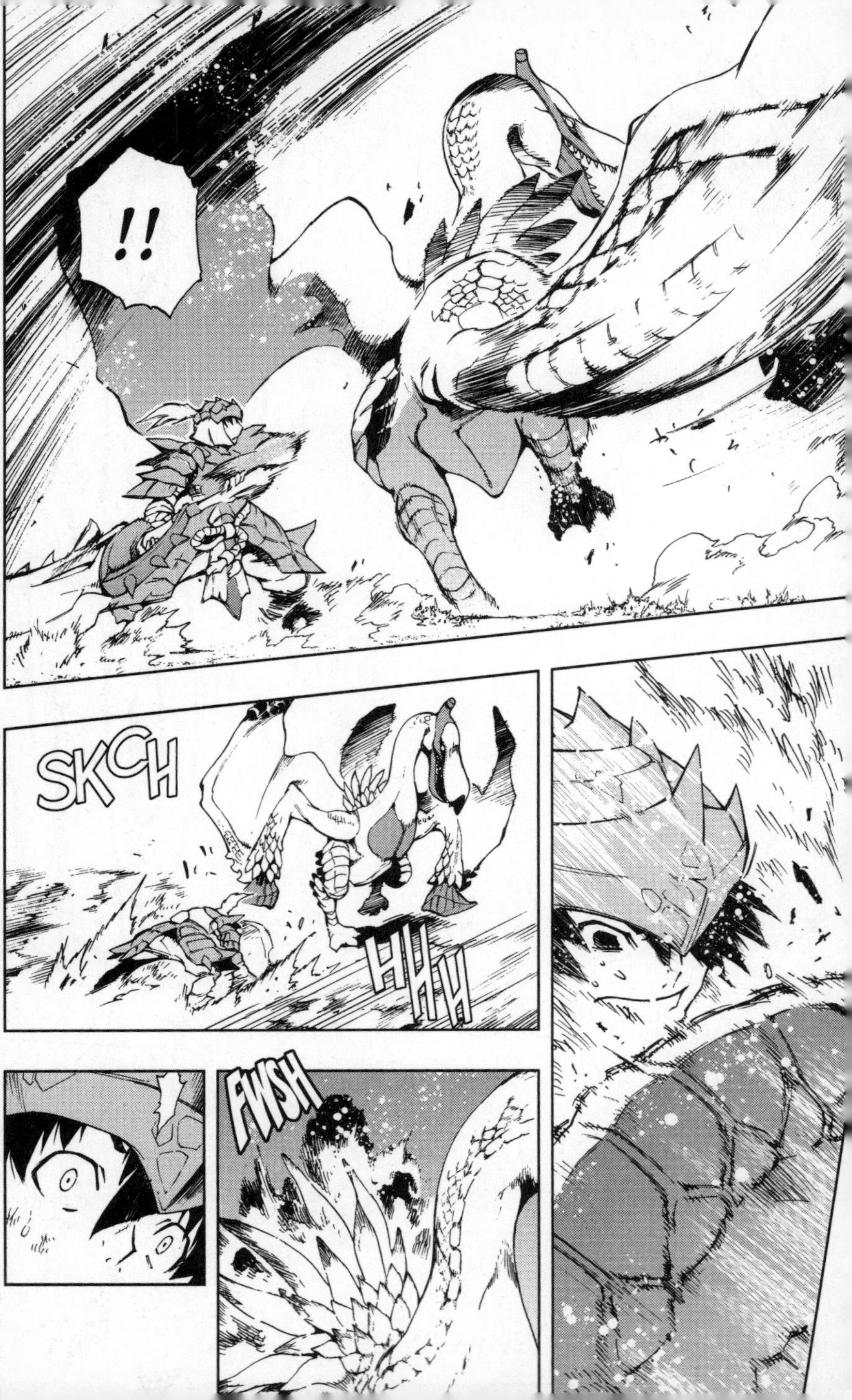
!!
SKCH
FWSH

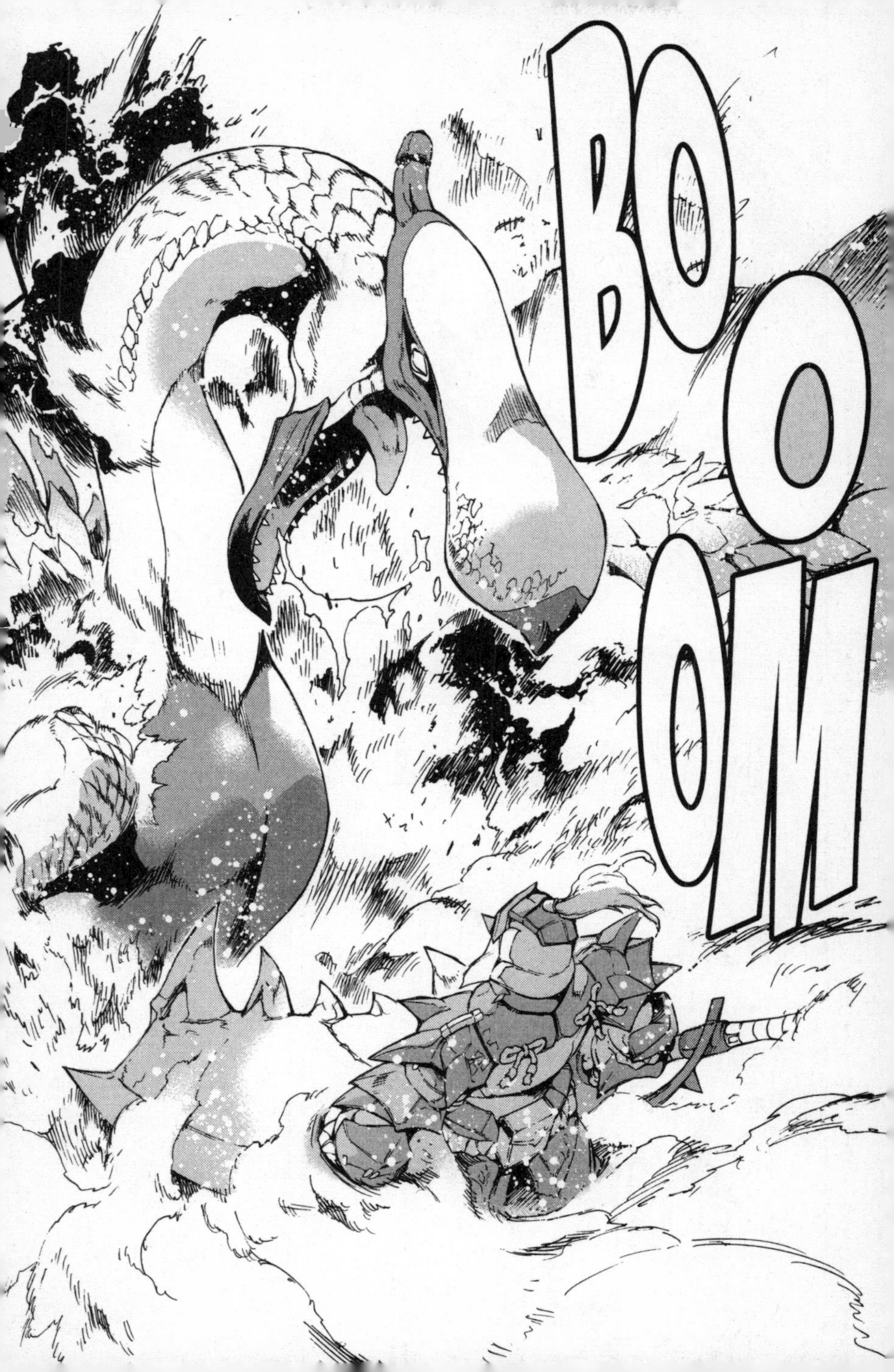
BOOOOM

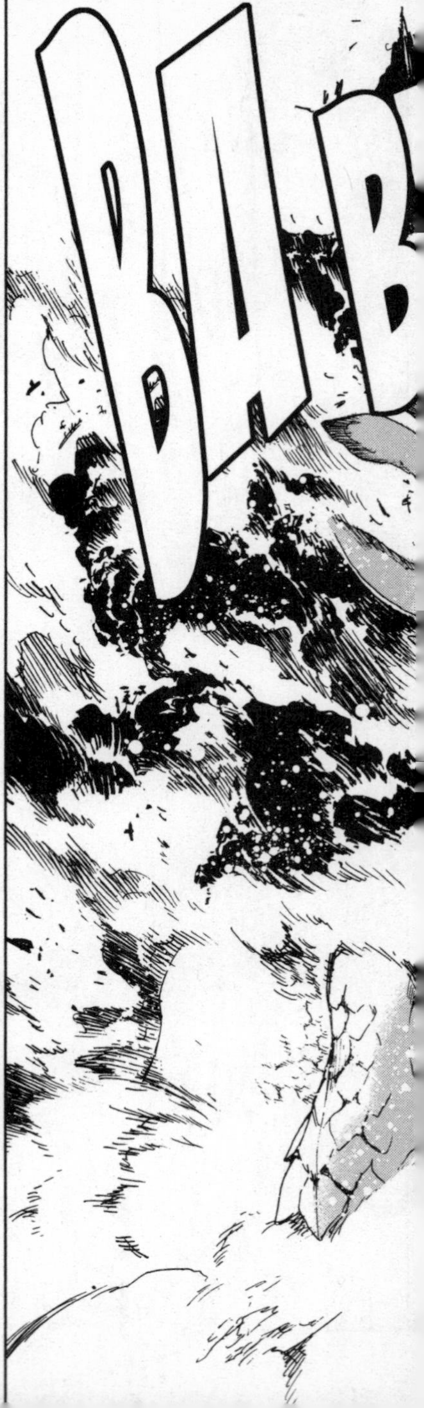
BAB

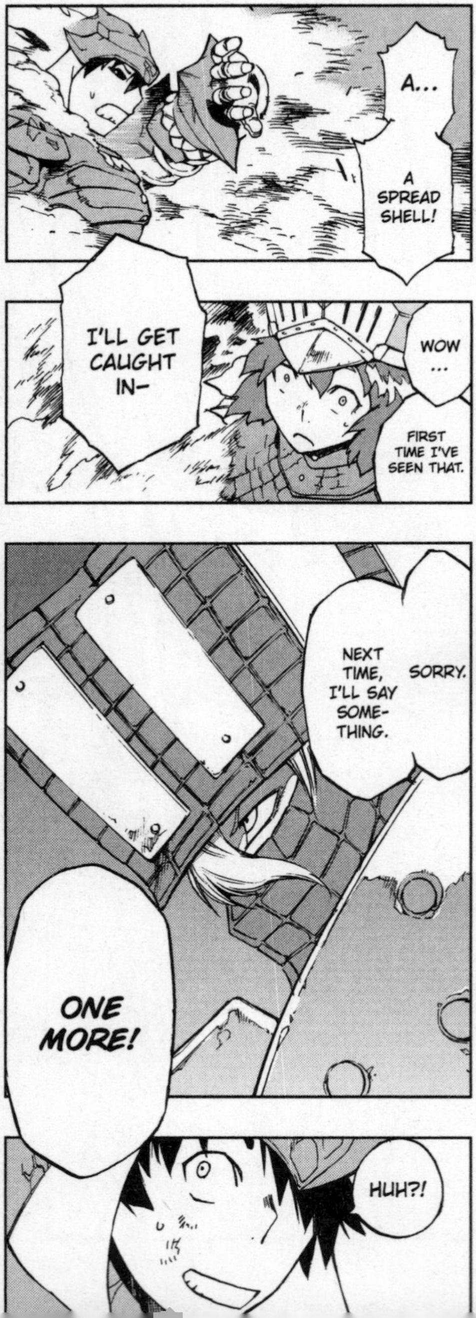
A...
A SPREAD SHELL!
I'LL GET CAUGHT IN–
WOW...
FIRST TIME I'VE SEEN THAT.
SORRY.
NEXT TIME, I'LL SAY SOMETHING.
ONE MORE!
HUH?!

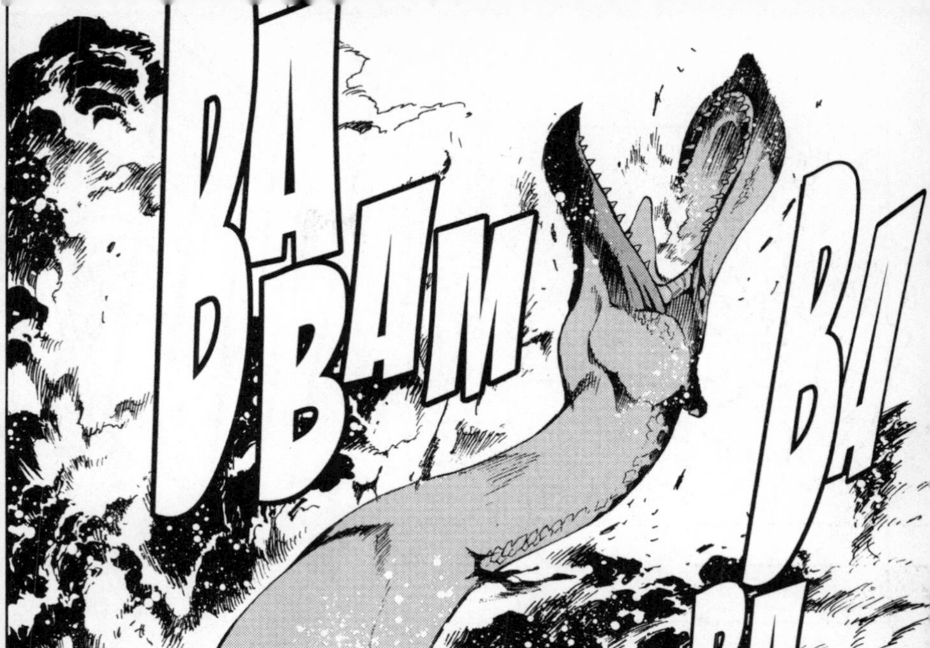
BA DA BAMM
DA DBAM

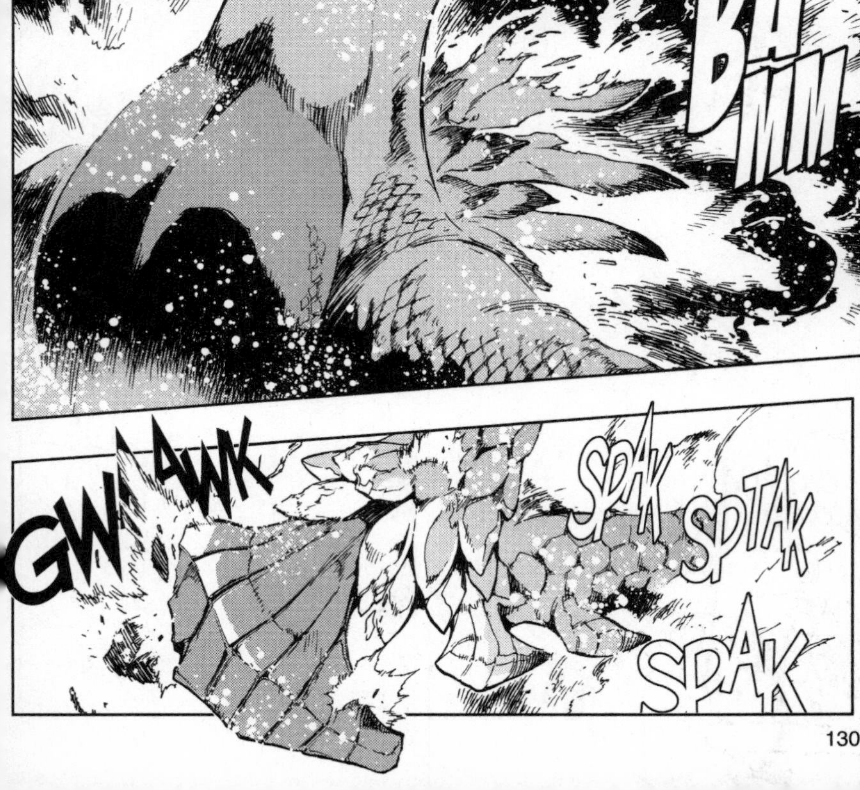
SPAK
SPTAK
SPAK
GWAAWK

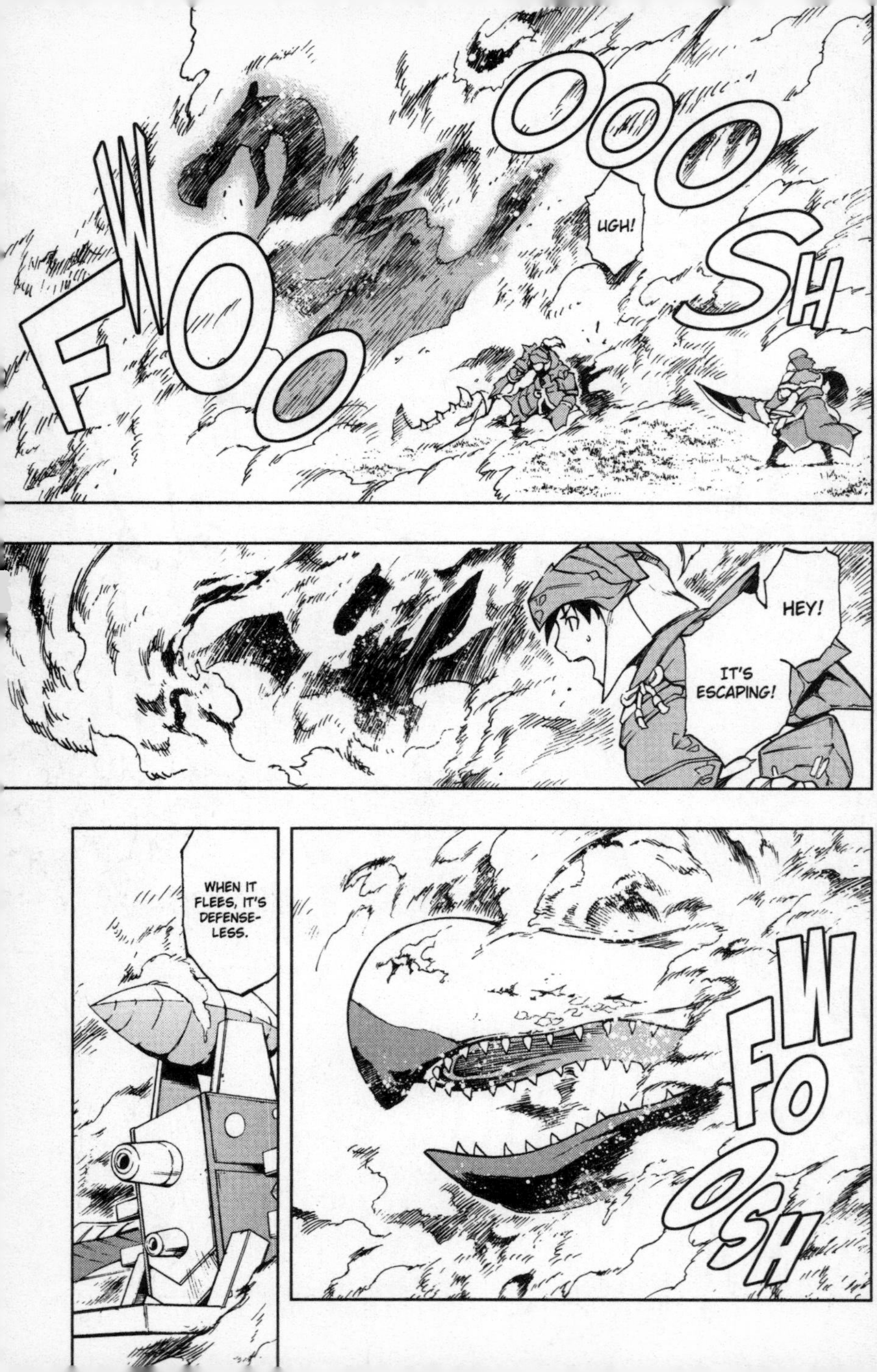
FWOOOOOOSH
UGH!
HEY!
IT'S ESCAPING!
FWOOOSH
WHEN IT FLEES, IT'S DEFENSELESS.

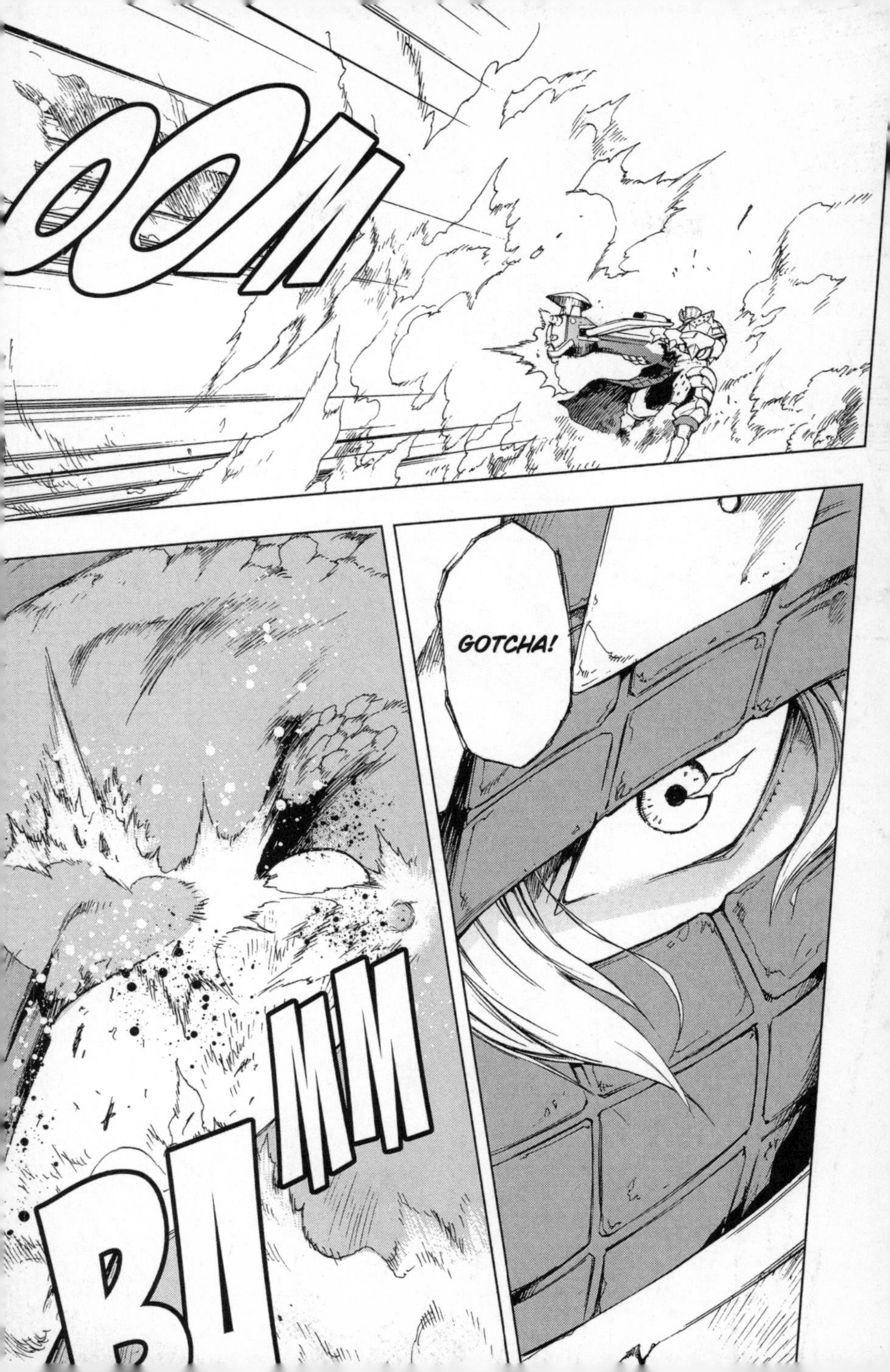
GOTCHA!
BAMMM

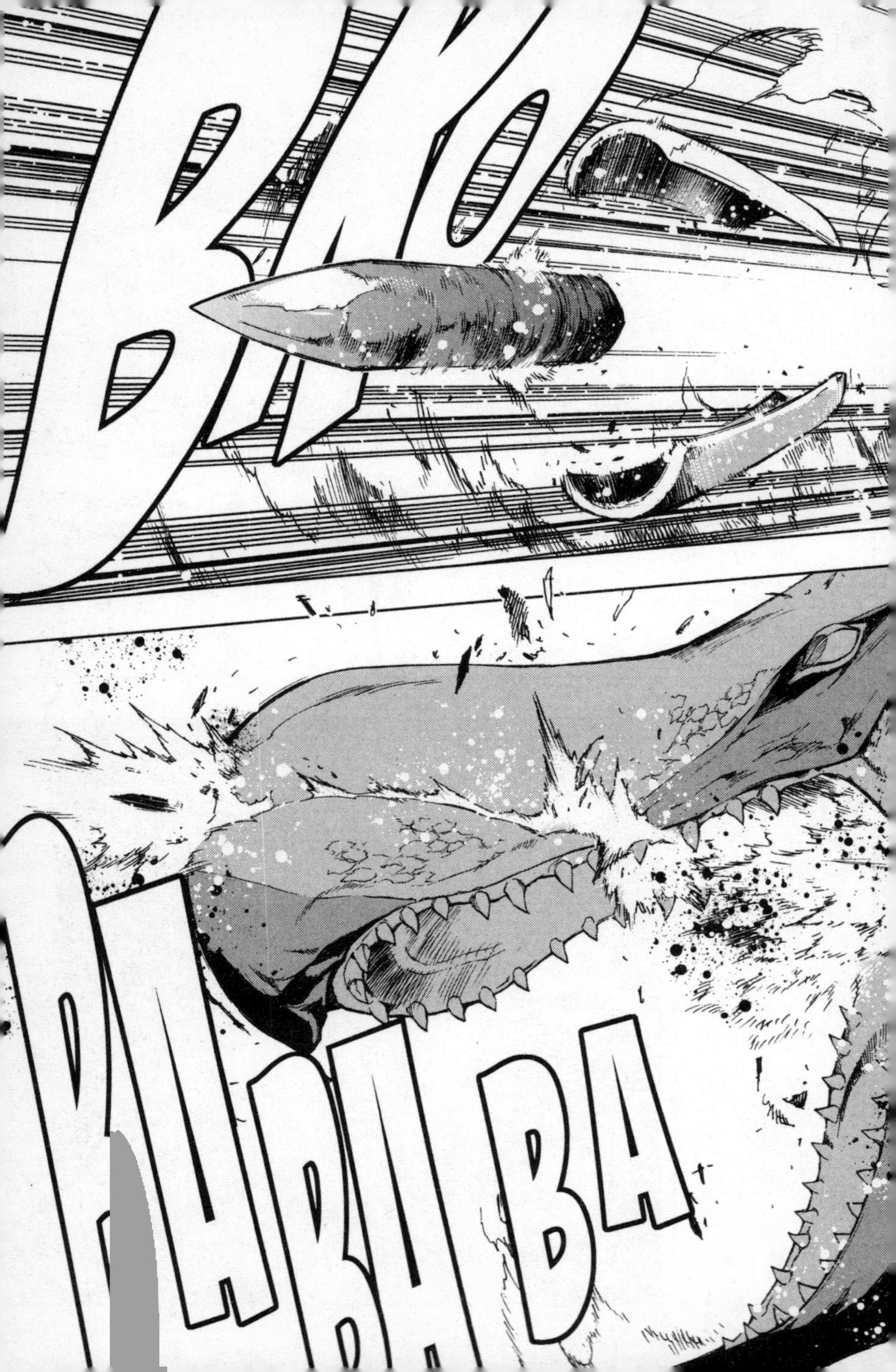
BABABA

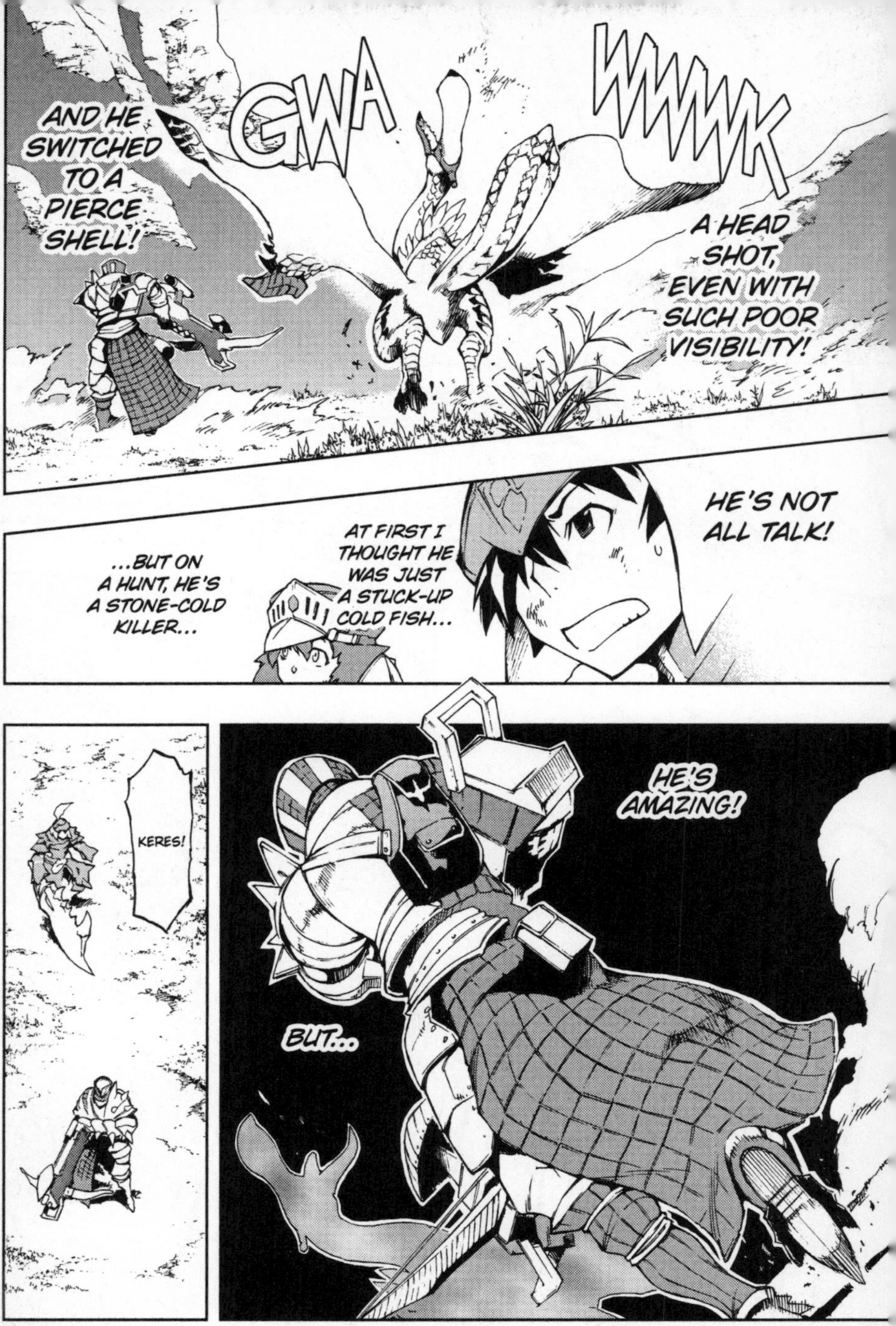
GWA
WWWK
A HEAD SHOT, EVEN WITH SUCH POOR VISIBILITY!
AND HE SWITCHED TO A PIERCE SHELL!
HE'S NOT ALL TALK!
AT FIRST I THOUGHT HE WAS JUST A STUCK-UP COLD FISH...
...BUT ON A HUNT, HE'S A STONE-COLD KILLER...
HE'S AMAZING!
BUT...
KERES!

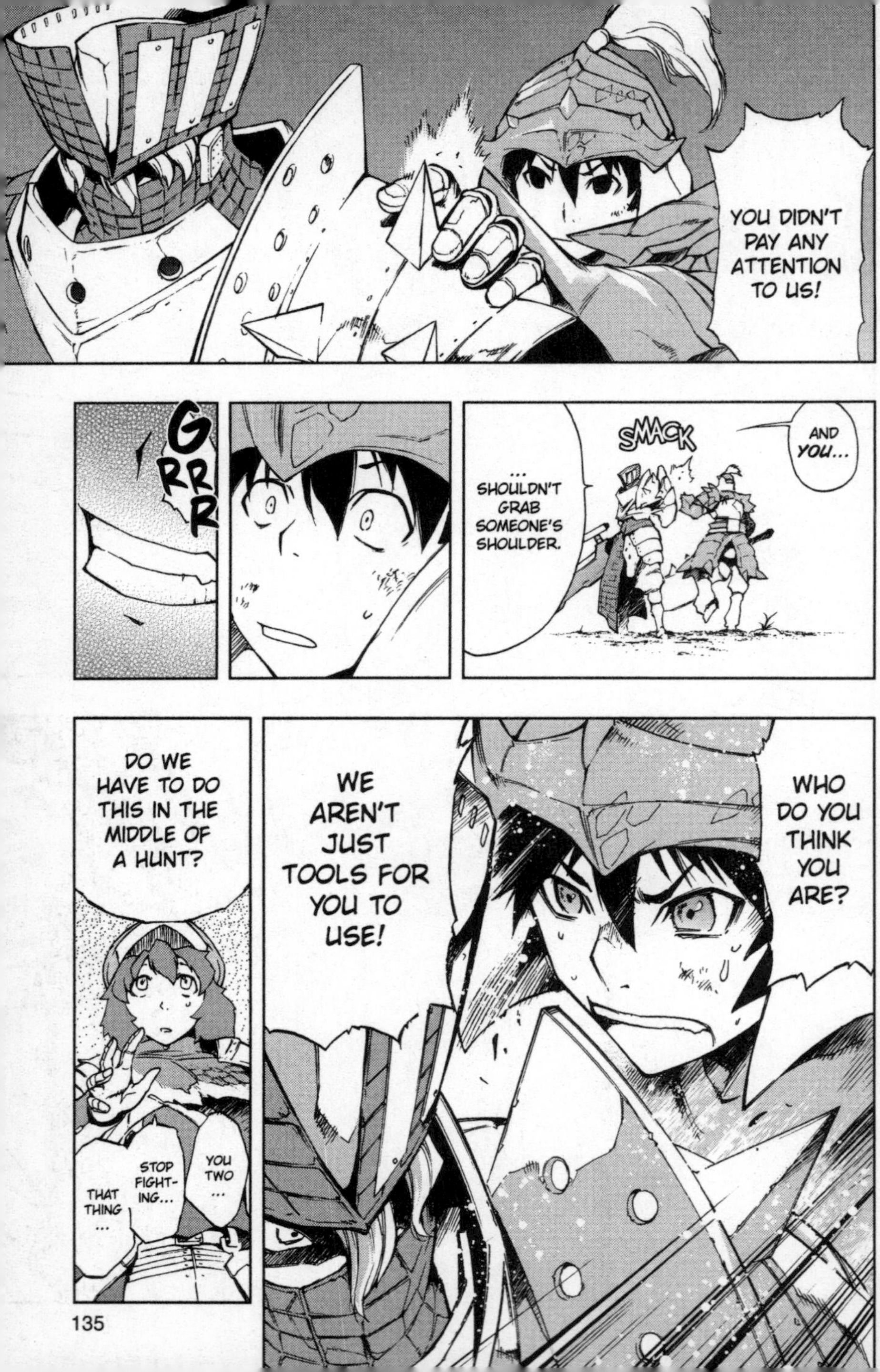
YOU DIDN'T PAY ANY ATTENTION TO US!
AND YOU...
SMACK
...SHOULDN'T GRAB SOMEONE'S SHOULDER.
GRRR
WHO DO YOU THINK YOU ARE?
WE AREN'T JUST TOOLS FOR YOU TO USE!
DO WE HAVE TO DO THIS IN THE MIDDLE OF A HUNT?
YOU TWO...
STOP FIGHT-ING...
THAT THING...

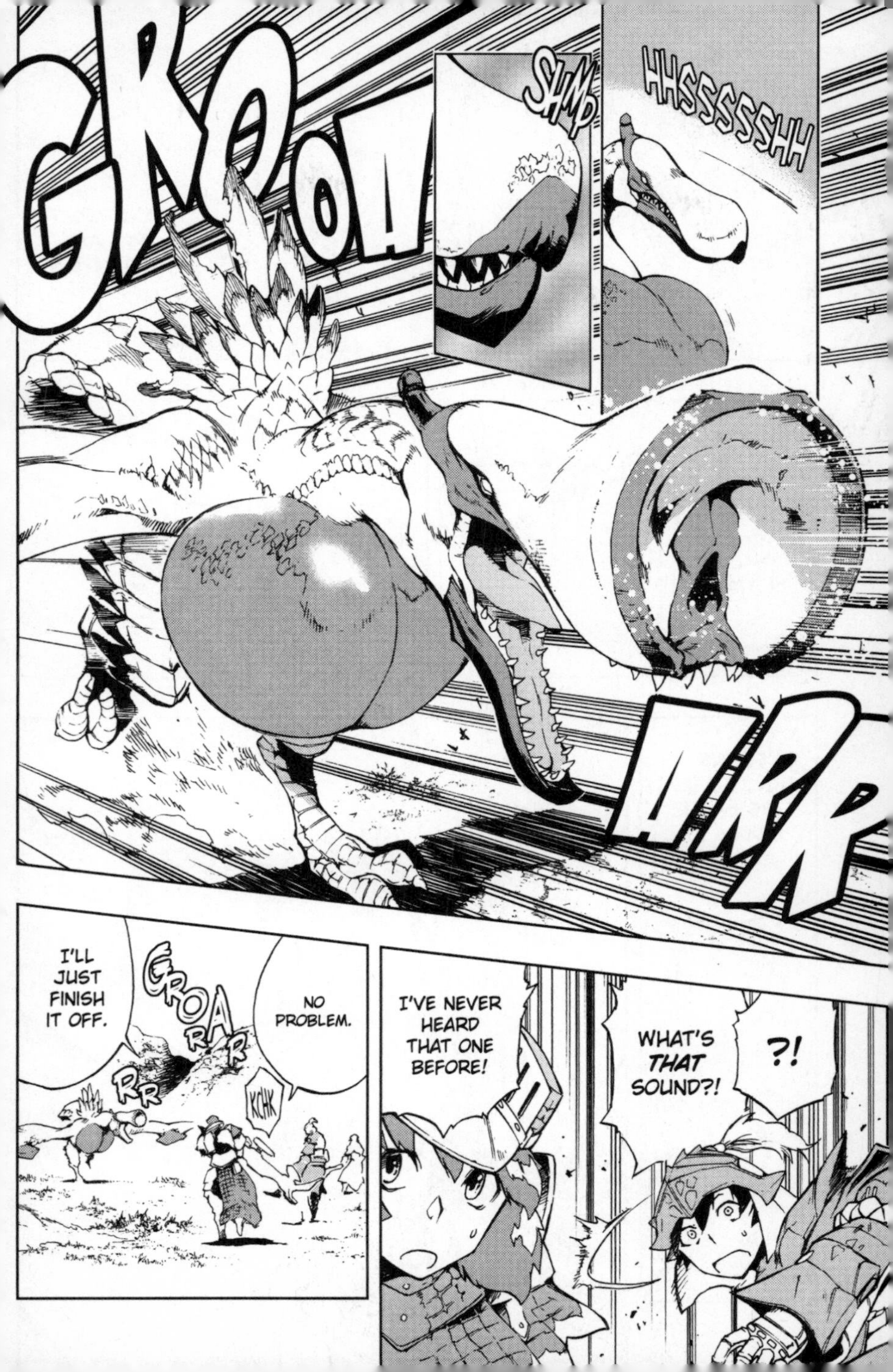
HHSSSSSHH
SHMP
GROOA
ARR
?!
WHAT'S *THAT* SOUND?!
I'VE NEVER HEARD THAT ONE BEFORE!
NO PROBLEM.
KCHK
GROARRRR
I'LL JUST FINISH IT OFF.

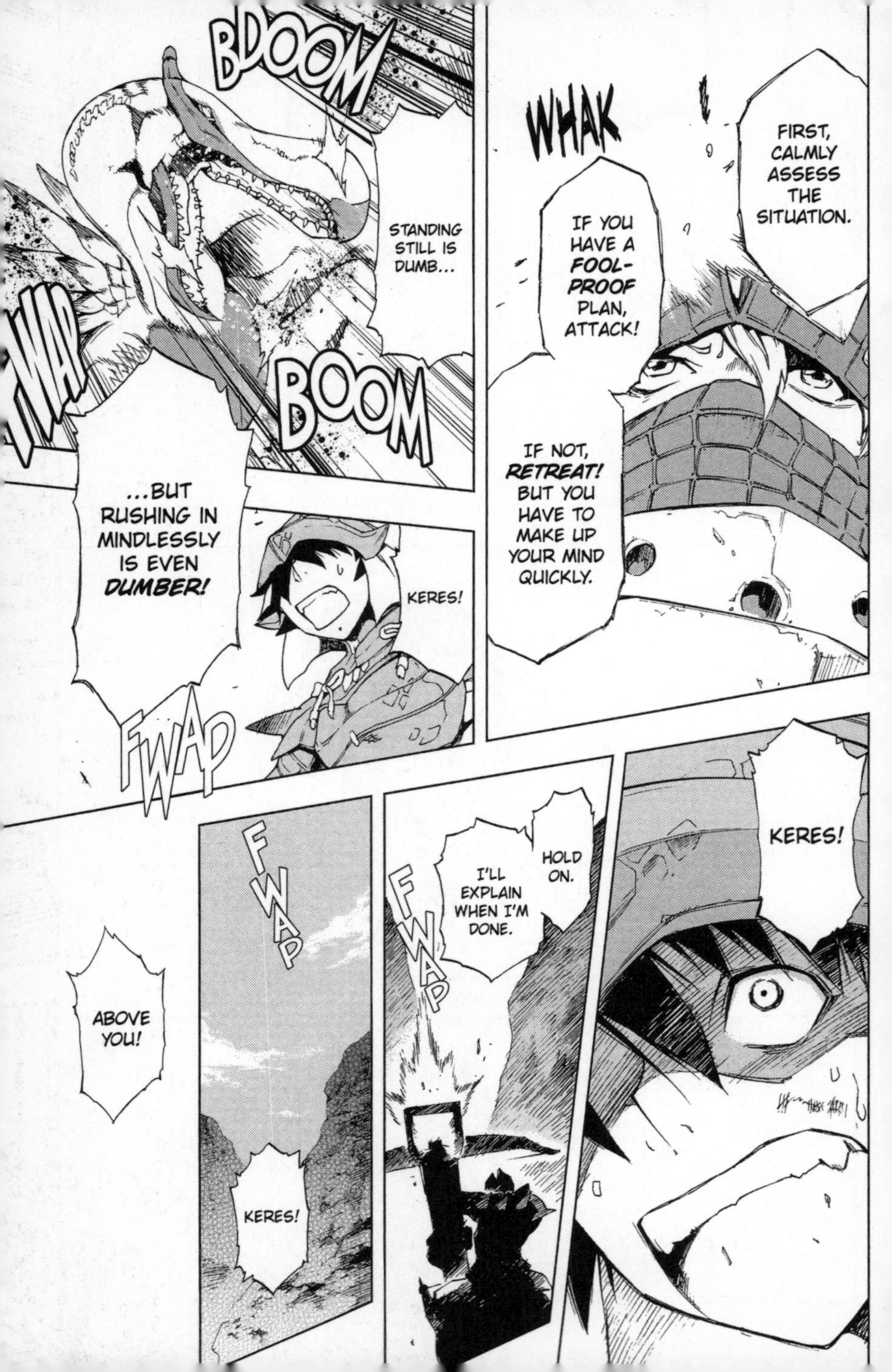
FIRST, CALMLY ASSESS THE SITUATION.
WHAK
IF YOU HAVE A ***FOOL-PROOF*** PLAN, ATTACK!
IF NOT, ***RETREAT!*** BUT YOU HAVE TO MAKE UP YOUR MIND QUICKLY.
BDOOM
STANDING STILL IS DUMB...
BOOM
FWAP
...BUT RUSHING IN MINDLESSLY IS EVEN ***DUMBER!***
KERES!
FWAP
KERES!
HOLD ON.
I'LL EXPLAIN WHEN I'M DONE.
FWAP
FWAP
ABOVE YOU!
KERES!

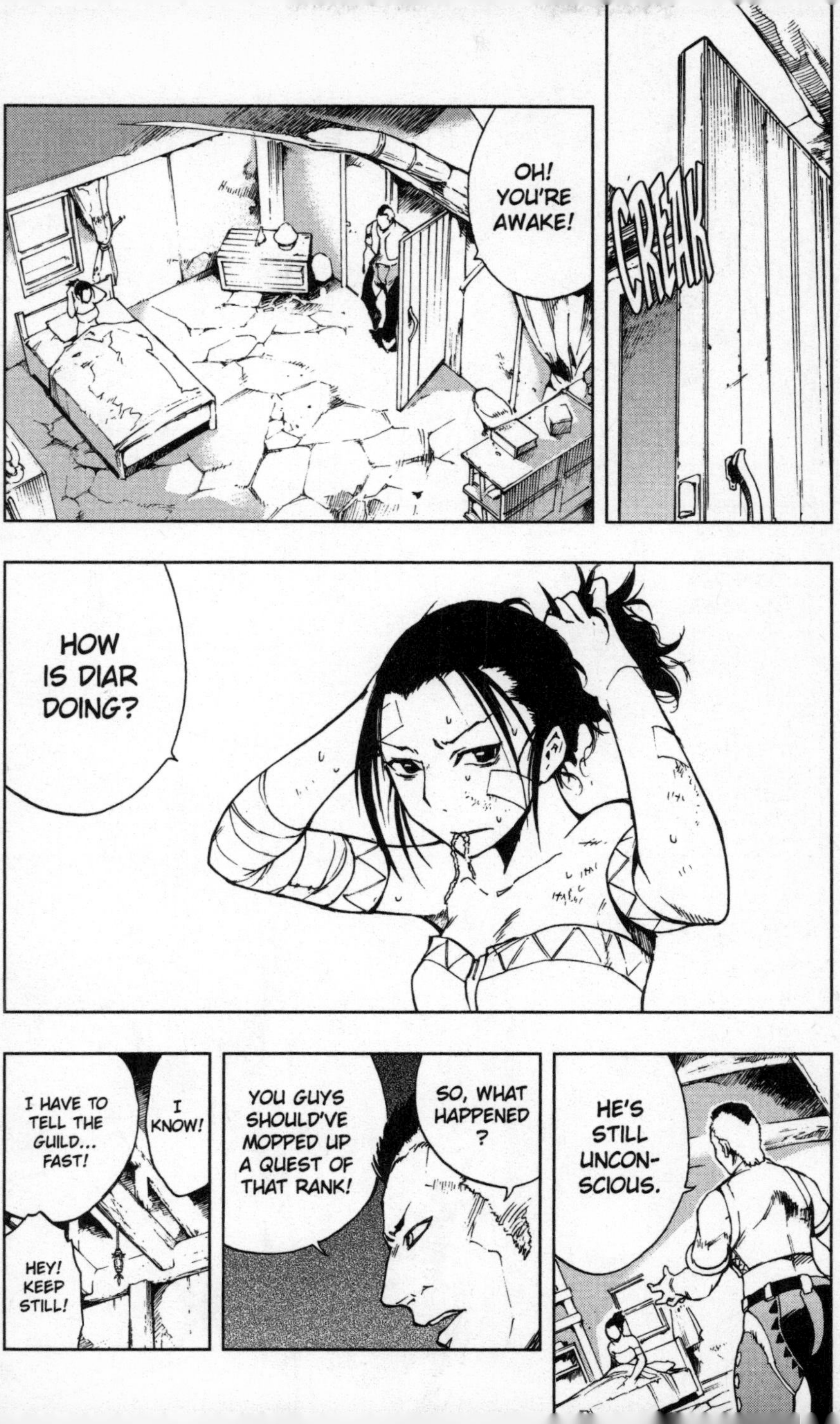
CREAK
OH! YOU'RE AWAKE!
HOW IS DIAR DOING?
HE'S STILL UNCONSCIOUS.
SO, WHAT HAPPENED ?
YOU GUYS SHOULD'VE MOPPED UP A QUEST OF THAT RANK!
I KNOW!
I HAVE TO TELL THE GUILD... FAST!
HEY! KEEP STILL!

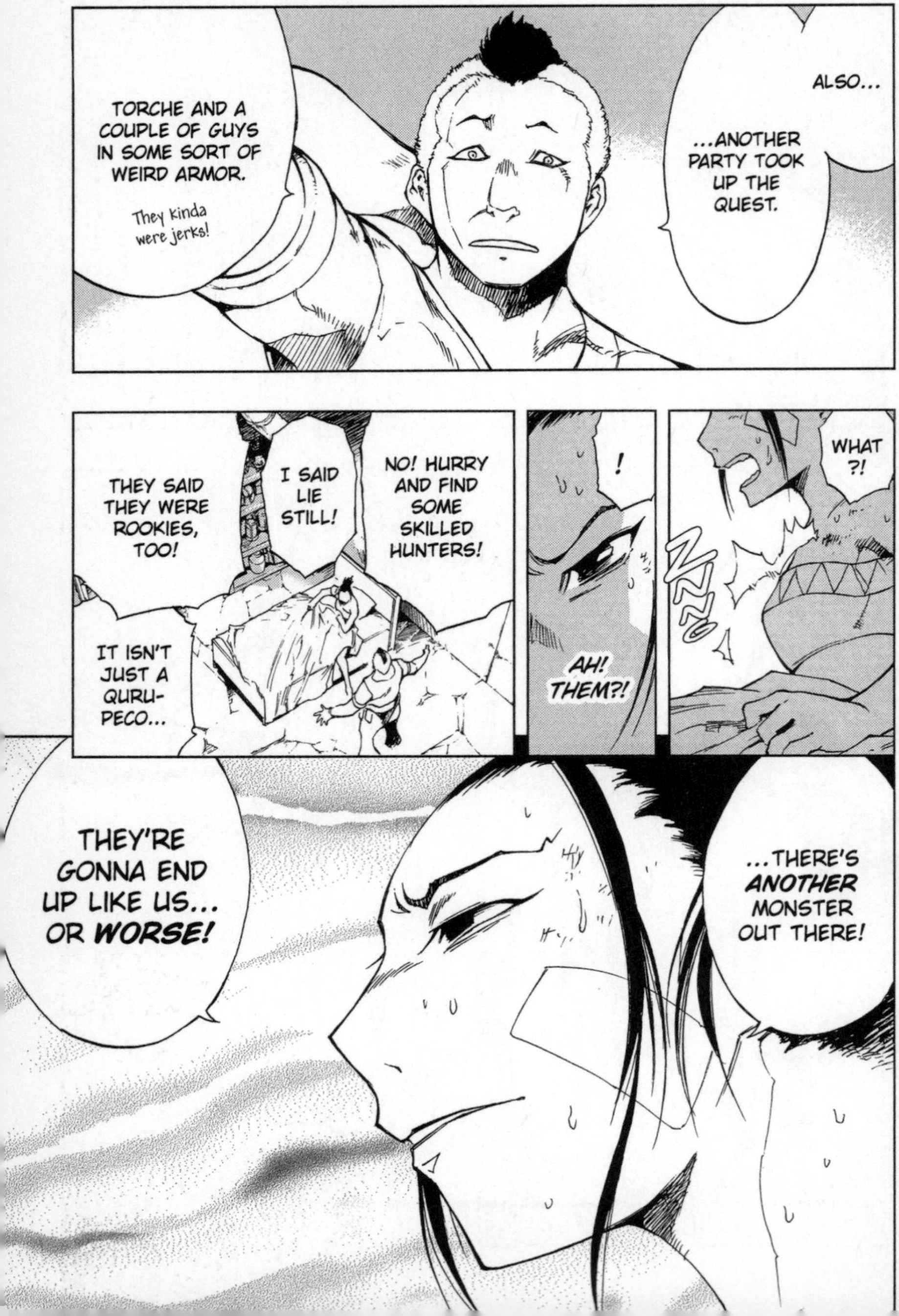
ALSO...
...ANOTHER PARTY TOOK UP THE QUEST.
TORCHE AND A COUPLE OF GUYS IN SOME SORT OF WEIRD ARMOR.
They kinda were jerks!
WHAT?!
!
AH! THEM?!
NO! HURRY AND FIND SOME SKILLED HUNTERS!
I SAID LIE STILL!
THEY SAID THEY WERE ROOKIES, TOO!
IT ISN'T JUST A QURU-PECO...
...THERE'S ANOTHER MONSTER OUT THERE!
THEY'RE GONNA END UP LIKE US... OR WORSE!

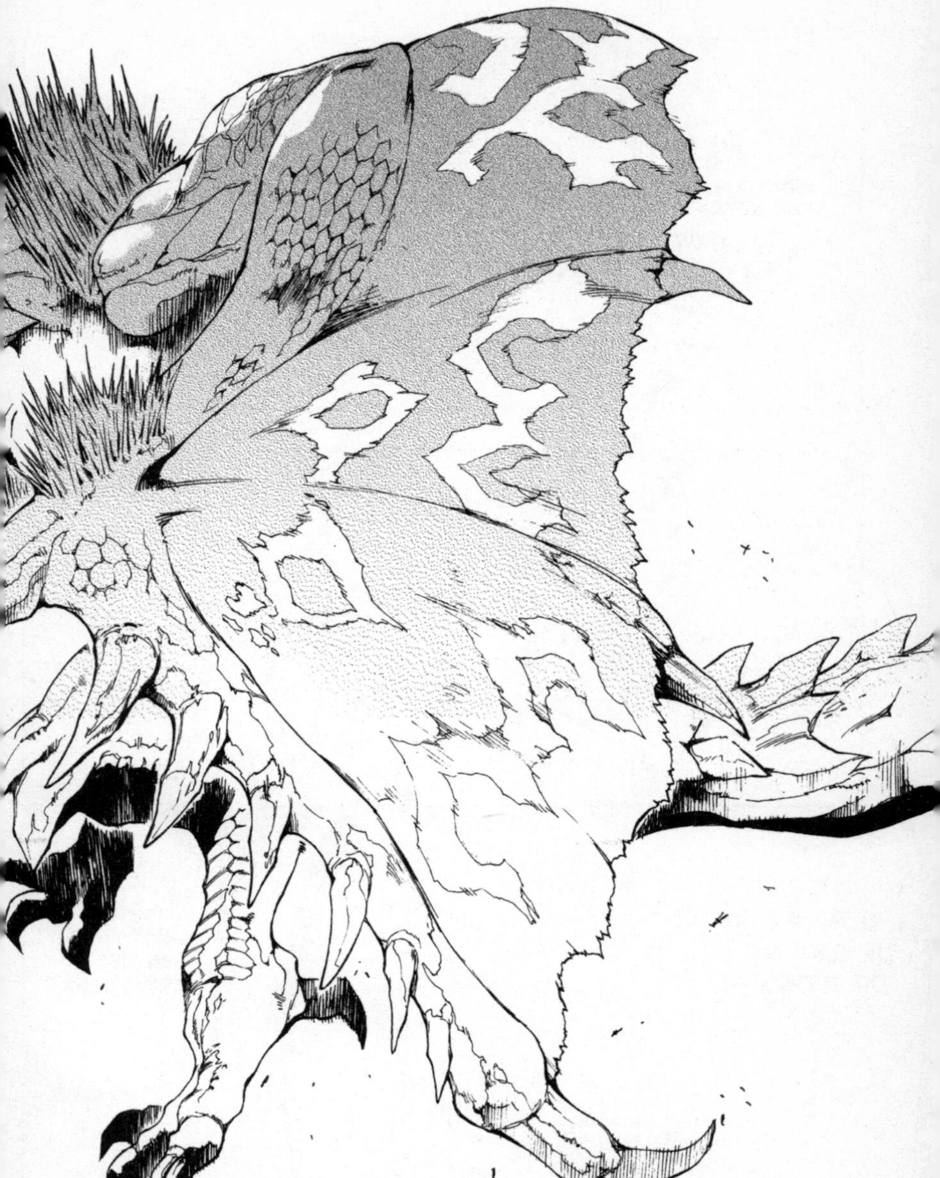

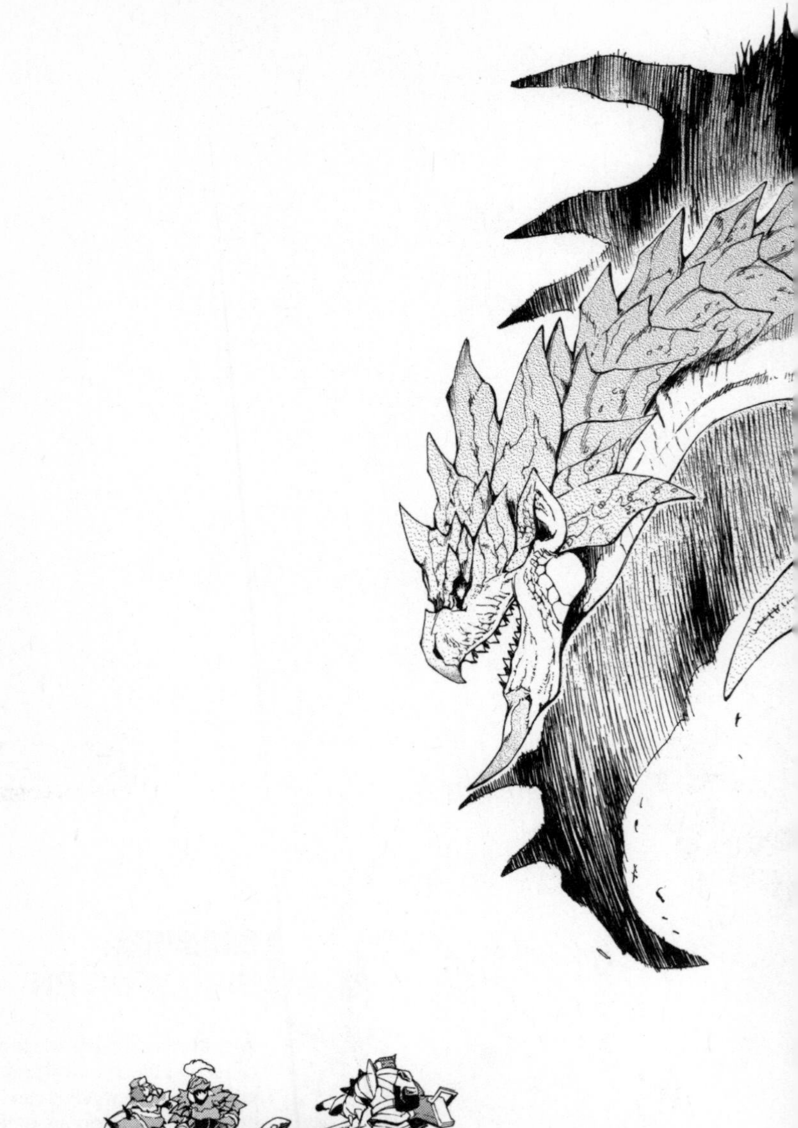

GWAAWK

QURUPECO
BIRD WYVERN

With its distinctively shaped
chest and the vocal organs in its
head, this bird wyvern can mimic
the cries of different monsters
to summon various other flying
wyverns. It can also perform a
peculiar dance that strengthens its
flesh and heals its wounds. (Also
called the "Colorful Bird.")

CHAPTER 5: QUEEN OF THE LAND

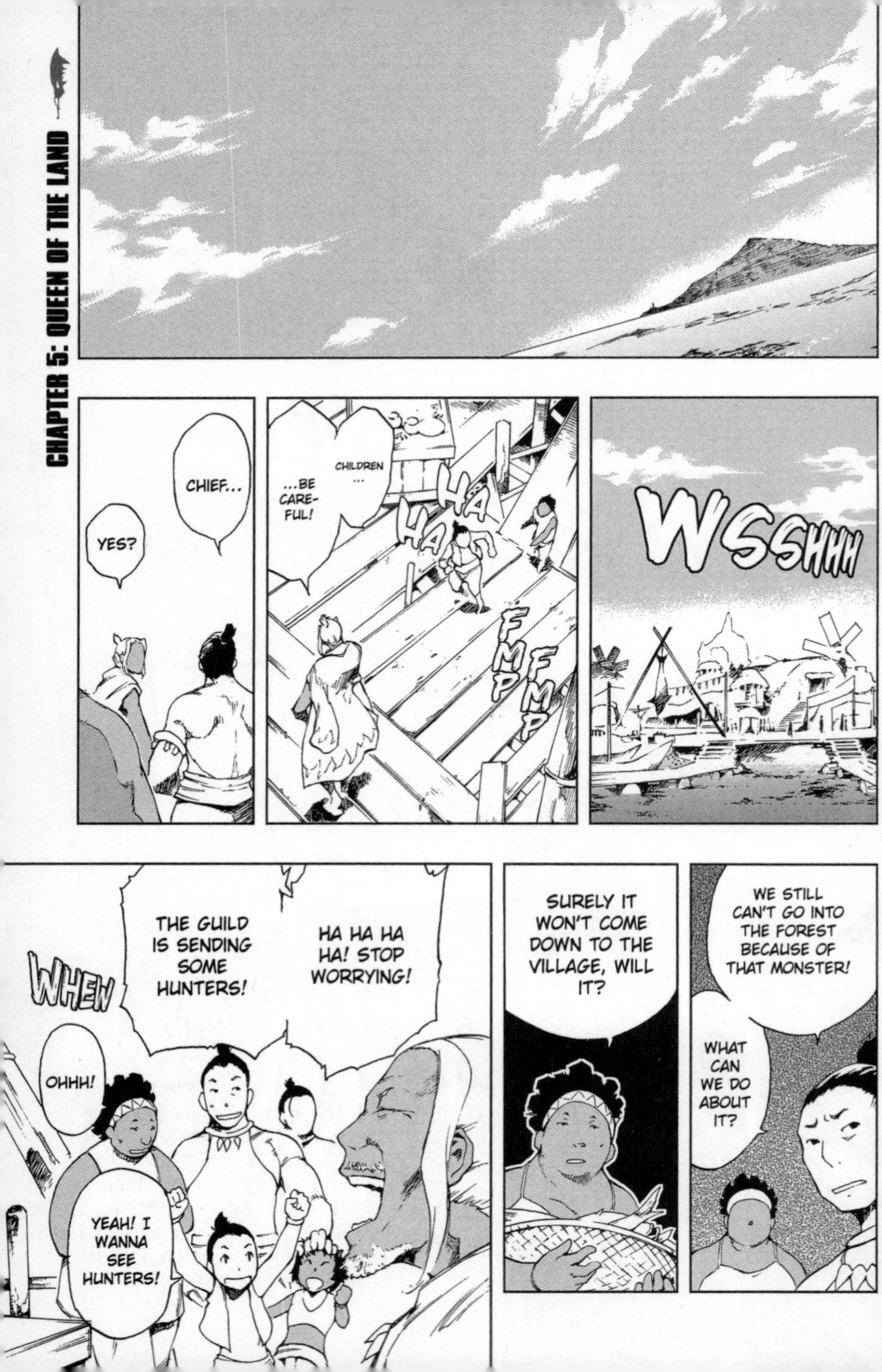

WSSHHH
CHILDREN ...
...BE CAREFUL!
HA HA!
FMP FMP
CHIEF...
YES?
WE STILL CAN'T GO INTO THE FOREST BECAUSE OF THAT MONSTER!
WHAT CAN WE DO ABOUT IT?
SURELY IT WON'T COME DOWN TO THE VILLAGE, WILL IT?
HA HA HA HA! STOP WORRYING!
THE GUILD IS SENDING SOME HUNTERS!
WHEW
OHHH!
YEAH! I WANNA SEE HUNTERS!

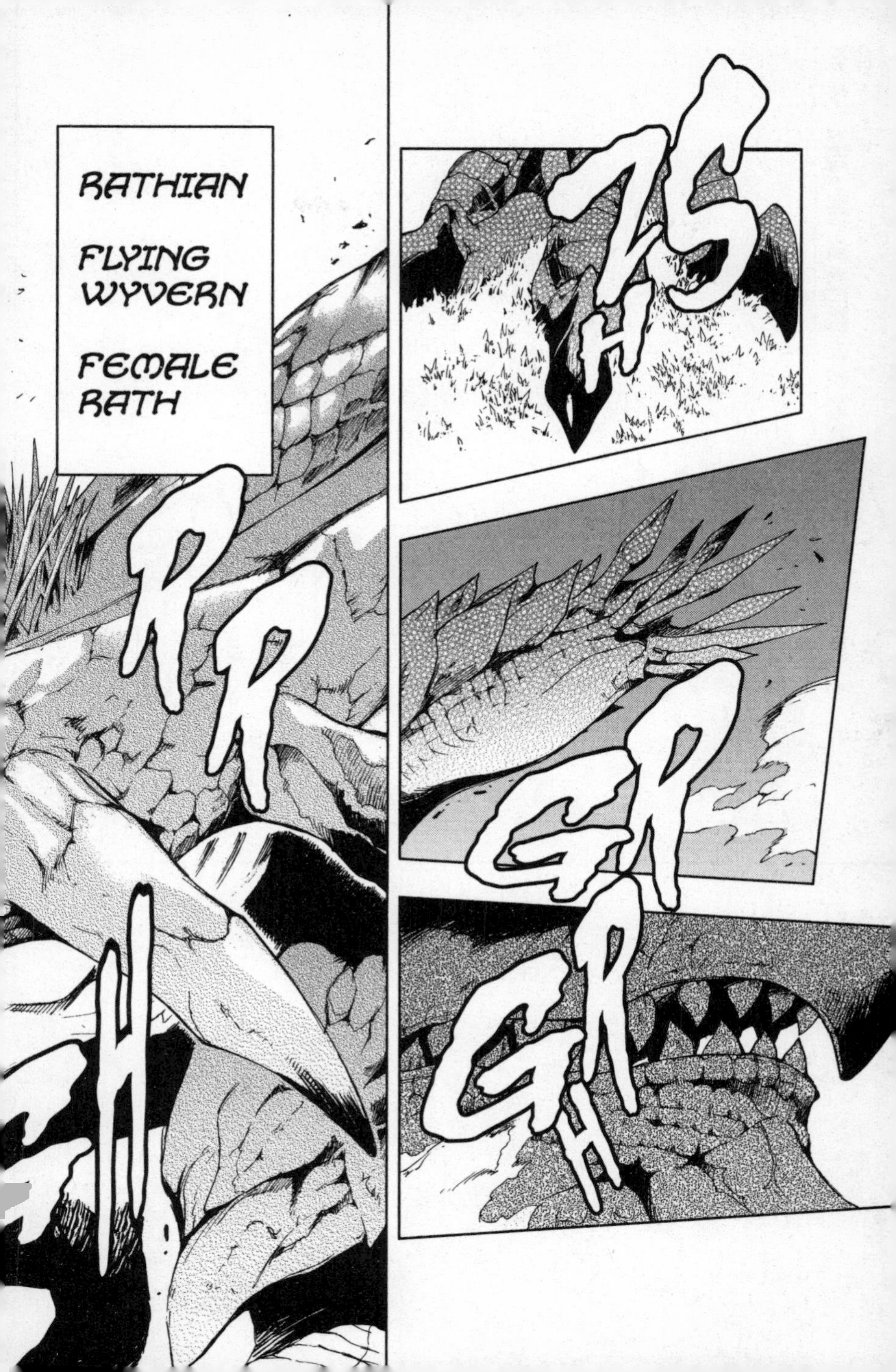
RATHIAN
FLYING WYVERN
FEMALE RATH
RRH

CHAPTER 5: QUEEN OF THE LAND

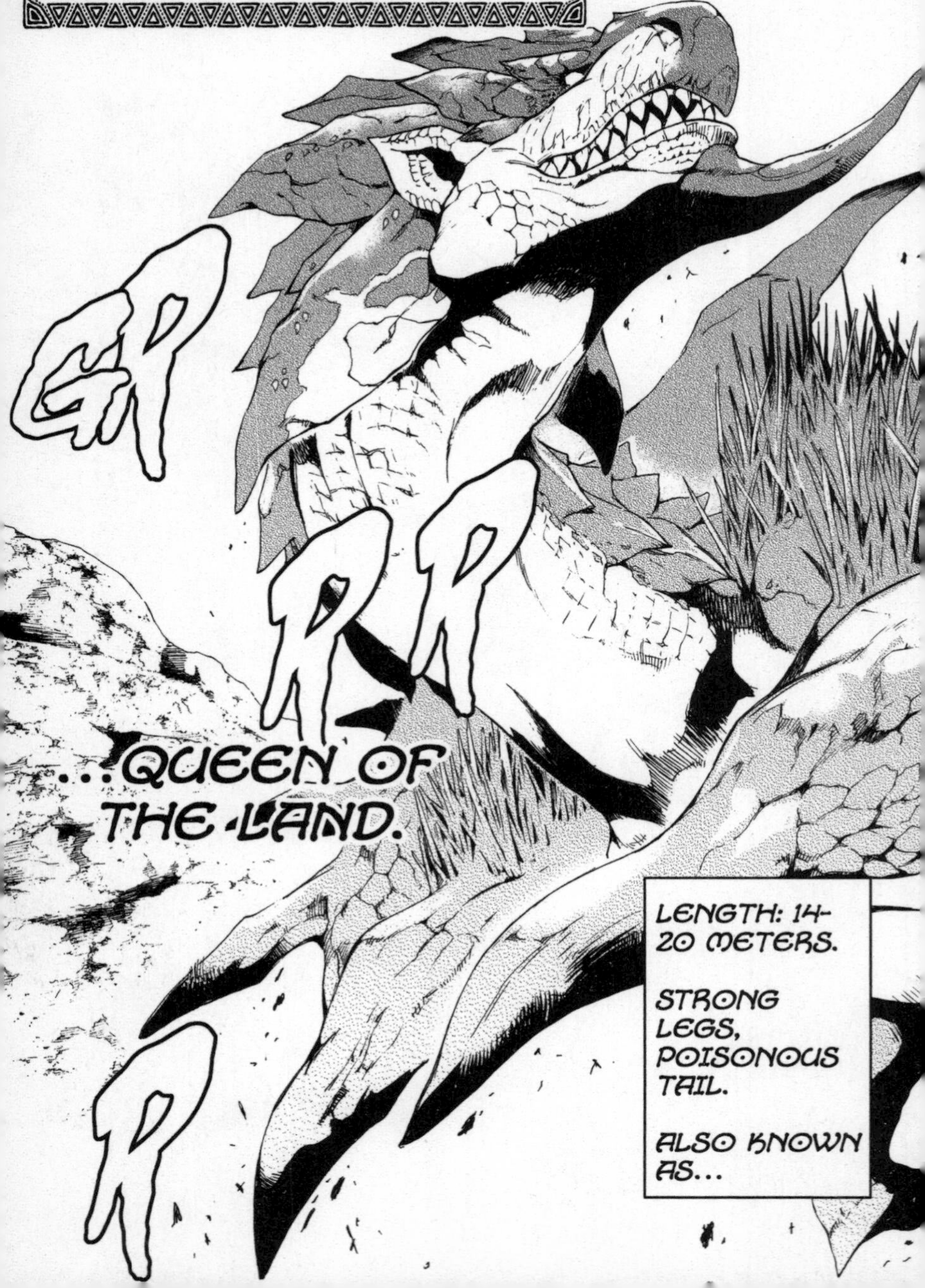
GR
RR
R
...QUEEN OF THE LAND.
LENGTH: 14-20 METERS.
STRONG LEGS, POISONOUS TAIL.
ALSO KNOWN AS...

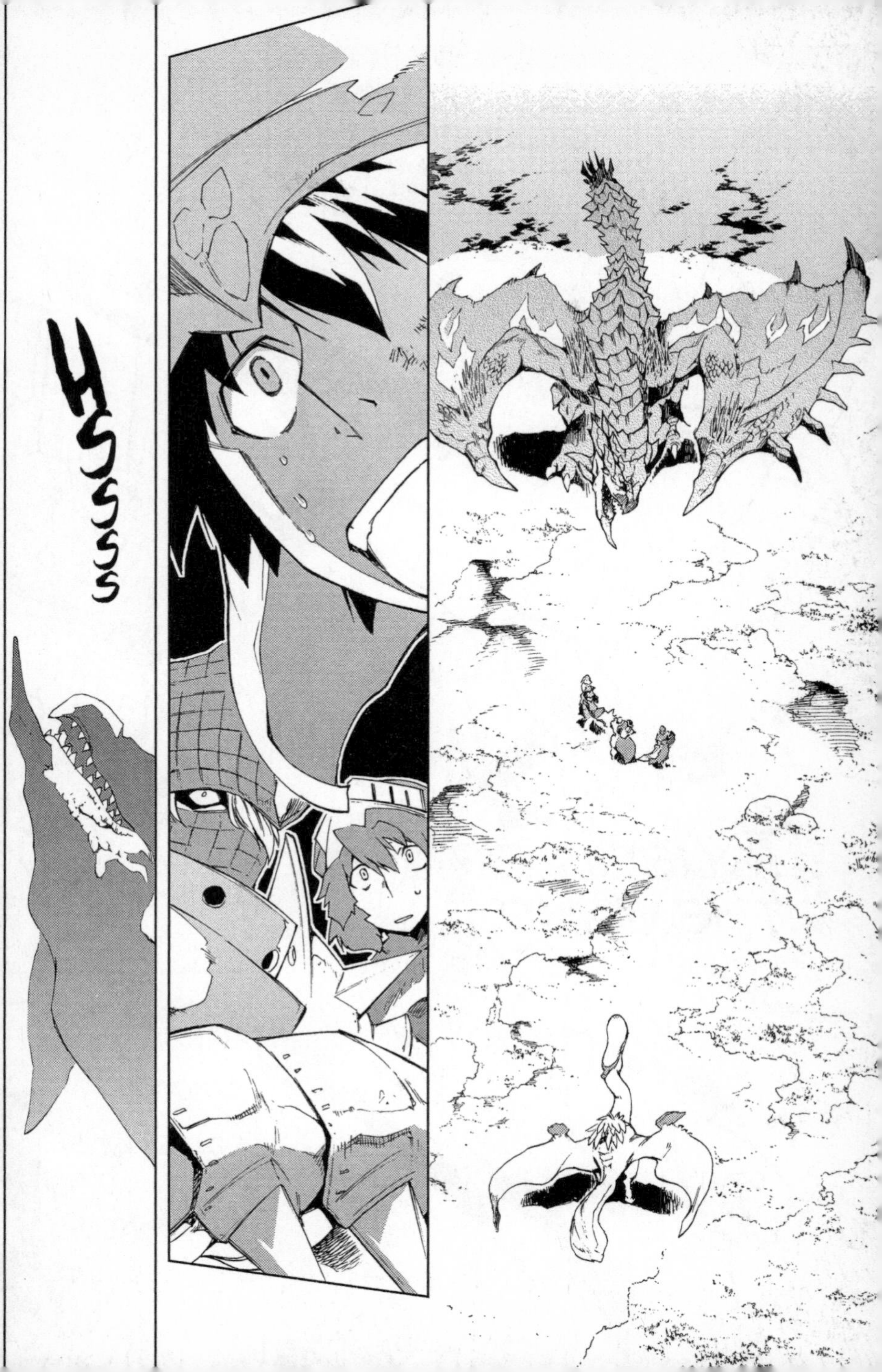
HSSSSS

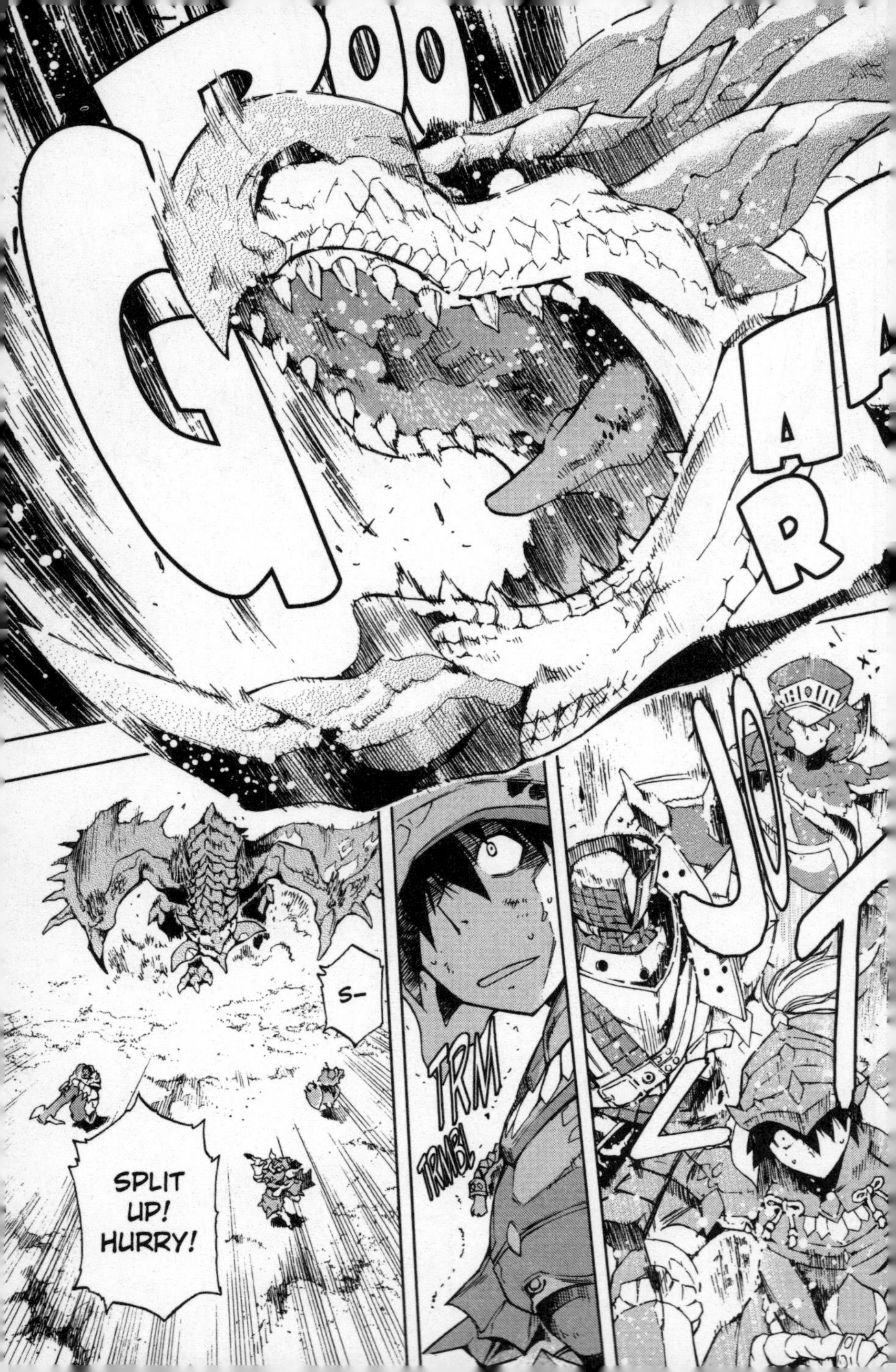
JOLT
TRM
TRMBL
S-
SPLIT UP! HURRY!

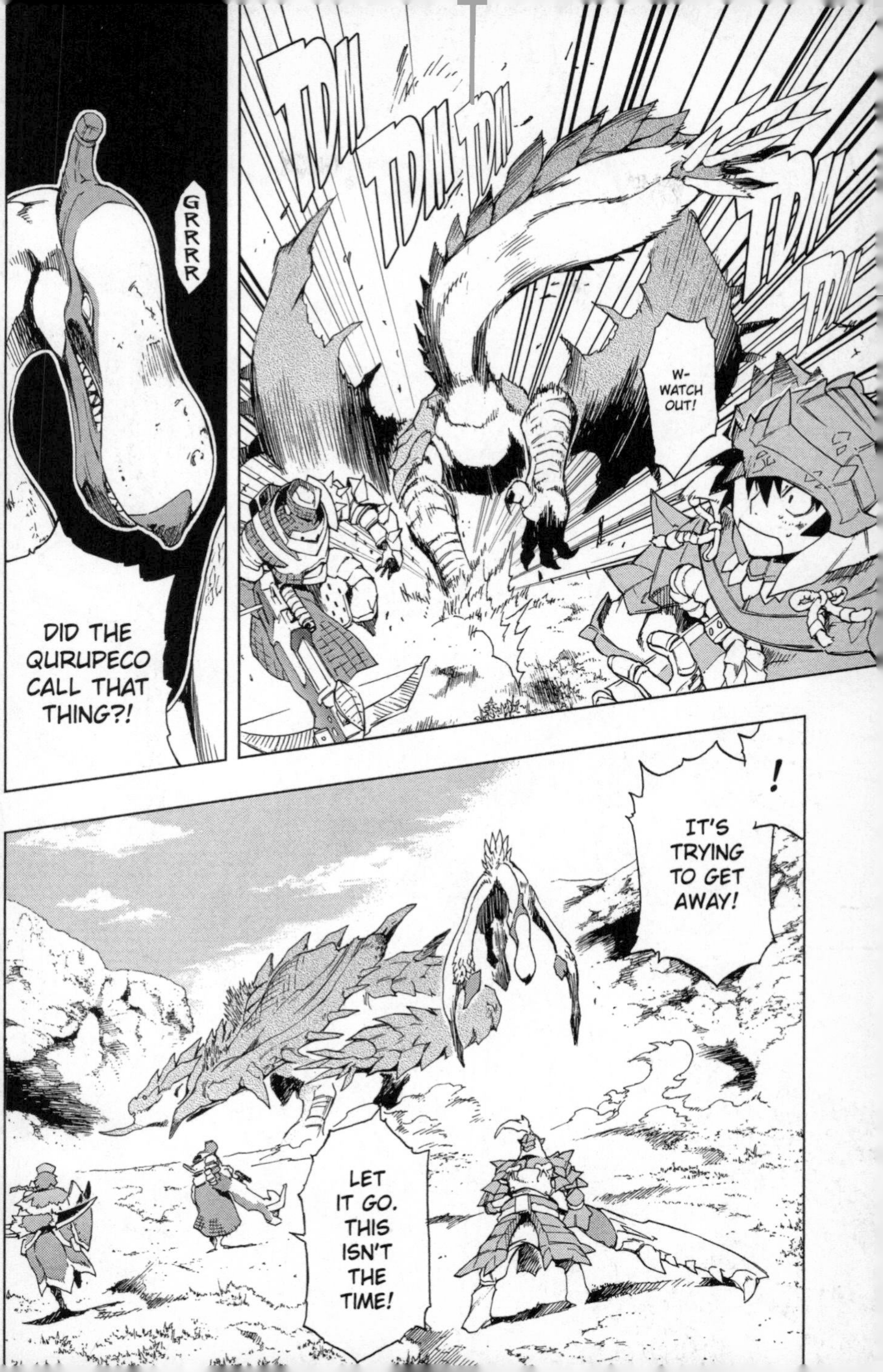
TDM TDM TDM
TDM TDM TDM
W-WATCH OUT!
GRRRR
DID THE QURUPECO CALL THAT THING?!
!
IT'S TRYING TO GET AWAY!
LET IT GO. THIS ISN'T THE TIME!

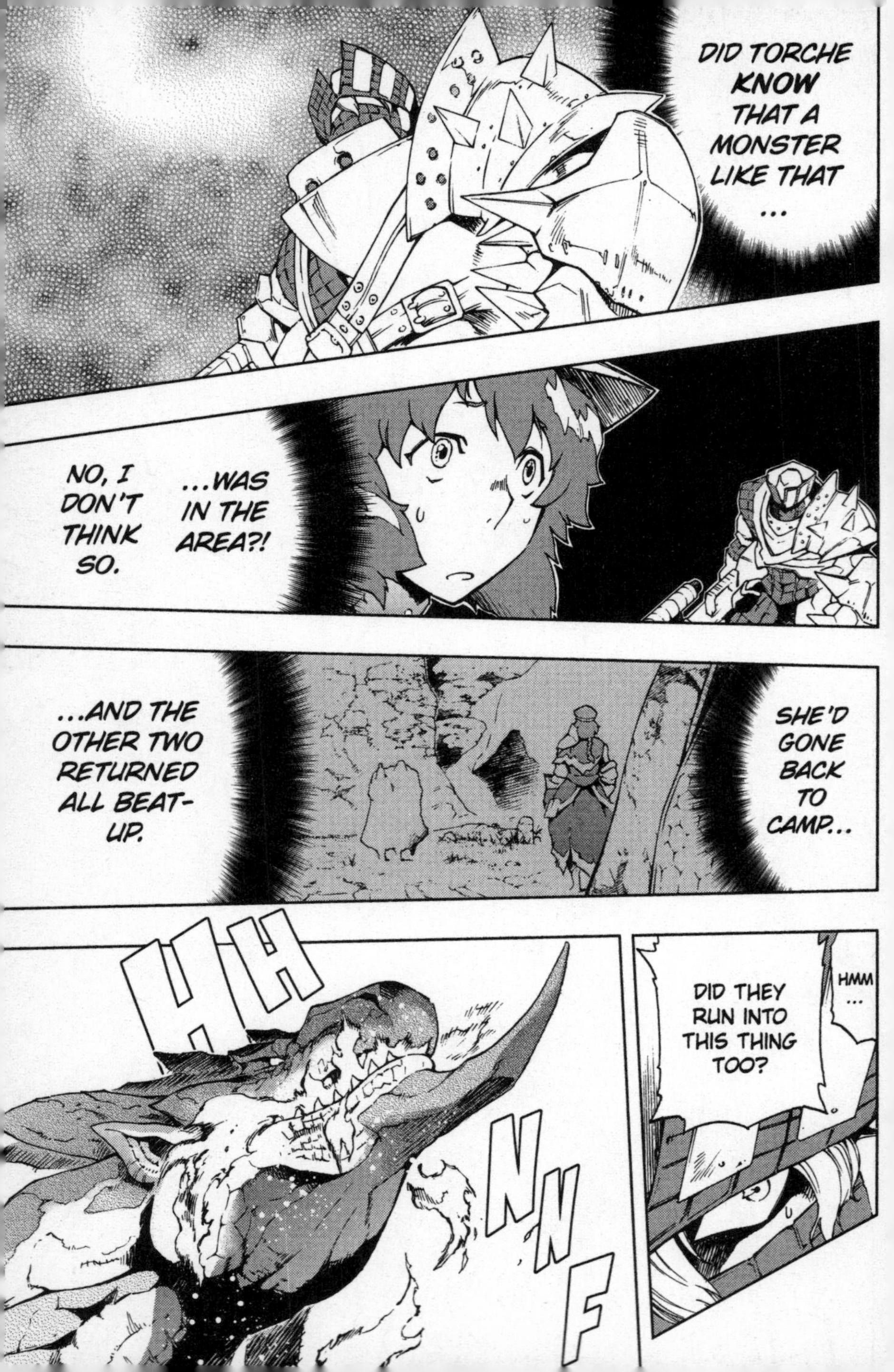
DID TORCHE KNOW THAT A MONSTER LIKE THAT ...
...WAS IN THE AREA?!
NO, I DON'T THINK SO.
SHE'D GONE BACK TO CAMP...
...AND THE OTHER TWO RETURNED ALL BEAT-UP.
HMM ...
DID THEY RUN INTO THIS THING TOO?
HH
NNNF

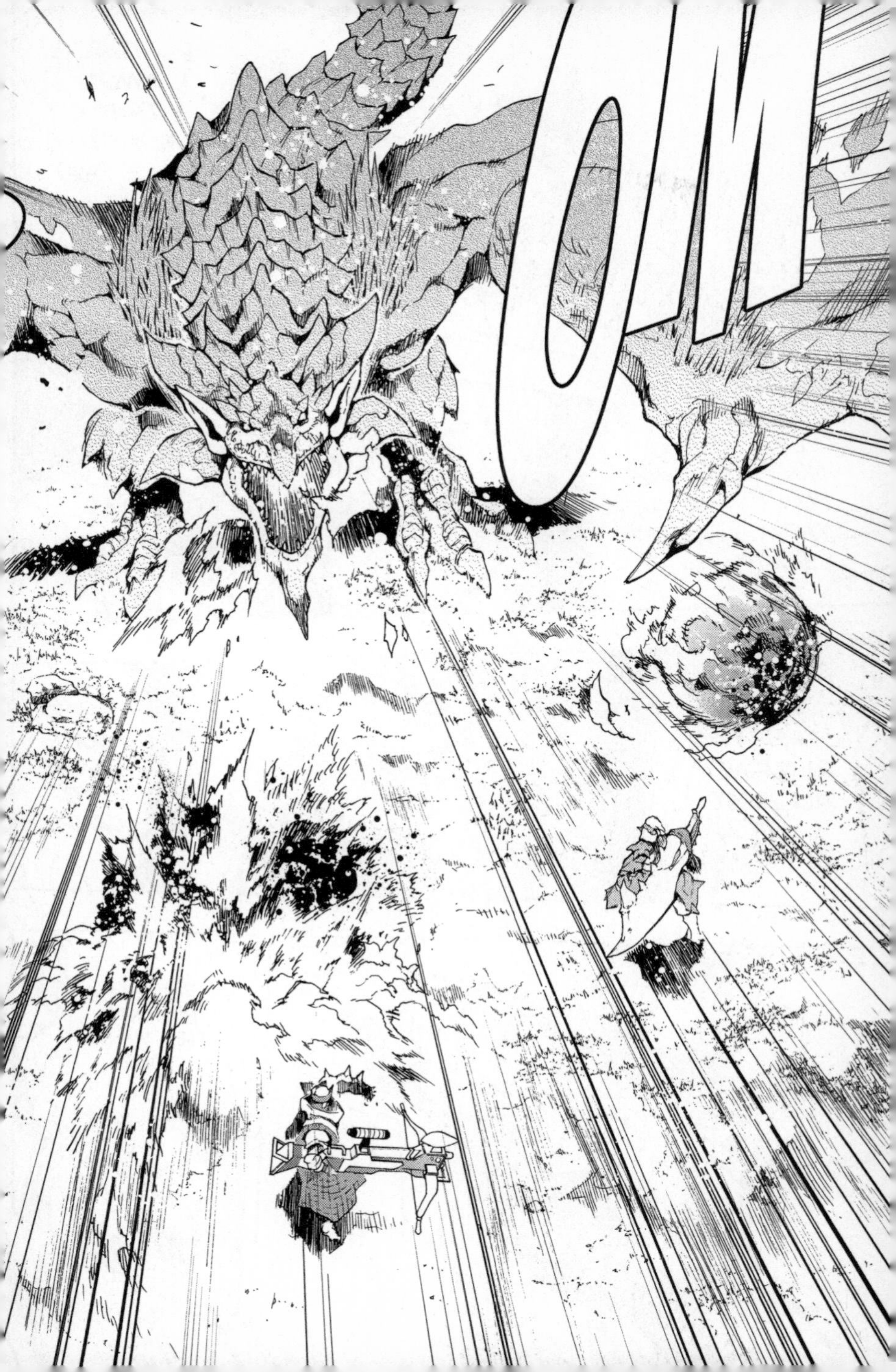
OM

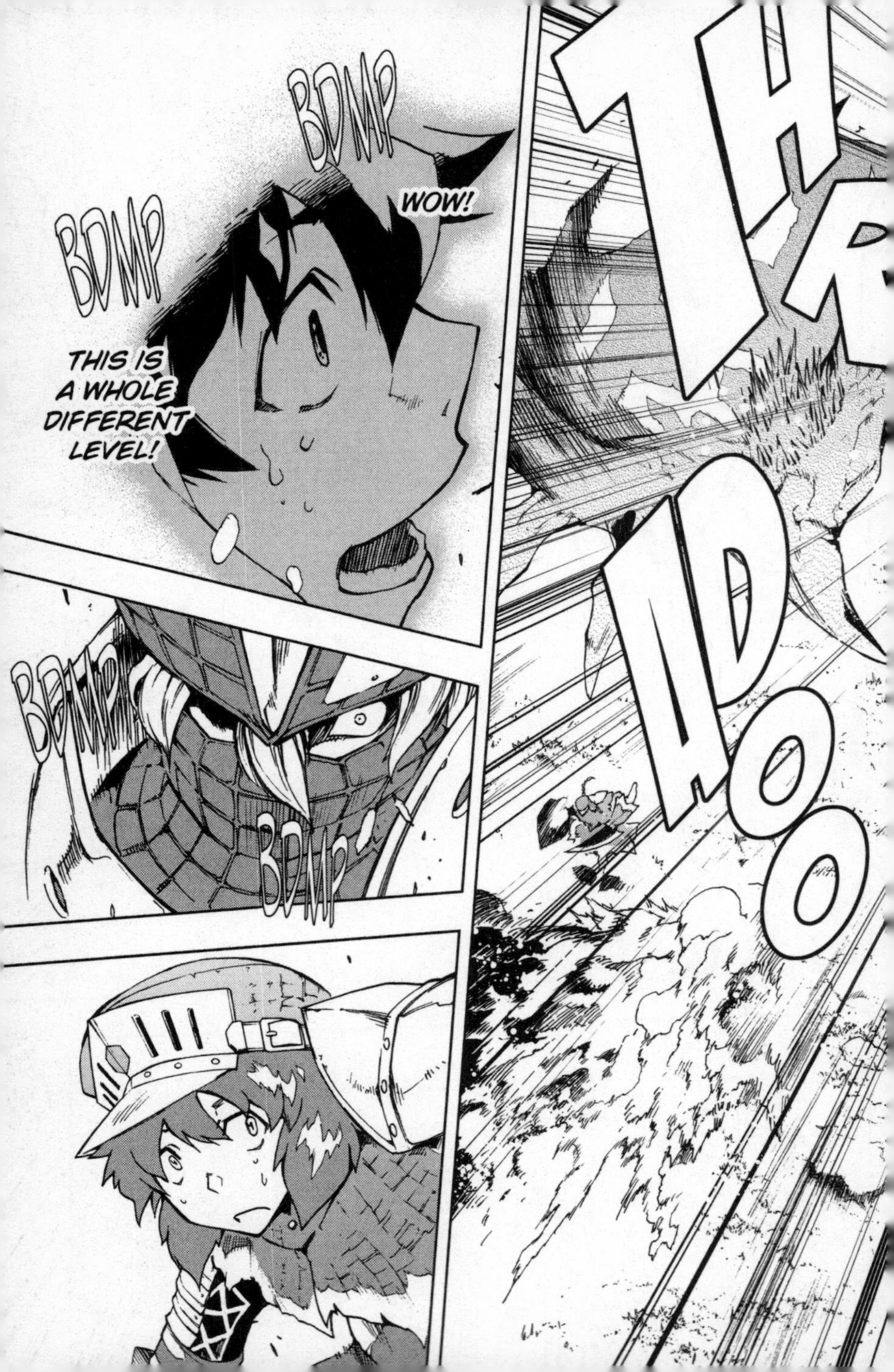
BDMP
WOW!
BDMP
THIS IS A WHOLE DIFFERENT LEVEL!
BDMP
BDMP

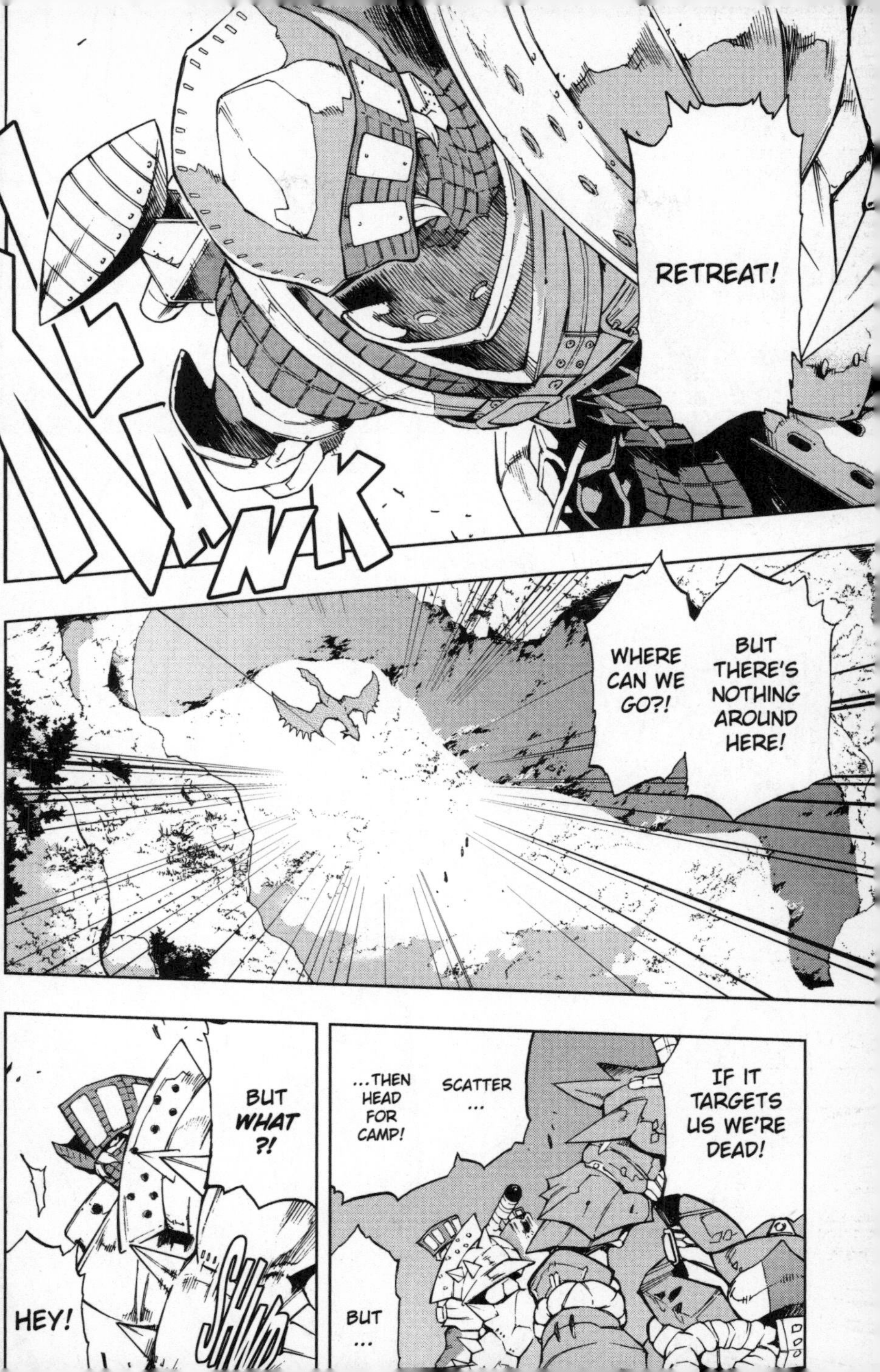
RETREAT!
WHANK
BUT THERE'S NOTHING AROUND HERE!
WHERE CAN WE GO?!
IF IT TARGETS US WE'RE DEAD!
SCATTER...
...THEN HEAD FOR CAMP!
BUT...
BUT ***WHAT*** ?!
HEY!

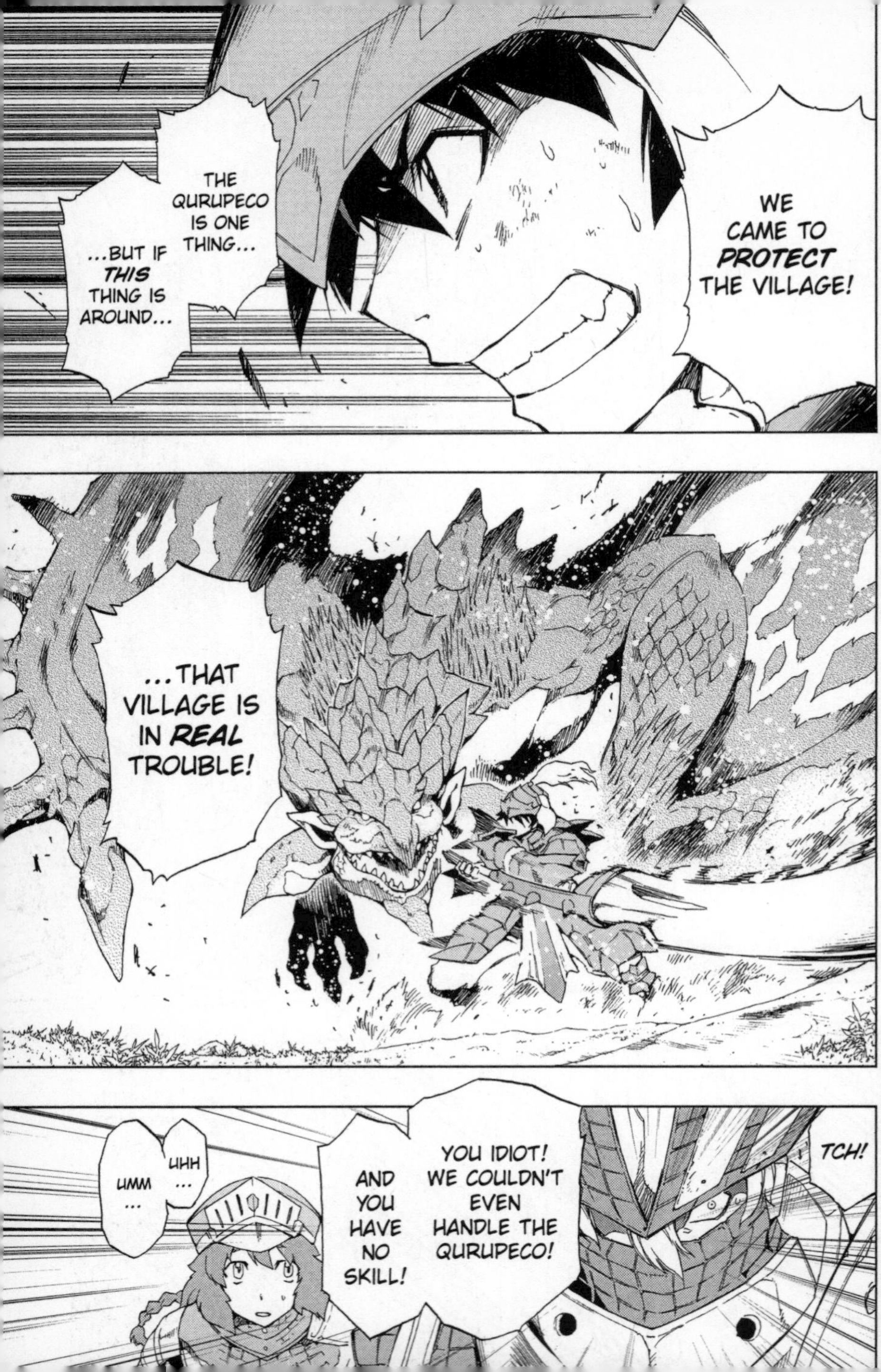
WE CAME TO PROTECT THE VILLAGE!
THE QURUPECO IS ONE THING...
...BUT IF THIS THING IS AROUND...
...THAT VILLAGE IS IN REAL TROUBLE!
TCH!
YOU IDIOT! WE COULDN'T EVEN HANDLE THE QURUPECO!
AND YOU HAVE NO SKILL!
UHH...
UMM...

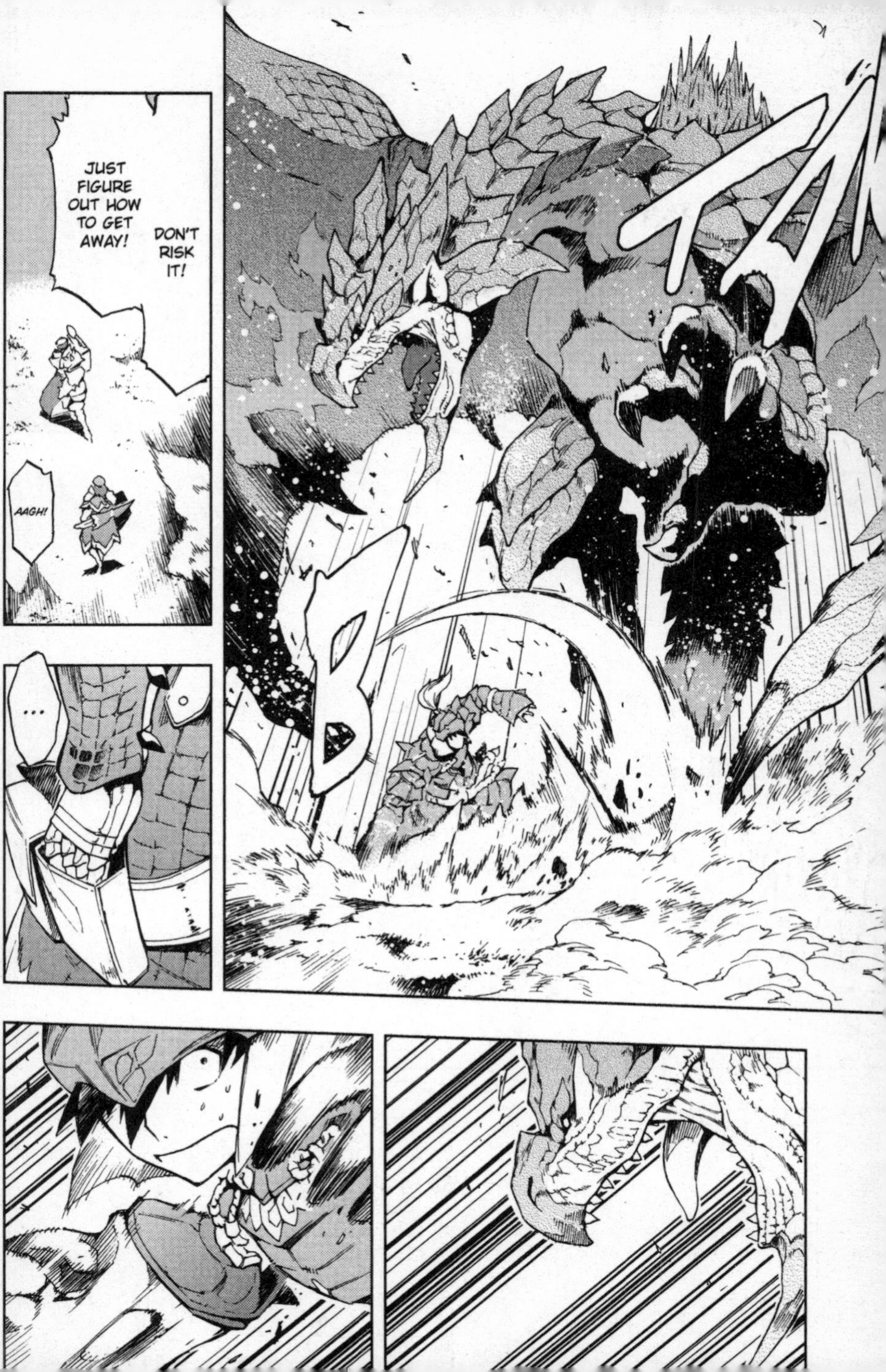
DON'T RISK IT!
JUST FIGURE OUT HOW TO GET AWAY!
AAGH!
...

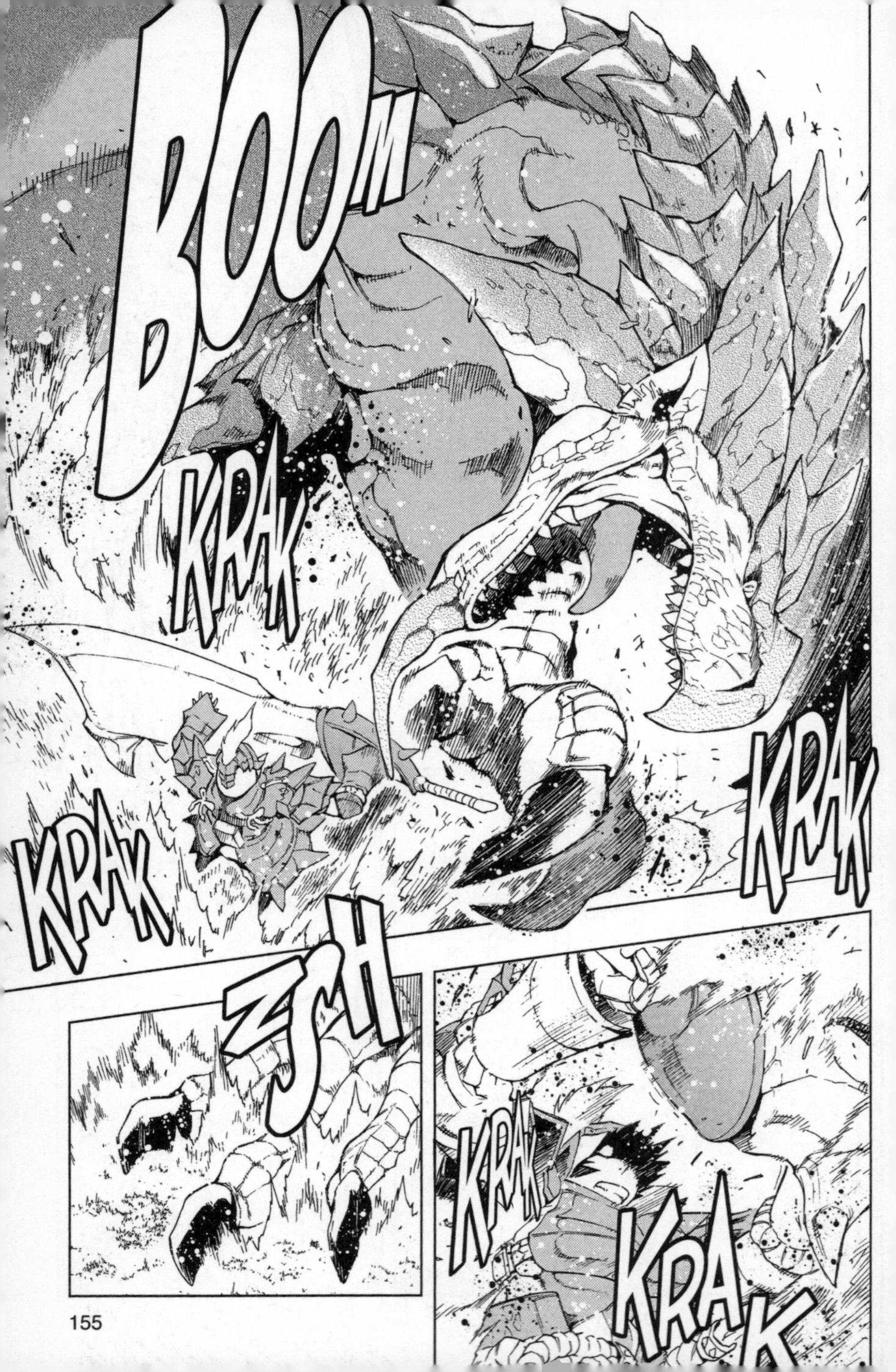
BOOOM
KRAK
KRAK
KRAK
KRAK
KRAK
ZSH

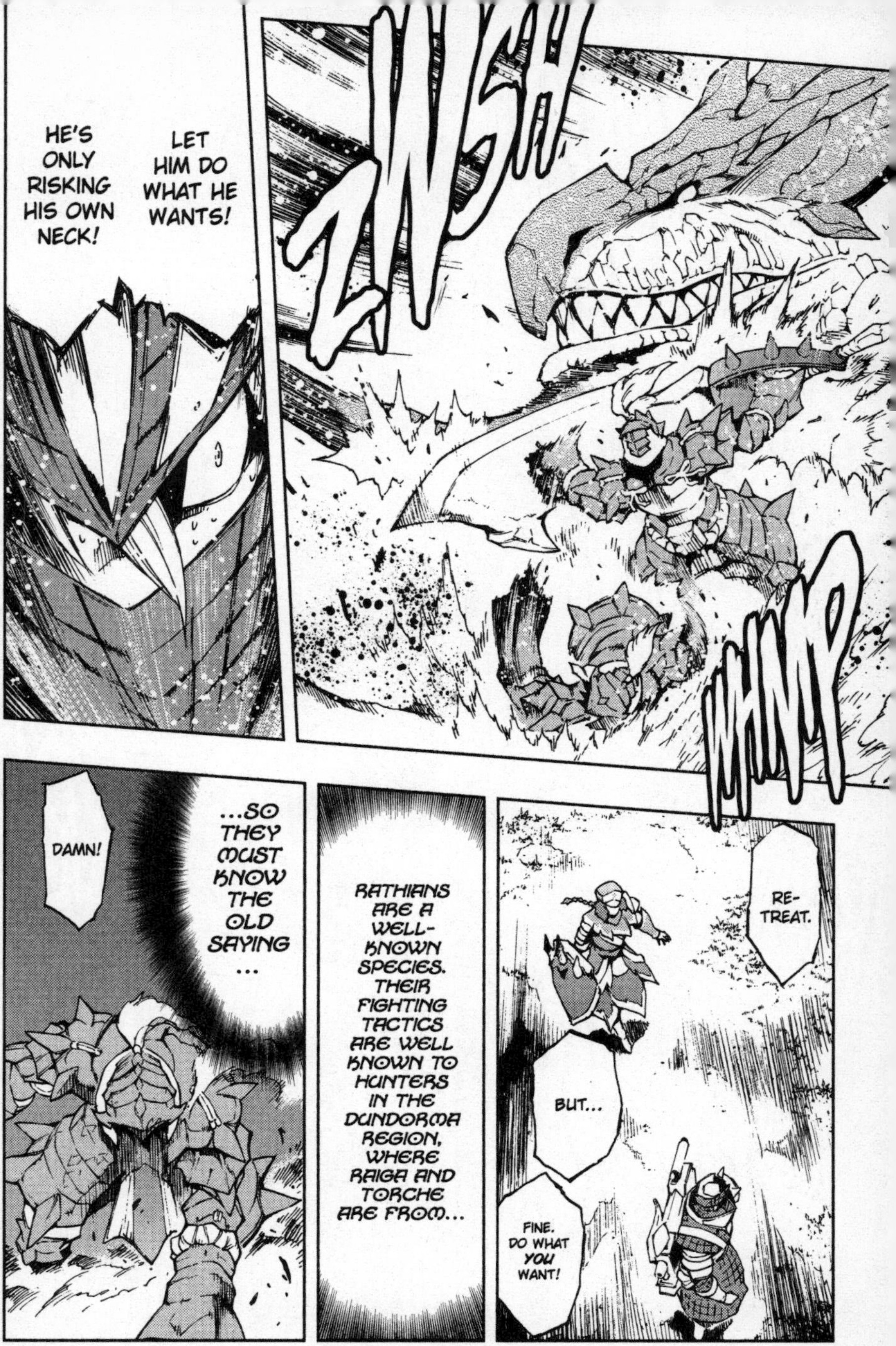
ZWSH
WHMP
LET HIM DO WHAT HE WANTS!
HE'S ONLY RISKING HIS OWN NECK!
RE-TREAT.
BUT...
FINE. DO WHAT YOU WANT!
RATHIANS ARE A WELL-KNOWN SPECIES. THEIR FIGHTING TACTICS ARE WELL KNOWN TO HUNTERS IN THE DUNDORMA REGION, WHERE RAIGA AND TORCHE ARE FROM...
...SO THEY MUST KNOW THE OLD SAYING...
DAMN!

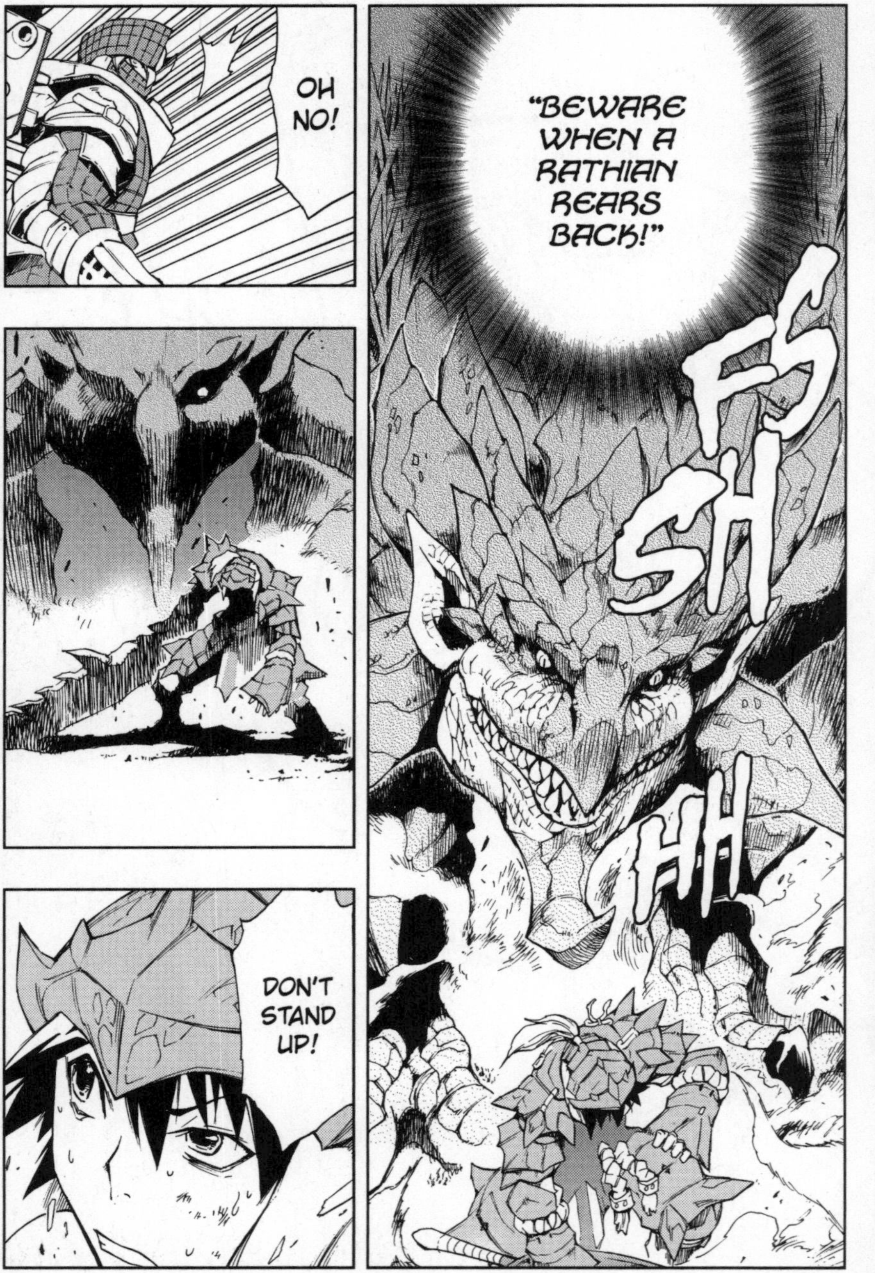
"BEWARE WHEN A RATHIAN REARS BACK!"
FSSHHH
OH NO!
DON'T STAND UP!

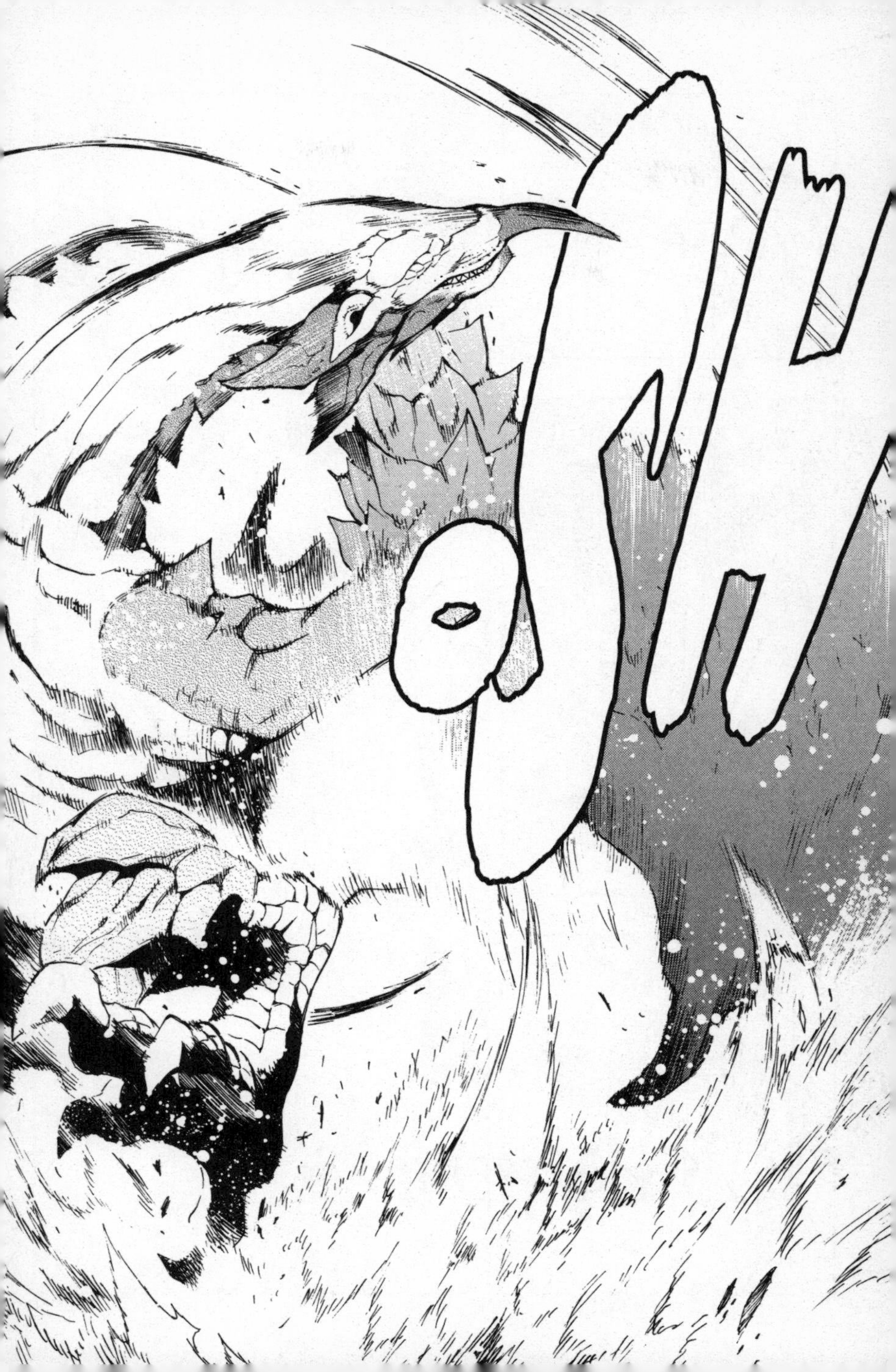

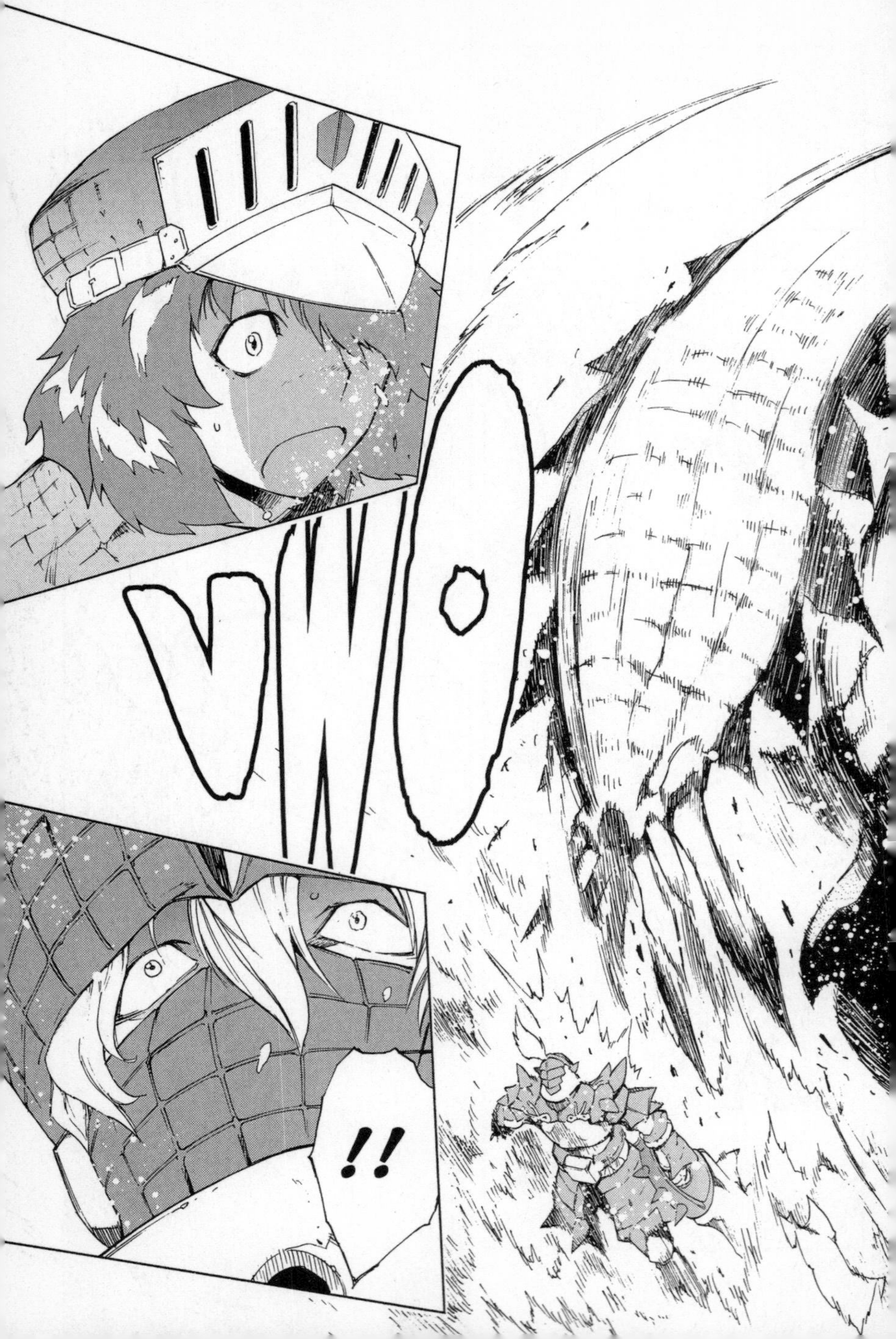
VWO
!!

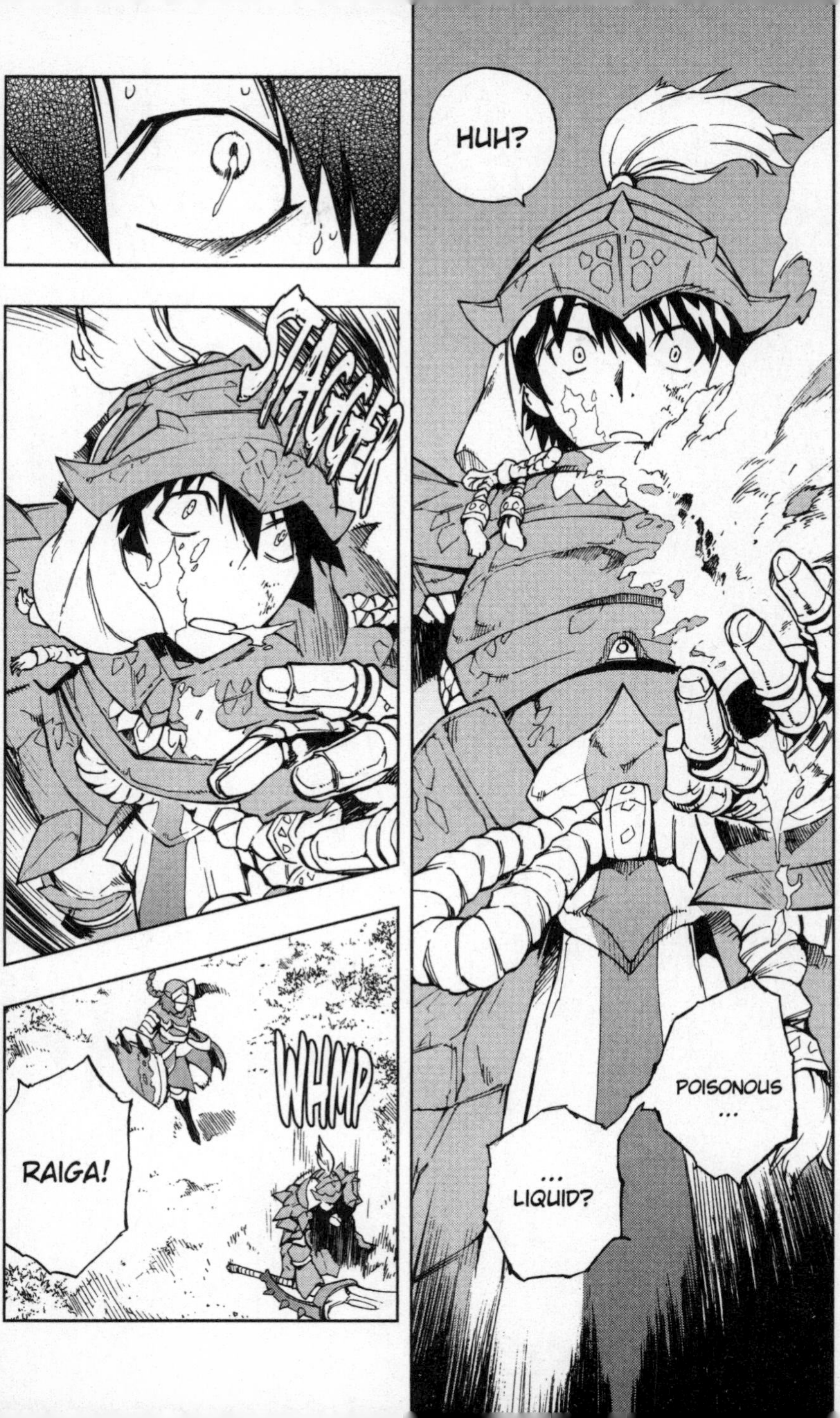
HUH?
POISONOUS ...
... LIQUID?
WHMP
RAIGA!

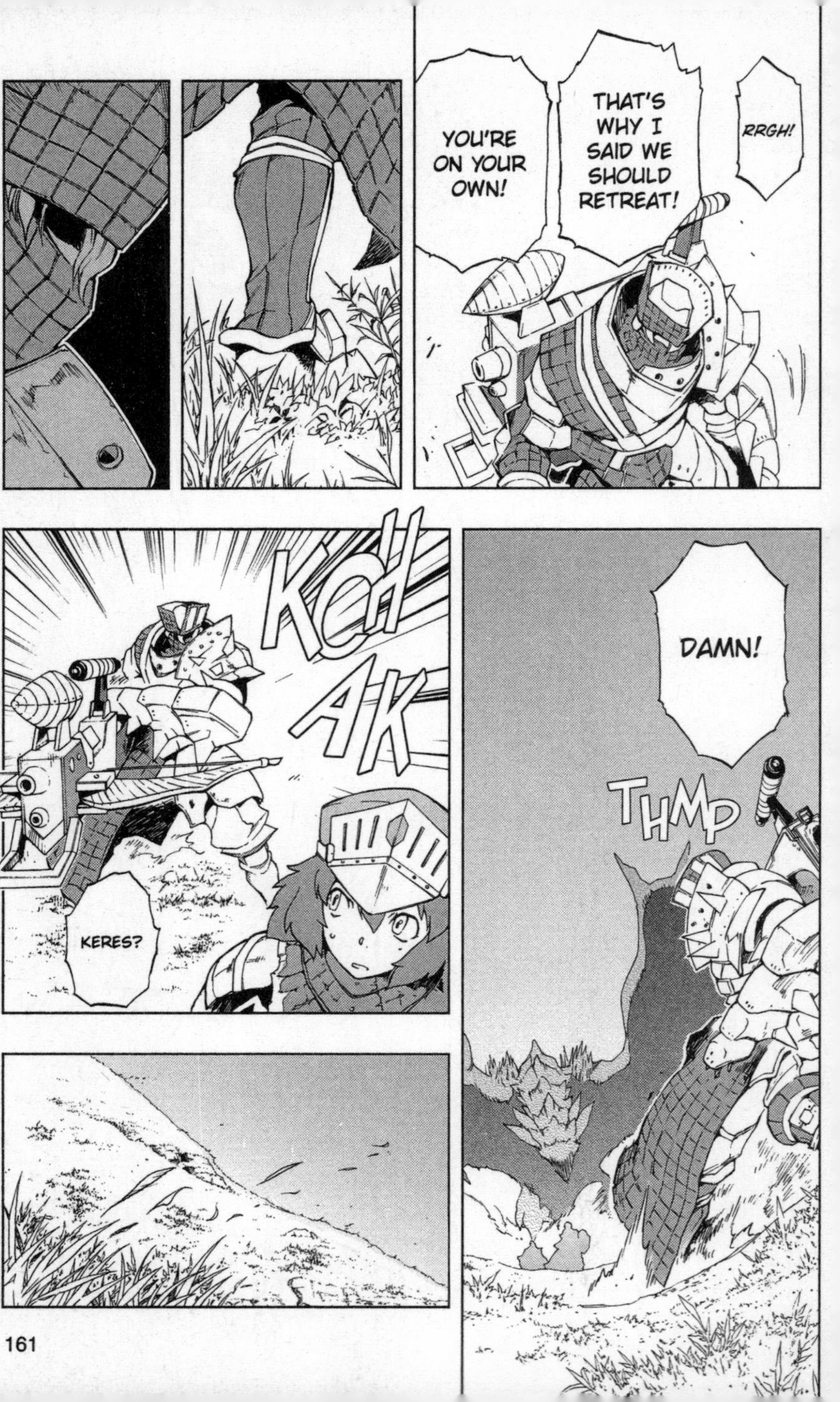
RRGH!
THAT'S WHY I SAID WE SHOULD RETREAT!
YOU'RE ON YOUR OWN!
DAMN!
THMP
KCHAK
KERES?

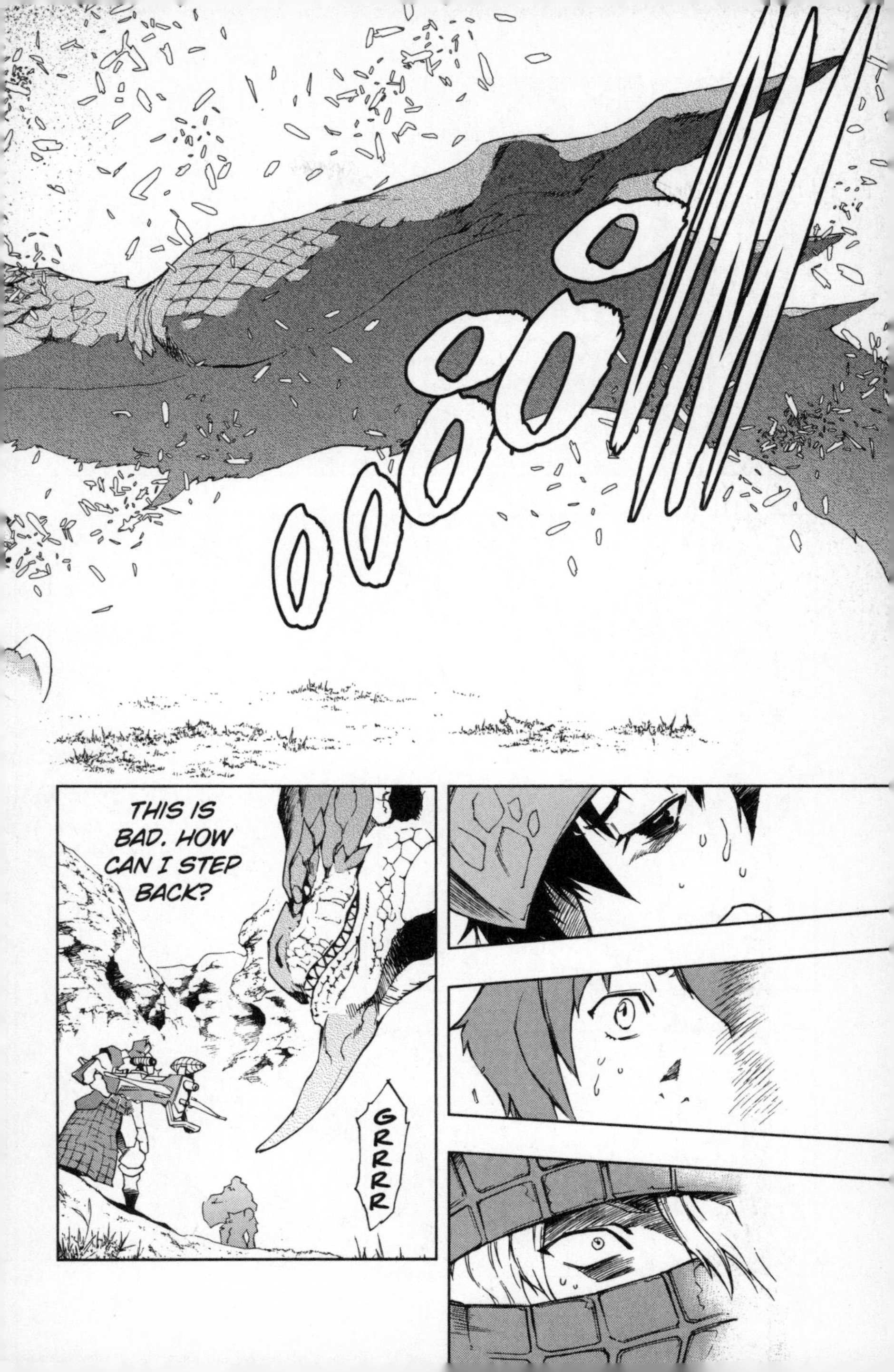
THIS IS BAD. HOW CAN I STEP BACK?
GRRRR

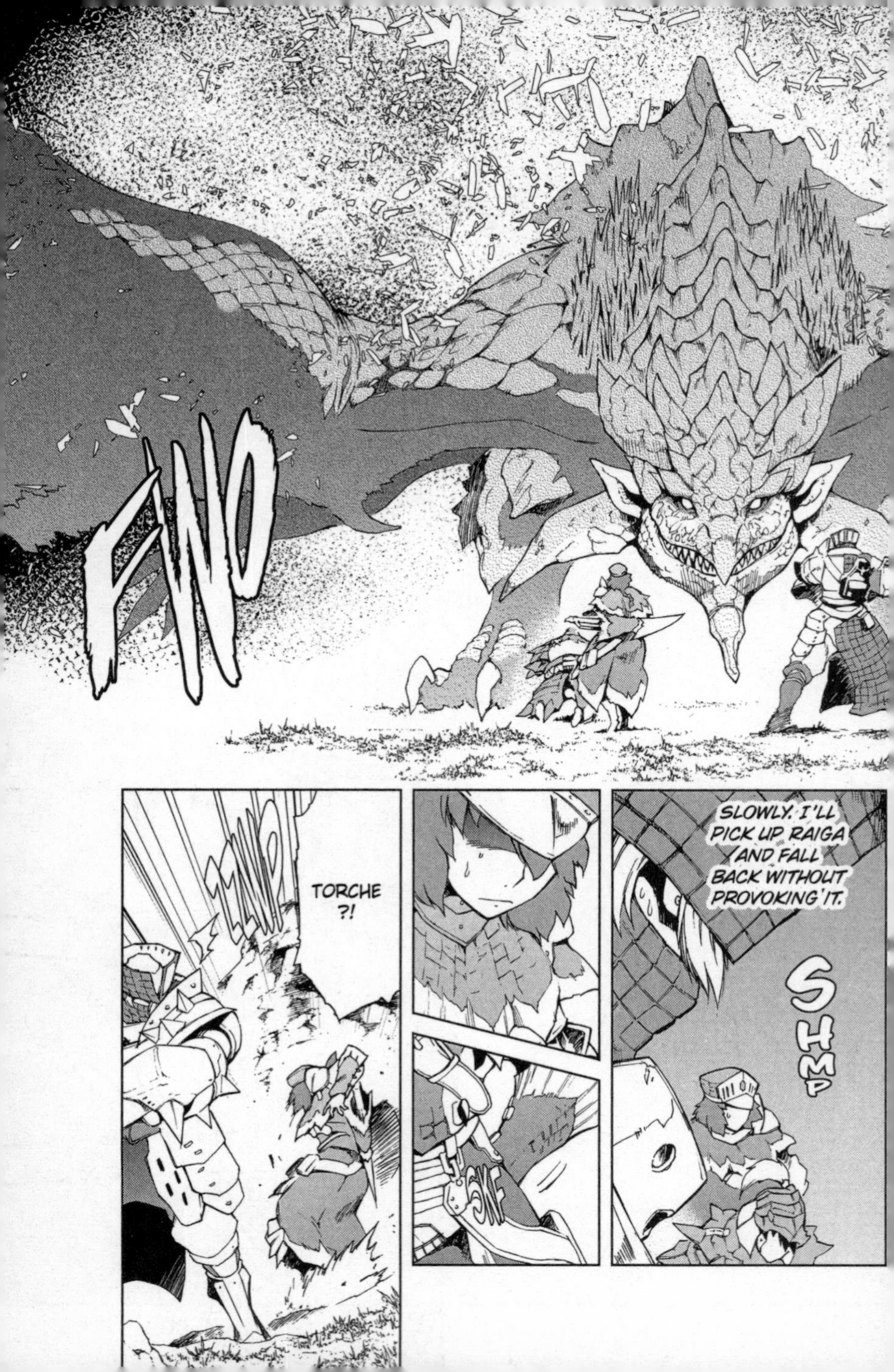
FNO
SLOWLY. I'LL PICK UP RAIGA AND FALL BACK WITHOUT PROVOKING IT.
SHMP
TORCHE ?!

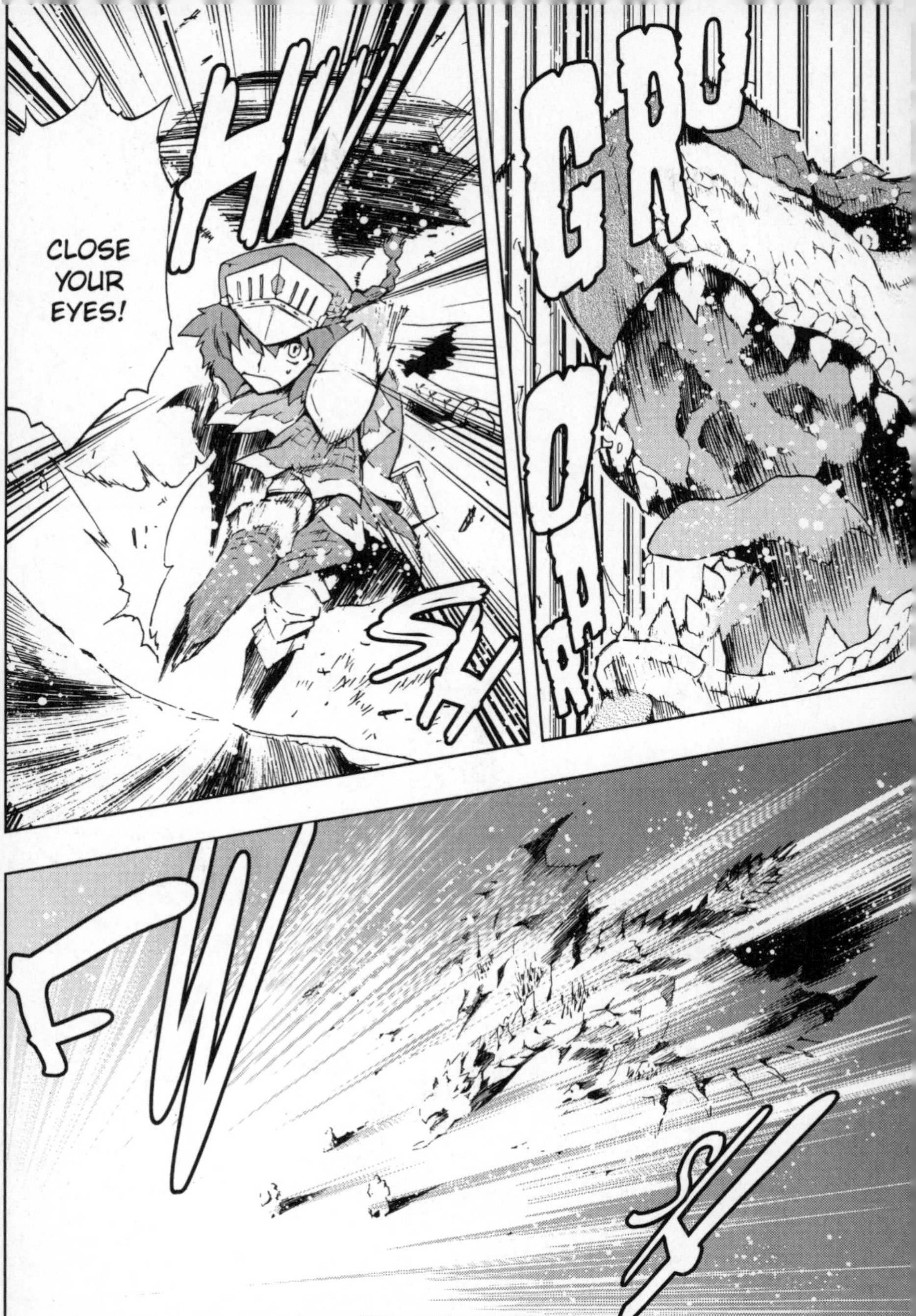
GROOAR
CLOSE YOUR EYES!
SH
SH

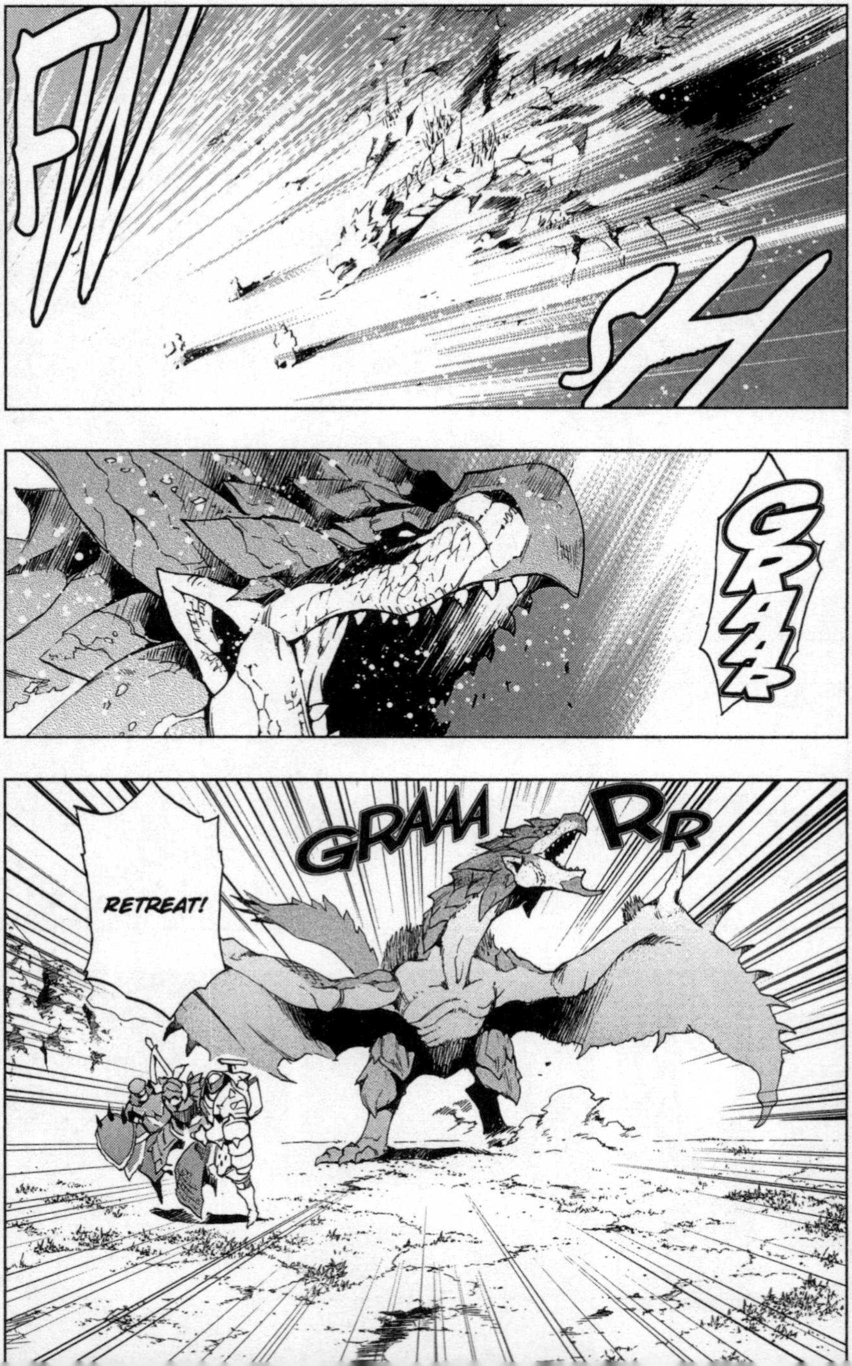
FW
SH
GRAAR
GRAAA RR
RETREAT!

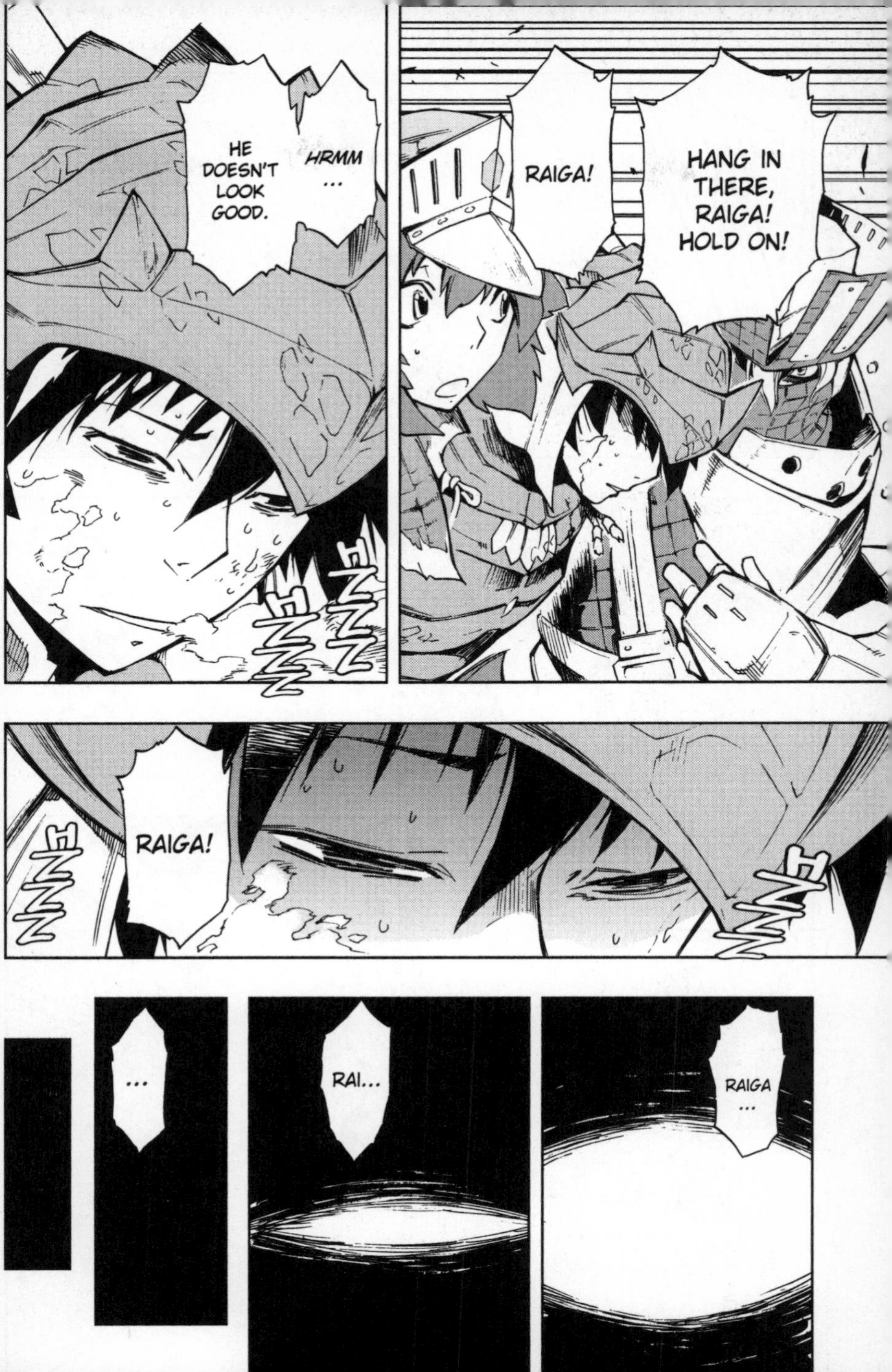
HANG IN THERE, RAIGA! HOLD ON!
RAIGA!
HRMM ...
HE DOESN'T LOOK GOOD.
RAIGA!
RAIGA ...
RAI...
...

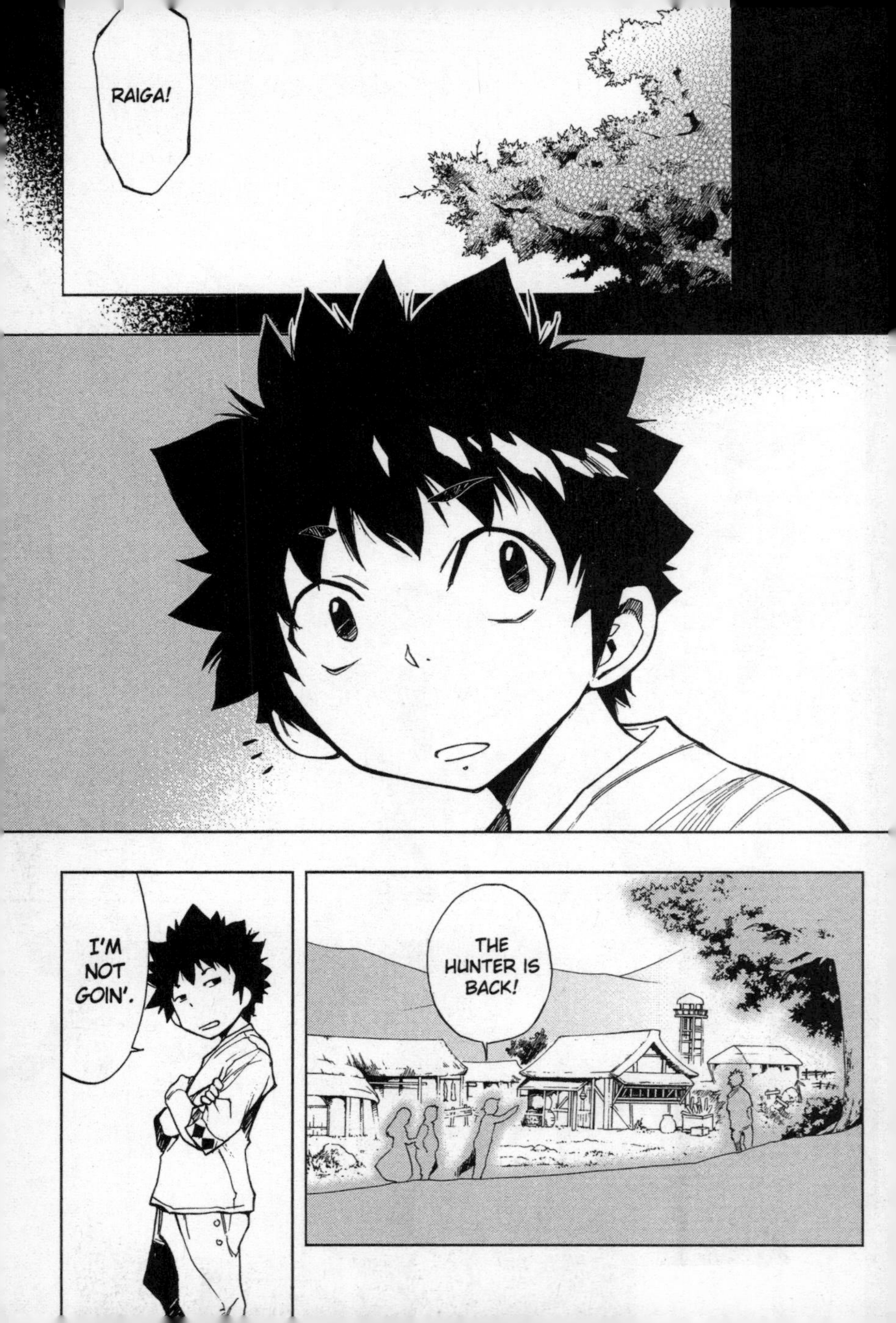
RAIGA!
THE HUNTER IS BACK!
I'M NOT GOIN'.

CHAPTER 6: BEXEL

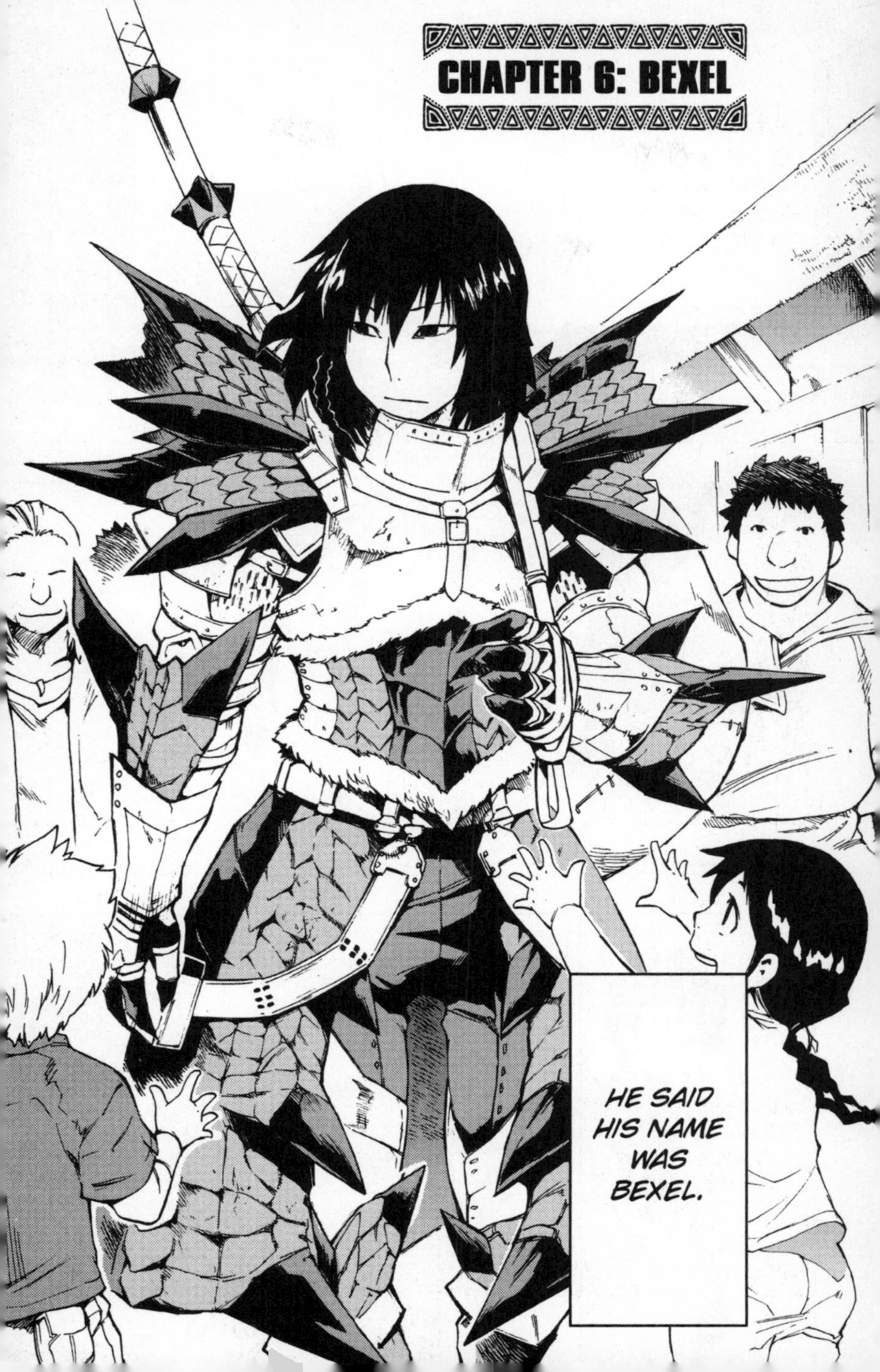
HE SAID HIS NAME WAS BEXEL.

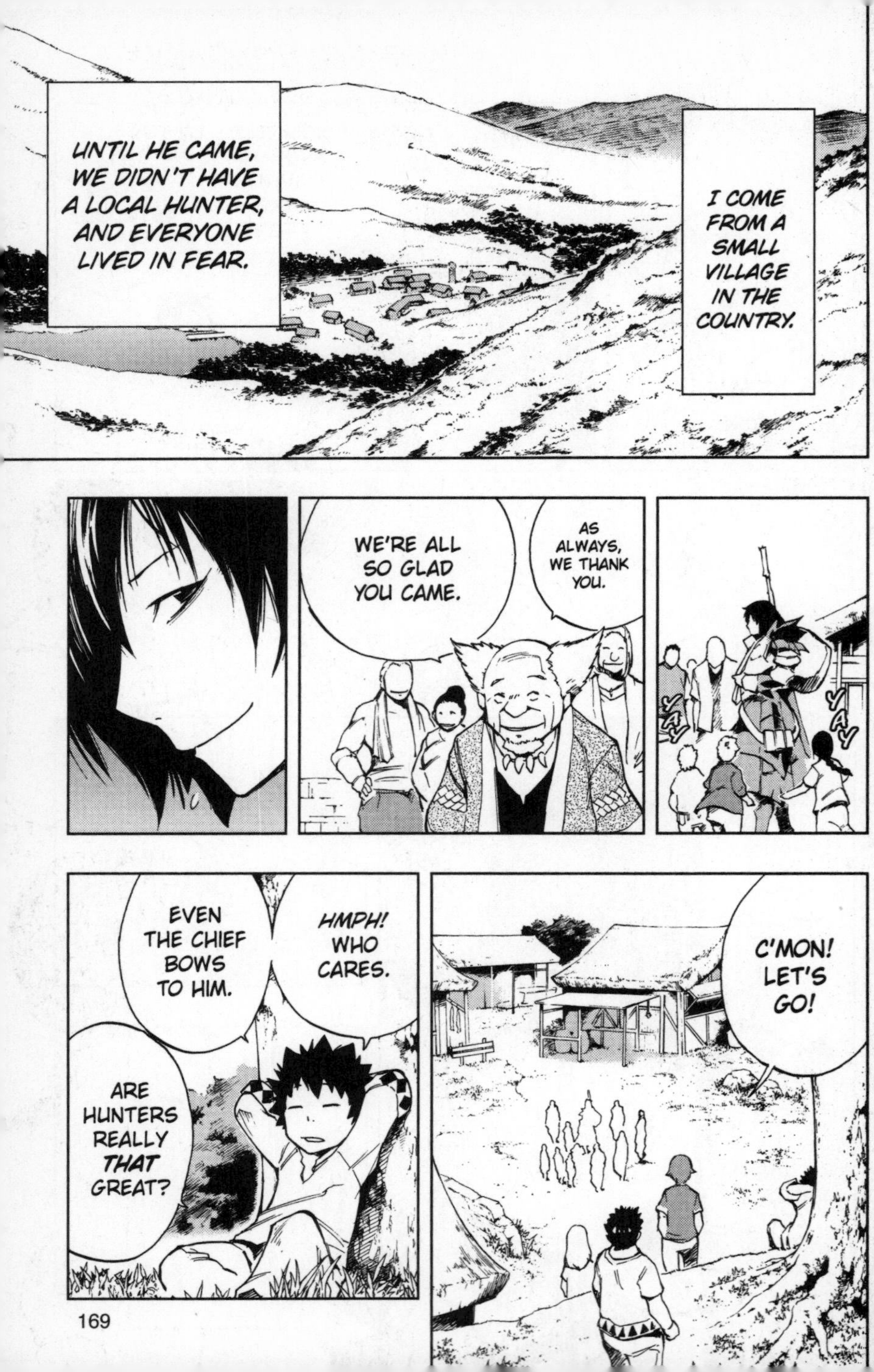
I COME FROM A SMALL VILLAGE IN THE COUNTRY.
UNTIL HE CAME, WE DIDN'T HAVE A LOCAL HUNTER, AND EVERYONE LIVED IN FEAR.
YAY
YAY
AS ALWAYS, WE THANK YOU.
WE'RE ALL SO GLAD YOU CAME.
C'MON! LET'S GO!
EVEN THE CHIEF BOWS TO HIM.
HMPH! WHO CARES.
ARE HUNTERS REALLY THAT GREAT?

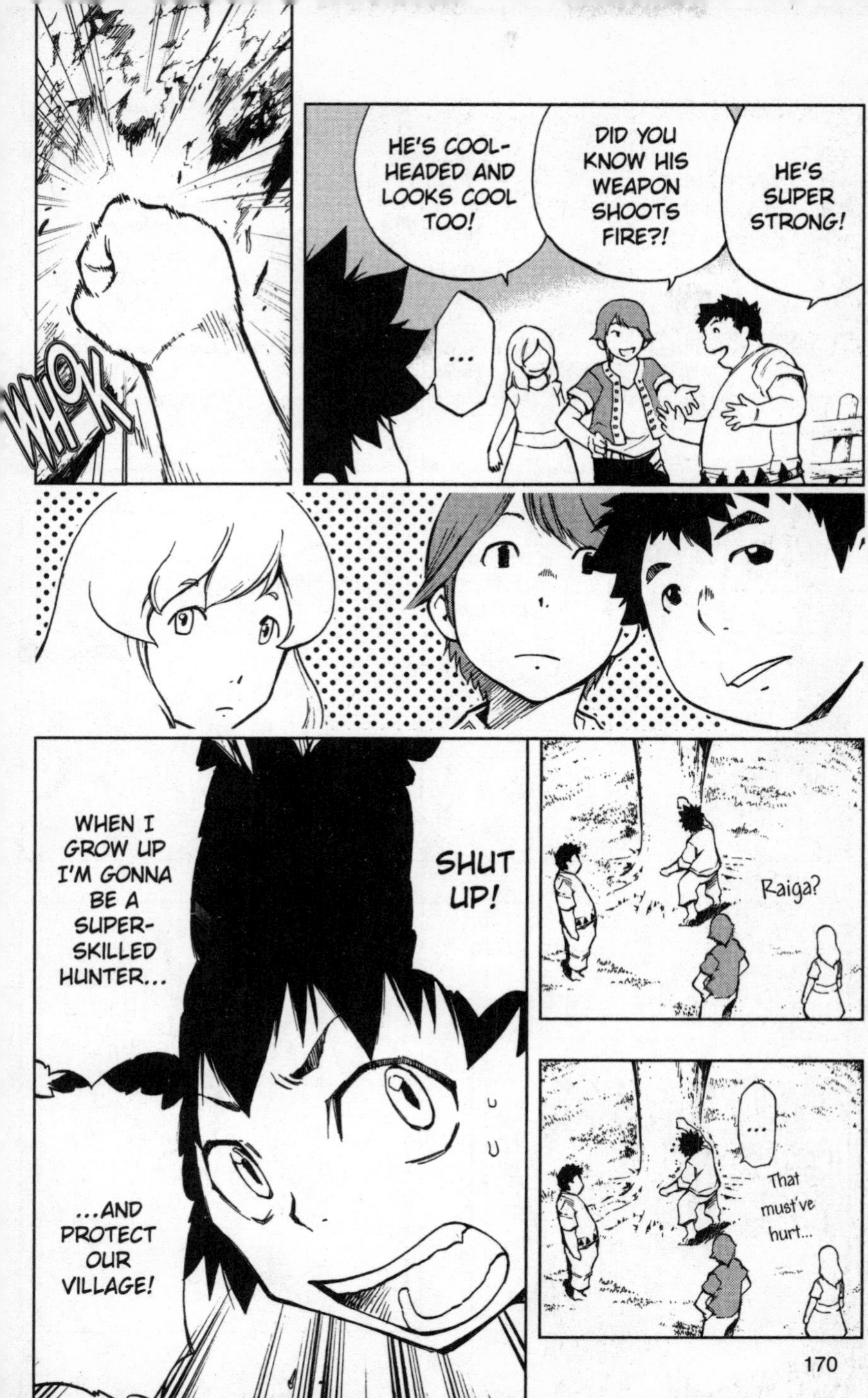
HE'S SUPER STRONG!
DID YOU KNOW HIS WEAPON SHOOTS FIRE?!
HE'S COOL-HEADED AND LOOKS COOL TOO!
...
WHOK
Raiga?
...
That must've hurt...
SHUT UP!
WHEN I GROW UP I'M GONNA BE A SUPER-SKILLED HUNTER...
...AND PROTECT OUR VILLAGE!

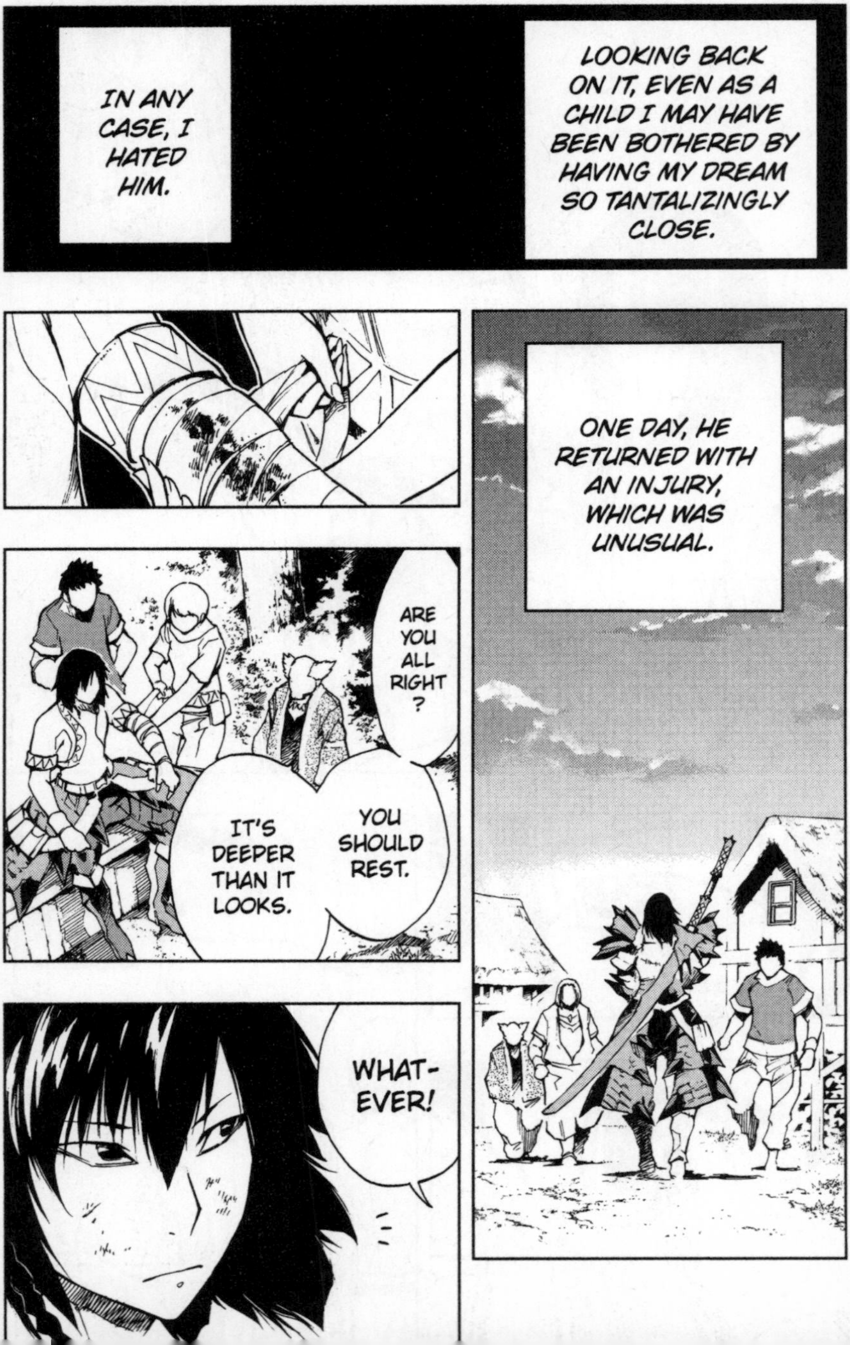
LOOKING BACK ON IT, EVEN AS A CHILD I MAY HAVE BEEN BOTHERED BY HAVING MY DREAM SO TANTALIZINGLY CLOSE.
IN ANY CASE, I HATED HIM.
ONE DAY, HE RETURNED WITH AN INJURY, WHICH WAS UNUSUAL.
ARE YOU ALL RIGHT?
YOU SHOULD REST.
IT'S DEEPER THAN IT LOOKS.
WHAT-EVER!

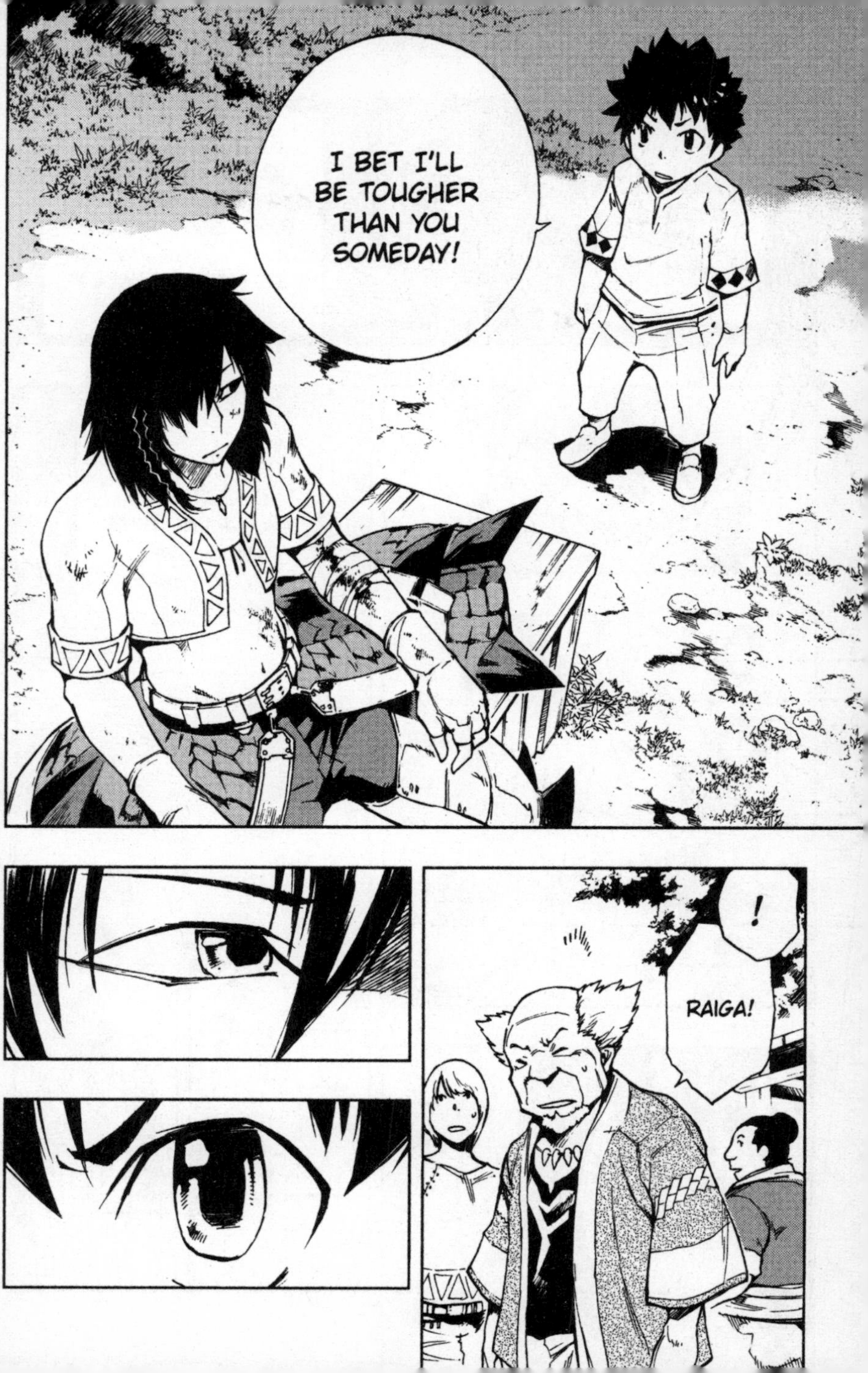
I BET I'LL BE TOUGHER THAN YOU SOMEDAY!
!
RAIGA!

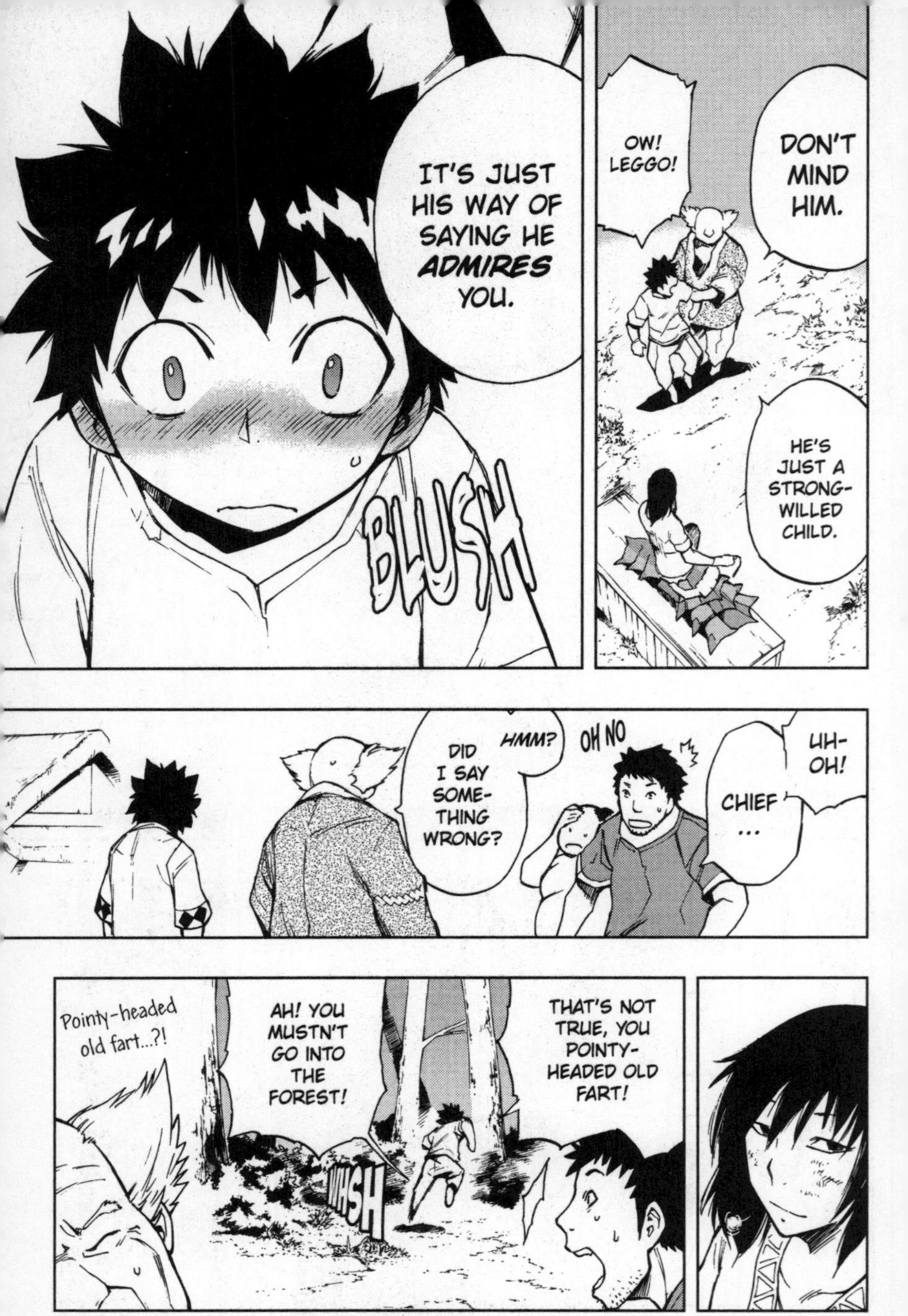
DON'T MIND HIM.
OW! LEGGO!
HE'S JUST A STRONG-WILLED CHILD.
IT'S JUST HIS WAY OF SAYING HE *ADMIRES* YOU.
BLUSH
UH-OH!
CHIEF ...
OH NO
HMM?
DID I SAY SOMETHING WRONG?
THAT'S NOT TRUE, YOU POINTY-HEADED OLD FART!
AH! YOU MUSTN'T GO INTO THE FOREST!
WHSH
Pointy-headed old fart...?!

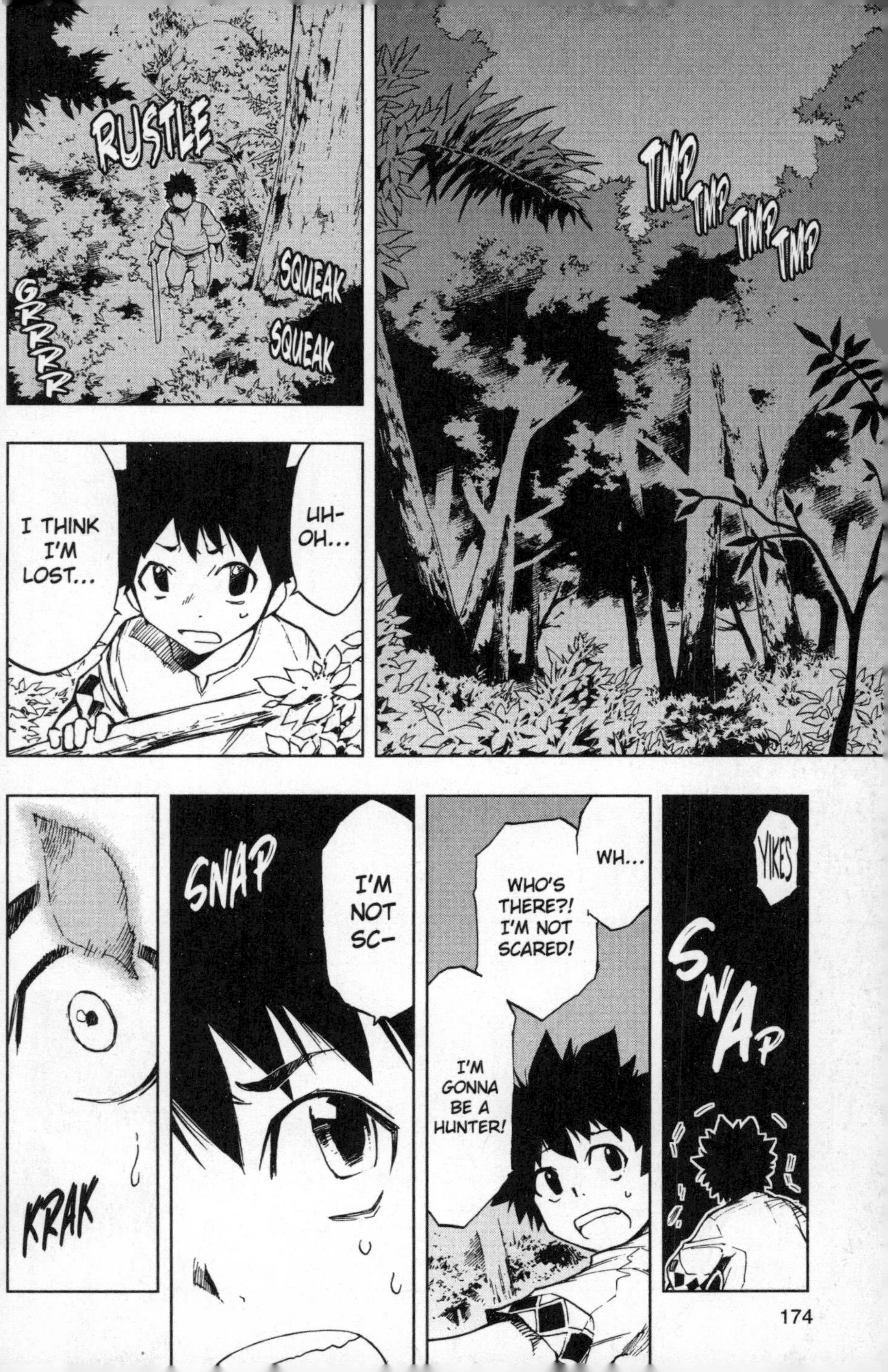
TMP TMP TMP TMP
RUSTLE
SQUEAK
SQUEAK
GRRRRR
UH-OH...
I THINK I'M LOST...
YIKES
SNAP
WH...
WHO'S THERE?! I'M NOT SCARED!
I'M GONNA BE A HUNTER!
SNAP
I'M NOT SC-
KRAK

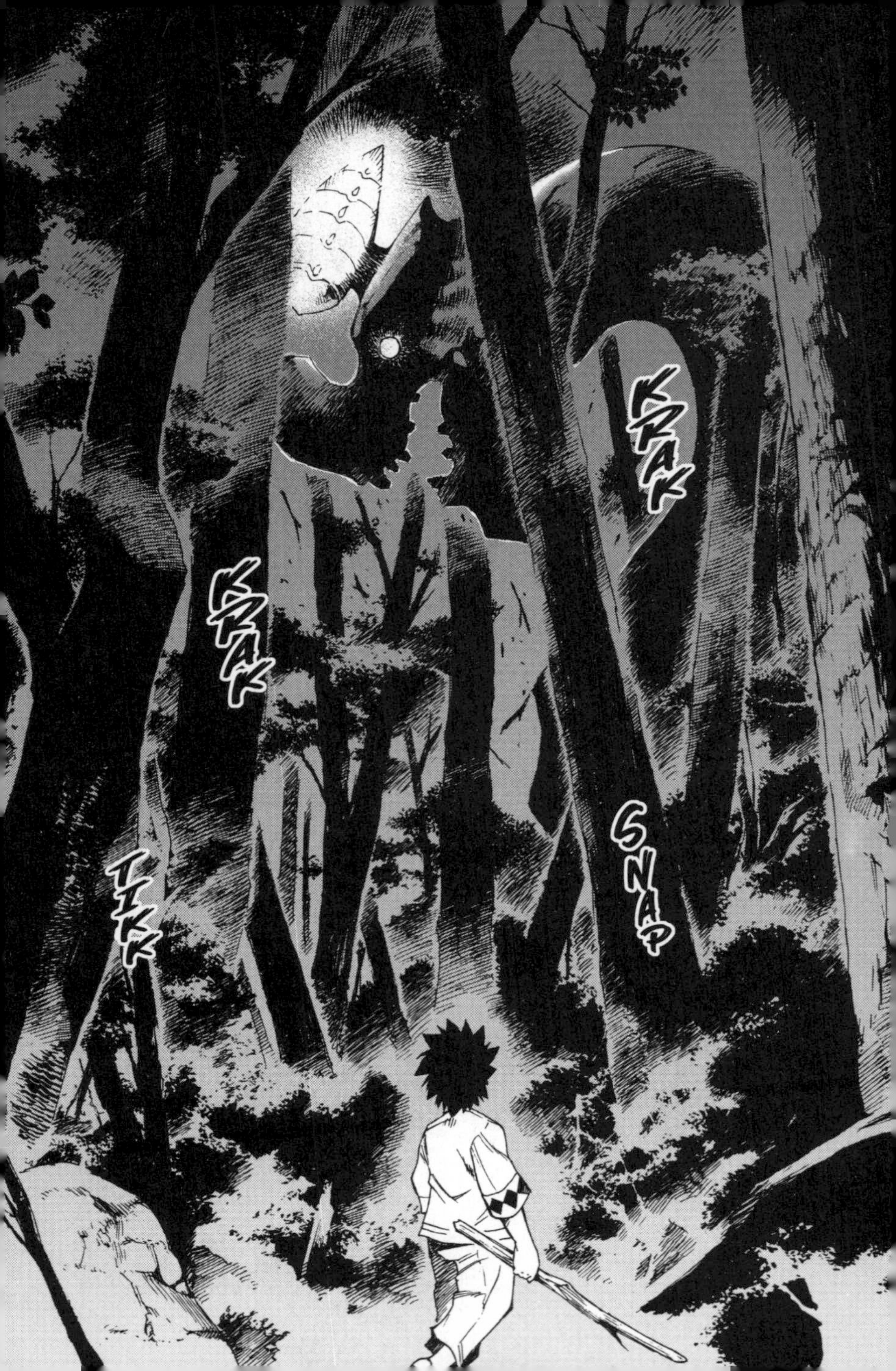
KRAK
KRAK
SNAP
TIKK

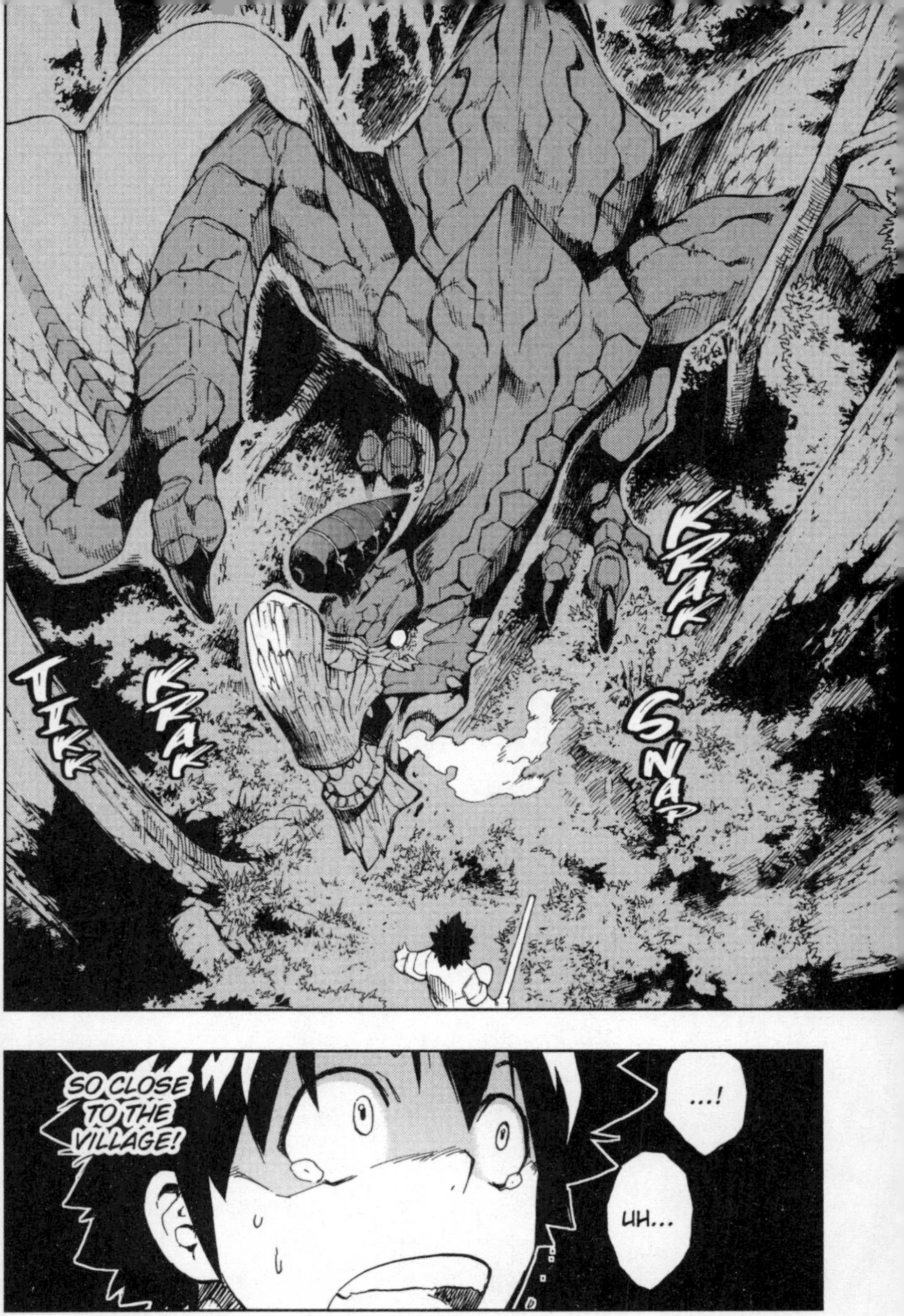
KRAK
SNAP
KRAK
TIKK
...!
UH...
SO CLOSE TO THE VILLAGE!

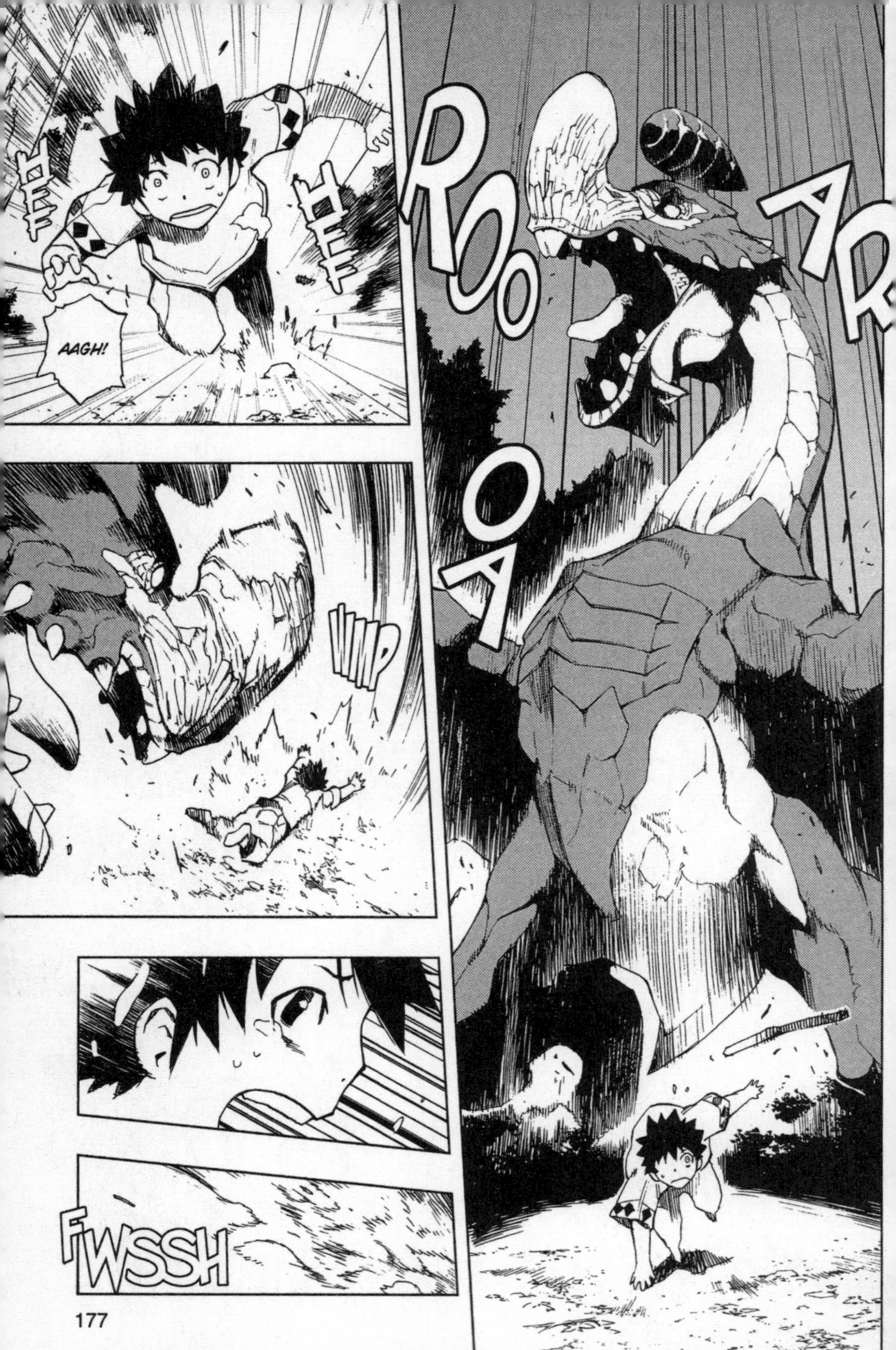
ROOOAAR
HEF HEF
AAGH!
WMP
FWSSH

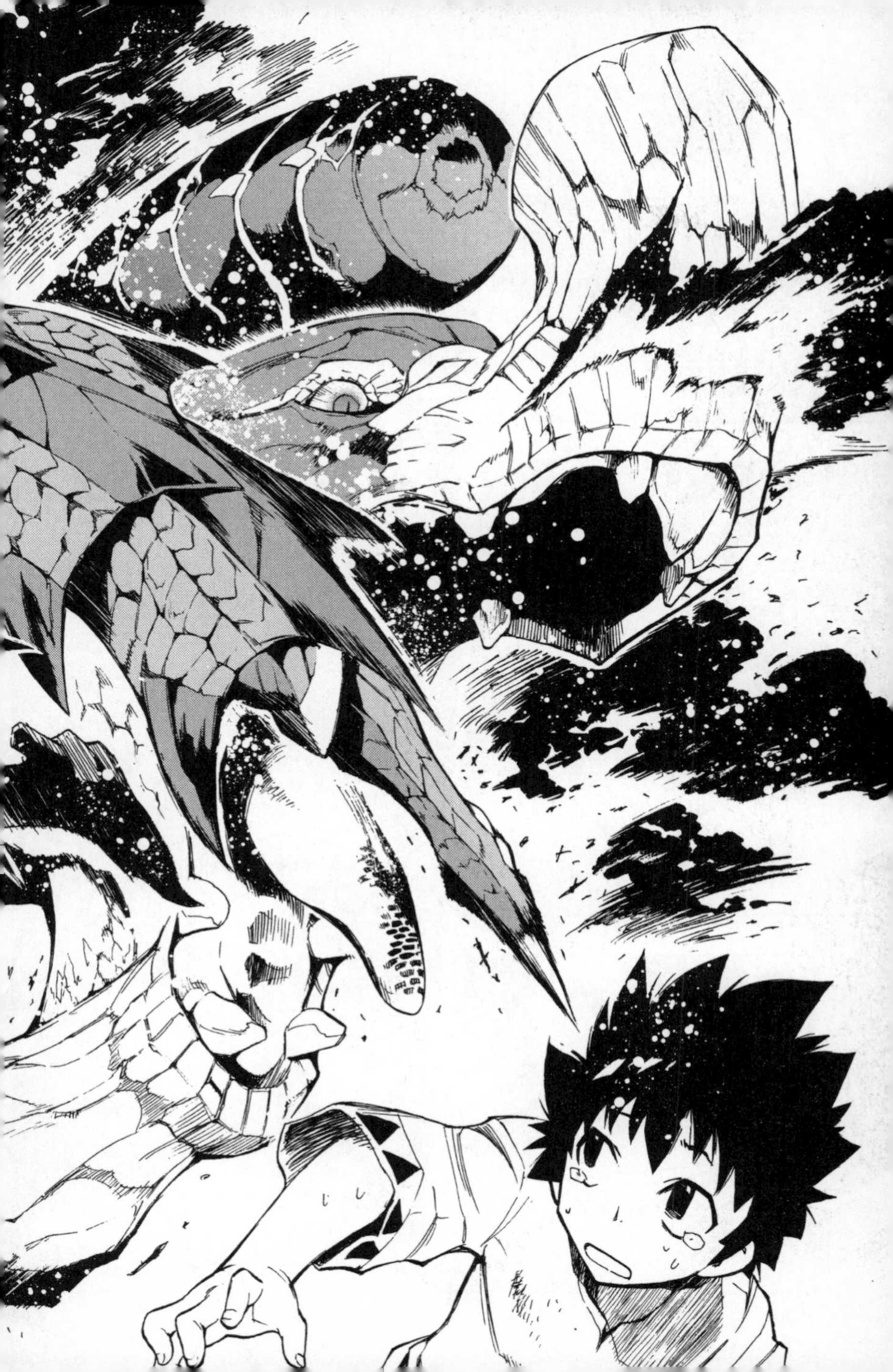

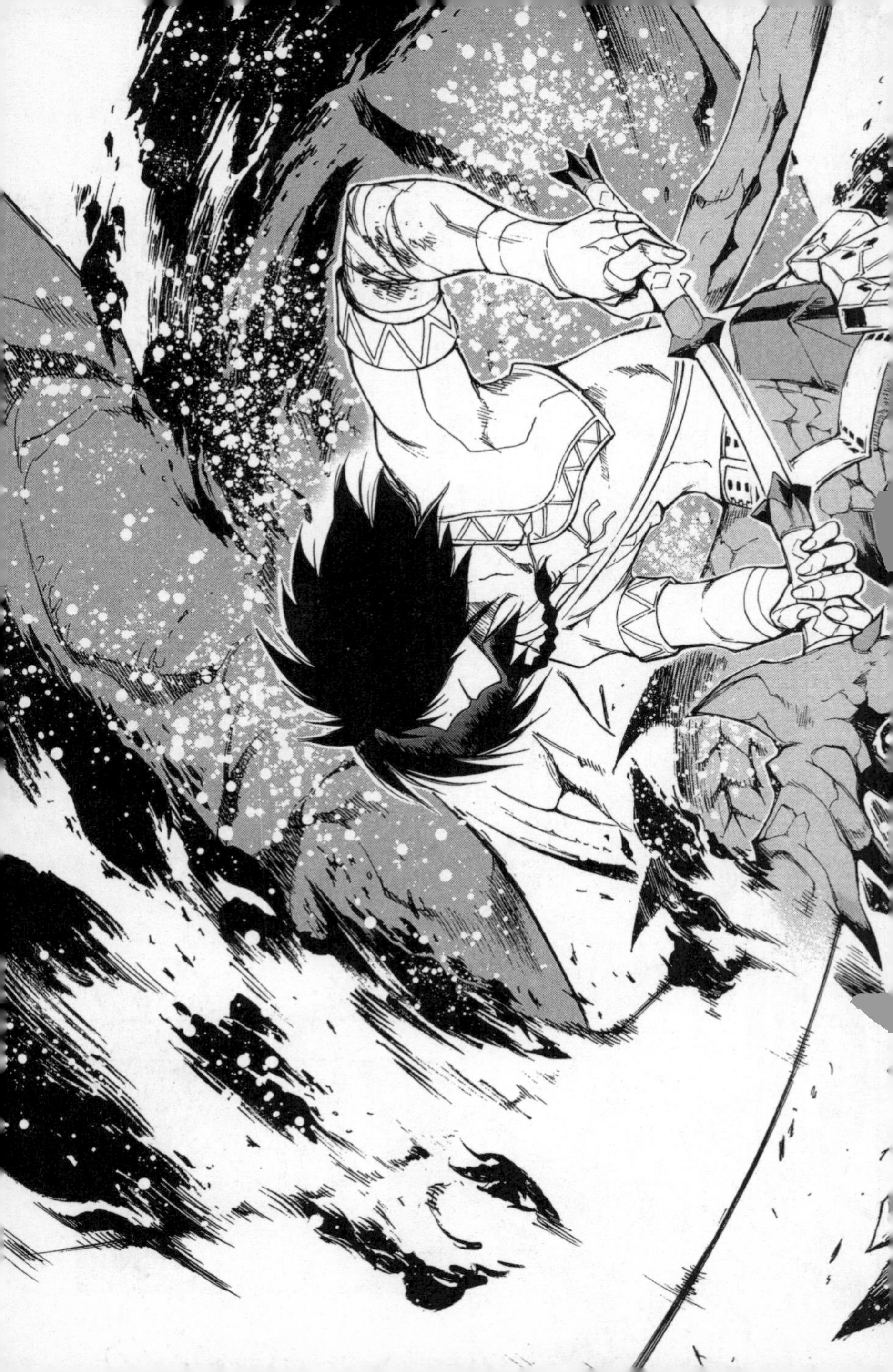

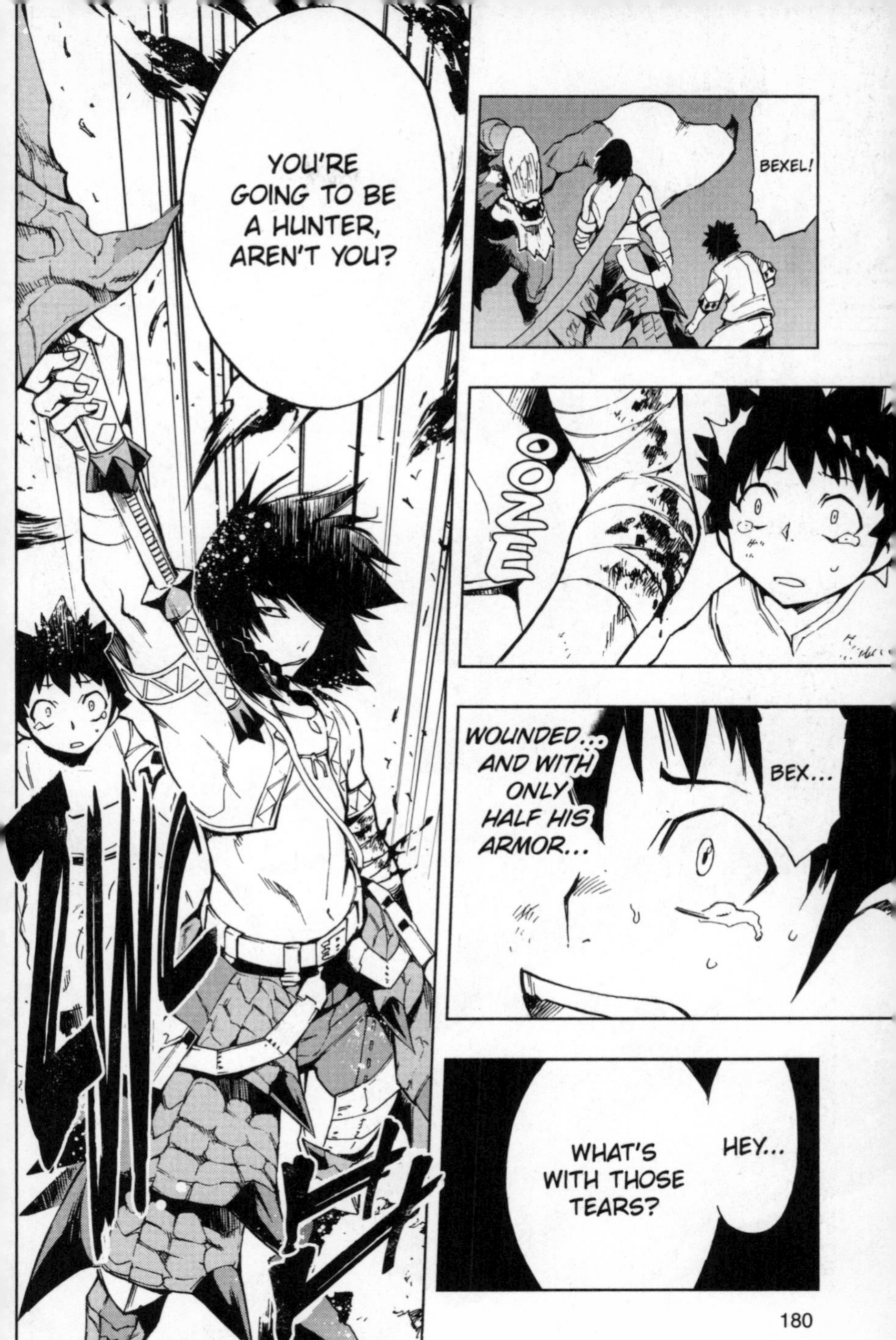
BEXEL!
OOZE
BEX...
WOUNDED... AND WITH ONLY HALF HIS ARMOR...
HEY...
WHAT'S WITH THOSE TEARS?
YOU'RE GOING TO BE A HUNTER, AREN'T YOU?

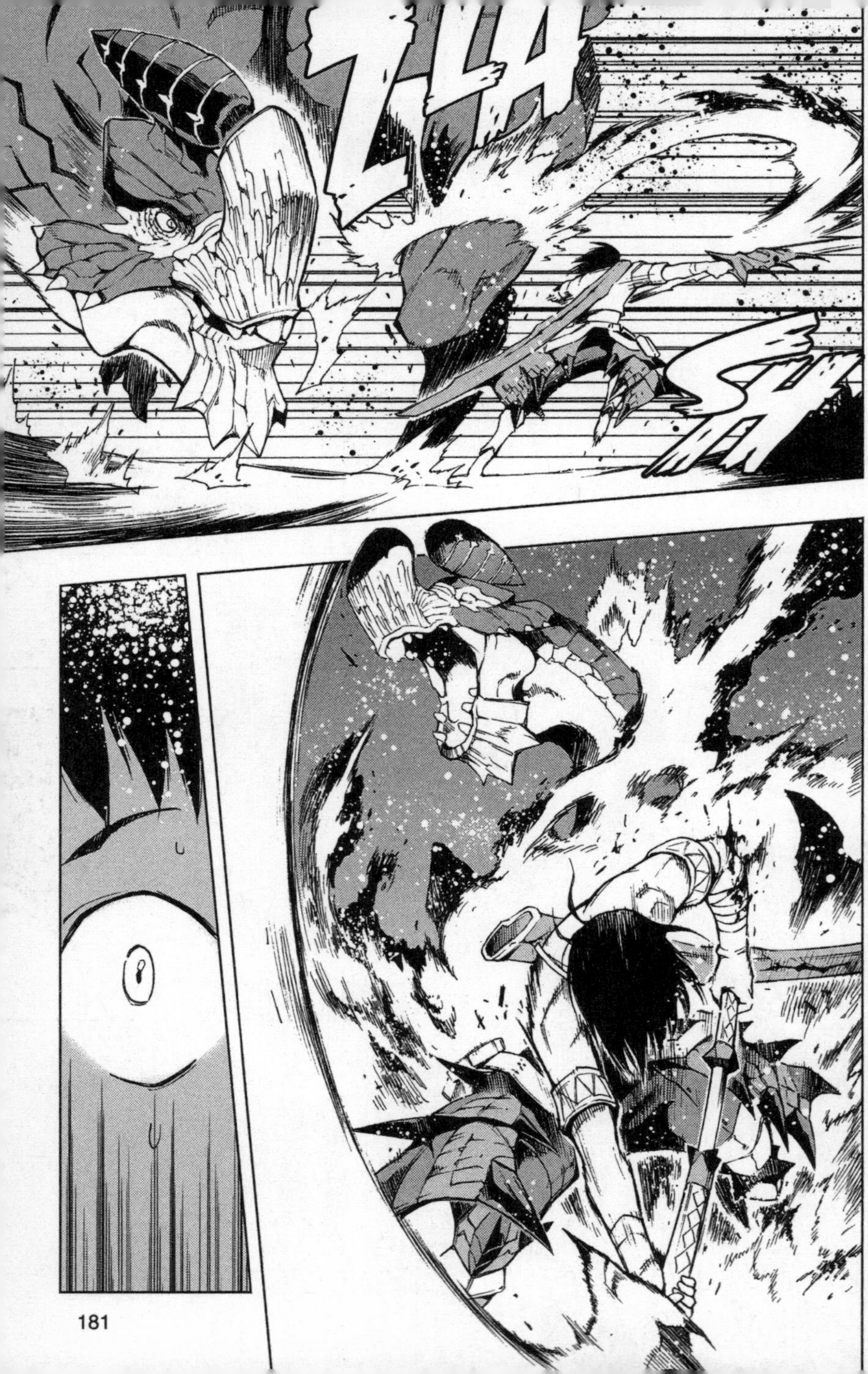
ZLA
SH

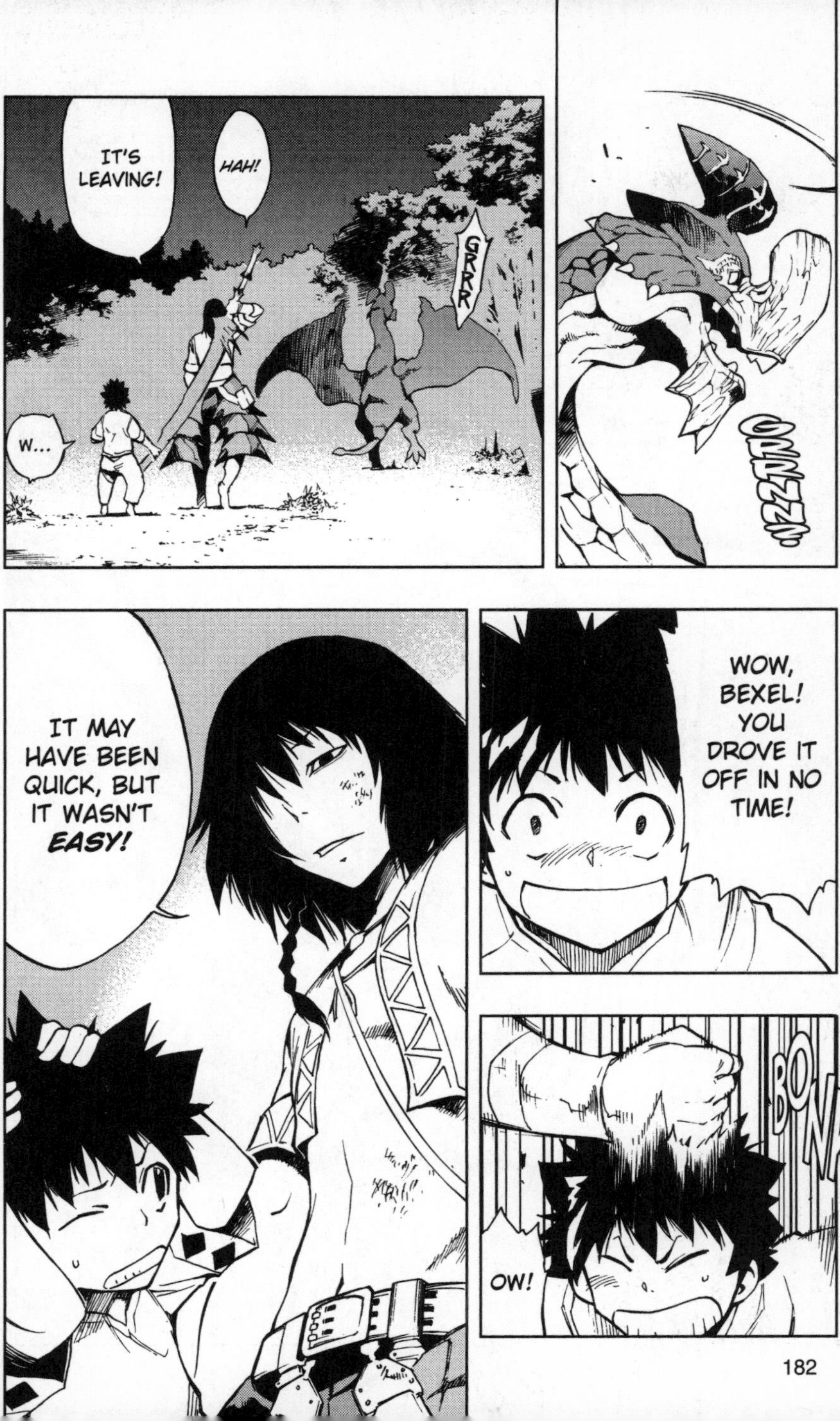
GRRR
HAH!
IT'S LEAVING!
W...
WOW, BEXEL! YOU DROVE IT OFF IN NO TIME!
BONK
OW!
IT MAY HAVE BEEN QUICK, BUT IT WASN'T *EASY!*

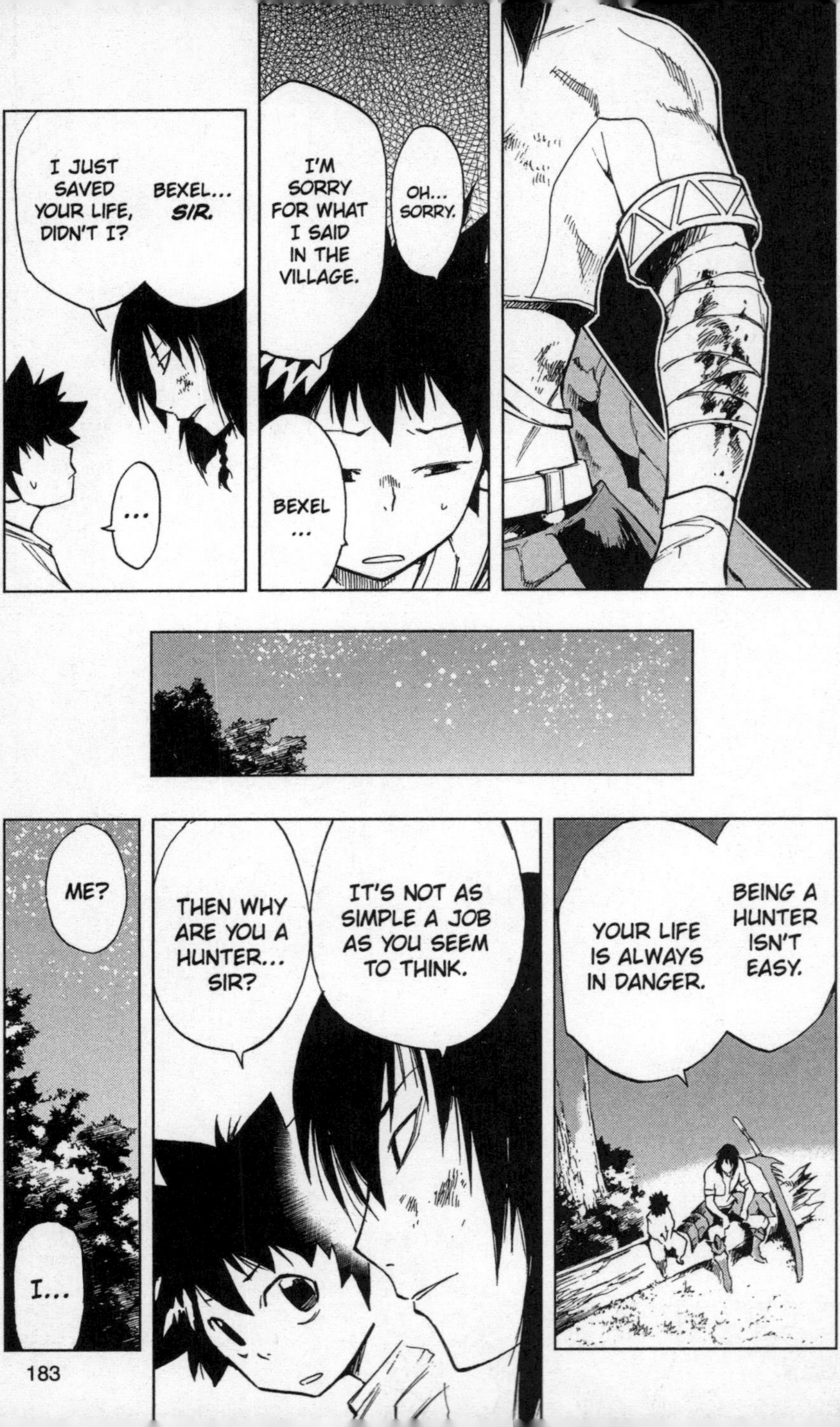
OH... SORRY.
I'M SORRY FOR WHAT I SAID IN THE VILLAGE.
BEXEL ...
BEXEL... *SIR.*
I JUST SAVED YOUR LIFE, DIDN'T I?
...
BEING A HUNTER ISN'T EASY.
YOUR LIFE IS ALWAYS IN DANGER.
IT'S NOT AS SIMPLE A JOB AS YOU SEEM TO THINK.
THEN WHY ARE YOU A HUNTER... SIR?
ME?
I...

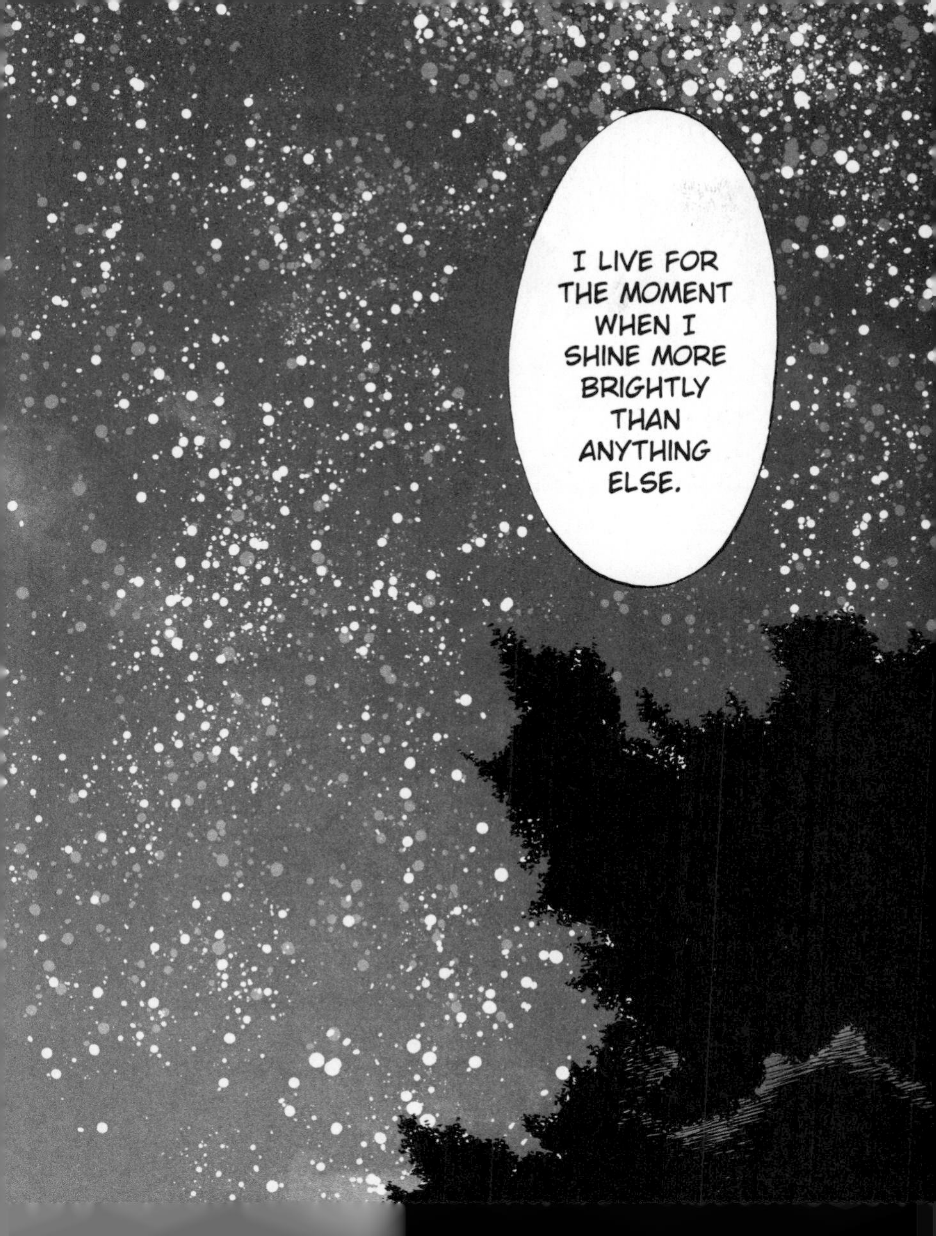
I LIVE FOR THE MOMENT WHEN I SHINE MORE BRIGHTLY THAN ANYTHING ELSE.

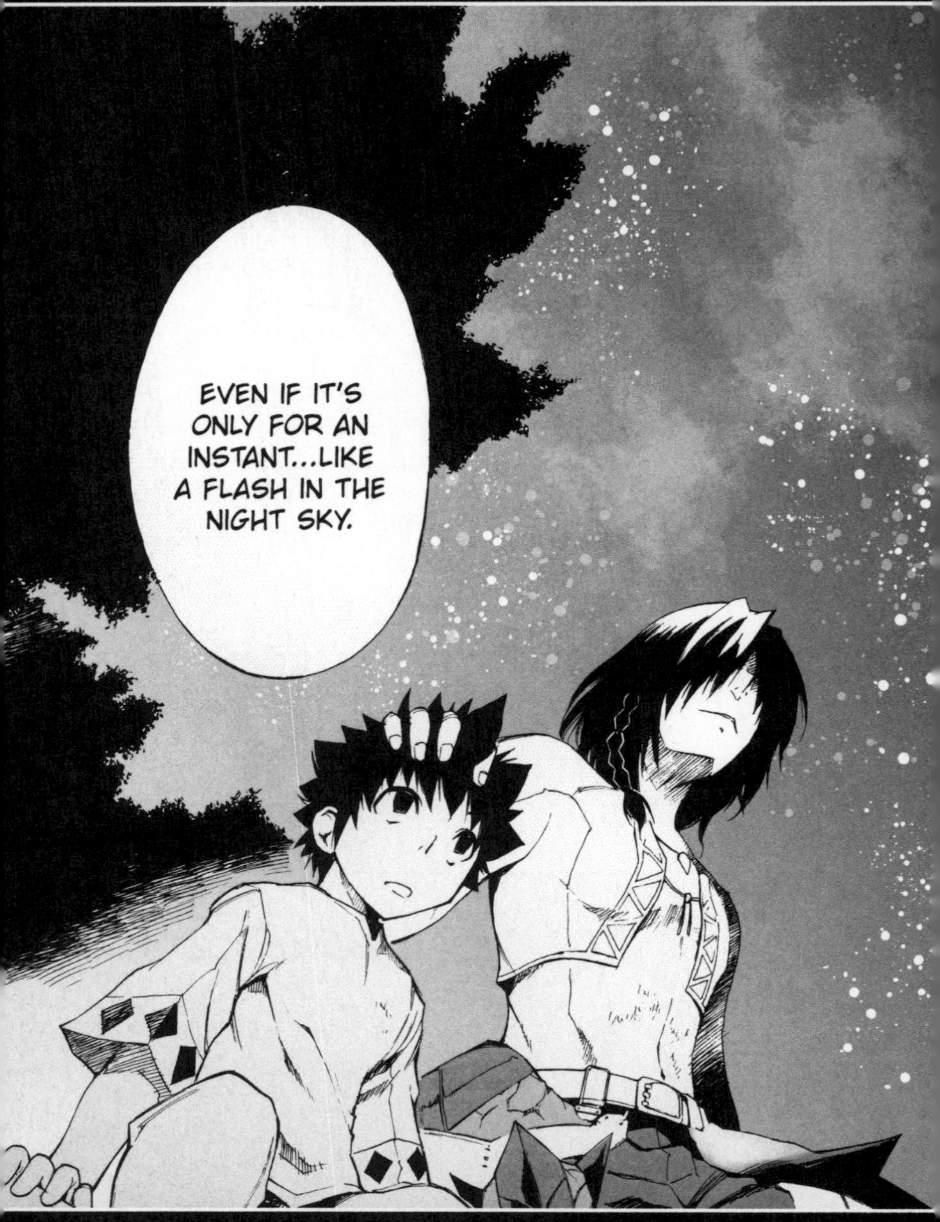
EVEN IF IT'S ONLY FOR AN INSTANT...LIKE A FLASH IN THE NIGHT SKY.

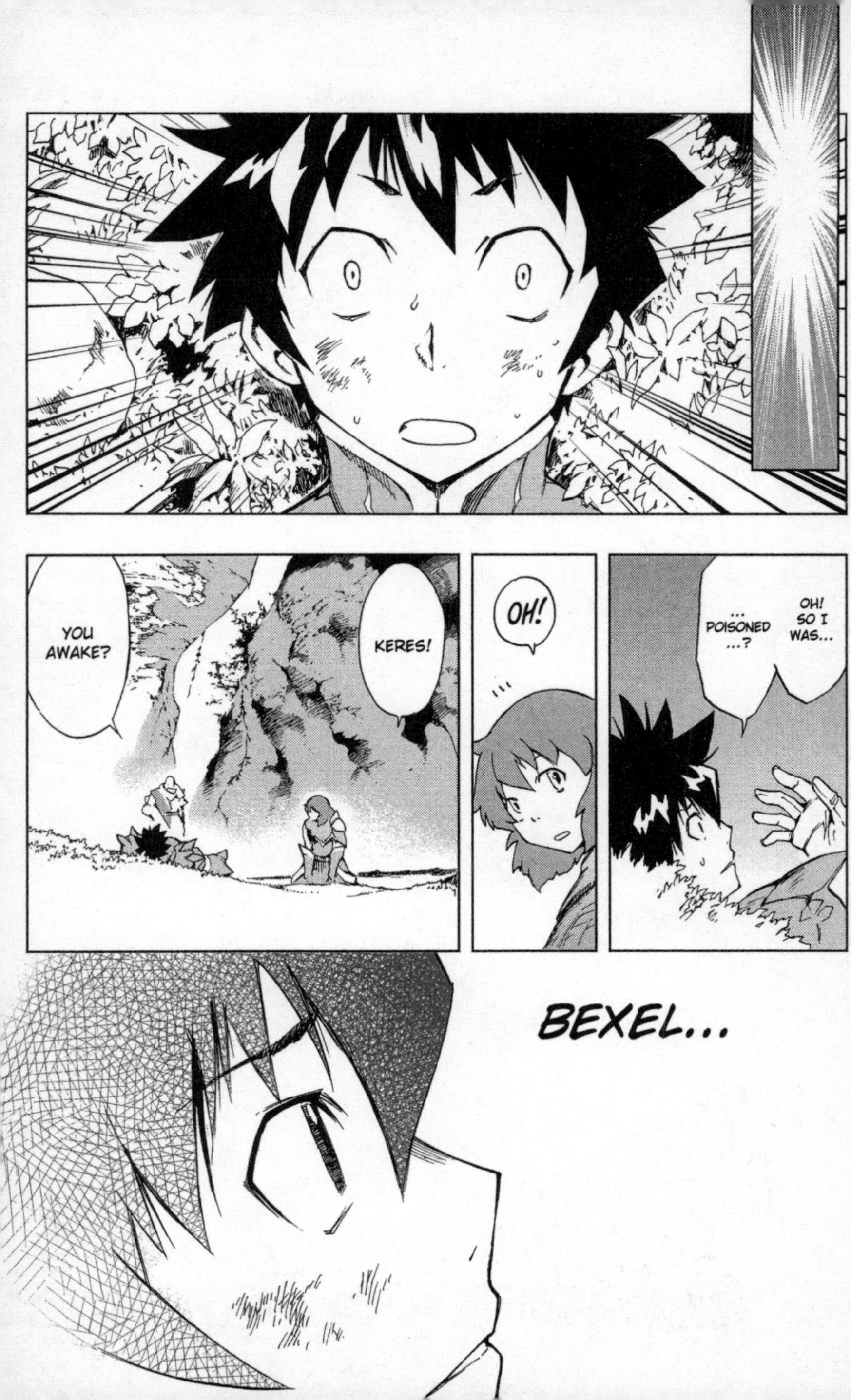
OH! SO I WAS...
... POISONED ...?
OH!
...
KERES!
YOU AWAKE?
BEXEL...

MONSTER HUNTER
FLASH HUNTER

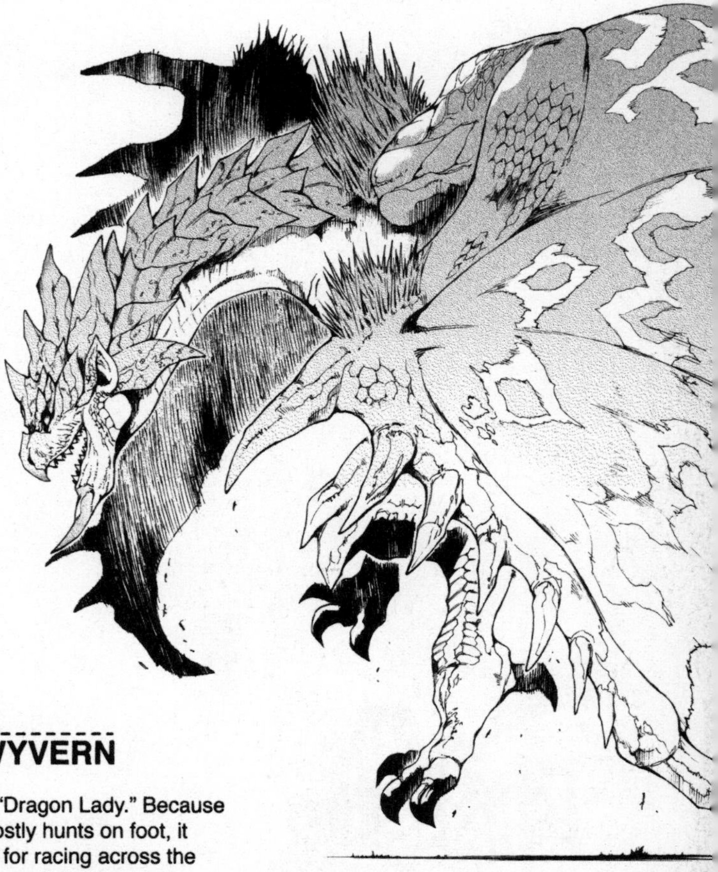

RATHIAN

FLYING WYVERN

Also known as “Dragon Lady.” Because this monster mostly hunts on foot, it has strong legs for racing across the countryside. It uses its poisonous tail to finish off prey. It has garnered the nickname "Queen of the Land" and often poses a great threat to inexperienced hunters.

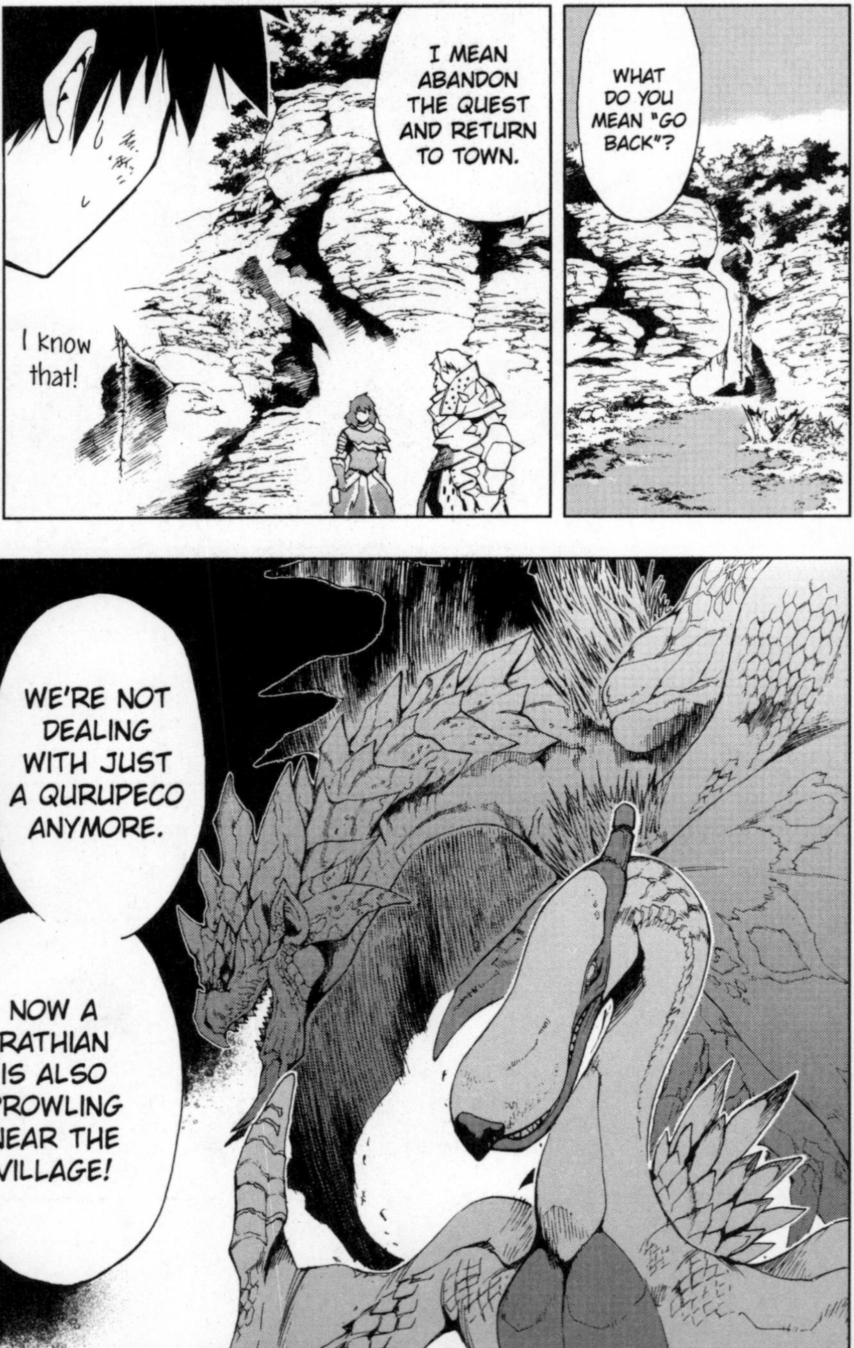
WHAT DO YOU MEAN "GO BACK"?
I MEAN ABANDON THE QUEST AND RETURN TO TOWN.
I know that!
WE'RE NOT DEALING WITH JUST A QURUPECO ANYMORE.
NOW A RATHIAN IS ALSO PROWLING NEAR THE VILLAGE!

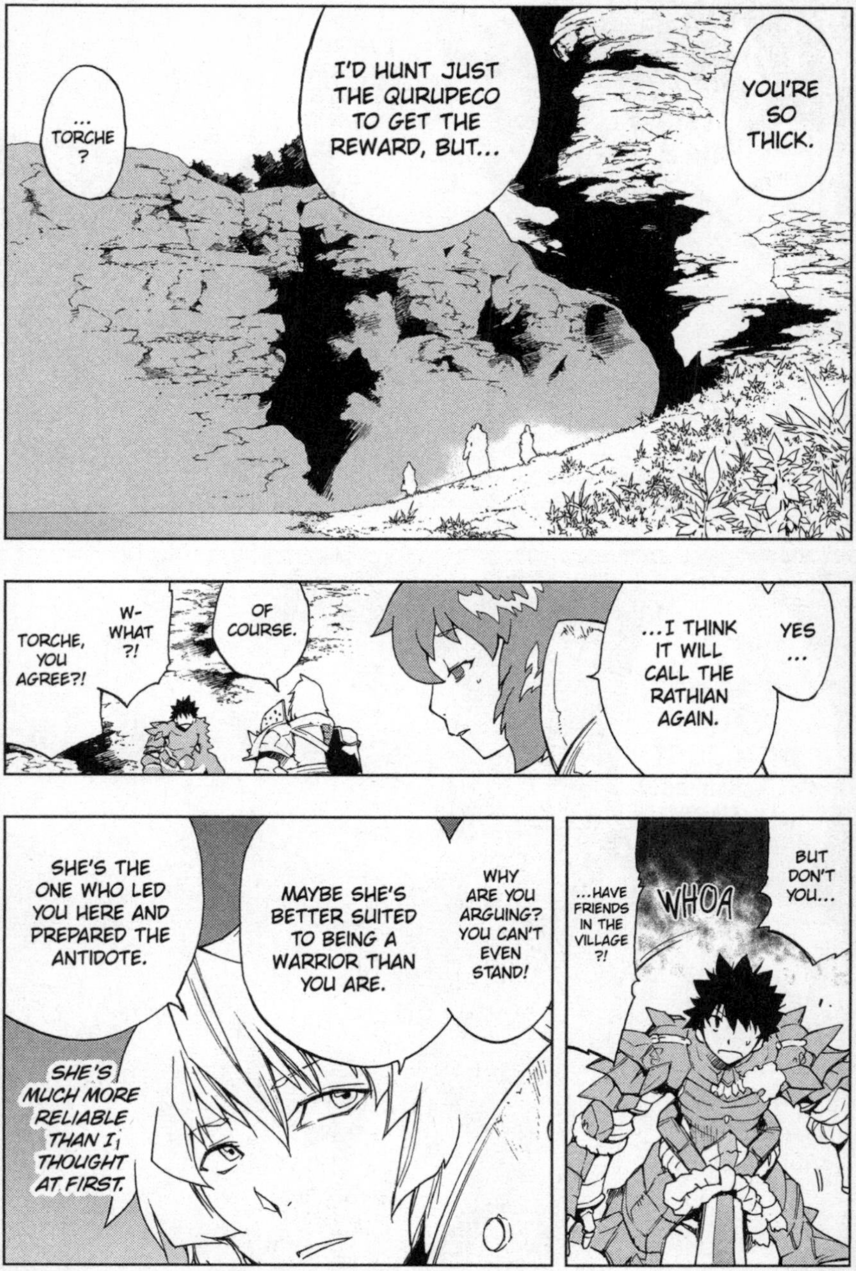
YOU'RE SO THICK.
I'D HUNT JUST THE QURUPECO TO GET THE REWARD, BUT...
... TORCHE ?
YES ...
...I THINK IT WILL CALL THE RATHIAN AGAIN.
OF COURSE.
W-WHAT ?!
TORCHE, YOU AGREE?!
BUT DON'T YOU...
WHOA
...HAVE FRIENDS IN THE VILLAGE ?!
WHY ARE YOU ARGUING? YOU CAN'T EVEN STAND!
MAYBE SHE'S BETTER SUITED TO BEING A WARRIOR THAN YOU ARE.
SHE'S THE ONE WHO LED YOU HERE AND PREPARED THE ANTIDOTE.
SHE'S MUCH MORE RELIABLE THAN I THOUGHT AT FIRST.

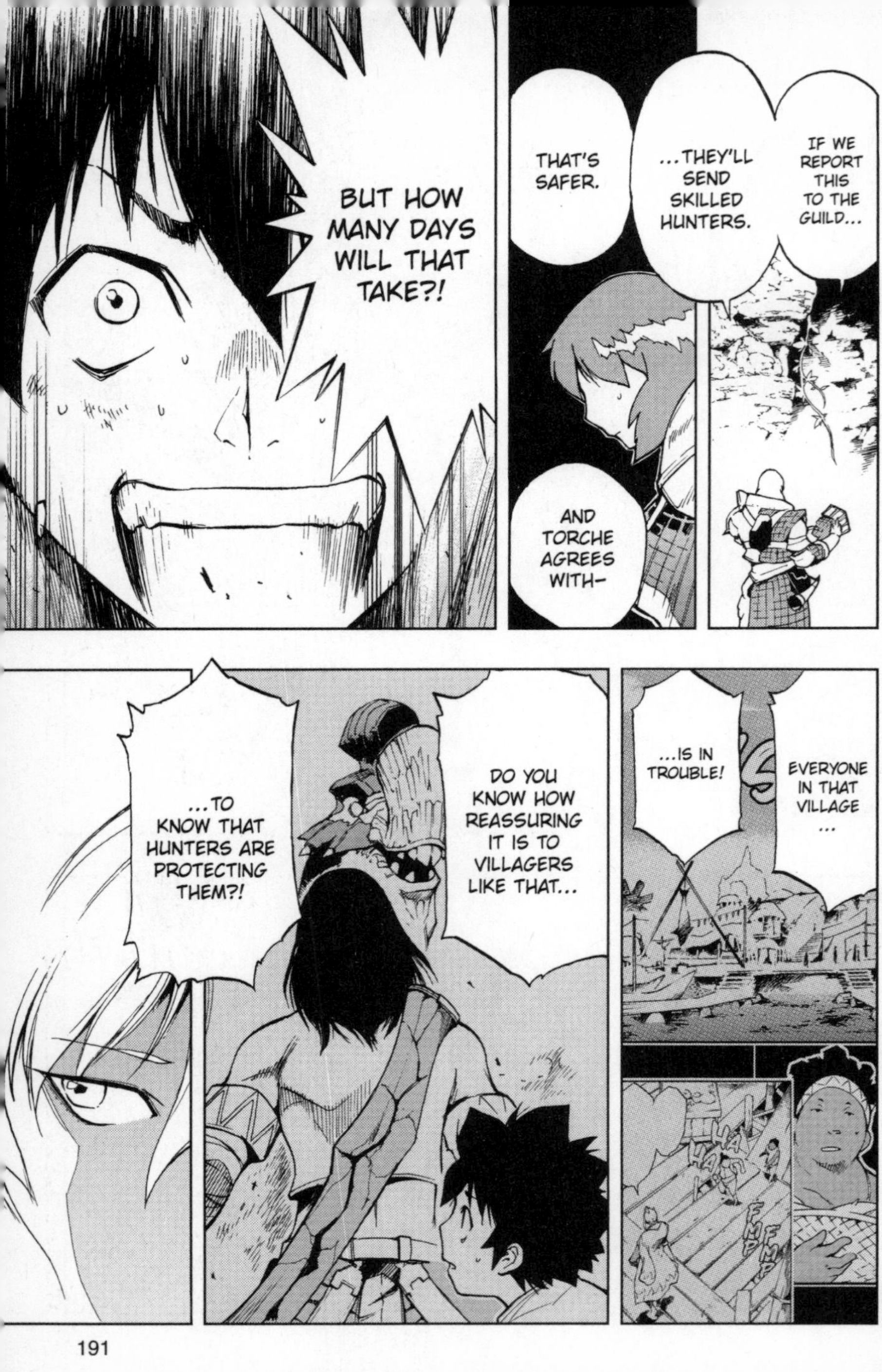
IF WE REPORT THIS TO THE GUILD...
...THEY'LL SEND SKILLED HUNTERS.
THAT'S SAFER.
AND TORCHE AGREES WITH-
BUT HOW MANY DAYS WILL THAT TAKE?!
EVERYONE IN THAT VILLAGE ...
...IS IN TROUBLE!
DO YOU KNOW HOW REASSURING IT IS TO VILLAGERS LIKE THAT...
...TO KNOW THAT HUNTERS ARE PROTECTING THEM?!

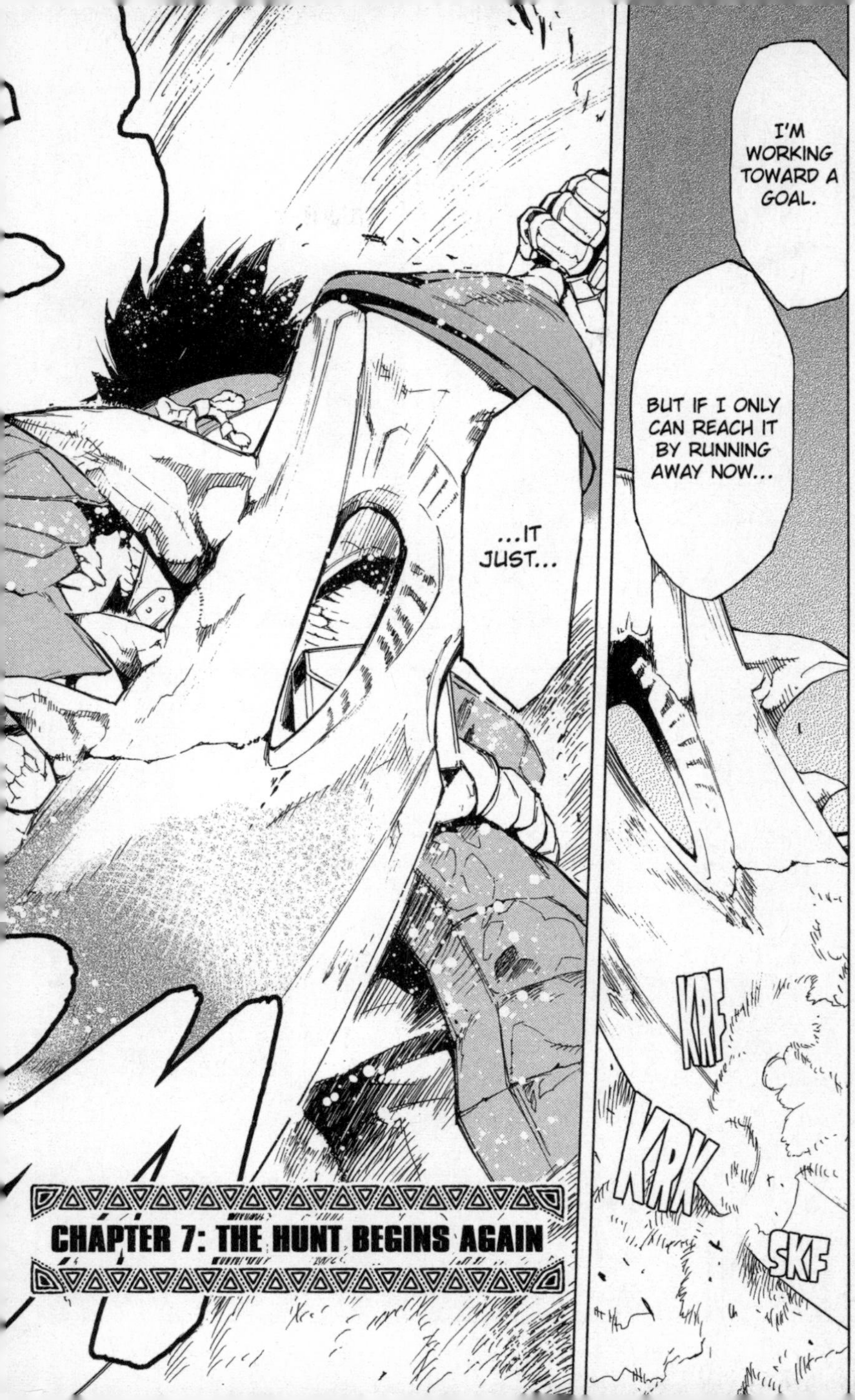
I'M WORKING TOWARD A GOAL.
BUT IF I ONLY CAN REACH IT BY RUNNING AWAY NOW...
KRF
KRK
SKF
...IT JUST...
CHAPTER 7: THE HUNT BEGINS AGAIN

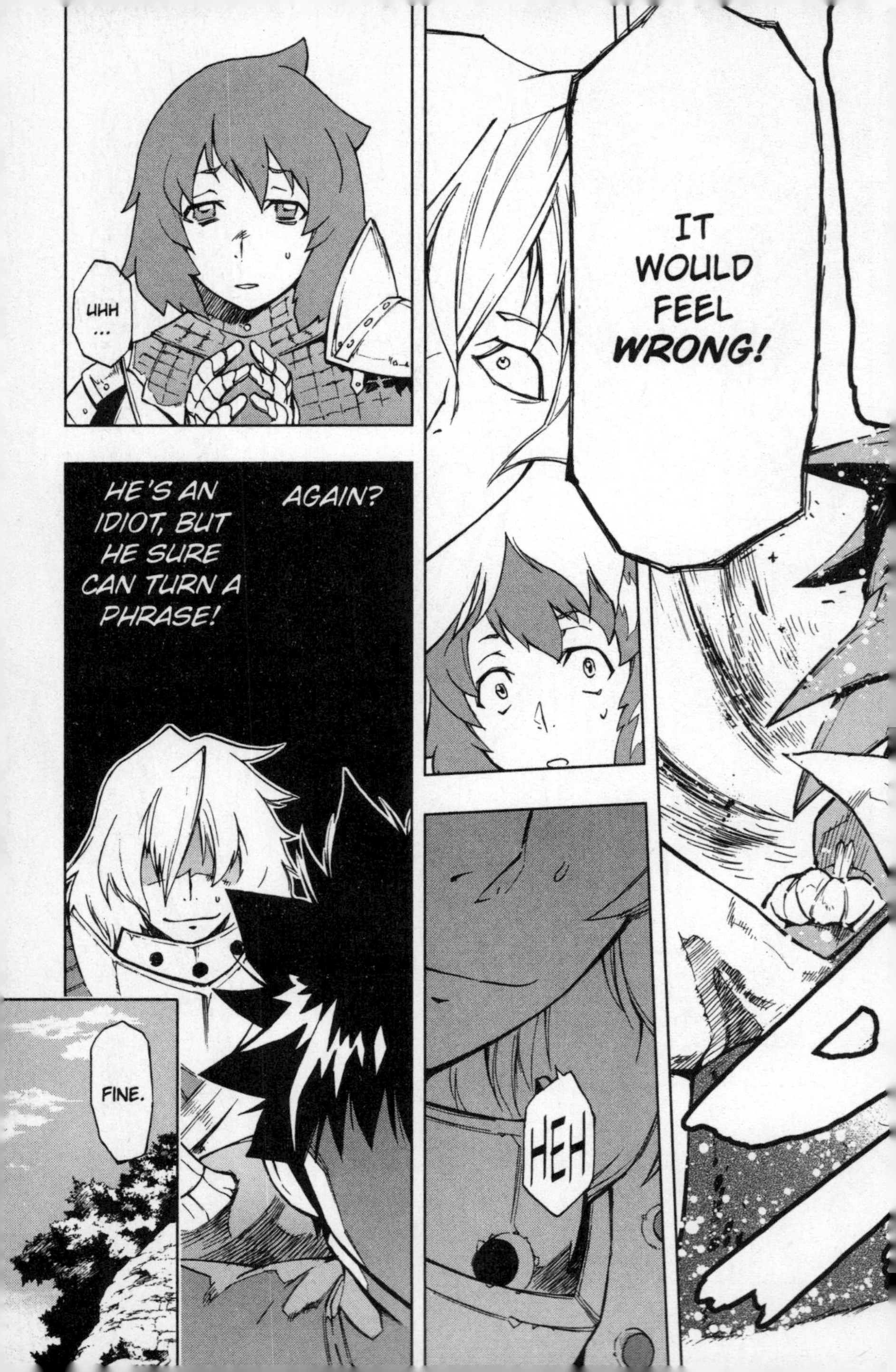
IT WOULD FEEL WRONG!
UHH ...
AGAIN?
HE'S AN IDIOT, BUT HE SURE CAN TURN A PHRASE!
HEH
FINE.

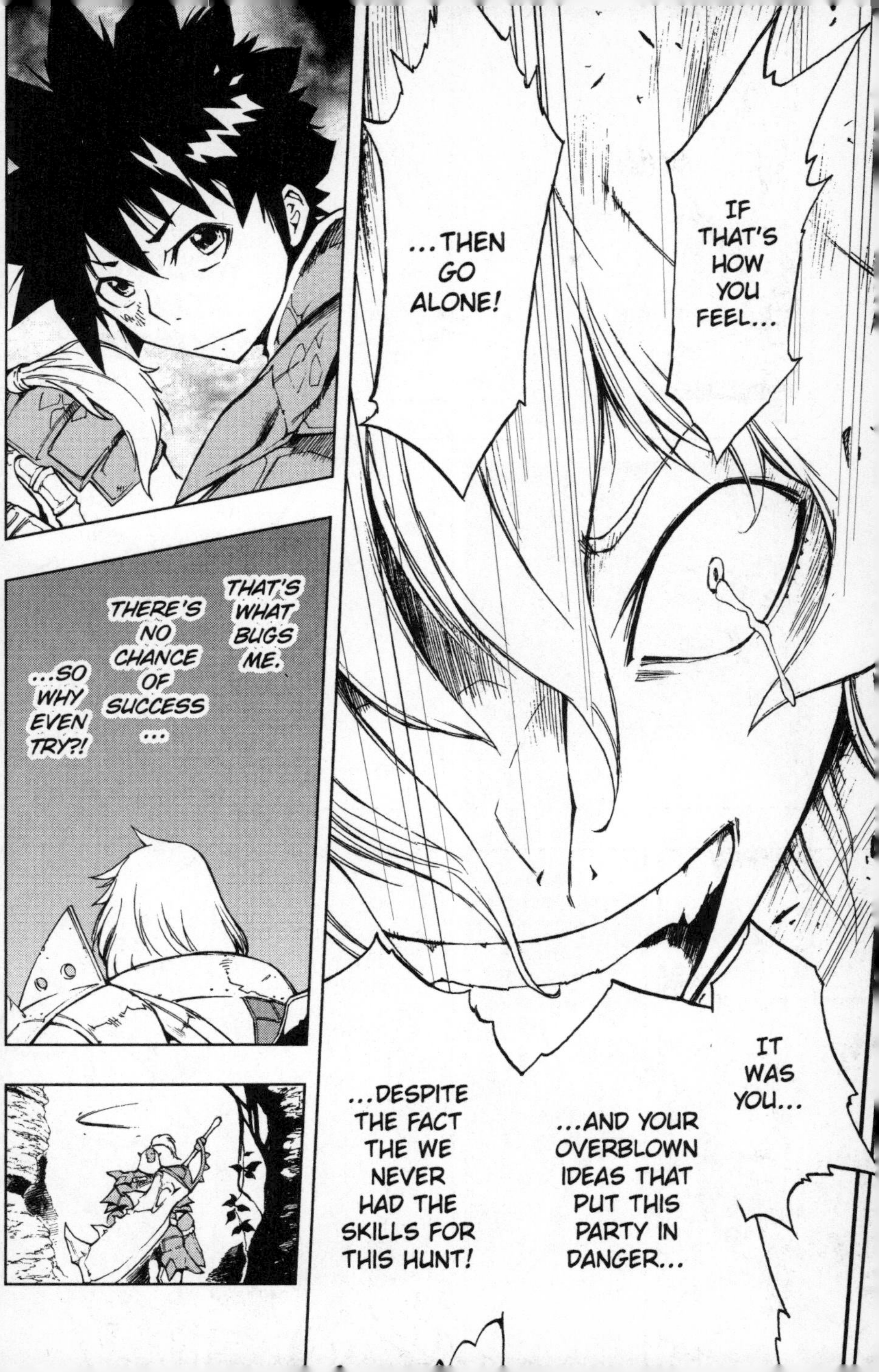
IF THAT'S HOW YOU FEEL...
...THEN GO ALONE!
IT WAS YOU...
...AND YOUR OVERBLOWN IDEAS THAT PUT THIS PARTY IN DANGER...
...DESPITE THE FACT THE WE NEVER HAD THE SKILLS FOR THIS HUNT!
THAT'S WHAT BUGS ME.
THERE'S NO CHANCE OF SUCCESS...
...SO WHY EVEN TRY?!

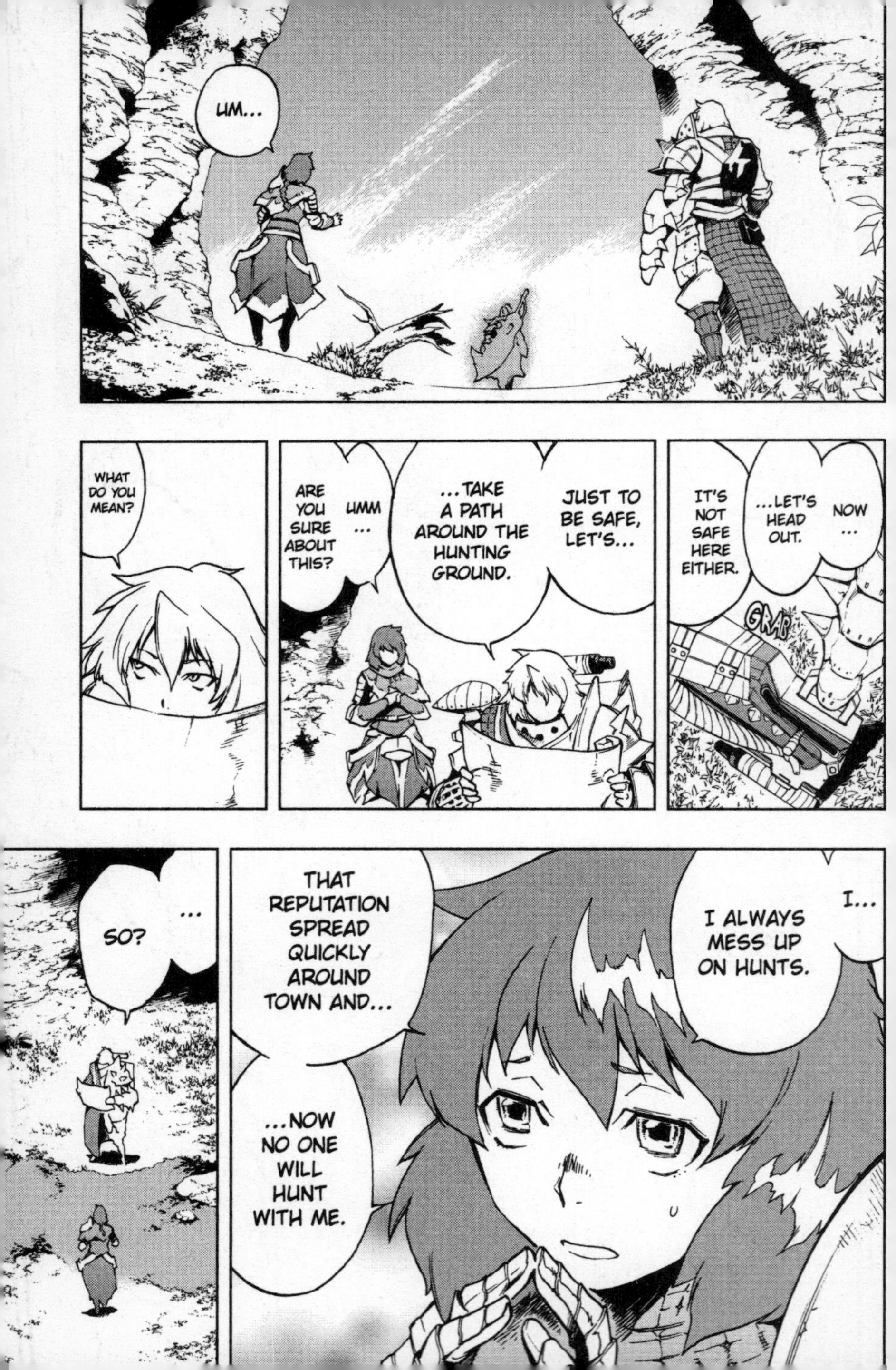
UM...
NOW...
...LET'S HEAD OUT.
IT'S NOT SAFE HERE EITHER.
GRAB
JUST TO BE SAFE, LET'S...
...TAKE A PATH AROUND THE HUNTING GROUND.
UMM...
ARE YOU SURE ABOUT THIS?
WHAT DO YOU MEAN?
I...
I ALWAYS MESS UP ON HUNTS.
THAT REPUTATION SPREAD QUICKLY AROUND TOWN AND...
...NOW NO ONE WILL HUNT WITH ME.
...
SO?

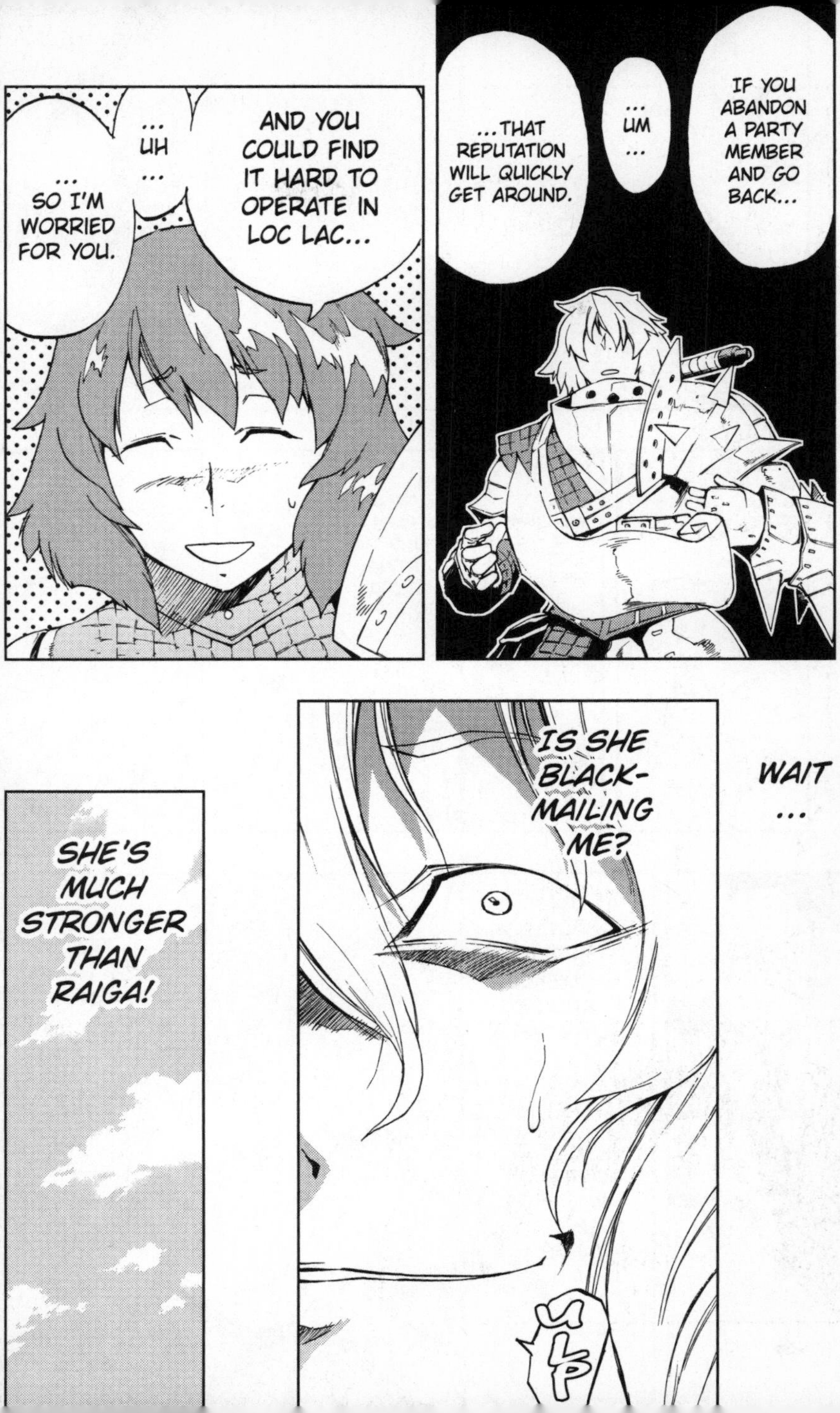
IF YOU ABANDON A PARTY MEMBER AND GO BACK...
... UM ...
...THAT REPUTATION WILL QUICKLY GET AROUND.
AND YOU COULD FIND IT HARD TO OPERATE IN LOC LAC...
... UH ...
... SO I'M WORRIED FOR YOU.
WAIT ...
IS SHE BLACK-MAILING ME?
SHE'S MUCH STRONGER THAN RAIGA!

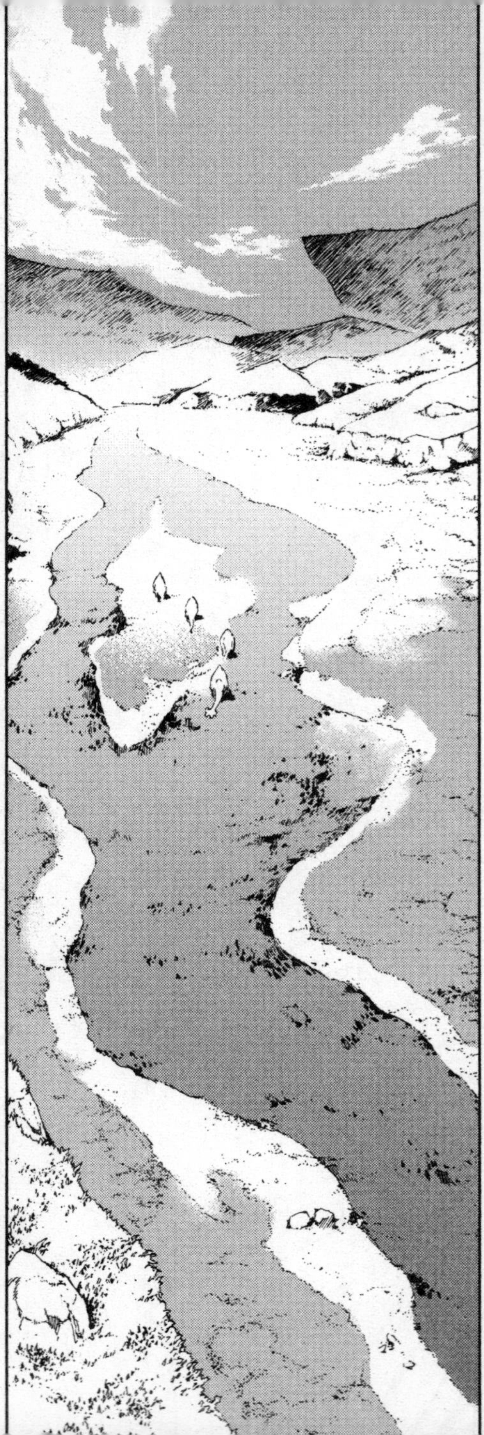

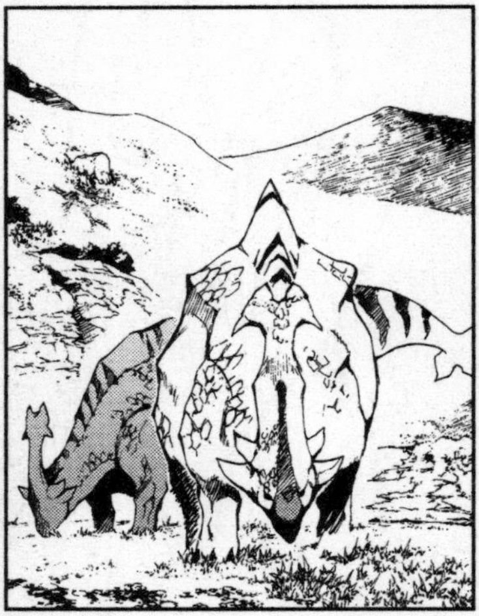

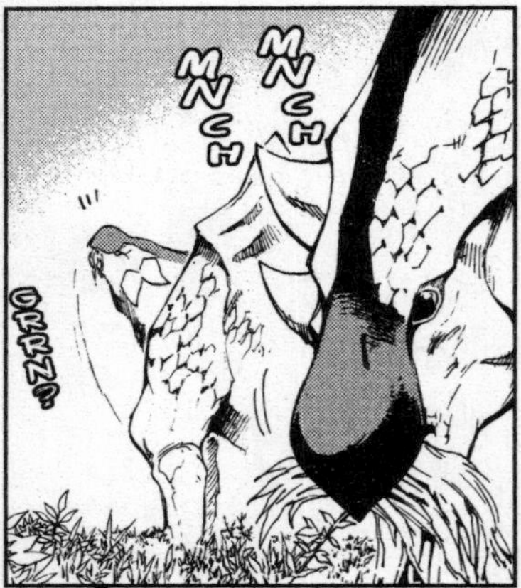
MNCH
MNCH
GRRN?

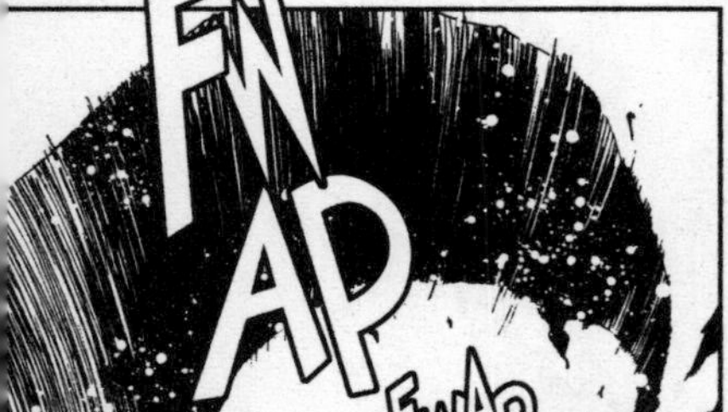
FWAP
FWAP

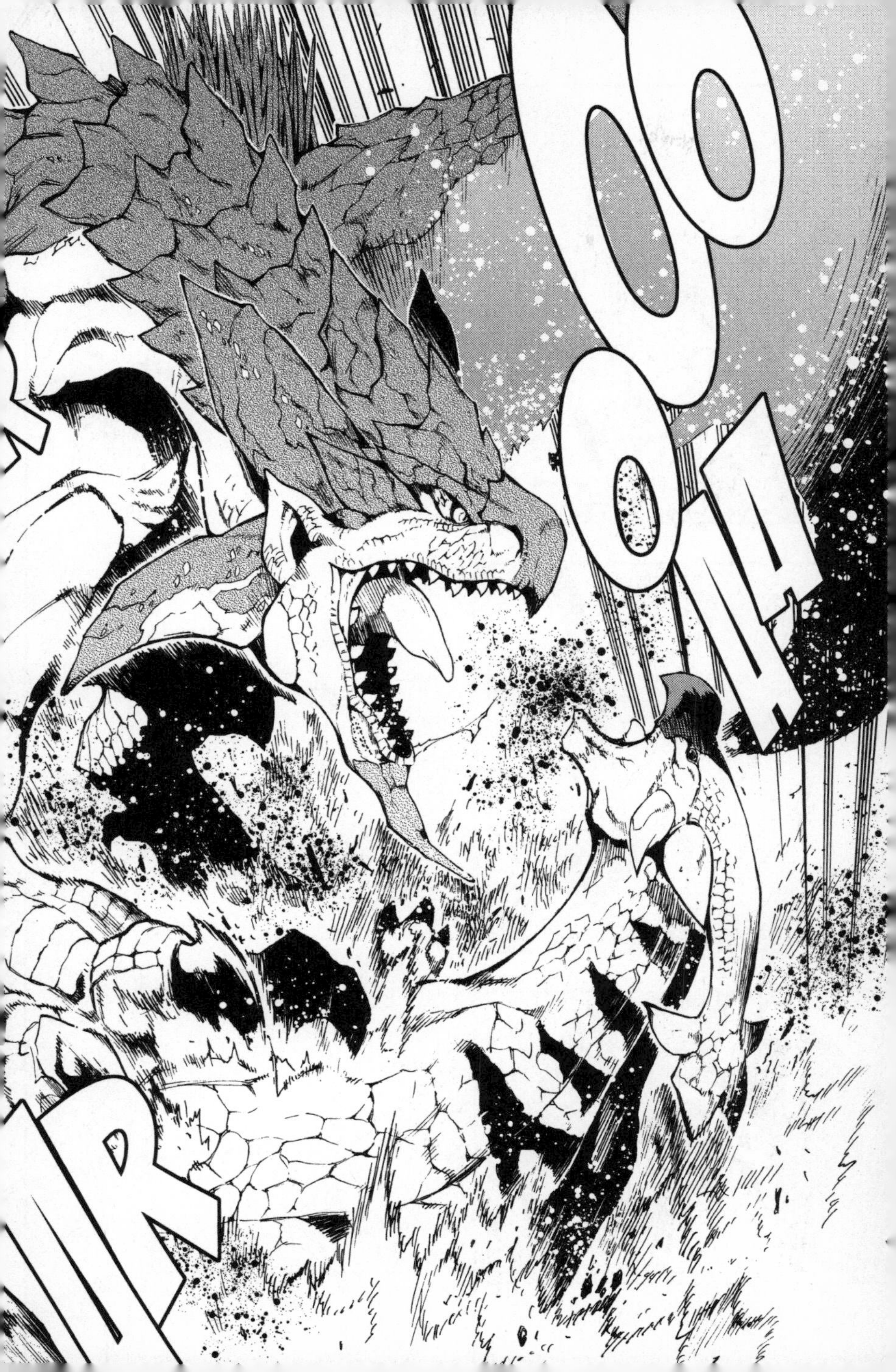

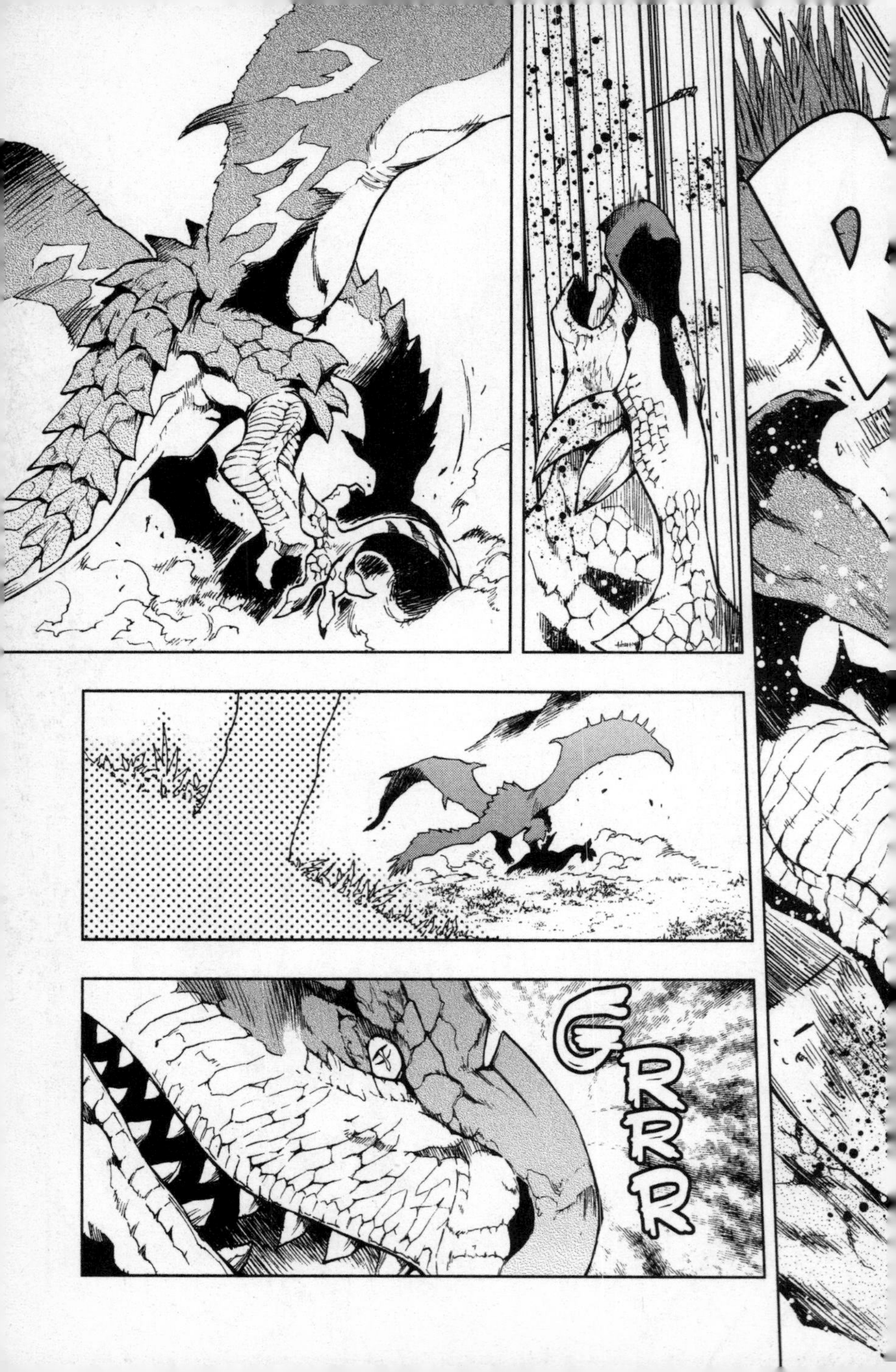
GRRR

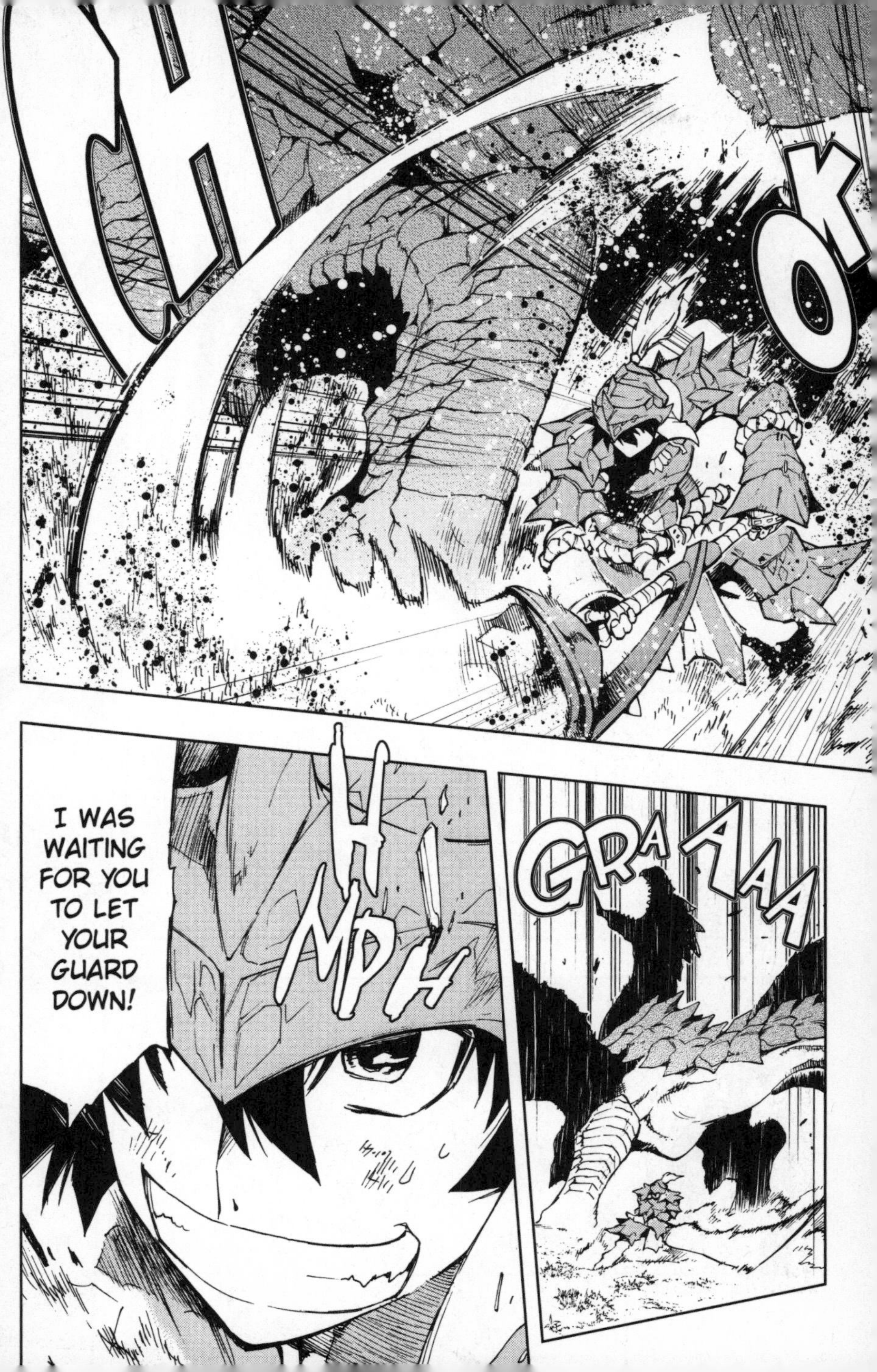
CH
OK
GRAAAA
HMPH
I WAS WAITING FOR YOU TO LET YOUR GUARD DOWN!

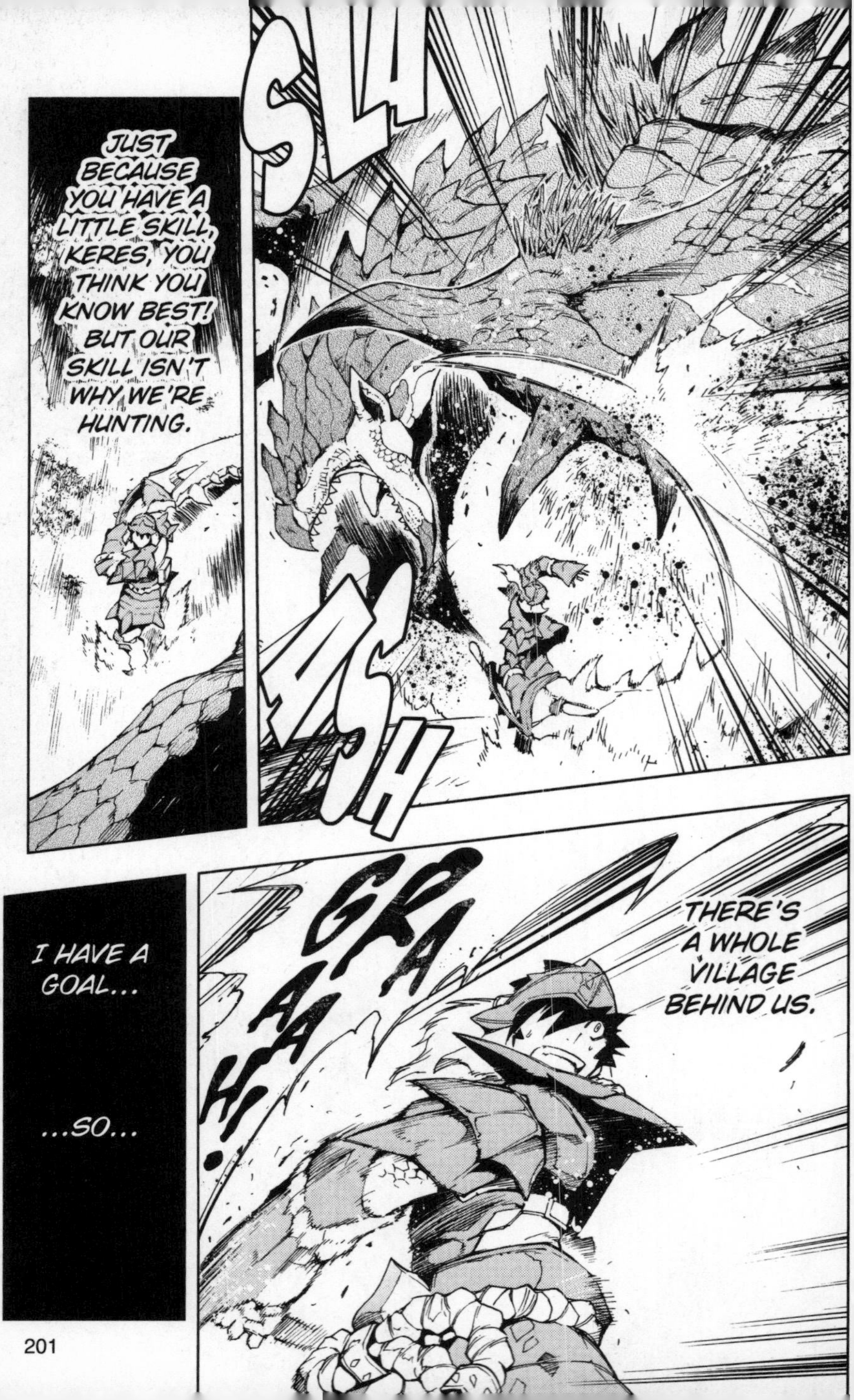
SLA
ASH
JUST BECAUSE YOU HAVE A LITTLE SKILL, KERES, YOU THINK YOU KNOW BEST! BUT OUR SKILL ISN'T WHY WE'RE HUNTING.
GRAAAH!
THERE'S A WHOLE VILLAGE BEHIND US.
I HAVE A GOAL...
...SO...

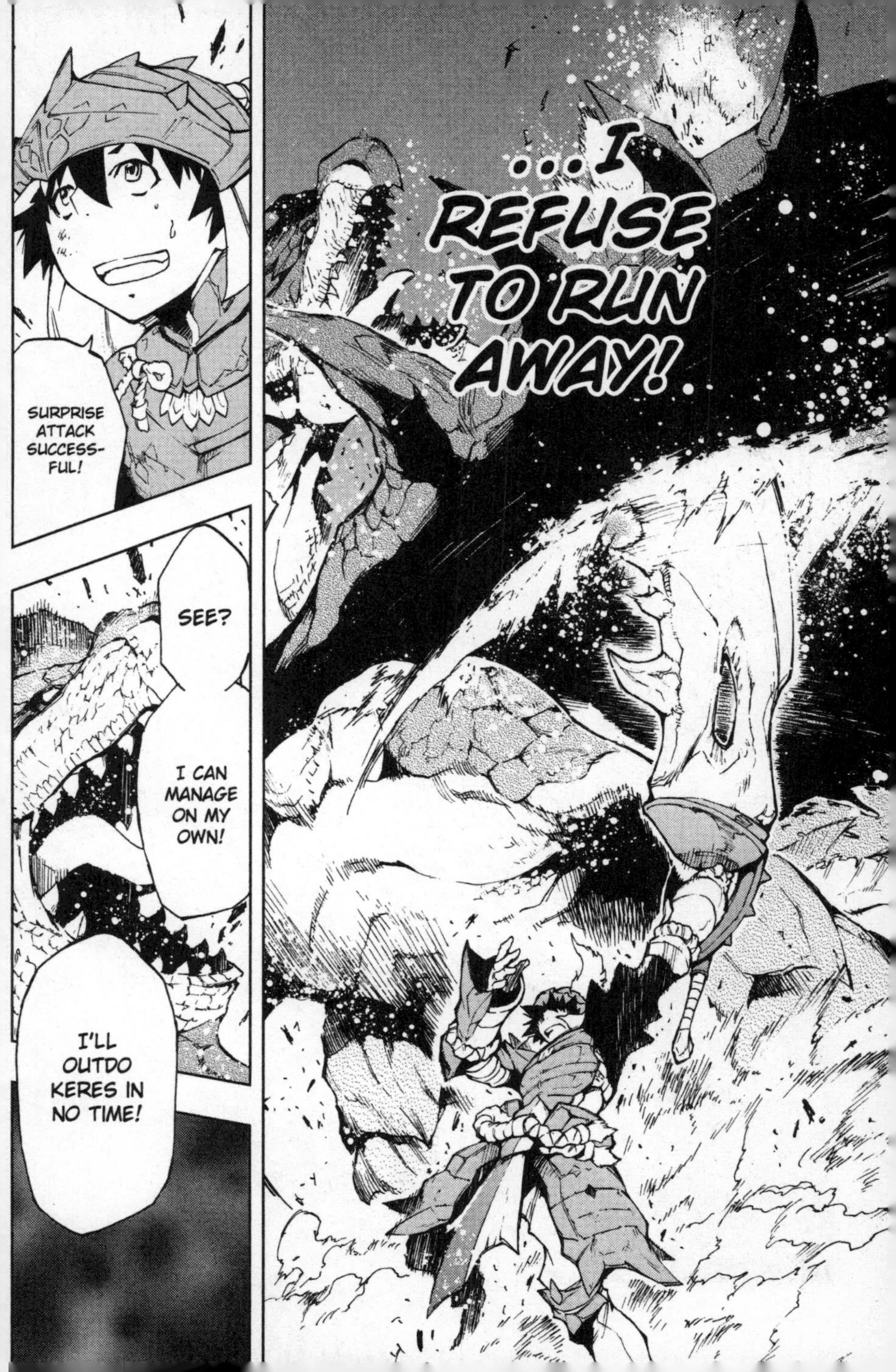
...I REFUSE TO RUN AWAY!
SURPRISE ATTACK SUCCESSFUL!
SEE?
I CAN MANAGE ON MY OWN!
I'LL OUTDO KERES IN NO TIME!

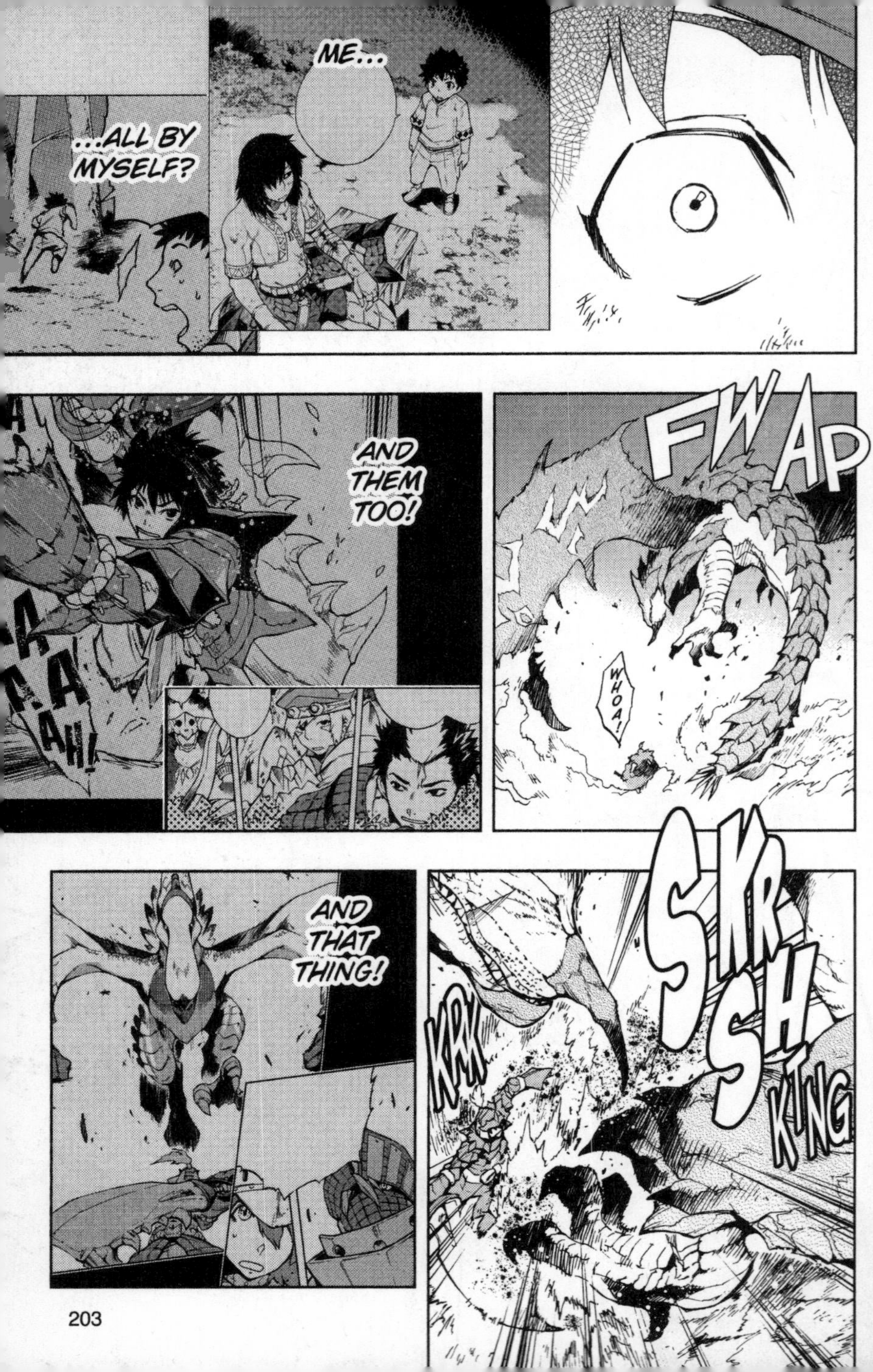
ME...
...ALL BY MYSELF?
FWAP
WHOA!
AND THEM TOO!
AAAAH!
SKRSH
KTNG
KRAK
AND THAT THING!

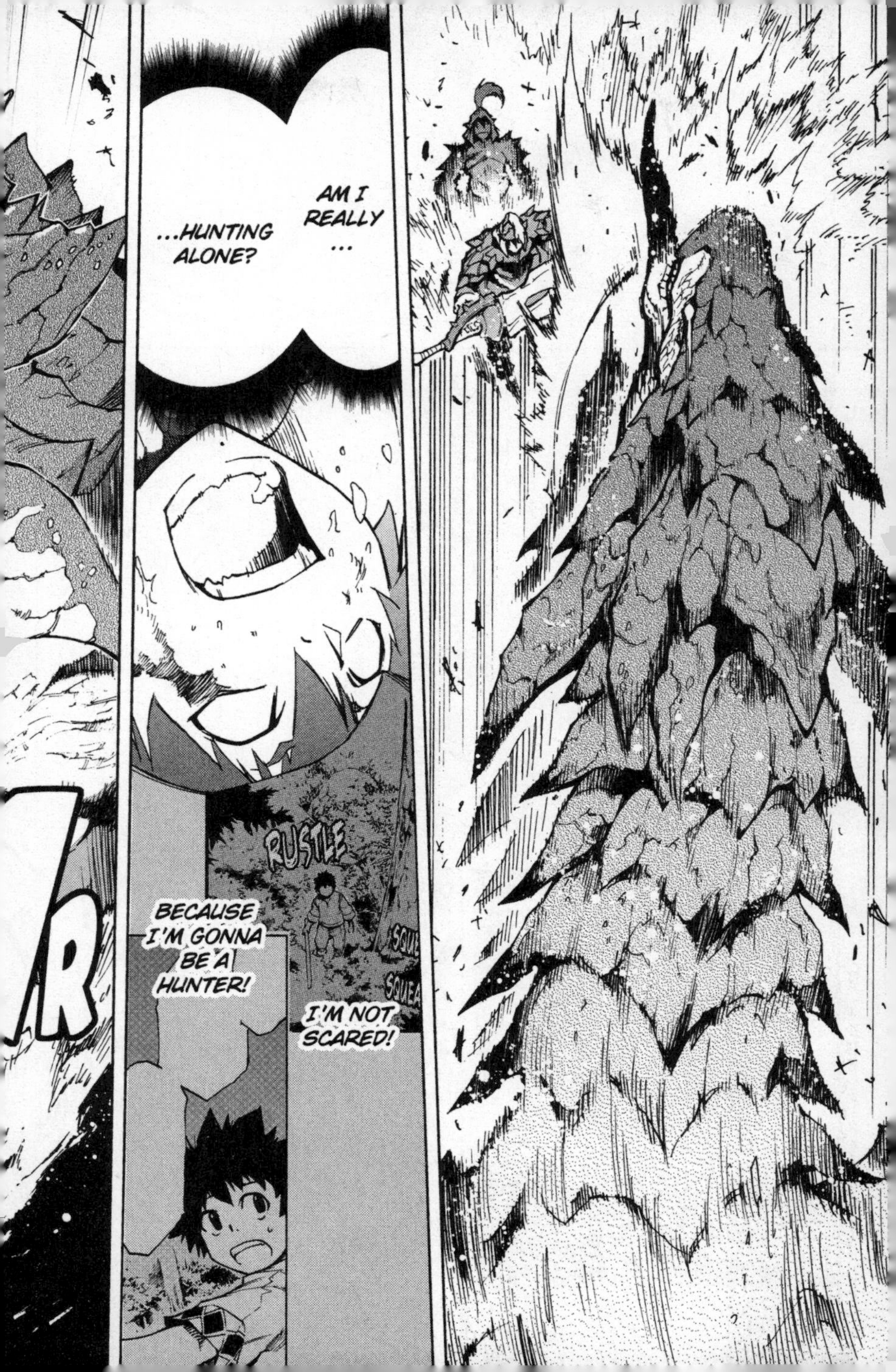
AM I REALLY ...
...HUNTING ALONE?
RUSTLE
SQUEA
SQUEA
I'M NOT SCARED!
BECAUSE I'M GONNA BE A HUNTER!

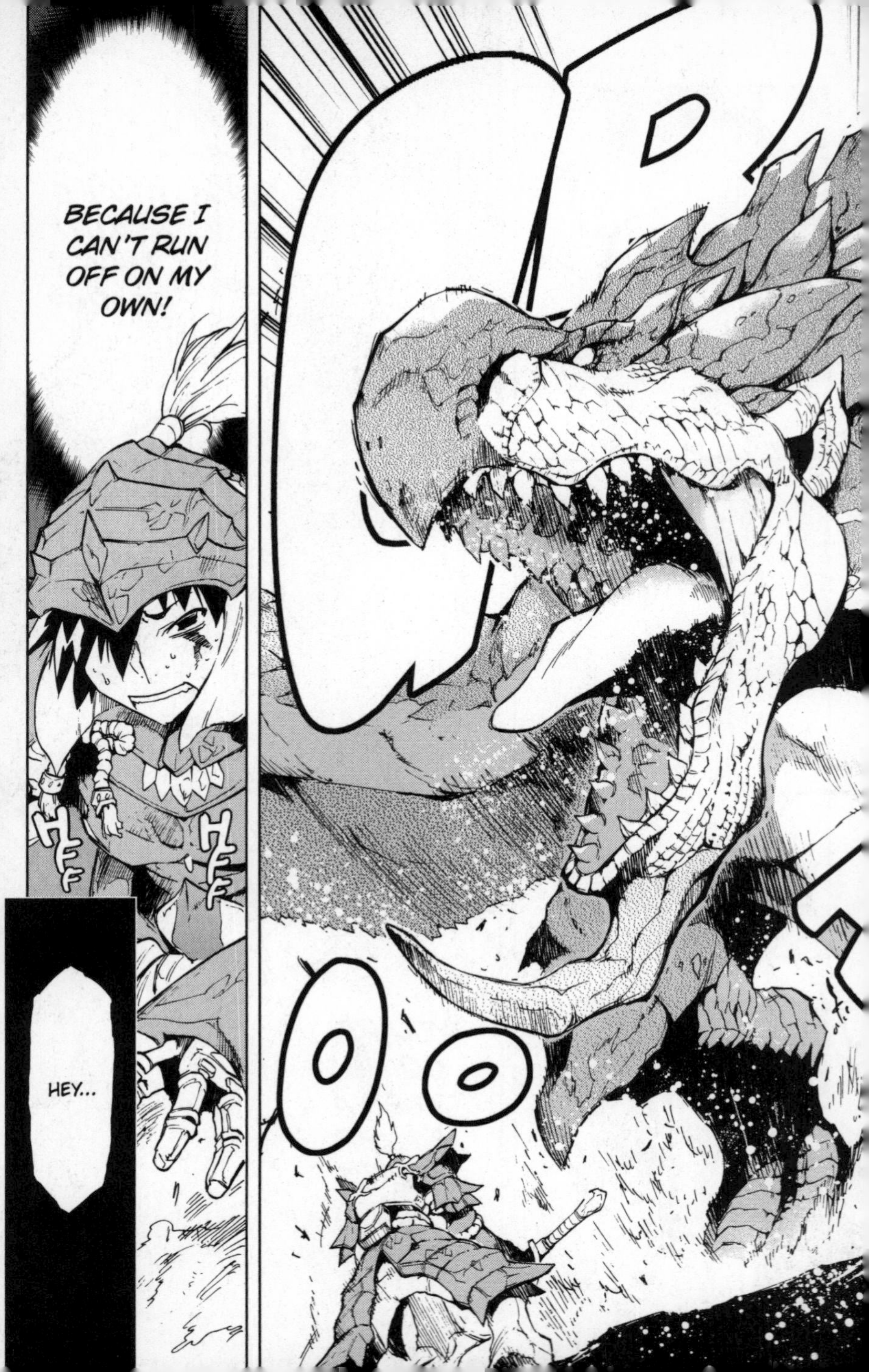
BECAUSE I CAN'T RUN OFF ON MY OWN!
HFF
HFF
HEY...

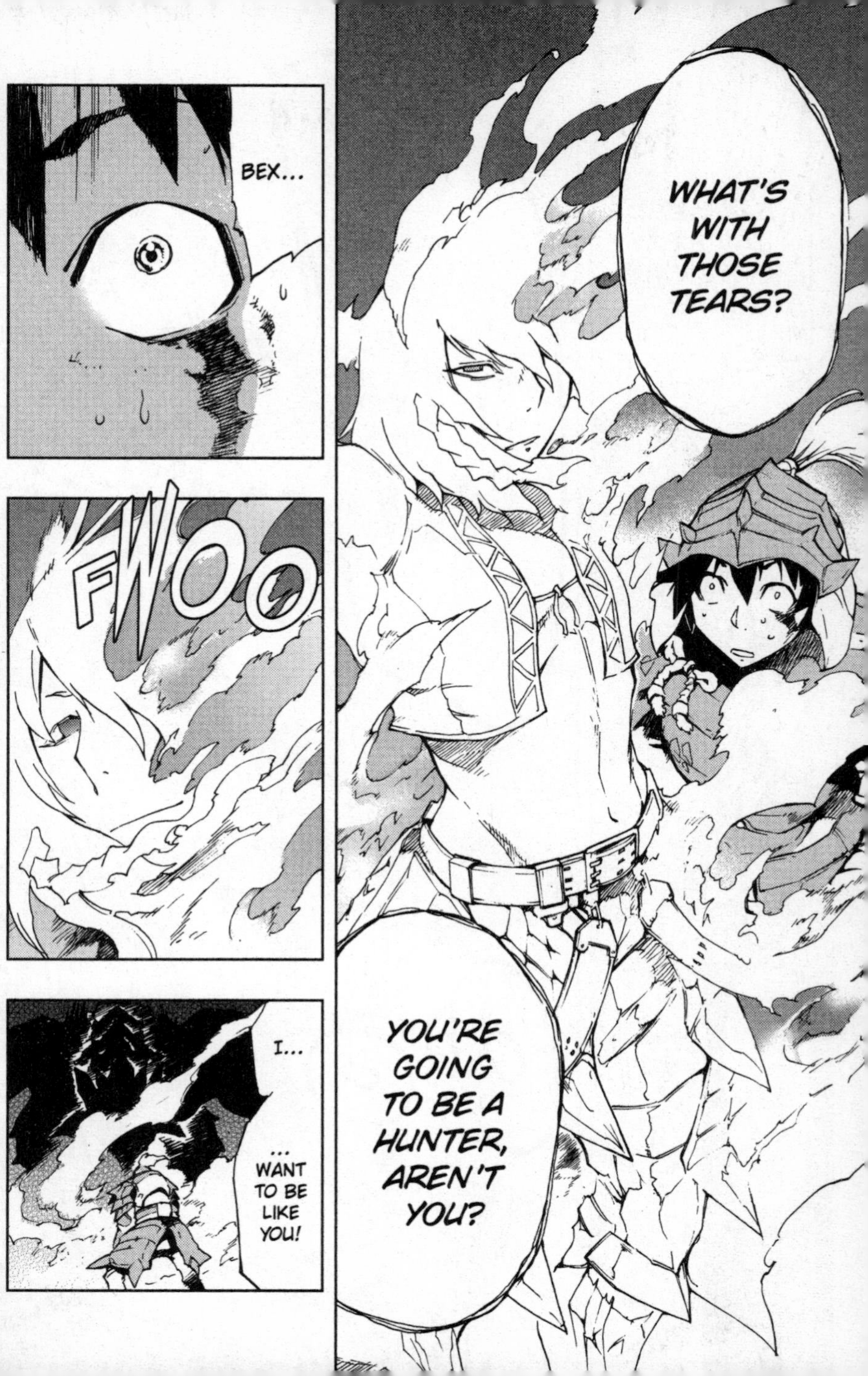
WHAT'S WITH THOSE TEARS?
YOU'RE GOING TO BE A HUNTER, AREN'T YOU?
BEX...
FWOOO
I...
... WANT TO BE LIKE YOU!

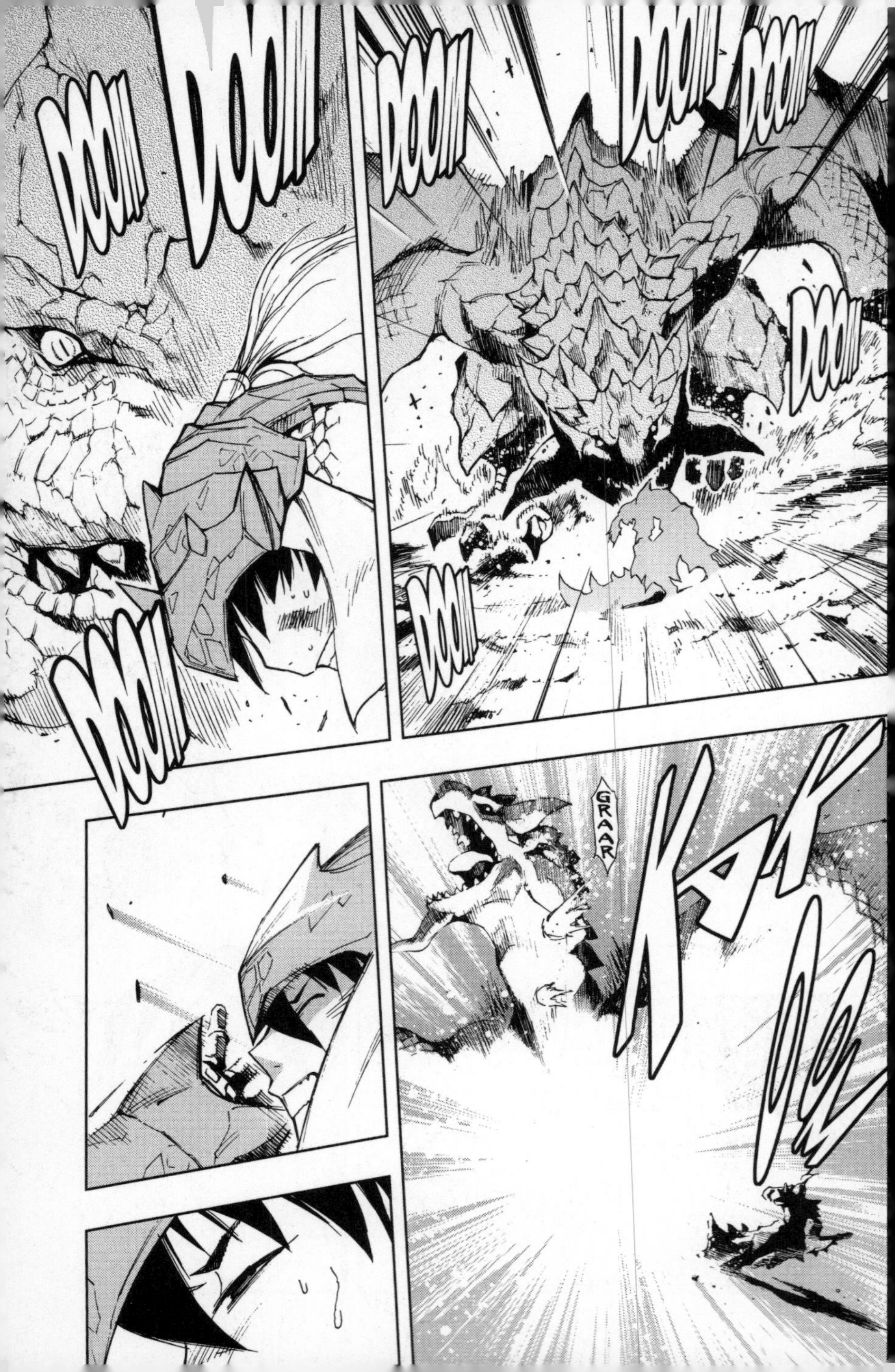
DOOM
DOOM
DOOM
DOOM
DOOM
DOOM
DOOM
DOOM
GRAAR
KAK

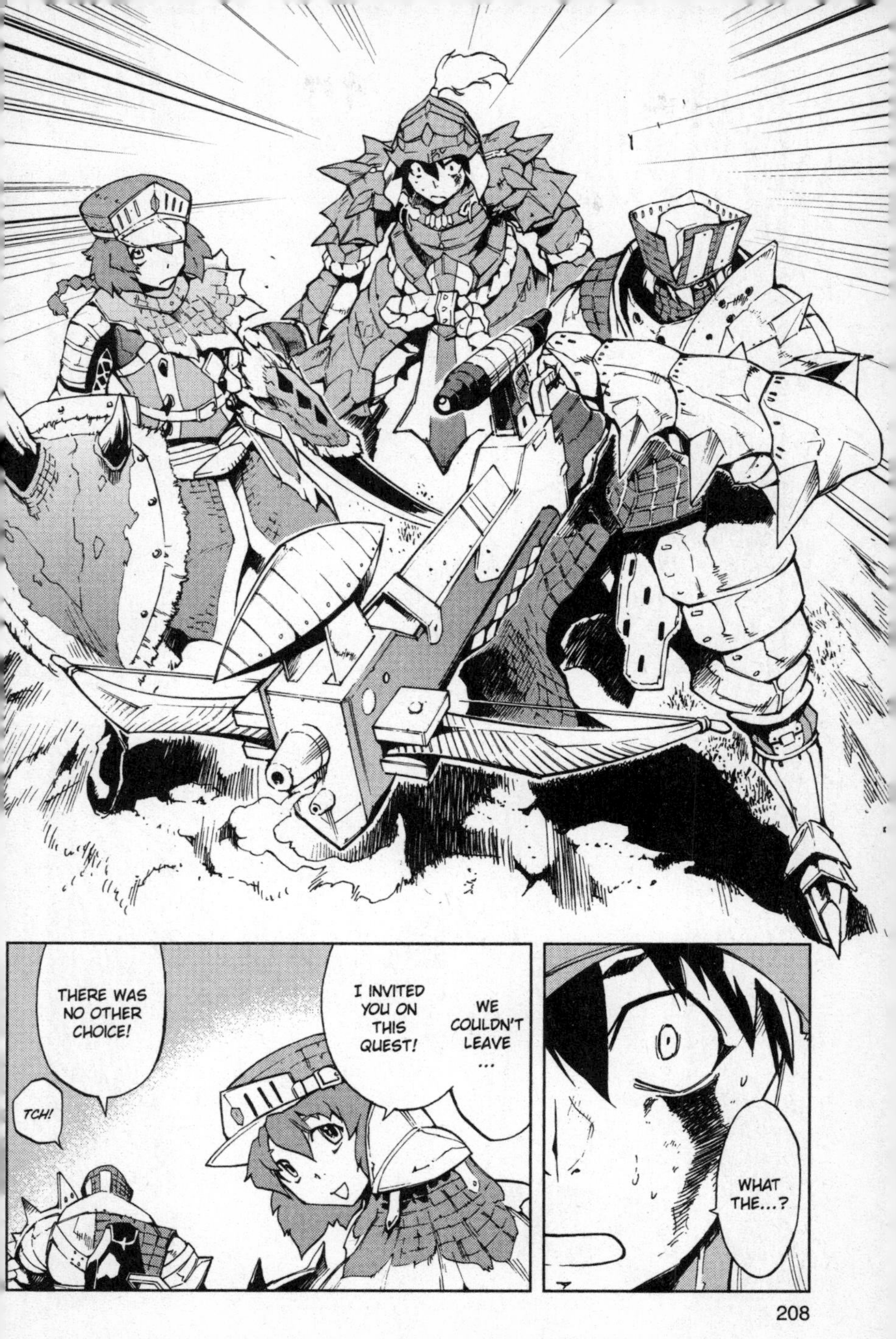
WHAT THE...?
I INVITED YOU ON THIS QUEST! WE COULDN'T LEAVE ...
THERE WAS NO OTHER CHOICE!
TCH!

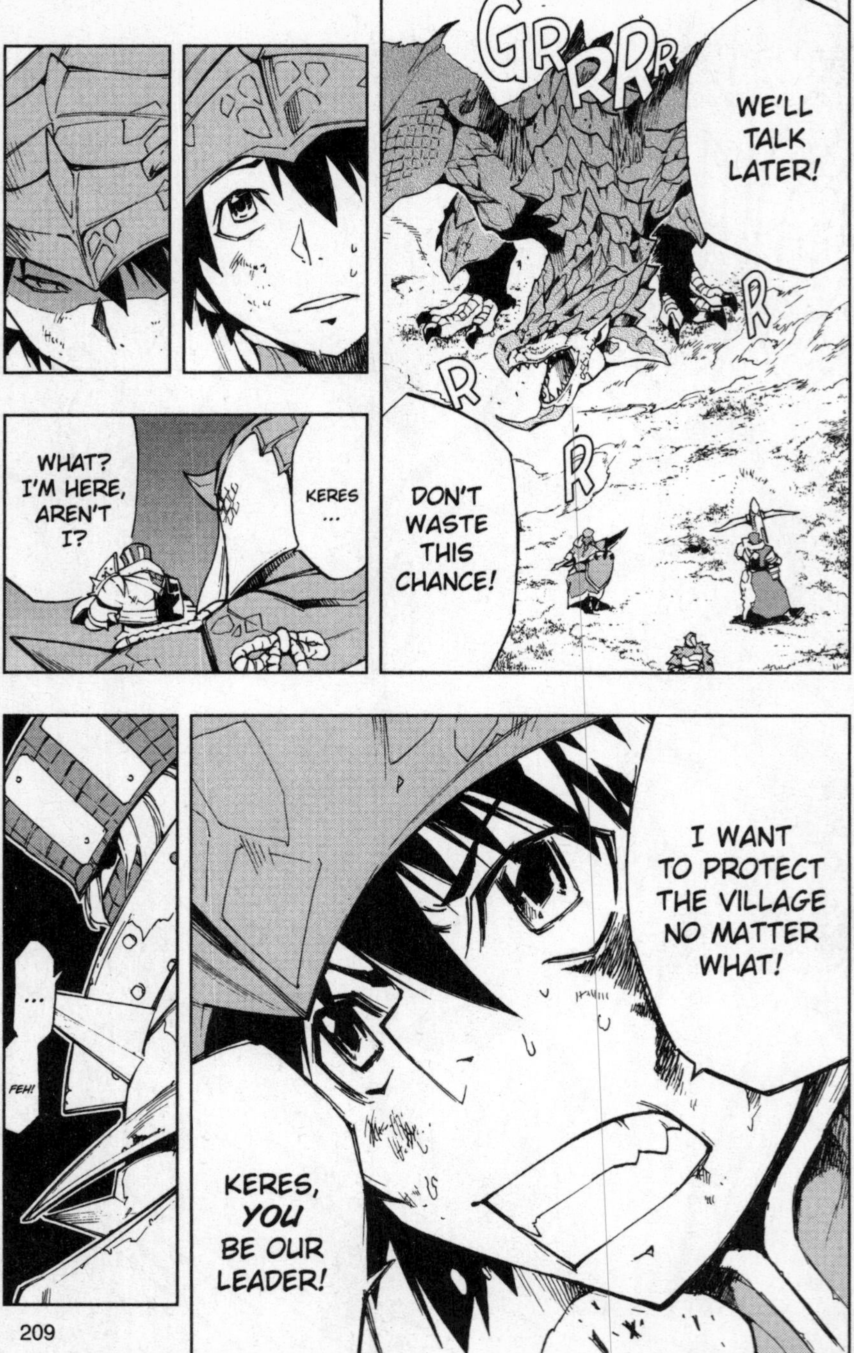
GRRRR
WE'LL TALK LATER!
R
R
R
DON'T WASTE THIS CHANCE!
KERES ...
WHAT? I'M HERE, AREN'T I?
I WANT TO PROTECT THE VILLAGE NO MATTER WHAT!
KERES, *YOU* BE OUR LEADER!
...
FEH!

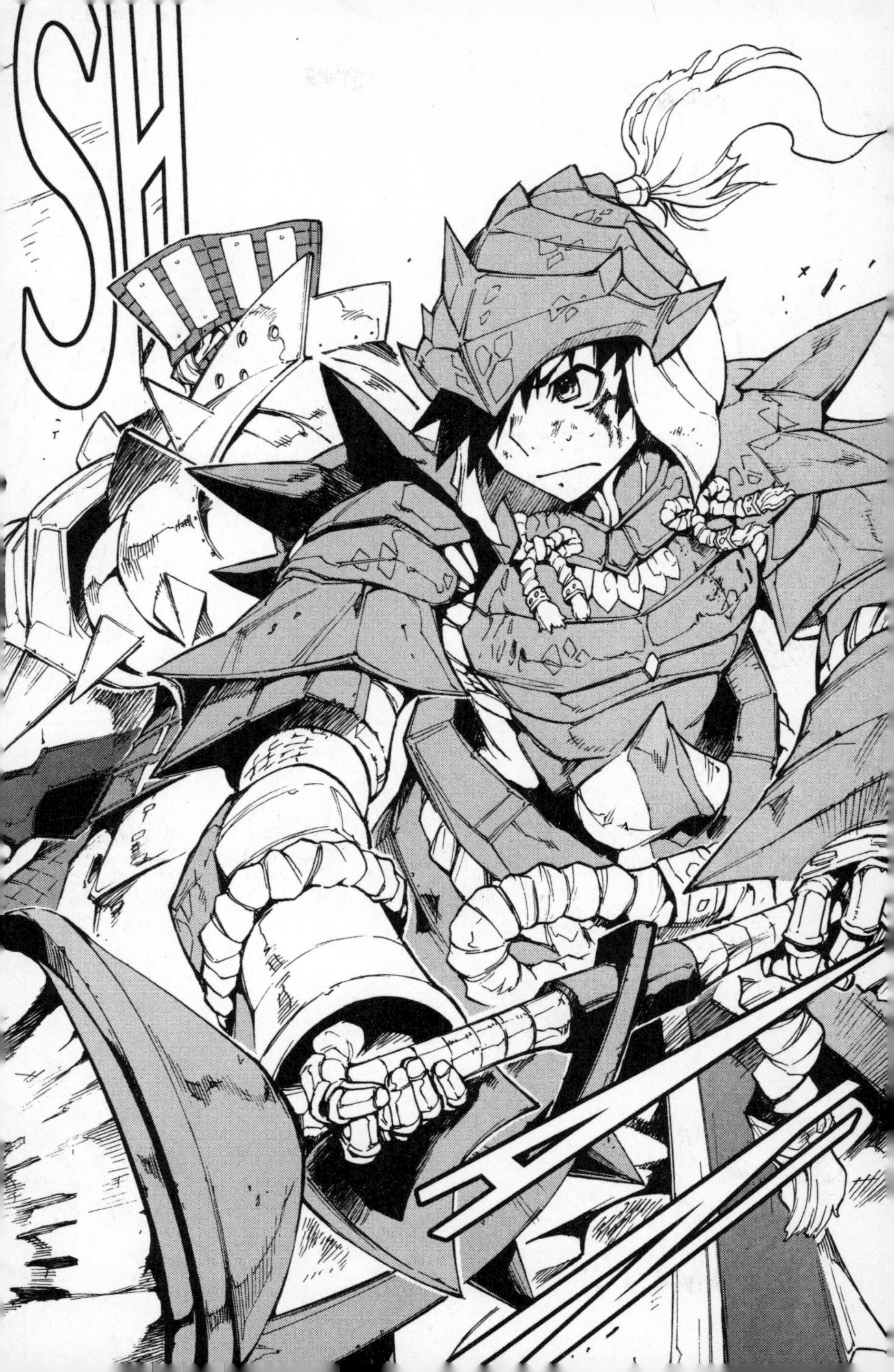
SHI

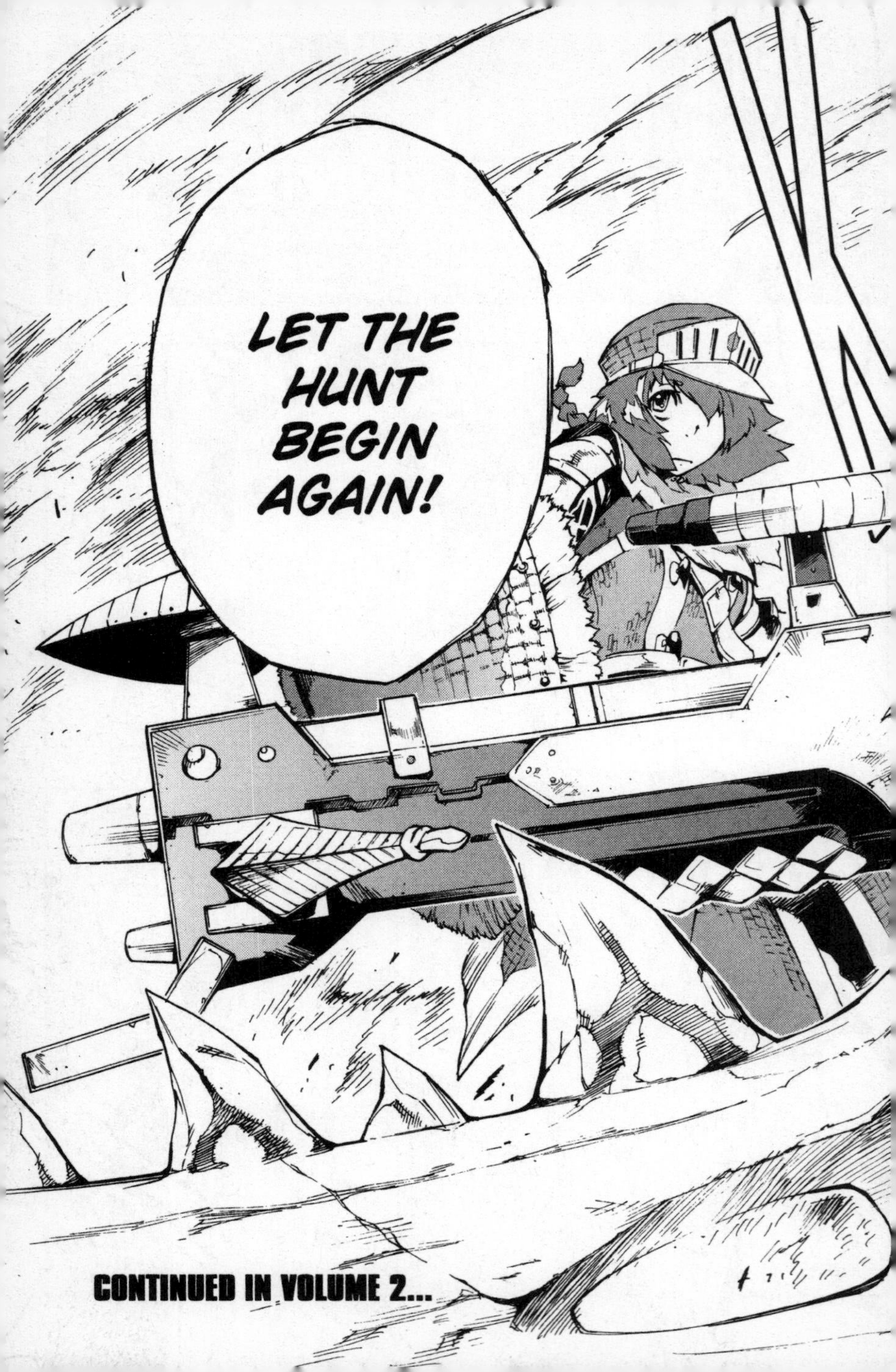
LET THE HUNT BEGIN AGAIN!
CONTINUED IN VOLUME 2...

ANOTHER HUNTER

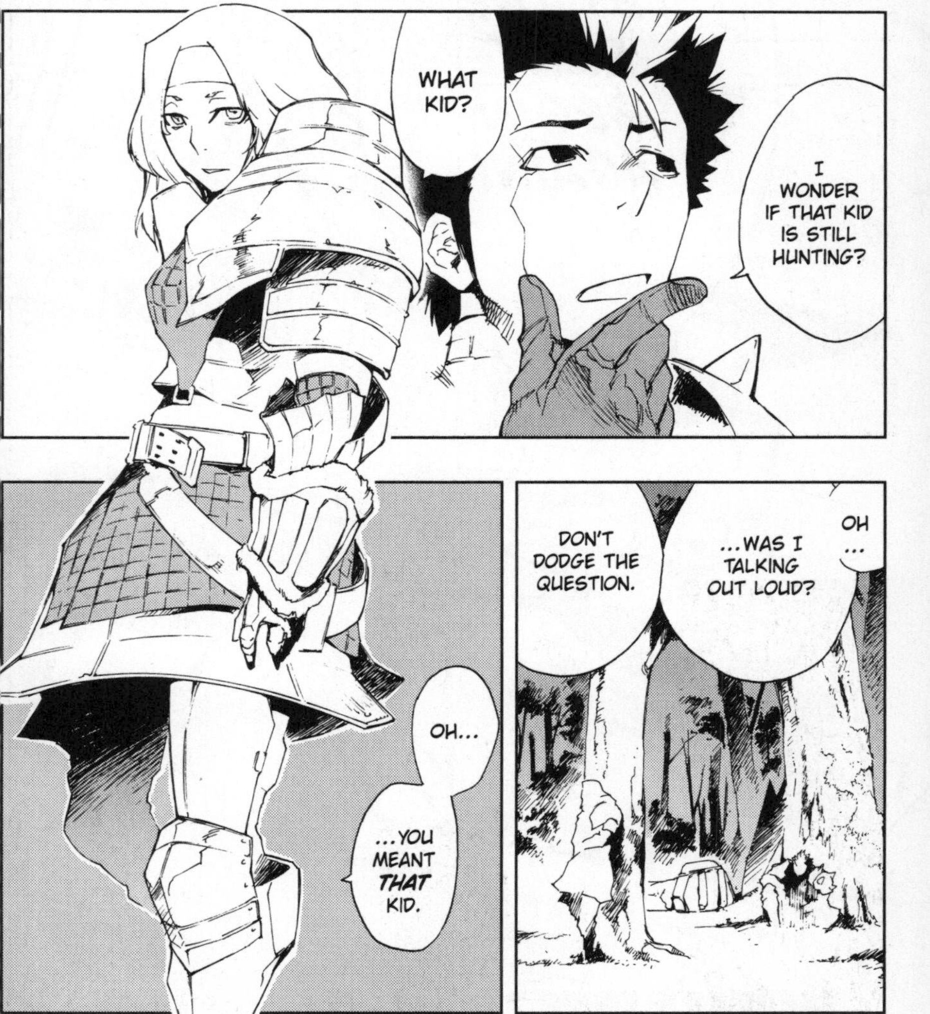
I WONDER IF THAT KID IS STILL HUNTING?
WHAT KID?
OH ...
...WAS I TALKING OUT LOUD?
DON'T DODGE THE QUESTION.
OH...
...YOU MEANT *THAT* KID.

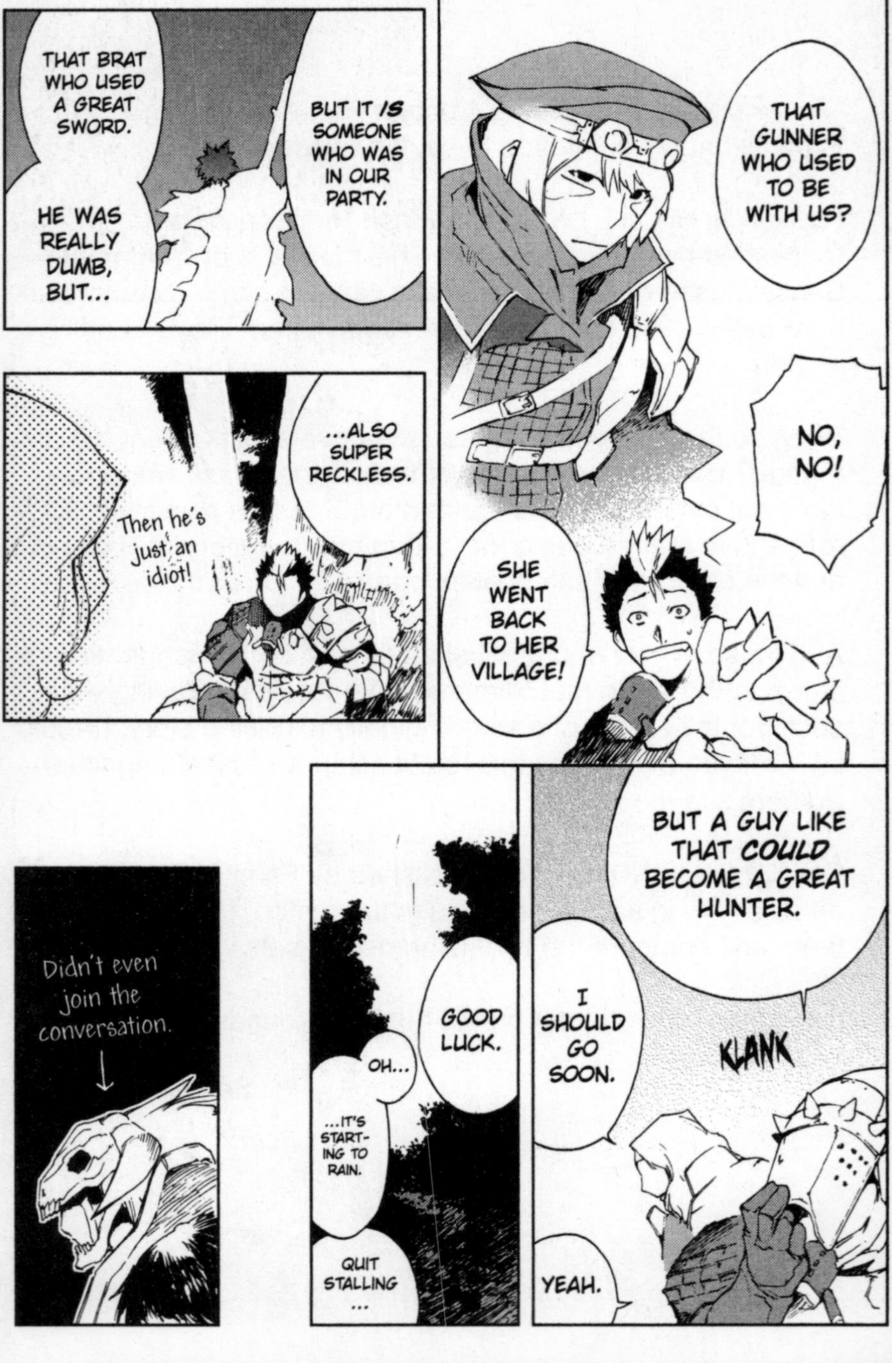
THAT GUNNER WHO USED TO BE WITH US?
NO, NO!
SHE WENT BACK TO HER VILLAGE!
BUT IT *IS* SOMEONE WHO WAS IN OUR PARTY.
THAT BRAT WHO USED A GREAT SWORD.
HE WAS REALLY DUMB, BUT...
...ALSO SUPER RECKLESS.
Then he's just an idiot!
BUT A GUY LIKE THAT ***COULD*** BECOME A GREAT HUNTER.
KLANK
I SHOULD GO SOON.
YEAH.
GOOD LUCK.
OH...
...IT'S STARTING TO RAIN.
QUIT STALLING ...
Didn't even join the conversation.

"Thank you for purchasing *Monster Hunter: Flash Hunter!*"
Is that what I'm supposed to say? (I'm nervous.)

I'm Keiichi Hikami. I wrote the *Flash Hunter* novels (published by Famitsu Bunko). This manga is by Yamamoto Sensei based on my novel. That's why I'm offering comments here at the start. But I'm worried it may seem like I'm butting in. (lol)

What do those of you who read the novels think about the manga? It's an interpretation of the original *Flash Hunter* story but overflowing with Yamamoto Sensei's own style. As a reader, I'm really looking forward to how the story of Raiga and the others will unfold over time.

And those of you who are just starting with the manga, are you enjoying the world that Yamamoto Sensei is portraying with such depth? As the one who originally wrote the story, I would love it if you did! I hope this relationship will last a long time! So here's to the future!

Oh, right, right! The novels published by Famitsu Bunko are on sale now in Japan, so if you're interested, please read them and compare the two! (Shameless sales pitch! (lol))

Okay then, see you out on the hunting grounds!

September 2011

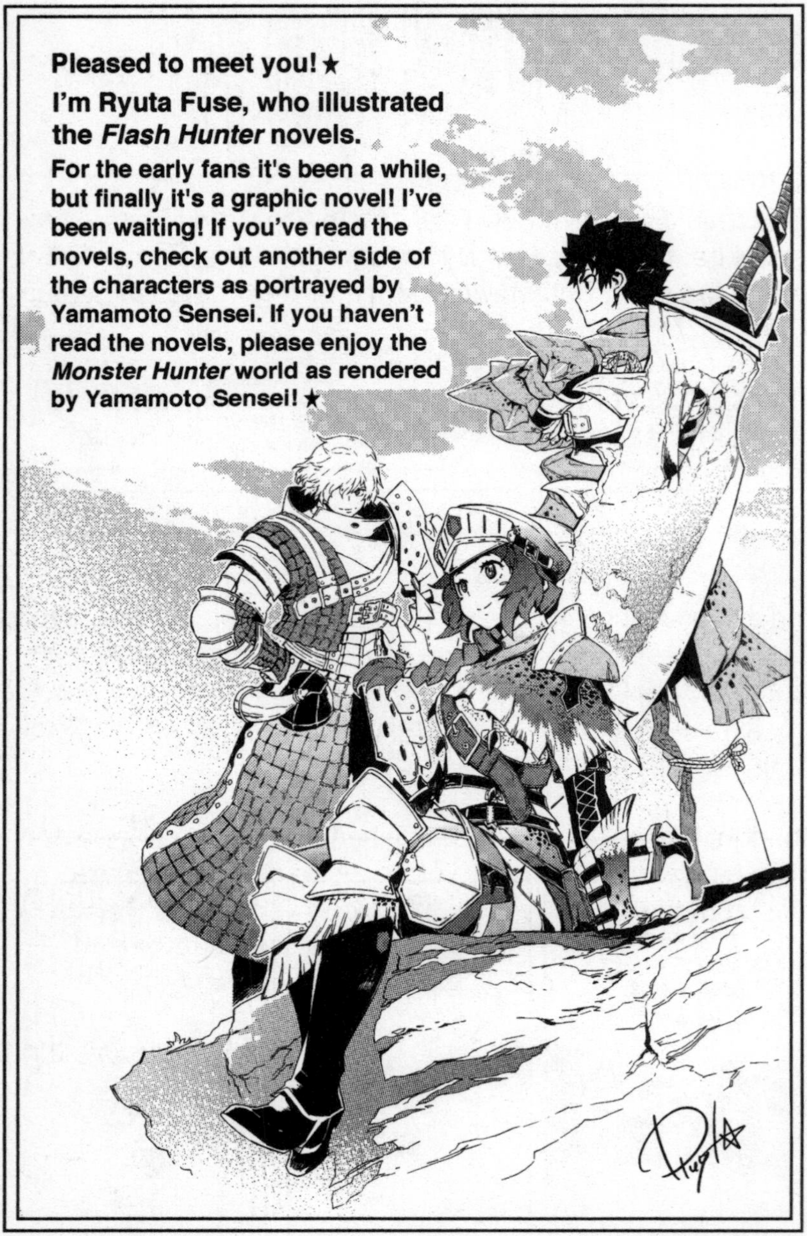
Pleased to meet you! ★
I'm Ryuta Fuse, who illustrated the *Flash Hunter* novels.
For the early fans it's been a while, but finally it's a graphic novel! I've been waiting! If you've read the novels, check out another side of the characters as portrayed by Yamamoto Sensei. If you haven't read the novels, please enjoy the *Monster Hunter* world as rendered by Yamamoto Sensei! ★

★Ryuta Fuse★

MONHUN AND ME

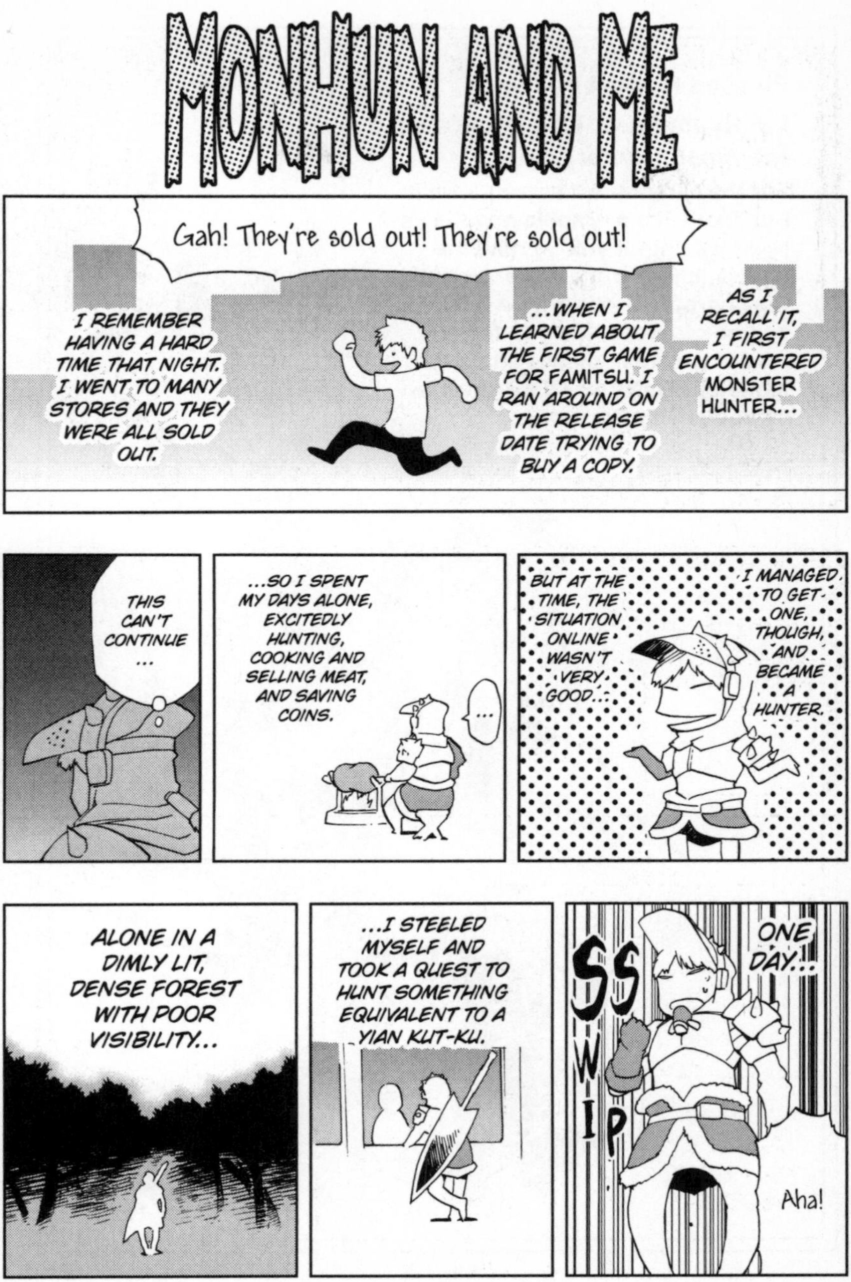
Gah! They're sold out! They're sold out!
AS I RECALL IT, I FIRST ENCOUNTERED MONSTER HUNTER...
...WHEN I LEARNED ABOUT THE FIRST GAME FOR FAMITSU. I RAN AROUND ON THE RELEASE DATE TRYING TO BUY A COPY.
I REMEMBER HAVING A HARD TIME THAT NIGHT. I WENT TO MANY STORES AND THEY WERE ALL SOLD OUT.
I MANAGED TO GET ONE, THOUGH, AND BECAME A HUNTER.
BUT AT THE TIME, THE SITUATION ONLINE WASN'T VERY GOOD...
...SO I SPENT MY DAYS ALONE, EXCITEDLY HUNTING, COOKING AND SELLING MEAT, AND SAVING COINS.
...
THIS CAN'T CONTINUE...
ONE DAY...
SSWIP
Aha!
...I STEELED MYSELF AND TOOK A QUEST TO HUNT SOMETHING EQUIVALENT TO A YIAN KUT-KU.
ALONE IN A DIMLY LIT, DENSE FOREST WITH POOR VISIBILITY...

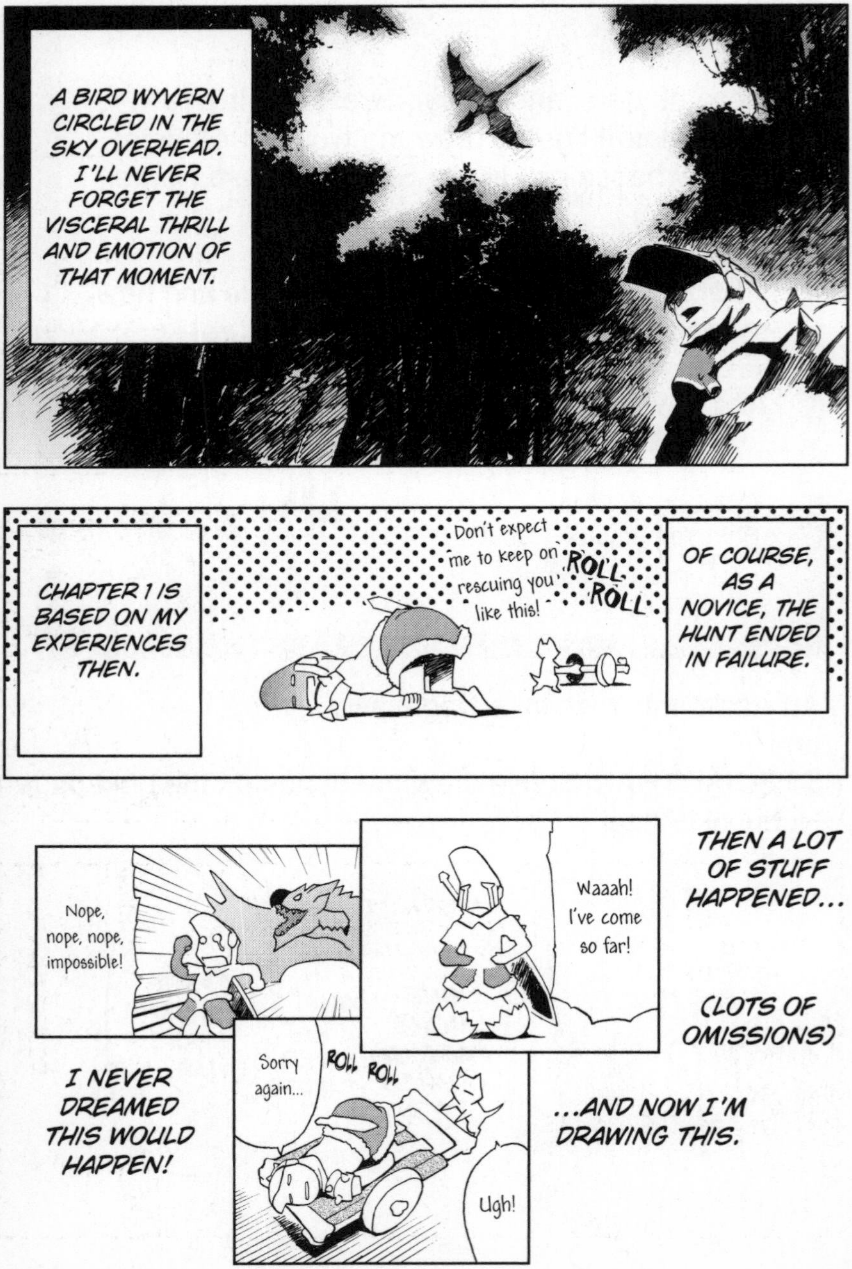
A BIRD WYVERN CIRCLED IN THE SKY OVERHEAD. I'LL NEVER FORGET THE VISCERAL THRILL AND EMOTION OF THAT MOMENT.
OF COURSE, AS A NOVICE, THE HUNT ENDED IN FAILURE.
ROLL ROLL
Don't expect me to keep on rescuing you like this!
CHAPTER 1 IS BASED ON MY EXPERIENCES THEN.
THEN A LOT OF STUFF HAPPENED...
(LOTS OF OMISSIONS)
Waaah! I've come so far!
Nope, nope, nope, impossible!
...AND NOW I'M DRAWING THIS.
ROLL ROLL
Sorry again...
Ugh!
I NEVER DREAMED THIS WOULD HAPPEN!

Hello hunters, and everyone else too!! This is Yamamoto!! I get to draw the world of *Monster Hunter* based on Hikami Sensei's *Flash Hunter* novels.

I'll work hard so that fans of the novels and new readers can enjoy it. Here's to the future!

And now…I'm going on a hunt!

October 15, 2011
Shin Yamamoto

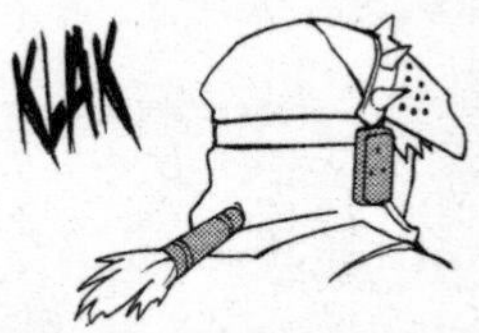
KLAK

Art Assistant: Yoshitaka Nagasawa
and
SPECIAL THANKS (He drew the bonus on the next page!)
Nobuyuki Anzai

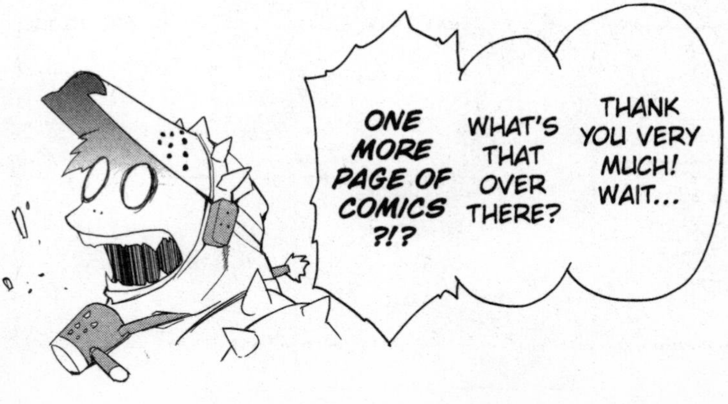
THANK YOU VERY MUCH! WAIT...
WHAT'S THAT OVER THERE?
ONE MORE PAGE OF COMICS ?!?

SHIN YAMAMOTO AND NOBUYUKI ANZAI

August 19, 2011

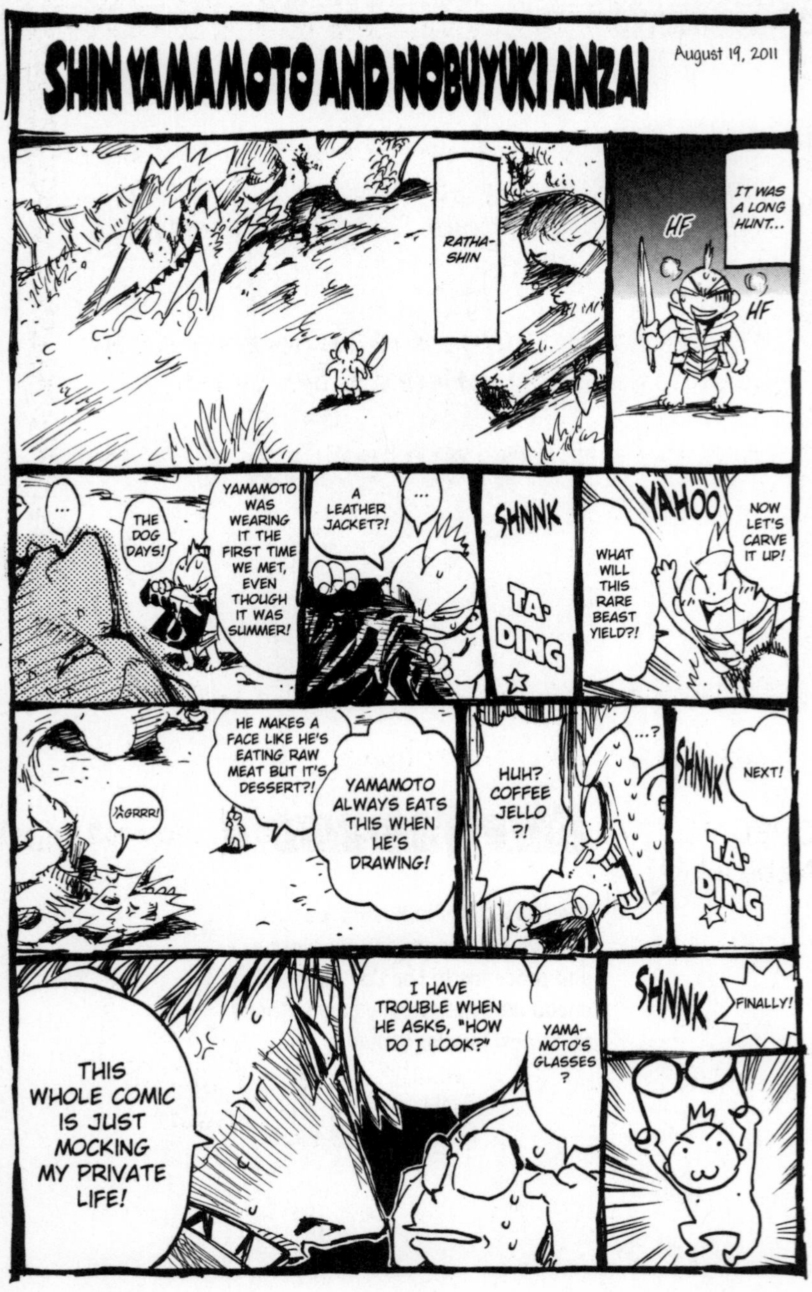
IT WAS A LONG HUNT...
HF
HF
RATHA-SHIN
NOW LET'S CARVE IT UP!
YAHOO
WHAT WILL THIS RARE BEAST YIELD?!
SHNNK
TA-DING
...
A LEATHER JACKET?!
YAMAMOTO WAS WEARING IT THE FIRST TIME WE MET, EVEN THOUGH IT WAS SUMMER!
...
THE DOG DAYS!
NEXT!
SHNNK
TA-DING
...?
HUH? COFFEE JELLO?!
YAMAMOTO ALWAYS EATS THIS WHEN HE'S DRAWING!
HE MAKES A FACE LIKE HE'S EATING RAW MEAT BUT IT'S DESSERT?!
GRRR!
FINALLY!
SHNNK
YAMA-MOTO'S GLASSES?
I HAVE TROUBLE WHEN HE ASKS, "HOW DO I LOOK?"
THIS WHOLE COMIC IS JUST MOCKING MY PRIVATE LIFE!

Shin Yamamoto

The story starts in Kokoto, passes through Minegarde and Dundorma, and proceeds to Loc Lac after encounters in several villages. Then on to new hunting grounds!!